W9-CUJ-195

Shaohsing: Competition and Cooperation
in Nineteenth-Century China

Monographs of the Association for Asian Studies

Published by and available from: The University of Arizona Press
1615 East Speedway Blvd., Tucson, Arizona 85719

XLIV. *Shaohsing: Competition and Cooperation in Nineteenth-Century China*, by James H. Cole. 1986.

XLIII. *Social Protest and Popular Culture in Eighteenth-Century Japan*, by Anne Walthall. 1986.

XLII. *Crime and Criminality in British India*, by Anand A. Yang. 1985.

XLI. *Chinese Religion in Western Languages: A Comprehensive and Classified Bibliography of Publications in English, French and German through 1980*, by Laurence G. Thompson. 1984.

XL. *Kerajaan: Malay Political Culture on the Eve of Colonial Rule*, by A. C. Milner. 1982.

XXXIX. *Academies in Ming China: An Historical Essay*, by John Meskill. 1982.

XXXVIII. *An Anthology of Modern Writing From Sri Lanka*, edited by Ranjini Obeyesekere and Chitra Fernando. 1981.

XXXVII. *An Introduction to Javanese Law: A Translation of and Commentary on the Agama*, by M. C. Hoadley and M. B. Hooker. 1980.

XXXVI. *Burmese Sit-tans 1764–1826: Records of Rural Life and Administration*, by Frank N. Trager and William J. Koenig with the assistance of Yi Yi. 1979.

XXXV. *Robe and Plough: Monasticism and Economic Interest in Early Medieval Sri Lanka*, by R. A. L. H. Gunawardana. 1979.

XXXIV. *Code and Custom in a Thai Provincial Court*, by David M. Engel. 1978.

XXXIII. *Philippine Policy Toward Sabah: A Claim to Independence*, by Lela Garner Noble. 1977.

XXXII. *Political Behavior of Adolescents in China: The Cultural Revolution in Kwangchow*, by David M. Raddock. 1977.

XXXI. *Big City Government in India: Councilor, Administrator, and Citizen in Delhi*, by Philip Oldenberg. 1976.

XXX. *The New Jerusalem: Aspects of Utopianism in the Thought of Kagawa Toyohiko*, by George B. Bikle, Jr. 1976.

XXIX. *Dogen Kigen–Mystical Realist*, by Hee-Jin Kim. 1975.

XXVIII. *Masks of Fiction in* Dream of the Red Chamber: *Myth, Mimesis, and Persona*, by Lucien Miller. 1975.

XXVII. *Politics and Nationalist Awakening in South India, 1852–1891*, by R. Suntharalingam. 1974.

XXVI. *The Peasant Rebellions of the Late Ming Dynasty*, by James Bunyan Parsons. 1970.

XXV. *Political Centers and Cultural Regions in Early Bengal*, by B. M. Morrison. 1970.

XXIV. *The Restoration of Thailand Under Roma I: 1782–1809*, by Klaus Wenk. 1968. O.P.

XXIII. *K'ang Yu-wei: A Biography and a Symposium*, trans. and ed. by Jung-pang Lo. 1967.

XXII. *A Documentary Chronicle of Sino-Western Relations (1644–1820)*; two volumes by Lo-shu Fu. 1966.

XXI. *Before Aggression: Europeans Prepare the Japanese Army*, by Ernst L. Presseisen, 1965. O.P.

XX. *Shinran's Gospel of Pure Grace*, by Alfred Bloom. 1965.

XIX. *Chiaraijima Village: Land Tenure, Taxation, and Local Trade, 1818–1884*, by William Chambliss. 1965.

XVIII. *The British in Malaya: The First Forty Years*, by K. G. Tregonning. 1965. O.P.

XVII. *Ch'oe Pu's Diary: A Record of Drifting Across the Sea*, by John Meskill. 1965. O.P.

XVI. *Korean Literature: Topics and Themes*, by Peter H. Lee. 1965. O.P.

XV. *Reform, Rebellion, and the Heavenly Way*, Benjamin Weems. 1964.

XIV. *The Malayan Tin Industry to 1914*, by Wong Lin Ken. 1965.

The Association for Asian Studies Monograph No. XLIV
Frank Reynolds, Anthony Yu, Ronald Inden, Editors

Shaohsing:
Competition and Cooperation in Nineteenth-Century China

James H. Cole

Published for the Association for Asian Studies by
THE UNIVERSITY OF ARIZONA PRESS / TUCSON

About the Author

JAMES H. COLE received his Ph.D. from Stanford in 1975. He has taught Chinese history at Stanford, the University of Washington (Seattle), and Yale, and has served as Curator of the Wason Collection on East Asia, Cornell University Libraries. In 1985 he was a Visiting Fellow in Cornell's China-Japan Program.

The publication of this volume has been financed from a revolving fund that initially was established by a grant from the Ford Foundation.

THE UNIVERSITY OF ARIZONA PRESS

Library of Congress Cataloging-in-Publication Data

Cole, James H.
  Shaohsing: competition and cooperation in nineteenth-century China.

  (Monographs of the Association for Asian Studies; 44)
  Bibliography: p.
  Includes index.
1. Shao-hsing fu (China) —History.   2. Elite
(Social sciences)—China—Shao-hsing fu.   I. Title.
II. Association for Asian Studies.   III. Series.
DS793.S417C65   1986   951'.242   86-7027

ISBN 0-8165-0994-8 (alk. paper)

To the memory of my aunt, Miriam Steinberg,
and to my friends in the Good Life Society

Contents

TABLES

ACKNOWLEDGMENTS

My interest in Shaohsing began twenty years ago with an undergraduate paper for Professor Yang Lien-sheng at Harvard. That interest eventually resulted in a doctoral dissertation at Stanford, completed ten years ago under the supervision of Professors Harold L. Kahn, G. William Skinner, and Lyman P. Van Slyke. This book is the metamorphosis of that dissertation.

The following all deserve thanks for their extremely helpful comments on either the original dissertation or my many revisions of it: J. G. Bell, David Buck, Stevan Harrell, Ross Isaac, Harold Kahn, Leo Ou-fan Lee, Susan Mann, Angus McDonald, Ramon Myers, Mary Rankin, John Schrecker, G. William Skinner, Jonathan Spence, and Lyman Van Slyke. In the final stages of revision several anonymous readers offered enlightening critiques. Ming Chan, Anthony Marr, Joseph McDermott, and Mary Rankin kindly brought a number of relevant sources to my attention.

A Foreign Area Fellowship in 1972-73, administered at that time by the Ford Foundation, helped to make possible my initial overseas research. Thanks are due also to Professor Skinner as director of the Ning-Shao Project at Stanford for assembling copies of the relevant gazetteers and genealogies from widely scattered collections. This is the first book to emerge from that Project. Thanks too to Tsurumi Naohiro and Tanaka Masatoshi of the Tōyō Bunko; Wang Erh-min of Academia Sinica (at the time of my visit); and the librarians of the following institutions: in the United States the Hoover Institution at Stanford, the Harvard-Yenching Library, the East Asian Library of the University of Washington (Seattle), Sterling Memorial Library at Yale, and the Wason Collection at Cornell University; in Taiwan the Fu Ssu-nien Library and the Institute of Modern History Library (both at Academia Sinica); in Hong Kong the Fung Ping Shan Library at the University of Hong Kong and the Chinese University of Hong Kong Library; and in Japan the Tōyō Bunko, the Institute of Oriental Culture (Tōyō bunka kenkyūjo) at Tokyo University, the National Diet Library, the Institute of Humanistic Studies (Jimbun kagaku kenkyūjo), Kyoto University Library, Tenri University Library, the Osaka Prefectural Library, the Naikaku Bunko, and the Seikadō.

Finally, my appreciation to Paul P. W. Cheng for the calligraphy.

J.H.C.

A NOTE ON ROMANIZATION

This book uses the Wade-Giles system of romanization, except for place names better known in another form and not part of a transliterated title: Thus, for example, Peking, Canton, Soochow, Hangchow, but *Hang-chou pai-hua pao*. I have taken the liberty of omitting the hyphen in Shaohsing and Ningpo. As a rule, Chinese terms in the text are italicized only upon their first appearance. In the index such terms are italicized throughout.

Major locales mentioned in the text.

xiii

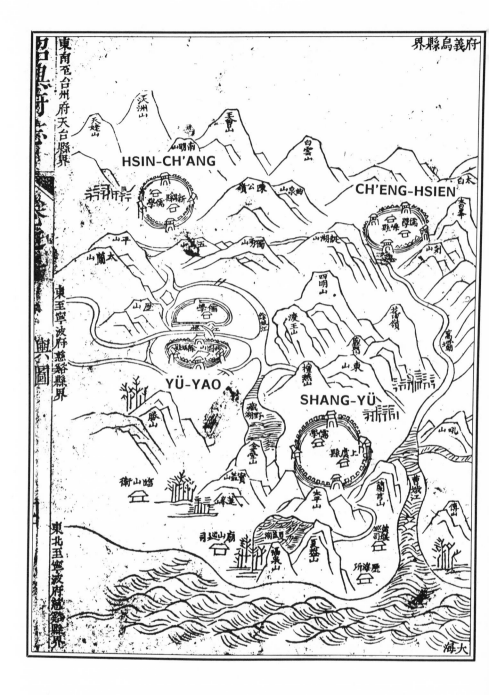

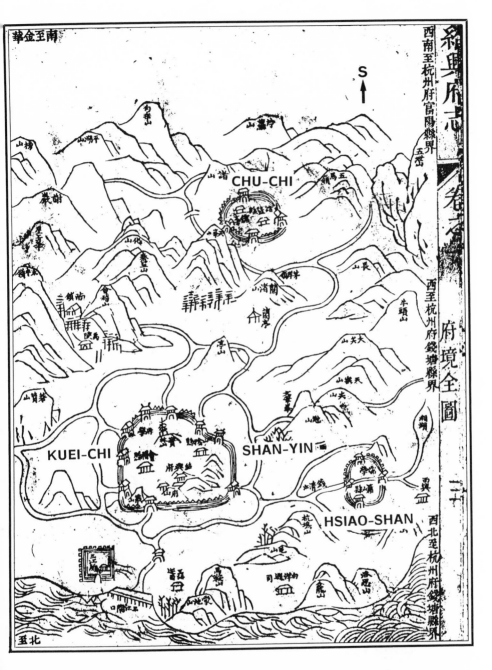

Shaohsing Prefecture from Shaohsing fu-chih, 1792.

Introduction

This is a book about survival - survival in one of the most fiercely competitive environments in human history, China during the Ch'ing dynasty (1644-1911). Too many scholars, too few jobs. Too many peasants, too little land. Too many people, too much struggle for survival. How did people live their lives in such circumstances? What strategies did they use to maximize their chances of success, or at least, minimize their chances of failure? How did they carve out spheres of influence, both geographical and institutional, that they could protect and perpetuate? How, in turn, did such domains protect and perpetuate them? And if people did manage to survive - and some even prosper - under such circumstances, generation after generation, what kind of society had they produced? What kind of people had they become?

To survive in the hostile environment of Ch'ing China required teamwork. The organization man had every advantage over the rugged individualist. People defined themselves by the groups to which they belonged, groups to which they gave their loyalty in return for sustenance and protection. Among these groups were the family, the lineage, and the locale - the native place which defined one's geographical identity. To share the same native place was a powerful tie that bound people together, imposing obligations of mutual aid when they were away from home. This book is a study of how at home, in their native place, the people of one prominent locale survived by cooperating as families and lineages, in competition with the other families and lineages, and how abroad, in the rest of China, they survived by cooperating as *t'ung-hsiang* ("fellow natives"), members of the same locale, in competition with members of other locales.

1

As a study in local history, this book adopts a mode of inquiry that has become well established among students of Chinese society. The work of Beattie on Anhui, Kuhn on Hunan, Meskill on Taiwan, Naquin on Hopei and Shantung, Perry on Anhui, Rawski on Fukien and Hunan, Schoppa on Chekiang, and Wakeman on Kwangtung (to name but a few of the studies published by Western scholars)[1] has demonstrated beyond any doubt the breathtaking diversity that China has encompassed within its borders. Indeed, the challenge for historians of China is no longer to demonstrate diversity but rather to start putting the pieces back together, uncovering patterns that will allow future scholars to offer confident generalizations founded on detailed, empirical case studies such as those cited above and, it is hoped, the present work as well.

Yet important as local history is, it will not fulfill its promise merely by accumulating case studies. The relationship between the parts and the whole must be considered not merely in some grand synthesis to be written far in the future (when all the case studies are done) but now, in the very process of writing local history. Accordingly, this book treats not merely one locale per se but also that locale's impact on China as a whole. For in studying nineteenth-century Shaohsing I have found that it is impossible to understand the locale itself without also understanding how it functioned within the broader context of the Ch'ing state.

Loyalty to one's native place is no monopoly of Chinese culture. But it is particularly noteworthy in a political system such as China's that was characterized not by a decentralized feudalism but rather by a precociously bureaucratic centralism. The traditional Chinese state managed to balance dual allegiances among its functionaries: on the one hand, allegiance to their families, lineages, and native places, which nurtured them; on the other, allegiance to the emperor and his dynasty, which employed them. The successful balancing of these centrifugal and centripetal forces would hardly have been possible in traditional China without the justly famous civil service examination system, which by linking the interests of local elite and dynastic polity served to maintain a symbiotic relationship between locale and center. The relationship was vulnerable, of course: Locales could declare their independence of the center, thus toppling the dynasty, as ultimately occurred in 1911. Conversely, the center could demoralize the locales by punishing local elites (e.g., for tax evasion, as occurred in 1661). At the beginning of a dynasty the center was eager to demonstrate its power over its constituent locales. By the end of a dynasty it had lost the ability to do so. Yet, precisely because the relationship between center and locale was symbiotic, not repressive, for most of a dynasty's span, the locales exerted their influence upon the center long before the dynasty's decline and fall. One of the major themes of this study is that one particular locale - Shaohsing prefecture in Chekiang province - exercised a disproportionate influence over the dynasty's administrative system, deriving from the symbiotic relationship between locale and center greater benefits than other jealously competing locales considered its fair share.

This competition between locales for the wealth and power deriving from successful penetration of the central government's administration was intense and perpetual, a virtual struggle for survival. Locales like Shaohsing that could produce a disproportionate share of government functionaries would reap disproportionate rewards. Locales that failed to produce government functionaries would remain perpetually victimized, paying out more in taxes and extortionate "squeeze" than they could hope to recover, unless they compensated by success in commerce, which was of course another means by which locales prospered at the expense of their peers.

The central government, ever fearful that the native-place allegiances of its officials might undermine their commitment to the center's interests, forbade them from serving in their home provinces. This strategy - the "law of avoidance" - succeeded in ensuring that functionaries would be strangers in the locales they administered, and thus unencumbered by particularistic ties that could easily interfere with their duties as representatives of the center. Precisely because they were strangers, however, functionaries had fewer compunctions about profiteering from the locales which they administered. Thus would a locale that produced a disproportionately large number of functionaries benefit from a system which in effect condoned mutual exploitation among locales, a situation considered preferable to the locales' exploitation of the center.

Nor was this administrative system necessarily considered corrupt by those who participated in it. For loyalty to kith and kin at the expense of strangers was orthodox Confucian doctrine. The higher a functionary's rank, the greater his moral obligation to provide for those near and dear. Thus making good was not an act of selfish individualism but rather the highest expression of filial devotion, of loyalty to one's roots. Profits extracted on alien soil in another part of China helped to finance, among other things, the ceremonies celebrating one's own ancestors back home.

The production of successful native sons could hardly be left to chance. The stakes were too high, and the pass rates in the civil service examinations - the royal road to the wealth and power attendant on official position - too minuscule. So locales devised at least two strategies to break the examination bottleneck. The first, and most widespread, was for the lineage to invest in the education of its brightest sons, so as to maximize its number of examination candidates and thus the number of potential passers. The second strategy was to outflank the examination system and enter the ranks of government functionaries via channels that were less honorable but more dependable - as subofficials, clerks, and expert advisers to officials, all of which positions afforded their own opportunities for wealth and power. As we shall see, Shaohsing prefecture succeeded in both strategies, which were complementary, not contradictory. Shaohsing's success in the examination sheds was outstanding. But its success through the back door was spectacular.

In the production of educated talent that was every locale's goal, the lineage played a crucial role. The resources of individual families, whether nuclear or extended, were too liable to fluctuation through time to ensure the proper education of deserving beneficiaries in each generation. Only at the lineage level could a poor but bright child stand a chance of receiving sufficient investment in his education - an investment which his possible future entry into the administrative system would more than repay. Obviously, the greater his lineage's resources, the greater his chance of eventual success. In this and in other ways it was far preferable to be a poor member of a rich lineage than a poor member of a poor lineage. Membership in a rich lineage provided both spiritual and material sustenance, not to mention protection in a world full of hostile strangers. (Those whose real kin ties proved insufficient or unrewarding could find a functional equivalent in the fictive kinship offered by secret societies.)

Thus did lineages serve to dampen down class conflict within each locale. Lineages split local society vertically, not horizontally. Just as locales competed with each other, so too did lineages compete within each locale. The most extreme form of inter-lineage competition, the vendetta, pitted tenant against tenant and landlord against landlord. Of course, there was no guarantee that locale-consciousness and lineage-consciousness would smother class-consciousness in every instance. Greedy members of the local gentry could easily incite trouble by failing in their moral obligation to provide for, or at least protect, their less fortunate relatives. If and when a lineage did fail some of its members, they could look for protection to the horizontal ties of class. But, when not abused, the institutions of local society contained the mechanisms to keep discontent within tolerable limits.

Unfortunately, by the last decades of the Ch'ing dynasty, which was established in 1644 after the fall of the preceding Ming dynasty and was in turn overthrown in 1911, the institutions of local society were being abused too often. The inequities of the ancien régime were reaching crisis proportions, and indeed remained endemic even after the dynasty fell. No observer expressed both the necessity for and the difficulty of social revolution more poignantly than did Chou Shu-jen (1881-1936), better known by his pen name, Lu Hsün. Generally regarded as modern China's greatest writer, Lu Hsün was a native of Shaohsing's Kuei-chi county. His name will reappear frequently in these pages.

> Imagine an iron house without windows, absolutely indestructable, with many people fast asleep inside who will soon die of suffocation. But you know since they will die in their sleep, they will not feel any of the pain of death. Now if you cry aloud to wake a few of the lighter sleepers, making those unfortunate few suffer the agony of irrevocable death, do you think you are doing them a good turn?
>
> ("Preface to 'A Call to Arms',"
> *Selected Works,* Vol. One,
> Peking, 1956, pp. 5-6)

Depressed by the abuses in Shaohsing's local society, Lu Hsün was equally troubled by the relations between Shaohsing and the rest of China. In a culture that highly prized loyalty to one's native place, Lu Hsün was sorely discomfited: How could he as an ethical person identify with a locale that, as we shall see, had an infamous reputation throughout China for producing scheming shysters? So when Lu Hsün was living in Peking, he did not like to admit that he was from Shaohsing. When asked his native place, he answered "Chekiang."[2]

The Shaohsing Milieu

During the Ch'ing dynasty Shaohsing, sometimes spelled Shaohing, was one of the eleven prefectures (*fu*) which together comprised Chekiang province. Located within the core area of the lower Yangtze macroregion,[3] Shaohsing was in turn composed of eight counties (*hsien*). In the following pages we shall be dealing for both the pre- and post-1911 periods with the area coterminous with the eight counties of Shaohsing prefecture. References to "Shaohsing" are to the prefecture unless otherwise noted.[4]

By the late Ch'ing most of these eight counties in Shaohsing prefecture possessed distinctive characteristics. Shan-yin and Kuei-chi, on the fertile alluvial plain stretching south from Hangchow Bay, were almost certainly the two richest counties in the prefecture, in terms both of agricultural productivity and inhabitants' aggregate income. Sharing the site of the prefectural capital, they were well known for their production of advanced civil service examination degree holders and, especially, legal experts. In contrast, Yü-yao and Shang-yü counties were known for their bankers. Hsin-ch'ang and Ch'eng-hsien were the most mountainous counties in the prefecture, although their county seats (like all others in Shaohsing) lay below the hundred meter line. Both Hsin-ch'ang and Ch'eng-hsien were known for their bandits and soldiers. If Shan-yin and Kuei-chi were Shaohsing's "inner core," Hsin-ch'ang and Ch'eng-hsien were its "outer periphery."[5] Of the two remaining counties, Chu-chi, combining both lowlands and mountains, tended to be peripheral, while Hsiao-shan, situated on the alluvial plain, tended to be core. Hsiao-shan's location oriented it westwards toward Hangchow, the provincial capital, just as Yü-yao's location oriented it toward the port city of Ningpo on the east, whose natives often cooperated with Shaohsing's in commercial ventures elsewhere in China, as we shall see.

How many people were living in these counties during the Ch'ing? Prior to 1933, the latest date for which population figures are available for all of Shaohsing's counties is 1791. The prefectural gazetteer in which these figures were published specifies that they include women and children as well as men: Shan-yin 1,002,582, Kuei-chi

266,526, Hsiao-shan 686,520, Chu-chi 956,556, Yü-yao 472,916, Shang-yü 176,517, Ch'eng-hsien 334,787, and Hsin-ch'ang 127,506.[6] Thus the total population of Shao-hsing prefecture in 1791 would be 4,023,910. The comparable figure for 1933 was only 3,843,777.[7] The Taiping Rebellion (1850-1864) clearly took its toll. In contrast, an amazing surge in Shaohsing's population seems to have occurred *not* between 1791 and 1933 but earlier, between 1683 and 1791: During the early Wan-li period (year not specified but prior to 1586), the population of Shan-yin (both male and female) was a mere 115,409 and the population of Kuei-chi (again both male and female) was only 62,004.[8] During the early K'ang-hsi period (year not specified but prior to 1683), the population of Shan-yin was 115,210 and the population of Kuei-chi was 62,768, both extremely close to the Wan-li figures.[9]

All these statistics are of course suspect. At the very least, they underrepresent the actual population pressure within Shaohsing, since they omit the Shaohsing natives who emigrated. But it seems reasonable to conclude that the demographic boom of early K'ang-hsi to late Ch'ien-lung contributed to the serious overpopulation problem which made the struggle for survival difficult for natives of nineteenth-century Shaohsing. Indeed, in 1820 Shaohsing was the fourth most densely populated prefecture in all of China.[10]

The beauty and richness of Shaohsing's physical setting was overpowering, the picture postcard image of rural China. E. H. Parker, a visiting British consul, described in 1884 the countryside surrounding Shaohsing's prefectural capital.

> Thence to Shao-hing Fu...and branch creeks intersect and irrigate the country in every direction. This is without exception the fattest stretch of land I have ever seen in China or elsewhere. The autumn crop of rice is gathered in two relays, called the early and late kinds, one six weeks or two months later than the other. Strange to say, the quality of land in the Shan-yin district differs so much from that in Siao-shan [Hsiao-shan] that there the rice crops are again reaped considerably later. Shan-yin and Kwei-chi are the prefectural districts, and seem to reek with richness. Substantial villages and market-towns, many as large as the more

Western district-cities, succeed one another at dis-
tances of half-a-mile, and are to be seen thickly
dotted over the country. There being no danger of
drought, husbandry is mathematically exact and
minute, cultivation being carried to the very water's
edge. With the exception of the substantial stone
pathways between the cities, there seems to be little
means of intercommunication except by boat, and
these boats are externally adorned by such consum-
mate art that they have the appearance of being
made of fine porcelain. Large and small, they are
fitted up with rainproof telescope mats, and can be
used as dwellings, cargo boats, or passenger and
pleasure barges; they fully merit the name gondola;
many of the small ones are worked with the feet,
and thousands are passed during a day's travel.
The country realizes to the full the 'willow pattern'
idea of China. Stone bridges of elegant shape are
seen or passed every few moments; remarkable
arches and monuments are thickly strewn about; the
willow, tallow, soap, and camphor trees adorn the
graves and villages; and all the ideal Chinese
scenes, such as goose and duck breeding, weir and
basket fishing, etc., recur at every moment. The
country is flat, but the graves (which waste a great
deal of good land) and village-clusters deprive the
landscape of monotony.[11]

Shaohsing was long the cultural center of the sub-
provincial region known since the Sung as Che-tung, "East
of the Che [River]," or more loosely, eastern Chekiang.
In contrast stands that portion of western Chekiang and
southern Kiangsu known as Che-hsi, "West of the Che
[River]." The two regions differed in intellectual styles
during the Ch'ing: To generalize outrageously, one may
state that Che-hsi's scholars tended to favor the philolog-
ical approach of native son Ku Yen-wu, who laid the foundation for empirical textual research on the Confucian
Classics, while Che-tung's scholars were more inclined
toward the historical approach of native son Huang Tsung-
hsi, who wrote a model intellectual history of Ming Confucianism as well as a searching critique of Ming despotism.[12]
Shaohsing's natives contrasted what they considered the
overrefined frippery of Che-hsi's cultural centers, Hangchow and Soochow, with the supposedly "pure," simple, and
unadorned customs of their own Che-tung.[13] Thus did

regional heritages and prejudices crosscut provincial boundaries.

In 1903 Ts'ai Yüan-p'ei, a native of Shaohsing's Shan-yin county and later to become famous as Chancellor of Peking University, gave a speech to a group of fellow Shaohsing natives living in Shanghai.[14] In his speech Ts'ai celebrated Shaohsing's glorious heritage, remarking on its fame as the home of Huang Tsung-hsi and the philosopher Wang Yang-ming as well as its renown as the wine capital of China. It was only when Ts'ai mentioned Shaohsing's fame as a producer of administrative clerks and *mu-yu* (legal experts hired by officials as their private secretaries) that he momentarily faltered. For in this sphere Shaohsing's reputation was less than glorious: During the last years of the Ch'ing, with corruption and national weakness on everyone's mind, the private secretaries were being dubbed "officials' pettifoggers"[15] and clerks were equally despised by reformers.[16]

A story gained wide circulation about five Shaohsing natives who pooled their resources and purchased a county magistracy. The partner whose outlay was greatest became magistrate, while the others became his private secretaries, each post being assigned in strict accord with the amount invested.[17] The story may be apocryphal, although indirect evidence to credit it does exist.[18] Most important is the tale's plausibility at the time - what it revealed about Shaohsing's reputation during the late Ch'ing. For Shaohsing, success had its price.

During the Han dynasty (206 B.C. - 220 A.D.) *tao-pi-li*, "functionary with blade [i.e., eraser] and writing brush," was a neutral term meaning "clerk." But by the Ch'ing it had acquired unsavory nuances of corruption and shystering chicanery, in short, pettifoggery.[19] During the late Ch'ing and early Republic, the term appeared in abbreviated form: It was common for Shaohsing natives to be labelled *Shao tao-kuei*.[20] Even more common was the term *Shaohsing shih-yeh*, the unsavory connotation of which can only be suggested by the translation "Shaohsing shyster."[21] Shih-yeh has usually been taken to refer to private secretaries, expecially the most important, those who dealt with judicial cases and taxation (*hsing-ming* and *ch'ien-ku* respectively).[22] But there is evidence that the term shih-yeh had a broader meaning, that it referred to clerks in the Six Central Administrative Boards in Peking, as well as to pettifoggers.[23] One critic of Lu Hsün wishing to discredit him made snide reference to Shaohsing's heritage of clerks, private secretaries, and pettifoggers,[24] lumping all three together. Lu Hsün's sensitivity to the reputation of his native place suggests that the barb did not miss its mark.

Shaohsing's notoriety was already established by the mid-seventeenth century. The Jesuit missionary Martini (1614-1661) claimed, "There are no legal counsels *(avocats)* more cunning or sly in all of China, such that no governor lacks a jurist from this town." In the late eighteenth century the Jesuit Grosier (1743-1823) echoed Martini's words: Shaohsing natives, he wrote, "are said to be the greatest adepts in chicanery of any in China; indeed, they are so well versed in the laws, that the governors of the provinces and the great mandarins choose their *siang-cong* *[hsien-sheng]*, or secretaries, from among them."[25]   As early as the Ming, clerks in fiction and drama were usually protrayed as Shaohsing natives.[26]   Chou Tso-jen (1885-1966, Lu Hsün's younger brother and a well-known author in his own right) commented on a Ming description of his native place and bemoaned Shaohsing's relative loss of innocence since those days, what with the increasing dominance of legal experts and "money shops" (native banks).[27] There was a saying that had become all too common by the early twentieth century: Shaohsing had hills but no wood, water but no fish, and men but no righteousness. "By local [Shaohsing] custom the saying was taboo, and whenever anyone got as far as 'no fish,' people would get mad and want to fight."[28]   Little wonder. That same bon mot had been making the rounds in Hangchow ever since the thirteenth century.[29] In China regional rivalries ran deep.

Late Ch'ing Shaohsing was typical of late Ch'ing China as a whole in its failure to solve problems of social pathology inherent in this locale but by no means unique to it - problems such as overpopulation, interlineage struggles, gentry abuse of privilege, and exploitation of commoners. What made Shaohsing unusual, however, was the ability of its populace to convert wealth into various kinds of bureaucratic positions more readily than the natives of other locales. The key factor explaining the success of Shaohsing natives in penetrating the Ch'ing bureaucracy was not wealth per se, but rather the existence of an extensive vertical network of Shaohsing natives throughout the Ch'ing administration, what can be called "the Shaohsing connection." Staffed predominantly by natives of Shaohsing's core area - especially its two most urban counties, in which the prefectural capital was located - this native-place network provided backdoor access to administrative positions. Throughout the Ch'ing dynasty, officials serving abroad were considered gentry at home, two sides of the same coin. Maintaining official position was the only sure way to maintain gentry status. Shaohsing's inordinate production of governmental functionaries meant an inordinate concentration of gentry within Shaohsing, with consequences that were not conducive to the locale's social harmony. Shaohsing natives' clique-like cooperation outside their locale was balanced by their fierce competition within it.

Yet competition and cooperation were by no means contradictory. Rather they were complementary, each appropriate to its context within a larger strategy of survival. Challenged by threatening competition at a given level, people responded by cooperating at the next lower level. Thus when the context was competition at the level of the locale, they cooperated at the level of the lineage *(t'ung-tsu)*. When the context was competition at the level of the empire-wide polity, they cooperated at the level of the locale *(t'ung-hsiang)*. And when, by the end of the nineteenth century, the new context was competition at the level of the international arena, people were beginning to appreciate the necessity of cooperating for the first time at the level of the empire-wide polity, the nation.[30] Like yin and yang, cooperation and competition defined themselves by reference to each other: To survive against external competition, social groups at any given level required cooperation among their constituent parts. It was precisely the external competition which motivated the internal cooperation.

How did this pattern of behavior work itself out in the reality of Shaohsing's local society?

PART ONE
Survival Through Competition:
Shaohsing's Local Society

"[S]crawled all over every page are the words,
'Virtue and Morality.' Since I could not sleep
anyway, I read half the night, until I began to see
words between the lines, the whole book being filled
with the two words - 'Eat people.'"
(Lu Hsün, "A Madman's Diary,"
Selected Works, Vol. One,
Peking, 1956, pp. 11-12)

In Part One we shall delve into the main strata of
Shaohsing's society, from the protean "gentry" at the top,
through the respectable but restless masses, down to the
outcasts and déclassés at the bottom of the social order.
In short, we shall survey the highly competitive society of
late Ch'ing Shaohsing, keeping in mind the following questions and hypotheses.

Although within Shaohsing competition was the norm,
we must distinguish between competition in the core and
competition in the periphery. In the periphery were
lineages the premier mode of social organization, binding
rich and poor together through the vertical ties of blood
relations? According to Johanna Meskill, describing Taiwan
during the eighteenth and nineteenth centuries, "[M]en
frequently struggled over economic issues but seldom
aligned on the basis of economic status. Instead, ties of
loyalty ran vertically, between wealthy leaders and poorer
followers, within such distinct segments of society as clans
and communal groups."[1] Does this generalization apply
equally well to Shaohsing's periphery (Hsin-ch'ang,
Ch'eng-hsien, and to a lesser extent Chu-chi)?

12

In Shaohsing's core (Shan-yin, Kuei-chi, and to a lesser extent Hsiao-shan, Yü-yao, and Shang-yü), cooperation seems to have occurred not only via the vertical bonds of lineage but also via the horizontal bonds of class. As we shall see in Chapter Two, it was overwhelmingly within the core counties that Shaohsing's incidents of class conflict occurred (e.g., landlord-tenant disputes and rice riots pitting have-nots against haves). Moreover, the disparity between the regressive tax rates on gentry and commoner households was greatest precisely in the core counties of Shan-yin, Kuei-chi, and Hsiao-shan. Likewise, the evidence that lineages were aware of the damage which class conflict could inflict on lineage solidarity comes from the core: It is a Shan-yin genealogy, as we shall see, which includes the warning that a lineage should engage tenants to work the lineage land from among members of *other* lineages, lest ensuing conflict between landlord and tenants weaken the lineage from within. One is tempted to hypothesize that in Shaohsing, cooperation along class lines varied directly with proximity to the core, and thus with the level of commercialization and urbanization.

Were social relations within Shaohsing more complex in the core than in the periphery? In the periphery, as we shall see, class consciousness seems to have remained embryonic during the Ch'ing. In the core, however, it seems that cooperation along lineage lines coexisted with cooperation along class lines. The lineage remained strong in the core as well as in the periphery. For the competition which made cooperation necessary occurred in the core *both* between lineages *and* between classes: Classes competed for scarce natural resources such as the share of the harvest (i.e., food); lineages competed both for scarce natural resources such as water and for scarce human resources such as examination degrees, which gave access to wealth.

Surprisingly, it was the poor, not the rich, who seem to have been better organized along class lines, as we shall see. For it was the poor who needed to supplement whatever protection they were receiving from their lineages by seeking further protection via horizontal associations. So long as landlords and tenants belonged to different lineages, there was no compulsion - nor incentive - to choose between lineage loyalty to one's relatives and class loyalty to one's peers. Thus, we may hypothesize, respectable commoners had more organizational options in the core than in the periphery, and took advantage of them to cooperate for survival in Shaohsing's hyper-competitive, "Eat people" society.

CHAPTER ONE
Local Elites

"According to Ah Q, he had been a servant in the home of a successful provincial candidate. This part of the story filled all who heard it with awe. This successful provincial candidate was named Pai, but because he was the only successful provincial candidate in the whole town there was no need to use his surname: whenever anyone spoke of the successful provincial candidate it meant him. And this was so not only in Weichuang but everywhere within a radius of thirty miles, as if everybody imagined his name to be Mr. Successful Provincial Candidate."

(Lu Hsün, "The True Story of Ah Q," *Selected Works*, Vol. One, Peking, 1956, p. 108)

1. *Who Belongs?*

As Lu Hsün suggests, success in the civil service examinations was the high road to elite status in Ch'ing China. But it was not the only road, especially from around 1850 on, when the sales of degrees, ranks, and offices became widespread as the central government strove to increase its revenues to meet the challenge of the Taiping Rebellion. Lu Hsün's younger brother, Chou Tso-jen, recalls that in Shaohsing (presumably his native Kuei-chi) around 1900 the village constables were commonly loafers and no-goods at the command of the gentry. According to Chou, the gentry consisted not only of the high degree holders but also of those landlords and rich merchants who had purchased at least a subofficial's status: Even the

purchase of assistant county magistrate rank gave the purchaser as much power over the village constables in his
home locale as did the purchase of a grander position in the
officialdom. If a commoner ran afoul of a member of the
gentry, Chou Tso-jen continues, and the matter was not
serious enough for the latter to demand satisfaction from
the magistrate, the village constable would be called upon
to act as the gentryman's "servant" in settling the problem.[1]

We see here the domestic consequences of Shaohsing
natives' favored position in the Ch'ing administrative network, a phenomenon analyzed in detail below in Part Two:
Shaohsing's production of unusually large numbers of subofficials and Shaohsing natives' backdoor connections for the
purchase of offices (via Shaohsing clerks in the Board of
Revenue) must have resulted in a disproportionately large
number of Shaohsing natives who could claim gentry status
and use that status for their own ends in Shaohsing's local
society. If even an assistant county magistrate by
purchase had the power to make "servants" out of the
village constables back home in Shaohsing, the task of local
officials attempting to administer Shaohsing would be all the
more difficult. Thus there was a direct link between
Shaohsing natives' success in penetrating the Ch'ing
bureaucracy and the excesses of its own local elite.
Indeed, the very success enjoyed by natives of Shaohsing's
core counties in penetrating the bureaucracy can only have
heightened tensions between classes in the core. Conversely, one reason why there seems to have been less class conflict in the periphery is that natives of the periphery were
less likely to penetrate the bureaucracy and thus were less
likely to achieve gentry status facilitating their depredations.

It clearly would be unjustified - as well as naïve - to
assume that in other locales lacking Shaohsing's success
abroad, domestic tranquility prevailed. It is in fact common
knowledge that, as in many societies, social tension and
conflict were widespread in many parts of Ch'ing China.
Yet it is also true that similar effects do not necessarily
imply identical causes. In the case of Shaohsing - or, more
precisely, Shaohsing's core counties - the locale's success
abroad was one factor which contributed to making its
domestic society all the more unbearable for those struggling for survival at the bottom of the social hierarchy.
And those who lacked either powerful protectors or the
financial resources to profit personally from the Shaohsing
connection suffered the most.

Like his two elder brothers, Chou Chien-jen (1887 – 1984) has left us a description of his native place, a sketch of society in Shaohsing's prefectural capital on the eve of the 1911 Revolution. It highlights the variety and diversity of those claiming membership in Shaohsing's local elite.

> The city's residents were more varied than the coun-tryside's: handicraft workers, vegetable growers, short-term laborers, gondoliers, boat captains, pa-lanquin bearers, all sorts of shopkeepers and shop clerks, landlords great and small, various gentry (*shen-shih*) and notables. The gentry's categories were the most numerous. There were the relatively upright and straight-forward; there were the ex-tremely crooked; there were those who were also pet-tifoggers, those who also ran gambling houses, as well as those with a haughty manner. . . . [One, for example, refused to receive the Kuei-chi magis-trate when he came to pay a visit.]. . . Among the gentry those who were comparatively upright and honest were colloquially called the straight gentry. The base and avaricious ones were commonly called the stinking gentry, the same as what the written language called the evil gentry (*lieh-shen*). Then there were those out for a selfish profit under the guise of doing good deeds. The gentry existed in a plethora of types and categories. There were those gentry who were landlords, as well as those who were propertyless and relied on ad hoc fundraising, such as collecting wharf money (*pu-t'ou ch'ien*) and a house percentage from gamblers to get along.[2]

As Chou Chien-jen's all too brief sketch suggests, defining the Chinese local elite precisely is an analytical swamp, into which we shall not venture here. The exist-ence of propertyless members of the local elite, if indeed true, is a rather startling phenomenon. Yet if property per se did not denote elite status, the testimony of both Chou Tso-jen and Chou Chien-jen suggests that to define Shaohsing's local elite solely in terms of examination degrees would be unrealistically narrow. And even limiting our-selves to such a narrow definition of elite membership would not avoid the controversy over just what degrees should be included: Most of this controversy has centered on the holders of the *sheng-yüan* academic degree, those who, as passers of the prefectural-level examination, were nominally government students. Some scholars argue that the sheng-yüan were not part of the gentry, whereas others contend that they were.[3]   But both sides make the same, faulty assumption.   For it is a mistake to look for *the* gentry or *the* local elite as an objective entity the parameters of which were agreed upon by all members of society. Rather, it is important to recognize that membership in an elite is a question of perspective: He who is accorded status has status.   The peasantry, looking up from below, considered sheng-yüan to belong to the elite and treated them as such.   We know for instance that among the simple folk living in the hill country of Chu-chi, where "men of seventy and eighty had never set foot inside a city wall," the local sheng-yüan were in fact "highly respected."[4]   As we shall see, the sheng-yüan examination in Shaohsing was especially competitive.   Little wonder that in Lu Hsün's "The True Story of Ah Q," becoming a sheng-yüan gave Mr. Chao's son great prestige in Weichuang village. Indeed, even as a *t'ung-sheng* (a candidate eligible to compete for the sheng-yüan degree), his prestige had been considerable, since he had little local competition.

But at the upper end of the status hierarchy, *chü-jen* and *chin-shih* (respectively holders of the far more exalted provincial and empire-wide academic degrees) had every motivation to exclude sheng-yüan from their definition of the elite, if for no other reason than that the prestige of membership in any elite varies inversely with its size. We shall have occasion in the following pages to refer to "the local elite" or "the gentry," especially when indicating a simple contrast to the common people, on the one hand, or to local officials, on the other.   Yet the perceived size - and thus the boundaries - of the local elite seems to have varied inversely with the social position of the perceiver: For those near the bottom of the hierarchy, the elite loomed large indeed, and the status gap between sheng-yüan and chin-shih appeared much smaller than it did to someone who was himself a chin-shih.

Thus to ask "Who was the local elite?" is to pose a false question, one that is by its very nature unanswerable. "The local elite" was not a fixed category amenable to objective definition, precisely because the boundaries of the elite varied with the subjective perceptions of the society's participants.   For example, in extreme circumstances such as the crisis precipitated by the Taipings' invasion of Shaohsing in 1861, a peasant with charismatic qualities from a backwoods village in Chu-chi county could emerge as a leader commanding a large and socially diverse following that included degree holders who flocked to his banner even from Shan-yin and Kuei-chi. The fact that this peasant was "objectively" low-class meant nothing compared to the subjective faith which even his upper-class followers placed in his powers.[5]   Clearly, the qualities which people seek in those whom they consider "elite" depend on the subjective perceptions which people have of the specific circumstances in which they find themselves at a given time. Peacetime leaders can become wartime followers.   If the crisis is severe enough, roles can be reversed.

Note too the urban-rural implications of these subjective perceptions. Sheng-yüan prestige was highest where degree holders were fewest, in the periphery - the countryside, and *a fortiori* the hill country, where the inhabitants were almost inevitably poorer and less educated than their lowland brethren. Cities, the urban cores, conversely attracted the holders of higher degrees, and sheng-yüan there were easily outshone by their superiors. Credentials sufficient for elite status in the periphery might not carry much weight in the core.

It is precisely the variability in the status of sheng-yüan that makes them the most fascinating stratum of all, to their contemporaries as well as to us. Sheng-yüan were clearly a problem as early as the fourteenth century, the beginning of the Ming dynasty, when Emperor T'ai-tsu issued his famous Horizontal Tablet *(wo-pei)* of 1382, specifically demanding that sheng-yüan everywhere desist from interference in local politics. Even simple farmers, merchants, and artisans, as well as higher degree holders, were permitted to voice their political opinions, but not sheng-yüan.[6]

In the seventeenth century Ku Yen-wu wrote a famous essay on the sheng-yüan problem.[7] Ku attacked them for, among other things, their motivation: Too many people were becoming sheng-yüan not as a first step on the orthodox road to an official career, but rather merely to obtain the prerogatives of the status, such as immunity from corporal punishment. Sheng-yüan of this sort, whom Ku estimated at 70 percent of the total,[8] were enjoying all the privileges of their position without due regard to its responsibilities. They were not setting a suitable example for their inferiors. Assuming his estimate's accuracy, it seems obvious that if "70 percent" of the sheng-yüan in Ku Yen-wu's day had taken the examination only for the privileges of the degree, the percentage who became sheng-yüan for the same reason in the late Ch'ing, when the degree could be purchased, must have been even higher.

Shaohsing's sheng-yüan were well represented among the pettifoggers, as we shall see. "The Gentry," a twentieth-century play by Ku Chien-ch'en, who was a native of Shaohsing county, describes one of its characters as "an impoverished *hsiu-ts'ai* [i.e., sheng-yüan] and a hack pettifogger as well."[9]   It has been said that in general sheng-yüan were troublemakers.[10]   During the 1890s the magistrate of Kuei-chi warned that local disputes were for the village constable *(ti-pao)*, the magistrate's delegated representative, to handle, "not something for sheng-yüan to concern themselves with. . . . For sheng-yüan to interfere in any matters that do not concern them is a transgression of the Horizontal Tablet."[11]   As this warning strongly suggests, Ming T'ai-tsu's pronouncement against sheng-yüan activism had become Ch'ing policy too.[12]   By the 1890s the issue of sheng-yüan meddling had taken on increased significance as the balance of power between local officials and the local gentry became increasingly precarious.   In a core county like Kuei-chi, mere sheng-yüan were obvious targets for a magistrate on the defensive.

Yet it would be a mistake to assume that all instances of sheng-yüan activism were necessarily evidence of sheng-yüan corruption.   They may be the very reverse - protest against corruption.   Such seems to have been the case during the early Hsien-feng period (1851-1861) when tax resistance *(k'ang-liang)* broke out in Ch'eng-hsien, having spread from nearby Yin-hsien and Feng-hua in Ningpo prefecture.[13]   The leaders of tax resistance in all three counties were rural sheng-yüan and holders of the purchased *chien-sheng* degree protesting against the double standard of tax collection whereby the gentry paid at a lower rate than commoners.[14]   The protesting sheng-yüan and chien-sheng had been forced to pay at the less desirable rate, an obvious indication of their insecure status.   Their inability to improve their tax position by negotiation - in other words the impotence of these sheng-yüan and chien-sheng vis-à-vis the magistrate and his clerks - was a major motivating factor in their protest, and stands in further contrast with the access to the magistrate which was the right of all holders of the more prestigious chü-jen and chin-shih degrees.

Again the urban-rural continuum must be taken into account: These protesting sheng-yüan and chien-sheng lived in the countryside, where they undoubtedly awed the peasantry, but where too their low status vis-à-vis the magistrate was compounded by their physical alienation from his yamen. Conversely, the higher degree holders tended to congregate in the county seat, where their right of access to the magistrate could be conveniently utilized. Thus in these instances of tax resistance, the rural sheng-yüan and chien-sheng, existing at the interface between gentry and commoner status, became the natural leaders of popular protest. The contradiction between their lack of elite tax privileges and, we may suppose, their insecure self-esteem as would-be gentry made this stratum especially volatile.

What of those indisputable members of the upper gentry, the chü-jen and chin-shih? Their relationship with the local magistrate, while more intimate than that of the sheng-yüan, was also more complex, especially in the late Ch'ing, when the balance of power was shifting from the magistrate, representative of a weakened central government, to the gentry. The polite fiction to be found in local gazetteers was that the upright local magistrate and the community-minded local gentry were natural allies in rooting out corruption among the yamen clerks. As the 1905 Chu-chi gazetteer relates, the county had only a few of the upper gentry *(ta-shen)*, and eliminating malpractices perpetrated by the clerks, such as overcollection of taxes, was very difficult. Malpractices "have been unavoidable. The situation awaits a pure and benevolent father-and-mother official [i.e., county magistrate] to take pity and punish the perpetrators of these malpractices."[15] Note the pious implication that a larger number of gentry would reduce the clerks' excesses. What gives the lie to the gazetteer's polite fiction is testimony from another source that in this very county, the gentry had overpowered the magistrate from the beginning of the Kuang-hsü period (1875),[16] so the gazetteer's expressed desire for a clean official to step in and rectify the situation is at the very least disingenuous. Perhaps if the proportion of upper gentry in Chu-chi had been higher, the incidence of corruption among clerks would indeed have been reduced, but there is no reason to assume so a priori: Shan-yin and Kuei-chi, which almost certainly had the highest proportion of upper gentry in any of Shaohsing's counties, were hardly havens of clerkly rectitude, as we shall see.

2. *Internal Cohesion and Conflict*

In the Chinese context, survival implied organization. Of importance in any study of the gentry are the mechanisms by which that elite acted, or failed to act, as a group. When issues arose of immediate concern to the gentry as a whole, such as taxation, we find extensive elite cohesion. In an instance cited by Ch'ü T'ung-tsu, undated but almost certainly from the late Kuang-hsü period (1875-1908), "On one occasion the gentry members of Shan-yin and Kuei-chi, Chekiang, complaining about the excessive charges demanded by the clerks for registering the transfer of landed property, held a meeting and decided that only 800 coins should be charged for such a transfer. They forwarded their resolution to the prefect, asking him to authorize this sum as the permanent official charge. The request was granted."[17] We may well imagine that a local official faced with such a solid gentry united front would find refusal difficult indeed. An even more impressive display of interest-group cooperation by the Shaohsing gentry occurred early in 1911 when the perfidious behavior of a mu-yu in the prefectural yamen towards an elderly literatus aroused the victim's peers from all eight of Shaohsing's counties to present a petition to the governor in Hangchow demanding the culprit's punishment on threat of taking the matter to Peking.[18]

Similarly, when foreign incursions threatened the locale, the Shaohsing gentry quickly alerted their influential contacts in Peking. Thus when in 1905 a Catholic mission highhandedly appropriated some property, "the gentry and people" (*shen min*) telegraphed their fellow natives holding office in Peking.[19] This channel was used on at least one other occasion in 1905, this time to rebuff a French attempt to establish rights to a proposed steamship link between Shaohsing and Shanghai. Antiforeignism per se was not the issue; rather, some Shaohsing gentry wanted to establish a steamship company themselves and wished to avoid French competition. To this end Shaohsing officials in Peking exerted themselves and convinced the Foreign Office to reject the French demand.[20] Another source confirms that a gentry-managed "Shanghai-Shaohsing Steamship Company" was indeed established in 1905.[21] Never a treaty port, Shaohsing was protected by its gentry from direct foreign attempts at incursion.

But if they could cooperate against external threats, Shaohsing's gentry could just as easily compete over issues originating within the locale. One such issue was water control. Water rights were a life-and-death concern that could quickly provoke discord, and even armed struggle, among members of the same class. Acting in the interests of the lineages which they led, and which looked to them for protection, gentry were in no position to unite along class lines when their respective lineages came into conflict.

In Che-hsi water control usually meant irrigation; but in Che-tung, including Shaohsing, it meant above all flood control.[22]   The establishment of an extensive water control system by local officials as early as the T'ang and Sung dynasties contributed to the locale's productivity of both goods and human talent.   Certainly by the fifteenth century Shaohsing boasted an elaborate network of dams, dikes, and other water control devices, as a Korean eyewitness testified.[23]   The locale had a saying, "A dike every ten *li*, a temple every seven feet."[24]

The famous mu-yu Wang Hui-tsu, a native of Hsiao-shan county, notes from personal experience a case during the eighteenth century where, in Ch'ü T'ung-tsu's words, "repairs on the dike of [the] Ch'ien-t'ang River were financed by the gentry of Hsiao-shan, Shan-yin, and Kuei-chi, who contributed 40,000 taels of silver, and by salt merchants in Shaohsing, who contributed 10,000 taels. Several conferences were held between the local authorities and the gentry, eleven of whom were appointed as directors of the bureau in charge of the project and of its funds."[25] This need for multi-county cooperation between gentry and local officials in Shaohsing prefecture was of course not unique to the eighteenth century.   During the 1890s the Kuei-chi magistrate called a similar conference of gentry from the three core counties of Kuei-chi, Shan-yin, and Hsiao-shan, all of which were affected by the "Three river sluice" (*San-chiang-cha*) flood control system, located at the entrance to Hangchow Bay north of the prefectural capital.[26]   The purpose of this conference was a "wide solicitation of public opinion."   But the Kuei-chi magistrate expressed disappointment that the participants "each had his selfish viewpoint" and "none came up with an overall plan."[27]   Clearly the widely perceived need for a common solution did not necessarily imply the achievement of that solution, especially when members of the gentry were split by their competing particularistic interests.

In considering water control as an object of local politics, at least two dimensions must be considered – relations between the gentry and local officials on the one hand, and among members of the gentry on the other. Satō Taketoshi has argued specifically in reference to Shaohsing's San-chiang-cha three-county water control system that from the Chung-chen period of the late Ming (1628-1644) through the Hsien-feng period (1851-1861), the government's role in managing the system and financing repairs gradually decreased and the role of the gentry correspondingly increased. Wang Hui-tsu's description of private financing for water control during the eighteenth century tends to corroborate this generalization. Specifically, during the Chung-chen period private contributions first began to be used to supplement tax monies in financing repairs of the network, while simultaneously the gentry began to join local officials in its management; at the same time, the repair force began to consist of hired workers rather than corvée laborers. Then in the early Ch'ing, repairs were managed jointly by officials and gentry, but were financed solely by private contributions. During the Ch'ien-lung period (1736-1795) gentry participation in management operations increased even more, and by Hsien-feng the gentry was dominating both management and financing.[28]

Evidence from the 1890s suggests, as we have seen, that the gentry, now unchallenged in water control, became divided among themselves, unable to agree on an overall plan. There is of course no necessary contradiction here: As the government's role in water control became reduced to providing a forum for interested private parties to meet and hopefully agree, the likelihood of that agreement shrank as the need for unity against possible government control decreased. With the government unable to impose a solution, interest-group politics precluded automatic cooperation among the gentry.

Nor can the effect of the Taiping Rebellion be overlooked, at least in the short term. For as we know from the autobiography of Tuan Kuang-ch'ing, an outside official who was called in by the Chekiang provincial government to help organize dike repairs in Shaohsing immediately after the Taipings' expulsion in 1863, members of the gentry proved extremely reluctant to work together on a large scale to repair the water control system and control the already serious flooding.[29] This despite both the urgency of the situation and the gentry's habitually leading role in such projects. Because of the destruction caused by the Taiping invasion, members of the gentry seem to have been more interested in reconstructing their immediate locales and looking after the survival of their own families and lineages than in contributing precious resources to a large-scale, multi-county project. "As for the Shaohsing gentry, I'm afraid that unless their relatives encourage them, they will never be willing to put up [the repair money]."[30] Tuan tells of meeting with a Hsiao-shan literatus who had just been appointed to the censorate and was about to set out for Peking. Tuan told him, "You advise the emperor in ruling the people of the whole empire. But the people in your own home area were harassed last year by the soldiers [i.e., the anti-Taiping fighting] and this year by floods. Can it be that you refuse to help them?" The new censor smiled and replied, "You, sir, are here, so there is already someone to help them."[31]

But when the provincial government finally agreed to lend the necessary repair funds, to be repaid out of Shao-hsing's next harvest, gentry opposition to Tuan's repair project ceased. Now that the project no longer threat-ened their immediate local interests, members of the gen-try began supervising the on-site repair work, together with official deputies (*wei-yüan*), whose presence indicates that, *pace* Professor Satō, the government was unwilling to leave matters entirely in gentry hands.[32]

In addition to government and gentry, there was of course a third party intimately affected by water control, namely the peasantry. The gentry's internal fractiousness, its difficulty in cooperating to keep the extensive flood control system repaired, often threatened dire consequences for the gentry's tenants. After extensive flooding in 1899 turned paddy into marshland, tenants implored their land-lords to finance repair of the drainage ditches. While each of the other landlords hemmed and hawed, waiting for some-one else to make the first move, one Madam Wu (discussed below) acted on her own and contributed "$2300 foreign silver dollars" to save an area of some 10,000 *mou* (1700 acres) despite the fact that not more than 20 percent of it belonged to her family. This land was all in Shang-yü county, across the border from her home in eastern Kuei-chi. Once Madam Wu had shamed them into action, other landlords in that part of Shang-yü finally got together and agreed on a plan for reconstruction.[33] From the very nature of the drainage system, it would have been impossi-ble for any one landlord to pay for salvaging his own prop-erty without also salvaging his neighbors'.

Scholars have often stressed that water control required considerable cooperation to be effective, but the converse was equally true: Water control was not always effective. For cooperation among the members of Shao-hsing's gentry was by no means inevitable, expecially in the absence of an external threat.

3. *"Gentry"* or *"Merchant"*?

Compared with the caste system of India and the aristocratic feudalism of Japan and Western Europe, Chinese social structure was remarkably fluid, permitting mobility in both directions. "From peasant to peasant in six generations" was the epigrammatic recognition of this social truth. Thus while there was little question who was or was not a brahman, samurai, or *homme de qualité*, the composition of the Chinese gentry was much more problematic precisely because it was not dictated by birth. Whereas the *bourgeois gentilhomme* was an object of ridicule in ancien régime France, the attempt of Chinese merchants to gain the acceptance of their "betters" by adopting their life-style was applauded. Imitation was indeed the sincerest form of flattery.

Previous researchers such as Fujii Hiroshi, studying Anhui, and Evelyn Rawski, studying Fukien, have documented the pattern whereby in late imperial China rich merchants and their sons converted commercial fortune into official position.[34] By their voluntary coöption into the officialdom, merchants of means gained increased prestige for themselves and their families. In so doing, they reaffirmed the vitality of the social order. Similarly in our account of the late Ch'ing gentry in Shaohsing, the close gentry-merchant nexus must be stressed.

As Thomas Metzger has pointed out, we have been far too ready to assume that the ancient Confucian bias against merchants applied in the late imperial period as well.[35] We have been slow to recognize that by the nineteenth century relations between merchants and gentry were extremely cordial, and that brothers in the same nuclear family often took different career paths, one seeking to become an official, the other a merchant.[36] Thus did a family seek to maximize its chances for success. Lu Hsün's own situation is a case in point. There were three possible occupations open to Lu Hsün and his brothers: the examination route to office, the mu-yu alternative, and the merchant alternative. Moreover, a sophisticated distinction was made between different kinds of merchants. According to Chou Tso-jen, if the son of a literati household in late Ch'ing Shaohsing were to go into trade, the most desirable establishment for him to join was either a pawnshop or a money shop.[37] Apparently the rationale was that if becoming a rich merchant wasn't as desirable as being a rich official, it certainly was preferable to becoming a poor merchant.

Given the usual turnover in elite families, and the almost predictable trajectory of downward mobility, it is no wonder that families seeking to prolong their stay at the top of the curve and thwart the pull of social gravity should rely at least in part on merchant capital, which was often as not the very means of surplus accumulation that had gotten them to the top in the first place. Lu Hsün's own lineal ancestors in the course of thirteen generations had gone from peasants to merchants to literati, then back down, then back up, before they headed downward once more during his childhood in the 1890s.[38]

The term most expressive of the gentry-merchant overlap in the late Ch'ing is *shen-shang*.[39] It can be taken to mean "gentry and merchants" as two separate groups, but there is considerable evidence that the term was also used to refer to individual persons. Consider the case of Wang Ch'in, a Shaohsing grain merchant who was active in a joint official-local elite philanthropic venture to sell rice at a discount in Shan-yin and Kuei-chi during the shortage of 1898. A document listing the participants in this undertaking begins with the names of the local officials involved, then lists the "gentry-managers" (*shen-tung*), and concludes with Wang's name, preceded by shen-shang, "gentleman-merchant."[40]

Marianne Bastid confirms that in late Ch'ing usage shen-shang frequently refers to persons possessing both gentry and merchant attributes rather than to the two as allied but distinct groups.[41] Doubtless the widespread sale of ranks and posts did much to blur the gentry-merchant distinction. Moreover, the education received by at least some merchants' sons in late Ch'ing Shaohsing reinforces the case for the "gentleman-merchant" hybrid. The elementary school that Lu Hsün attended was located in the eastern part of the prefectural capital. Not a lineage school, it was run by an old sheng-yüan. The curriculum was standard Confucian, including the Five Classics, the Great Learning, the Rites of Chou, and the Erh-ya. Significantly, according to Chou Tso-jen, as of the late 1880s and early 1890s, when Lu Hsün was in attendance, the majority of students in this school were the sons of merchants and shopkeepers. They had no intention of ever taking the civil service examinations, but merely wished to receive a classical education.[42] Apparently the cachet of the Classics appealed to the parents of these *bourgeois gentilhommes*-to-be.

Dramatic evidence of this gentry-merchant overlap in late Ch'ing Shaohsing - especially in its highly commercialized core - is contained in the biography of a ninety year old matriarch named Madam Wu, written by her stepson.[43] As will become evident, one is hardpressed to decide whether the family into which she married is best characterized as a merchant family with a gentry lifestyle or as a gentry family with extensive commercial interests.

Madam Wu (*Wu t'ai-fu-jen*) was born in 1815 and raised in T'ang-p'u, a market town in eastern Kuei-chi. She married Tung Ch'ing-chang of Yü-tu, a village five li (about two miles) away in the same county. In the distant past, five generations back and further, the Tungs had held examination degrees, including the chin-shih. But within the last four generations none of Tung Ch'ing-chang's ancestors had achieved any examination success. The Tungs had resided in Yü-tu village for nineteen generations, since the Yüan dynasty (1279-1368) and traced their ancestry back a total of forty generations. Ch'ing-chang's great-grandfather had founded a money shop and prospered moderately, leaving an estate of sixteen mou (about three acres). A tradition of classical education clearly persisted in the family: Ch'ing-chang himself was classically educated, studying with various teachers soon after his marriage to Madam Wu and composing a volume of poetry. But in the examinations he had no more success than any of his recent ancestors. During his years in fruitless pursuit of a degree Ch'ing-chang's income was minimal, and the family lived in genteel poverty. His father, obviously educated but of no great means, taught elementary school to help out. In 1842, after having failed several times to achieve the sheng-yüan degree, he finally abandoned the examination path.

Ch'ing-chang's luck thereupon changed quickly for the better. His first break came the very next year (1843) when he began selling silkworms raised by his wife. "The accumulated debts of several decades were cleared up in a day, with capital to spare."[44] From this point on Ch'ing-chang demonstrated considerable entrepreneurship, with highly profitable results. In 1853 a relative from Hangchow, whose silver refining business had gone bankrupt, came to him for help. The relative's eldest son was in the firewood business, also in Hangchow, probably supplying his father's smelter. Ch'ing-chang proposed the following plan. He himself would put up the capital for his relative to buy firewood in the hills - it being cheap at the time - with the relative's son retailing the wood in Hangchow. Ch'ing-chang would enjoy 70 percent of the profit but absorb all the expenses in case the plan failed. His relative, who would get the remaining 30 percent of the profit, gladly agreed. The plan was implemented and proved successful. Ch'ing-chang made a tidy sum for himself, while doing his relative a good turn at the same time.

The Taiping Rebellion's invasion of Chekiang brought new dangers, but also new opportunities. As Ch'ing-chang analyzed the situation, "The times are dangerous, markets are closed, but if we are willing to run the risk and carry on with business, we can't help but monopolize the profits."[45] Realizing that circumstances were presenting him with an opportunity to achieve every businessman's dream, a monopoly, he summoned up more than enough risk-taking entrepreneurship[46] to seize the chance. So with Hang-chow's silk merchants panicking at the approaching Tai-pings, Ch'ing-chang bought their merchandise for a song. He bought more silk in Hu-chou, also at a cut rate. He branched out into the tea trade. When the actual invasion came in 1861, he shifted operations to Shanghai. Soon after Shaohsing was recovered in 1863 he returned, and the following year established a loan agency with several part-ners in Shaohsing city. Then in 1865, while land values were still down, he took the opportunity to acquire 900 mou in Shang-yü county. That same year he purchased the rank of expectant subprefect (*hou-hsüan t'ung-chih*), rank 5A, thus helping to safeguard his wealth and perhaps com-pensating for the disappointment of his unsuccessful exami-nation years.[47]

When this whirlwind of activity began to take its toll on his health in 1866, Ch'ing-chang followed his wife's advice and decided to give up his tea interests. But he had much to keep him busy. A money shop in Hangchow in which he had a financial stake was suffering from a part-ner's poor management and required attention. With anoth-er partner he also opened a pawnshop in Shang-yü. His younger brother opened another pawnshop with three more partners. In 1867, with steamships beginning to come into their own, the price of old-style wooden ships soon became very reasonable. Ch'ing-chang quickly purchased one, scrapped it, and made a profit on its wood.

His sons, to his great regret, were having no more success at the examinations than had he. So, like their father, they took up more practical pursuits. One learned the banking business in Shaohsing city, while another seems to have handled rent collections on the extending family's very extensive landholdings (which were to swell to 3000 mou by 1899).

Madam Wu's stepson-biographer tells us little about those from whom this groundrent was collected. But from the description of her seventieth birthday festivities in 1884, we learn that apparently in honor of the occasion the family's tenants were granted a rent reduction of over 10 percent. And when serious flooding occurred in 1899, Madam Wu ordered that all her affected tenants be excused from paying rent; simultaneously a pawnshop in which the family held half-ownership allowed its customers to redeem their goods without having to pay the usual interest. Perhaps the fact that she had lived on modest means early in life made her unusually sympathetic to the poor when she became rich. Perhaps the fact that she and her husband were not absentee landlords but remained in his ancestral village kept her aware of the peasants' hardships. Perhaps she was simply by nature a charitable person.

For it would be unfair indeed to imply that the fruits of his considerable business acumen were selfishly hoarded by Ch'ing-chang and his immediate family. When it was found desirable to reconstruct their ancestral hall to provide a larger stage and seating capacity for the performance of operas, he volunteered fully 80 percent of the cost. In 1867, moreover, he had even planned to establish a lineage charity estate *(i-chuang)* for his poor relations, for whom the Taiping invasion had proved less than a blessing. But this plan was still to be implemented when Ch'ing-chang died in 1874. He was buried on his property in Shang-yü. Thirty-one years later his widow, Madam Wu, finally established the charity estate with a donation of 1200 mou, consciously modeling it on the famous charity estate of the Fan clan in Kiangsu, founded in the Sung by Fan Chung-yen and still in operation in Madam Wu's day.[48] Commemorating her ninetieth birthday, the founding of the charity estate was the capstone and institutionalization of decades of extensive philanthropic activity, the benefits of which were not limited to lineage members but assisted a great number of the poor in her own and neighboring villages. Whether they would have been less poor if she had been less rich is of course another question.

After Ch'ing-chang's death his younger brother became the family's business manager. This arrangement permitted Ch'ing-chang's son, Chin-chien, to continue his examination studies, as Madam Wu desired. The relationship between Chin-chien and Madam Wu was very close despite the fact that he had been borne by one of her husband's secondary wives. Obviously valuing the examination route even above her husband's stupendous business success, Madam Wu exhorted the lad with memories of his late father's early unfulfilled examination dreams. "Your father loved to study. He would keep on even late at night. When he had a little money to spare, he would buy books. Finally, because of the family's circumstances, he became unable to satisfy this habit. Now your uncle is handling the family's affairs, so you are not sullied. You are just at the right age to revive the old scholarly heritage and have an [official] career."[49]

When, however, the uncle died in 1882, Madam Wu, by now a strong matriarch, was forced to tell Chin-chien that he would have to abandon the examination route and take over management of the family's business interests. She did permit him, however, to continue his studies on a part-time basis, and he annotated one of the works of the Han philosopher Tung Chung-shu. Apparently Chin-chien either passed or, more likely, purchased the sheng-yüan or chien-sheng degree, for he made one more attempt at the chü-jen examination in 1888, but failed. Madam Wu consoled him with the words, "Better to make yourself secure than to seek fame."[50] The next year his younger brother purchased the rank of expectant subprefect, thus maintaining for another generation the family's hold on the rank purchased by their father. Chin-chien thereupon devoted himself fulltime to the family's business interests, including a new money shop in Shaohsing city which he had established with a partner in 1885, three years before attempting the chü-jen examination for the last time.

Examination success continued to elude the family. A second younger brother kept trying, and failing, the chü-jen examination. Apparently having one expectant subprefect by purchase in the family was insufficient. Finally, in 1897, a lineage member succeeded in passing the chü-jen examination, the first time in the lineage since 1837. The family's triumph was vicarious but real. "Madam joyfully said, 'This is what our lineage has lacked for decades. It insures our local prestige.'"[51] The lingering insecurity of the nouveaux riches was now a thing of the past. She felt that finally they had arrived.

So once again we must ask, was this a gentry family with extensive commercial interests? Or a merchant family with deeply held gentry values? The answer is not ambiguous, for ambiguity itself is the answer.

CHAPTER TWO
Respectable Commoners:
The Struggle for Survival

In December, 1919 Lu Hsün returned home to Shaohsing for a final visit, to say goodbye and take his family
back with him to Peking. The episode is immortalized in
his memoir *Ku Hsiang* ("My Old Home"). In this memoir Lu
Hsün recounts meeting his boyhood friend, the peasant
Jun-tu.

> When I asked how things were with him, he just
> shook his head. 'In a very bad way. Even my
> sixth can do a little work, but still we haven't
> enough to eat . . . and then there is no security
> . . . all sorts of people want money, and there is
> no fixed rule . . . and the harvests are bad. You
> grow things, and when you take them to sell you
> always have to pay several taxes and lose money,
> while if you don't try to sell, the things may go
> bad.'. . . After he had gone out, mother and I
> both shook our heads over his hard life: many
> children, famines, taxes, soldiers, bandits, officials
> and landed gentry, all had squeezed him as dry as a
> mummy.
>
> > (Lu Hsün, "My Old Home,"
> > *Selected Works*, Vol. One,
> > Peking, 1956, p. 72)

1. *Tenancy and Taxation*

The overwhelming majority of Shaohsing's respectable
commoners were quite obviously peasants. In an evaluation
of the peasants' condition, the burden of taxes and rent

under which they labored is of course crucial. Even within Shaohsing prefecture we can expect considerable local diversity. Moreover, although the laboring classes composed the bulk of Shaohsing's society, they certainly did not compose the bulk of the written record documenting that society. In attempting to reconstruct the life of this silent majority, the historian must deal with bits and snatches, fragmentary but authentic, and thus preferable to a spuriously whole cloth. Consequently, the evidence to be presented is suggestive, not exhaustive.

Our first significant data on taxation and landlord-tenant relations in nineteenth-century Shaohsing come from Shang-yü county in the 1840s. According to Shang-yü's "Complete Regulations of Tax Payment" (*Wan-fu ting-chang ch'üan-an*), dated 1847, the various surcharges added to each silver tael (ounce) of the land tax resulted in a pre-1847 exchange rate of somewhat over 2500 copper *wen* per silver tael. But in 1847 over 3000 wen were collected per tael, resulting in a protest by the local gentry to the magistrate; they demanded that the clerks reduce their illegal surcharges. As a result the "Complete Regulations of Tax Payment" were drawn up by the magistrate to clarify the situation.[1] In 1839 the gentry of neighboring Ch'eng-hsien protested successfully to Peking in their efforts to have their magistrate revise the silver exchange rate which he had established.[2] Such disputes were common, for it was by manipulation of the silver-copper exchange rate that taxes were usually adjusted in the nineteenth century.

It was of course the landlords of Shang-yü (together with the land-owning peasantry) who had to pay the land tax. Yet while they were being squeezed by the tax surcharges, these same landlords were having increasing difficulty controlling their tenants, who paid no tax but whose rent was the basis for the landlords' tax payments. The Shang-yü gazetteer describes the increasing unruliness of tenants from the Opium War period on, and rather disingenuously places all the blame on the unrest stirred up by the British invasion of Ningpo at that time.[3] "After the British barbarians stirred things up, unruliness increased daily. Tenants transferred land to [other] tenants without asking the landlord's permission. As a result the new tenants had no rental contract with the landlord."[4] These tenants further confused their landlords by concealing and switching plots, and overpowered them by defiantly organizing themselves and taking de facto possession of the land they rented.[5] "Landlords had no way of controlling their property. From this point [the Opium War period] on, tenant abuses accumulated and rents decreased daily, as did the price of land."[6]

Evidence such as this, and more to be presented below, tends to validate the thesis put forward most strongly by Imabori Seiji that tenants in the lower Yangtze during the nineteenth century were capable of giving their landlords almost as much trouble as their landlords gave them.[7] Tenants did not passively accept their own exploitation, nor was their struggle for survival always futile.

The evidence from Shaohsing in the 1850s indicates substantial anti-tax unrest by landowners and anti-rent uprisings by tenants. The center of such activity was Yü-yao,[8] which had close marketing ties with Ningpo and thus was affected by the major anti-tax struggles that were breaking out in that prefecture during the 1850s, struggles which in turn spread from Yü-yao to Shang-yü.[9] A rare Chinese-language missionary newspaper, *Chung-wai hsin-pao* (The Sino-Foreign News), published in Ningpo during the 1850s, records widespread tenant violence in 1858 against the large-scale landlords of Yü-yao. Especially prominent among these landlords was the Hsieh lineage, which owned "several tens of thousands of mou" and was "long hated." Overdue rent payments caused the lineage in the tenth month of 1858 to make violent reprisals against its tenants, resulting in several deaths. In revenge, the local peasants attempted to "exterminate the Hsiehs." Part of the lineage did escape to Ningpo. There they hired twenty "braves" (i.e., mercenaries) and were on the way home with them when they were attacked by Yü-yao peasants, who killed sixteen.[10]

This incident raises the question of tenancy on lineage land. It is probably safe to state that most of the collective property of most Shaohsing lineages took the form of land. Thus it was the tenants to whom this land was rented who provided lineages with much, if not most, of their corporate income. What is known about tenants on lineage land in Shaohsing?

Most Shaohsing lineages which include information on their tenants in their genealogies seem to have had a deliberate policy of renting land to tenants from lineages other than their own, so as to avoid disharmony within the lineage if a rent dispute should arise. This policy was first enacted in 1083 by the famous charitable estate of the Fan lineage in Soochow.[11] In the words of a Shan-yin genealogy published in 1884, "Do not allow lineage members to become tenants on [lineage] land. Model yourself on the regulations of the Soochow Fans, lest there be persistent

defaulters the dunning of whom will injure lineage con-
cord."[12]

It was common for Shaohsing lineages to include documents relating to lineage lands in their genealogies. These
documents often list the lineage's tenants, and from these
lists it is clear that the lineage instructions cited above
were actually followed in practice. For the tenants' surnames almost always differ from that of the lineage.[13]

Hand in hand with renting to nonlineage tenants went
the practice of seeking assistance from the local magistrate
in collecting overdue rent, a phenomenon discovered first
by Muramatsu Yūji in documents relating to Soochow.[14] We
now know that the same practice occurred in Shaohsing's
core. The same Shan-yin lineage instructions quoted above
also state, "If there are persistent defaulters who don't pay
up, send an official to dun them."[15] Thus did lineages
shrewdly deflect tenant enmity away from themselves and
redirect it against the local magistrate, whose yamen runners did their dirty work.

Apparently the Hsiehs were following the standard
practice of renting to tenants from other lineages, thus
attempting to avoid weakening their own lineage with inter-
necine rent disputes. But this time the strategy backfired
disastrously, for their tenants, once provoked, had no compunctions about massacring them. Although we differentiate
between vendettas and landlord-tenant rent struggles, it is
not at all clear that in practice the participants themselves
made such an ironclad distinction. What we see as class
struggle may well have also appeared to the participants as
inter-lineage conflict.

Another landlord-tenant incident broke out in Yü-yao
the same year (1858). A rich absentee landlord named Li,
living in the county seat but owning 600 to 700 mou of paddy, refused to grant a rent reduction despite the year's
bad harvest. Another rich landlord family, the three Shih
brothers, who together owned "ten thousand mou," also
proved heartless. The aroused peasantry erected a plaque
stating that the magistrate's policy was to permit rent to be
paid at a 30 percent reduction in years of bad harvest.[16]
But the landlords remained adamant.

> The poor people got organized and remained reso-
> lute. Yamen runners arrested the leader of the
> tenants, Wang Ch'un-sheng. He was a t'ung-sheng
> [i.e., candidate for the sheng-yüan degree] who,
> seeing the peasants' suffering, acted as their chief
> strategist. When the assembled people saw him

being taken away, they entered the county seat en masse. Thinking that Wang must be in jail, they forced the warden to open the jailhouse door and free the prisoners. After most of the prisoners had escaped but there was still no sign of Wang, the magistrate in the crisis threw himself into the water twice [apparently attempting suicide] but was rescued by the people. At latest word the affair had not yet been settled. We have heard that on the twenty-eighth day of the second month and thereafter, local braves *(hsiang-yung)* [apparently in the landlords' employ] clashed with the local people on the bridges and roadways.[17]

This account is especially noteworthy for its explicit reference to the tenants' leader, Wang Ch'un-sheng, a t'ung-sheng. Lowly as Wang's examination status must have seemed to the magistrate who ordered him arrested, it must have given him great prestige among the illiterate tenants who looked to him for leadership. The account quoted above strongly implies, although it does not explicitly state, that Wang was not himself a tenant. In fact, another source claims that he was a "small, non-absentee landlord."[18] The question arises why even a small landlord would be leading a tenants' rent resistance uprising. But it is known that some of the tenant protestors whom he led shared his surname.[19] I take this fact to suggest that they were related to him. On his part, blood seems to have been thicker than class consciousness.

A related account, quite possibly of this same incident, has survived in the diary of Li Tz'u-ming, a native of Kuei-chi who was serving at the time as an official in Peking. The sources of Li's account are not known, but must have included letters from friends and relatives back in Shaohsing. Note especially that in his version the protesting tenants are termed "tenant bandits." In reading literati sources we must be careful not to accept such characterizations at face value. To the establishment any protestor could be branded a bandit.

Heard that tenant bandits[20] *(tien-fei)* of Yü-yao repeatedly killed soldiers and militiamen. The trouble cannot be resolved. Yü-yao is situated on the seacoast, where the inhabitants are ferocious and wealthy families are used to oppressing the common people. Last year, some rural inhabitants went to the hsien [yamen] to report a famine; they petitioned that rent be reduced. The magistrate, Ts'ui Chia-yin, listened to them. [With his authorization] an association was promptly formed and a bureau established; special dry-measures were made to be used in rent collection. Three of the big families, Shao, Hung, and Hsieh, refused to comply [with the new arrangements]. Violent fights broke out immediately. It happened that at this juncture a new magistrate arrived [at Yü-yao to replace Ts'ui Chia-yin]. The Shao family, in conjunction with others, forced the new magistrate to recruit local militiamen and to order them to arrest the tenants; they increased the rent further, inscribed the new rates on stone tablets, set up special bureaus [to collect the rent], and demanded prompt payment [from the tenants]. The rural inhabitants were infuriated. Hsüan Hsi-wen and Huang Ch'un-sheng,[21] both bandits *(fei)*, together with some others, incited the tenants to make trouble. After having surrounded and burned down the homes of some of the wealthy people, the mob attacked the hsien city in the same evening and set free all [tenants] that were previously imprisoned [by the new magistrate].[22]

The mechanisms by which protesting tenants organized themselves deserve further attention. As suggested above, landlord-tenant disputes were quite possibly transformed into disputes between lineages. Another, smaller unit of organization was the parish – the *miao* or *she*. Since single-lineage villages existed in Shaohsing, the terms miao and she in these cases may have had consanguineal as well as spatial significance. Both rural townships and villages in late nineteenth-century Shaohsing are said to have been divided into she. Each she had its own *she-miao* (parish temple) containing the statue of the local divinity but also used as a community storehouse for farm tools. Each she staged an annual parish opera *(she-hsi)*, described in Lu Hsün's story of the the same name.[23] We know that in Kuei-chi during the 1890s the peasants used their local parish temples to store grain which they had expropriated from a hoarder.[24] Thus the she and the miao, which were apparently interchangeable terms, were spontaneous, natural units of organization rather than artificial, administrative ones.[25]

Indeed it seems clear that the parishes (she) were also centers of local cults, about which the Confucian literati had grave misgivings. I have no evidence from Shaohsing, but the famous scholar Ch'üan Tsu-wang (1705-1755) from nearby Yin-hsien, Ningpo prefecture, has left a very suggestive essay entitled "On the Origins of the Parish."[26] In this essay Ch'üan condemns the contemporary proliferation of local shrines with the distaste of an Enlightenment Deist for Sicilian Catholicism. Ch'üan viewed local shrines as breeding grounds of idolatry and superstition, "just the thing to be promoted by the ignorant multitude." Equally deplorable to him, the she-miao institutionalized local divisions at the expense of greater unity. "The ancients united but today men divide." "So nowadays if you wish to rectify sacrificial rites, all you have to do is rectify those in the parish." From another viewpoint, however, the parishs' very "heterodoxy" testifies to their vitality - that they played a significant role in the lives of the local common people whom they served, that they were, in short, a meaningful mechanism of local social organization.

It was common for the members of the separate miao in a locale to join together periodically for religious processions or carnivals *(sai-hui)*. Again the Sicilian analogy is perhaps not amiss. The importance of such religious festivals as mechanisms of social organization and mobilization is underscored by the following account, again from Yü-yao in 1858.

> The Hsiehs of Ti-ssu-men, Yü-yao, are a rich and powerful lineage. Last year [1858] when major contributions *[chüan,* i.e., special taxes, apparently here for charity relief] were being solicited, the magistrate assessed them several millions [cash?]. The Hsiehs agreed to only several hundred thousands. The magistrate had no recourse. But when that year's returns showed a deficit, he promptly issued a proclamation instructing the impoverished to seek charity from the Hsiehs. The Hsiehs didn't cooperate. So the poor people plundered the Hsiehs, who brought charges several times. But the magistrate treated their charges as mere slanders. So the Hsiehs hired mercenaries *(yung)* and set up their own instruments of punishment. In the eighth month of last year a young scion of the Hsieh house was out riding his horse when he came across the local people holding the autumn festival procession with a dragon winding and revolving [i.e., a dragon dance]. Fearing that they would scare his horse, he harshly ordered them to cease. But the twenty-

odd men holding the winding dragon were unable to stop short, and the frightened horse threw him. The young lord returned home seething with anger. Later, when the procession reached his house, he ordered his minions to take revenge. Many in the procession were injured. The procession's participants represented a total of seventeen temples (miao).[27] The populace [from these seventeen temples] assembled and pressed forward in a swarm, bent on revenge. The Hsieh residence was surrounded on all four sides by lakes, with two bridges. Seeing the approaching horde, the Hsiehs pulled down one of the bridges, allowing access by only one [and thus setting a trap]. Ti-ssu-men [where the Hsiehs lived] is a market town (shih-chen). Its shops were all closed, with the Hsiehs' mercenaries hidden inside. After the mob had passed by, the mercenaries emerged from ambush and slaughtered over a hundred of them. From that day on the populace was at war against the Hsiehs. The original cause of the imbroglio was the Hsiehs' private usurpation of the official prerogative to torture. The horse and festival revenges were of lesser importance. People say that Yü-yao's rent disturbances are due to the Hsiehs. Actually, the number of people injured in the rent protest was not great [i.e., it was not the rent problem alone which was responsible for the continued violence].[28]

This passage suggests that a strictly economic interpretation of landlord-tenant relations in Shaohsing would be oversimple, for neither tenants nor landlords conceived of themselves in purely economic terms. They also played other roles, and their motivations were thus multiple.

Although lineage consciousness remained strong in all parts of the prefecture, class consciousness among Shaohsing's tenants seems to have been furthest developed in the core counties. Evidence from Hsiao-shan indicates that tenant power increased significantly from the 1850s through the Kuang-hsü period (1875-1908). During the Hsien-feng reign landlords were still able to evict deadbeats and bring in new tenants, who were required by contract to assume the previous defaulters' debts.[29] It has been claimed that in Hsiao-shan "during the Taiping occupation landlords were powerless and the people's mentality changed greatly."[30] This assertion should not be taken at face value, however,

for there is other strong evidence that the Taipings in
Hsiao-shan tacitly accepted landlord-tenant relations as they
found them and did not in fact implement any local social
revolution.   A Taiping period landlord's rent receipt from
Hsiao-shan has survived.

This interesting document, dated October, 1862, was
issued by a Taiping local administrator at Hsiao-
shan, Chekiang, authorizing a landowner to collect
4.6 piculs of rent in grain from his tenant.   This
printed document, though issued to the landowner,
was intended to become a receipt for the tenant after
the rent was paid. . . . As in many other localities
in Kiangsu and Chekiang, the land tenure situation
in Hsiao-shan seems to have been unchanged.[31]

Thus it is more likely that the temporary anarchy
caused by the Taiping invasion in 1861, and the flight of
Shaohsing's wealthy stratum to Shanghai, did more to
strengthen tenants' de facto control over the land they
rented than any implementation of a Taiping ideological mas-
terplan.   In any event it is said that in post-Taiping
Hsiao-shan "the tenants were organized and the landlords
were not."[32]   As of 1867 tenants were setting their own
rent rates, and landlords were usually no longer able to
evict deadbeat tenants.   Even when eviction did take place,
no new tenant was willing to scab for the landlord.[33]   It
seems reasonable to assume that what gave tenants in the
post-Taiping period such increased power was the fact that
the man-land ratio had been improved, for at least several
decades, by depopulation during the Taiping period.   Large
numbers of Shaohsing peasants emigrated to Chia-hsing,
north of Hangchow Bay, and to other now underpopulated
areas after the Taipings were driven out.   Thus Shaohsing
landlords no longer had population pressure on their side,
at least for a while.   As population crept back up toward
its pre-Taiping levels, the tenant's position vis-à-vis his
landlord did worsen.[34]   Yet it is my impression that Shaohsing tenants managed to maintain a better bargaining position through the end of the dynasty - although not necessarily much beyond - than they had had before the Taiping
invasion.   Rent rates in Hsiao-shan reflect this improvement.   During the Hsien-feng period landlords usually collected 70 to 80 percent of the stipulated rent rate, but
during the T'ung-chih and Kuang-hsü periods (1862-1908)
they were collecting only 60 to 70 percent of the rate in

good years, 20 to 30 percent in bad, and new tenants' customary payment for the privilege of renting was eliminated.[35]

Violent rent resistance continued in Shaohsing's core
counties during the Kuang-hsü reign. In Kuei-chi we find
tenants destroying rent contracts and beating up yamen
runners – indirect evidence that landlords were using
official authority to help collect rents.[36] "Tenants have all
kinds of perverse schemes. . . . They cannot be recon-
ciled to their lot."[37] Rent resistance in Kuei-chi was
especially common after floods,[38] probably because many
landlords were unwilling to grant temporary rent reductions, at least to the extent that tenants desired. It would
be unfair, however, to imply that all landlords were so
heartless. As we have seen, Madam Wu was one who did
grant reductions, and there were others: In Shan-yin the
Hsüs, one of "Chekiang's great houses," canceled all rent
(*mien-tsu*) on 1000 of their mou due to the poor harvest of
1889, as did the Chous the same year on all 4000 of their
mou.[39]

A nationwide survey of land tenure conditions conducted by missionaries in 1888 on behalf of the Royal Asiatic Society is instructive concerning the situation on the
"plain of Shaohing," i.e., Shan-yin and Kuei-chi counties,
as reported by Bishop Moule: "[N]ear Shaohing [city]
there are estates of several thousand, perhaps not 10,000
[mou]." In Jen-ho county, Hangchow prefecture, "working
farmers till at most one or two hundred mou, more in Shaohsing."[40] The "at most" should be emphasized. Certainly
the size of the average peasant landowner's holdings was
not that large.   In fact, Lu Hsün's family in Kuei-chi
(which, far from peasant, was definitely gentry – his
grandfather being a chin-shih and former Hanlin Academy
official) owned no more than 40 to 50 mou at the time of Lu
Hsün's birth, and this was enough to make it "a large
landlord by Kiangnan standards."[41]

Bishop Moule's description continues:

> Hired labor is employed, but not in any large propor-
> tion. My informants thought hardly 20 per cent of
> field work was hired. . . . My informants could not
> strike a proportion between freehold of the cultivator
> and leasehold. It is common for a small owner to
> add a few mou on lease. . . . Large owners employ
> an Agent to let their farms. . . . The landlord is
> paid, always in either paddy [rice] or dressed rice;
> usually that later; never in silver. The proportion

is said to be nearly, if not quite, one-half of an average crop of rice. It is, however, a fixed amount, except in bad years, when a composition [i.e., an arrangement] may be come to, the small tenants (who usually pay more) being let off at the same rate as large holders. All the other crops go to the tenant, e.g., wheat and barley, pulse, mulberry, sesamum, etc . . . etc . . . Good land, well-tilled, will yield 3 stone *[tan]* of paddy [rice]. Price and measure vary greatly according to locality. But the above yield was understood to be taken at the standard weight of the [tan].[42]

Another nearly contemporaneous Western account, based on a visit to Shan-yin and Kuei-chi in 1884, confirms Moule's information concerning the rent rate: "Cultivators' rack-rents range from 250 to 300 catties of paddy (equals half the weight of rice) a *mu* [mou], that is, nearly one-half of an average harvest. The landlord pays the tax, and the tenant pays for the beasts and implements."[43]

It will be noted that Moule mentions large estates of several thousand mou (almost certainly composed of a large number of small, scattered plots) in the vicinity of Shao-hsing city. Such estates were doubtless owned by rich gentry and merchants living within the walls of the prefectural capital, where the action (and protection) was.

Unlike tenants, peasants who owned their land and thus had to pay tax on it did not benefit even for a few decades from the post-Taiping depopulation. If anything, taxation got worse. According to Li Tz'u-ming's diary, elite households in Kuei-chi and Shan-yin as of 1859 (i.e., prior to the Taiping invasion)

paid only 1.25 to 1.3 taels for [what was nominally] 1 tael of land-and-labor service tax, whereas the medium rate was 1.4 taels, and the small households [i.e., peasant proprietors] paid as much as 1.5 or 1.6 taels for 1 tael of tax. [Li's] own family paid 1.38 taels. Li also mentioned that only his and other big [i.e., elite] households paid in rice for grain tribute, and as a rule, for every *hu* (half picul) of grain, they paid 6 or 7 *sheng* in excess of the legal tax. The commoners always paid in copper coins instead of rice.[44]

Here again we see the centrality of the exchange rate, or rather rates, to the whole tax problem. Members of the gentry were allowed to pay their taxes at rates lower than were commoners. Thus the tax structure (like the rent structure, as Bishop Moule indicated) was clearly regressive. The poor paid more. It was for the purpose of annually negotiating one's tax rate that the gentry's access to the magistrate was crucial. Yet note too that even the elite's tax rates exceed the legal (i.e., statutory) limit. Both gentry and commoners were paying more, because of surcharges, than the law specified; but the gentry was paying at more nearly the legal limit.[45]

The phenomenon of multiple tax rates for gentry and commoners was common throughout the lower Yangtze,[46] but it was apparently especially egregious in Shaohsing. Immediately after the Taipings' two-year occupation of the prefecture (1861-1863), Tso Tsung-t'ang, who was then governor-general of Fukien and Chekiang, wrote a widely reprinted memorial describing the post-Taiping tax situation in Shaohsing.[47] In it he urged both that the tax quota be reduced and that the multiple rates be abolished. "Upon investigating the tax quotas in the eight prefectures of Che-tung we find that Shaohsing's is the highest. The malpractice of overcollection is also most serious in Shaohsing.[48] In the tax payments of Shan-yin, Kuei-chi, and Hsiao-shan counties[49] there has been a disparity between the gentry and commoner households" (*shen-hu min-hu chih fen*). Tso continues,

If a fixed set of regulations is not clearly established and excess payments eliminated, the malpractices will get ever worse. . . . But if we stick firmly to a policy of tax payment in full at a uniform rate by both gentry and commoner households, the people will save over two billion cash and over 3000 piculs of rice within ten years. Thus there would be no need to assess [charity] contributions from those above to aid those below. . . . Poor households would not fret over insufficiencies. If official levies have fixed rules, then relations between those above and those below will be respectful. If the people's payments have fixed amounts, then clerks' malpractices will be eliminated. . . .

If the Shaohsing gentry proves recalcitrant, "the facts must be ascertained and punishments strictly meted out, to serve as a warning." In short, Tso was proposing nothing less than a complete overhaul of Shaohsing's tax procedures to force the elite in the core counties to pay a larger share, eliminate peculation, and thus ease the burden on the taxpaying peasantry.

The T'ung-chih Emperor's response was highly favorable:

> Let it be done as proposed. From now on let there be fixed tax regulations to be respected in perpetuity. No further shall a tax distinction between gentry and commoner households be permitted. . . . If gentry households fail to respect the regulations and do not pay in full, let the governor-general and governor ascertain the facts and punish severely, so that the State's revenues be increased and the people's suffering assuaged. Respect this.[50]

Was the attempt successful? Did the central government bend the elite in Shaohsing's core to its will? The answer is no. The double tax standard for gentry and commoners remained. In Hsiao-shan, one of the counties specifically mentioned by Tso, we find that as of 1877, thirteen years after his memorial, the old double standard was still in effect, and "a commoner-taxpayer had to pay about 1000 to 2200 more coins per tael" than did a gentry taxpayer.[51] And as late as 1904-1905, fully forty years after Tso's memorial, we find that in Shan-yin and Kuei-chi the clerks were still overcollecting,[52] the gentry was using its legal expertise to commit serious tax fraud,[53] and the prefect, ironically, was citing Tso's memorial in his futile railings against the longstanding abuses.[54]

As with rent resistance, antipathy against overtaxation in Shaohsing often became violent. Outbreaks of tax resistance occurred in Shaohsing, as in Ningpo, by the Hsien-feng period if not before.[55] Resistance was typically led, as we have seen, by rural sheng-yüan and chien-sheng,[56] whose status was insufficient to give them access to the magistrate to negotiate lower tax rates, but whose prestige was high in the eyes of their peasant neighbors – a potentially explosive contradiction. Particularly serious anti-tax outbreaks occurred in Yü-yao during the 1890s. To cite one example among many, just ten days after a new tax office was opened in 1898, over a thousand rioters, "sounding gongs and brandishing bamboo staves," destroyed the office and killed the tax collectors.[57] This incident was typical in its motivation: What infuriated the taxpayers in Shaohsing during the last decades of the Ch'ing was not so much the land tax, which though a burden[58] was long established. Rather, it was the new

commercial taxes, usually termed chüan but indistinguish-
able from *likin*, the tax on goods in transit, which proved
to be the proverbial last straw. Throughout Shaohsing
there was one attack after another on the new tax offices,
which seem to have slapped fees on almost any commodity
that moved - rice, tea, silk, cotton, tobacco, salt, wine,
etc.

The official rationale for imposing the likin tax in post-
Taiping Shaohsing was that the funds were to be used to
finance postwar reconstruction.[59] The extent to which they
were actually used for that purpose is impossible to determine, doubtless varying with the scruples of individual
officials and gentry. We are told, for instance, that in
Hsin-ch'ang county a new foundling home was opened in
1903 with the proceeds from the cocoon tax.[60] A contemporaneous Western source, on the other hand, took a more
jaundiced view, claiming that after the Boxer Rebellion of
1900 canny local officials throughout Chekiang attempted to
shift the blame for new imposts onto the foreigners' demand
for a huge indemnity. The foreigners retorted that more
often than not the new taxes went simply to line official
pockets. As the Hangchow correspondent for the *North-
China Herald* wrote in 1902,

> Every Chinese, from highest to lowest, is too well
> aware of the imposition of the 'indemnity' and every
> Chinese groans under it. . . . The amount appor-
> tioned to the province of Chekiang for payment
> yearly is $1,400,000. . . . Under cover of collect-
> ing this amount, the officials have strained every
> nerve to collect all the additional taxes they can in
> every direction. . . . [T]he whole province of
> Chekiang has increased tax receipts for the year by
> the sum of over $4 million dollars! Thus do the
> officials borrow the title of the indemnity for the
> purpose of extorting the highest possible amount of
> extra funds from the people, without the odium
> accruing to themselves.[61]

Western scholars have usually dealt with likin as a
mainstay of regional fiscal autonomy and as an impediment
to internal trade and merchant development. There is no
doubt that these perspectives are valid. Indeed, even
limiting our data to Shaohsing, we find that the merchants
in the market town of Tou-men, Shan-yin, staged a general
strike in August, 1911, to protest the levying of new commercial taxes.[62] But what has not been generally

appreciated, although Japanese scholars have made it clear, is that the ultimate victims of the likin and similar commodity taxes during the Ch'ing were not the merchants so much as the peasantry. Peasants had in effect to pay likin three times: First, directly, when they passed collection stations while taking their goods to market. Then indirectly, when the goods which they purchased were more expensive because the merchants had increased their prices to cover their own likin expenses. And, from the 1890s on, again indirectly when peasants received a lower price for the goods they sold, since the wholesale brokerage guilds purchasing their cash crops monopolized the market for each commodity; the wholesale brokers forced prices down in order to recoup the likin expenses which they themselves would incur when they resold the peasants' produce to retailers.[63] For example, as of 1900 in Shaohsing the cocoon brokerage guild *(chien-yeh kung-so)* monopolized the cocoon market, and peasants had no choice but to sell at prices set by the guild.[64] The whole inter-relationship between these local guild monopolies, the Shanghai market, and patterns of economic imperialism awaits its historian.[65]

Thus all those with whom the peasant came into commercial contact – the merchants from whom he bought, the brokers to whom he sold – passed on their own tax costs to the peasant. From the late nineteenth century on, peasants were not dealing with free markets in which they could bargain to sell their cash crops at the best price. Madam Wu's husband, as we remember, made his first money selling cocoons before the Taiping Rebellion. Fortunately for him, the likin tax was as yet unknown, and the brokers' market monopoly system was apparently not yet as firmly established as it was to become after the Sino-Japanese War (1894-95).[66] Otherwise his feat of social mobility might never have been possible.[67]

It was precisely in the economically most developed areas of China such as the lower Yangtze region that the likin taxes were most oppressive. For it was there that the division of labor was greatest, and thus the need to transport commodities at different stages of the production process most frequent.[68] For example, in Shaohsing the tinfoil for the spirit money burnt in religious ceremonies was hammered out in the urban workshops of the prefectural capital, but attaching the tinfoil to its paper backing was a major cottage industry for housewives both urban and rural.[69] Obviously the materials had to be transported back and forth between city and countryside in the course of the production process, and they were subject to taxation at each stage.

Although both merchants and peasants were victimized by likin, the merchants had an enormous advantage, in addition to being able to pass the cost of the tax on to the consumer: Merchant guilds negotiated on their members' behalf with the likin tax collectors, securing lower rates than an individual merchant would get on his own. By this procedure, called *jen-chüan* or *pao-chüan*, a guild would pay in advance all its members' likin expenses for a given period of time, thus saving each merchant the red tape and extortions attendant on paying likin each time he trans- ported his goods past a collection station.[70]   Increased exports, for example, led Shaohsing's several cotton-dealer guilds to ally in 1901 to form a cotton tax associa- tion *(hua-chüan kung-so)*, which handled their total month- ly likin payments "in order to avoid the various malprac- tices of stealing and leakage."[71]   There is some evidence that, as we might expect, merchants' success in negotiating reduced likin rates varied directly with the power and influence of the merchant guilds involved.   As with the land tax, the poor paid more.[72]   This situation helps explain the general strike in the Shan-yin market town men- tioned above.   In 1878 an even more serious protest broke out in several counties of Ningpo, as well as Yü-yao, when middle and small merchants went on strike to support the peasants' wholesale destruction of likin stations and even the murder of tax collectors.[73]

Thus there were definite contradictions within the merchant class.   Likin hurt poor merchants much more than rich.   Yet the fact remains that merchants were able - al- beit to varying degrees - to reduce the harmful effect of likin by what was in effect collective bargaining.   Contrast the peasants who sold produce in the marketplace - in short, the vast majority of Shaohsing's peasantry.   They were compelled to deal individually with the likin collectors, not to mention the wholesale brokers.   Whereas merchant guilds varied from strong to weak, comparable peasant guilds, such as cooperatives to market their commodity pro- duction, were nonexistent.   The state recognized the right of merchants to organize and negotiate for their common benefit.   No such rights were accorded the peasants.

It was said with good reason that to be a likin collector was more lucrative than to be a county magis- trate.   In 1880 Chekiang's likin revenue exceeded its land tax revenue.[74]   The likin rate in Che-tung during the late nineteenth century was no less than 10 percent ad valorem, compared to under 6 percent in Che-hsi.[75] The original definition of likin as a tax of one-thousandth had been long forgotten. Thus it is hardly surprising that peasants in Shaohsing, as elsewhere, branded as bandits whenever they attempted to organize themselves, expressed their outrage violently by burning likin stations and murdering their exploiters.

In addition to being an economic scourge, Shaohsing's likin stations *(ch'ia)* had a definite counter-insurgency function. Although they could not withstand attacks by well-armed "bandits," the likin stations did help discourage peasant uprisings, not only by keeping a close watch for the transport of weapons, but also by having at their disposal fifteen gunboats to intimidate the populace.[76] From 1898 on, Shaohsing prefecture contained 61 likin collection stations, compared to Hangchow's 51 and Ningpo's 23.[77] It is highly unlikely that all, or even the majority, of the tax collectors manning these stations were officials; according to Ch'ü T'ung-tsu, speaking of China as a whole, "many posts in the likin bureaus and stations were occupied by gentry members."[78] That gentry were engaging directly in tax collection demonstrates how the local balance of power had tilted in their favor towards the end of the dynasty. Yet such a development was not without its dangers, for it made a mockery of the gentry's pretense of protecting the peasantry against rapacious local officials. The peasantry's anti-likin violence had unmistakable implications of anti-gentry class conflict.

2. *Inflation and Rice Riots*

In addition to rent and taxes, the people of late Ch'ing Shaohsing faced another equally serious economic burden, inflation.

Inflation was a common end-of-dynasty phenomenon. Ramon Myers, reviewing the collected essays of the economic historian Ch'üan Han-sheng, notes that Ch'üan's "studies measuring price change during the northern and southern Sung and the early and mid-Ch'ing periods show that long periods of moderate price rise were soon followed by price fluctuations and rapid price increases by the end of a dynastic period."[79] Psychological uncertainty during a time of troubles played perhaps as great a role as objective scarcity in driving prices up. To cite an extreme example, the fall of Shaohsing city to the Taipings in November, 1861 sent the price of rice from 5000 cash per picul (tan) before the fall to 13,000 after.[80]

But this inflation was not merely a sporadic reflection of temporary shortages: The Hangchow native Hsü K'o found that commodity price inflation was substantial and endemic from the end of the Taiping Rebellion into the 1920s (the time of his writing). Since wage increases did not keep pace, a decrease in consumers' purchasing power was inevitable.[81]   Wang Yeh-chien confirms this picture of late Ch'ing inflation. He writes,

From the mid-80's [1880s] onward prices were unmistakably on the rise. . . . Given 1875 as the base year, prices had increased by one half by 1895 and by one and a half at the end of the dynasty. . . . The remaining years of the dynasty (1875-1911) witnessed the most inflationary phase, with the exception of the period of the Taiping Rebellion.   The index number remained stable around 240 for about a decade from 1875 to 1885, but shot up thereafter to 600 on the eve of the 1911 Revolution.[82]

People took to the streets to protest the rising cost of rice.   Sometimes rice protests were peaceful demonstrations.   At other times they were riotous lootings of grain merchants' shops.   Even after the Taiping depopulation, Shaohsing still had to import rice to feed itself in normal years.   In lean years it was of course all the more vulnerable to shortages.   As early as the Sung dynasty, when most of the lower Yangtze was still self-sufficient, Shaohsing was importing rice.   Wrote Chu Hsi, "Shaohsing is overpopulated and produces insufficient rice for its needs. Even when the harvest is good it is supplied from neighboring prefectures.   It is not like Che-hsi, where rice is plentiful."[83]   In the Ch'ing the usual suppliers for Shaohsing's perennial deficit were Chin-hua and Ch'ü-chou, both in Chekiang.   But in bad years, when these locales suffered from bad harvests, Shaohsing had to look further afield, as we shall see.

Although natural disasters, especially floods, increased Shaohsing's rice deficit and contributed to the rising price of rice there, another factor was the peasants' tendency to plant more lucrative cash crops such as cotton on land previously used for paddy.   We find this phenomenon, for example, in Yü-yao in the early 1920s.   Living in one of Chekiang's most highly commercialized areas, Shaohsing peasants were sensitive to the best-paying cash crops, and this sensitivity left them vulnerable to fluctuations.   Unlike subsistence farmers, they were not immune to the "unethical merchants" *(chien-shang)* who hoarded and profiteered from grain shortages.[84] Shaohsing's magistrates criticized merchants for such behavior,[85] but seem to have had no means other than persuasion to compel them to change their ways. The Shaohsing correspondent for the *North-China Herald* wrote from the prefectural capital in March, 1907,

> I know that the magistrate has for some time been exhorting the rice shops to cease raising their prices, but without avail. This is the result. A large crowd, chiefly of women and old people from the country, visited the District [i.e., county] magistrate, who promised to insist on the rice being sold at a cheaper rate, and told them to come again in three days, by which time he would have made some arrangement. That would be tomorrow, but I hear that the [rice] shops are still determined to hold out, and one fails to see what means, beyond exhortation, he can take to compel them to sell at a cheaper rate.[86]

Local officials and gentry did organize to purchase large quantities of grain and resell it to the needy at below market price, but such relief measures were less than fully effective if only because of their limited spatial scope, as we shall see.

On the very eve of the 1911 Revolution, flooding brought famine to Shaohsing, and prices soared. In the words of the local *North-China Herald* correspondent, published on October 7, 1911,

> According to the Governor's report to the Throne, Huchow and Shaohsing prefectures have suffered more severely than others in the province. In the Chuki [Chu-chi] district of Shaohsing, more than half the crops have been utterly destroyed. In Chuki city the water rose to within 18 inches of the top of the city wall. . . . The price of rice in the city of Shaohsing is $8.80 per shih, the highest ever reached here.[87]

Little wonder then that such desperate circumstances provoked a succession of rice riots. It is not possible to give a statistical accounting of such outbreaks in Shaohsing, since the sources are fragmentary and many incidents were doubtless never recorded. There is absolutely no doubt, however, from newspaper reports and the like, that these outbreaks occurred not only in Shaohsing but widely throughout the Yangtze valley during the final decades of the dynasty.[88]   To pick but a few examples, we read of Kuei-chi in 1902, "The harvest this year has been poor, and each rural township *(hsiang)* has been distributing rice at a discount to the needy.   The sufferers are massing together, and the houses of the rich have been destroyed in countless numbers."[89]   In Shaohsing dialect such outbursts were known as "pinning down the rich" *(chuang ta-chia)*. [90]   We read too of K'o-ch'iao, a central-market town in Shan-yin, where in the fifth month of 1911 over two hundred crudely armed residents decimated the rice shops.   Gunfire from the recently formed police force scattered the rioters, but they reassembled in a teahouse, where they "raged" and "loudly threatened to expropriate rice to eat."   Only after being given cash and rice by the merchants did they disperse.[91]

Fragmentary accounts of similar incidents abound. The magazine *Tung-fang tsa-chih* records that during the first month of 1907 "peasants of Shaohsing prefecture, owing to the high cost of rice, demolished rice shops."[92] The same source reports laconically that in the fifth month of the same year, "the poor took rice by force."[93]   A more detailed account in the Shanghai newspaper *Shih pao* (The Times) described a rice riot in May, 1911, in the town of Lin-p'u, Hsiao-shan.   This town contained a large number of rice merchants, according to the county gazetteer.[94] The owner of a rice shop there pleaded that his shop be spared destruction while he prepared his inventory for distribution (apparently at a discount).   The populace agreed; but when the time for distribution arrived, the rice shop, along with all others in the town, had closed its doors, and there was no food for sale.   Outraged at this trickery, the populace sacked many shops, and had to be subdued by gunfire (whether from private guards or police is unclear). Most of those killed were lacquer workers or perhaps painters *(ch'i-kung)* who, as urban artisans, obviously depended on market conditions for their food even more than peasants.   The local rice merchants' guild paid a token seventy dollars' compensation to the relatives of the deceased, to which the lacquerers' boss added another thirty dollars. The total sum was used for spirit money to be burnt in memoriam, whereupon the matter was considered closed.   A day or so later the Hsiao-shan magistrate visited the town and "forcefully exhorted all shops to reopen for business as usual."   The shops complied.[95]   Note that official exhortation was effective in this case, perhaps because it was perfectly timed to coincide with commercial self-interest.

We do not know the native places of Shaohsing's grain merchants, but it is quite likely that they were not Shaohsing natives, or at least were not natives of the locales in which they conducted their business. This informal mercantile law of avoidance doubtless made it psychologically easier for them to deny grain to the starving populace, just as the formal administrative law of avoidance resulted in reduced official compunctions about profiteering from one's post. We do know that the tea merchants in Shaohsing city were overwhelmingly natives of Hui-chou, Anhui; they spoke Shaohsing dialect to customers and their own dialect among themselves.[96] In Chu-chi city as of the early 1920s the pharmacists were from Yin-hsien (Ningpo), the leather merchants were from Tung-yang (T'ai-chou), the sugar merchants from I-wu (Chin-hua), the dealers in "foreign and Cantonese groceries" from Hsiao-shan, the pawnbrokers again from Hui-chou, and the potters from T'ien-t'ai (T'ai-chou).[97] This pattern of reciprocal profiteering among locales extended of course to crime as well. When Ah Q's gambling winnings were stolen, "where could he look for the culprits? . . . [M]ost of the people who ran gambling tables at the Festival were not natives of Weichuang."[98]

Local officials, although similar to merchants in their lack of emotional ties to the locality in which they served, were unlike merchants in that they were expected to set a moral example and keep the welfare of their subjects in mind. We do find them in not a few cases siding with the local populace against selfish grain merchants. But when, conversely, they chose not only to profiteer covertly but even to engage in overt and brutal repression of law-abiding commoners peacefully assembling to dramatize their legitimate grievances, such officials lost in a real sense their mandate to rule. Lu Hsün's youngest brother, Chou Chien-jen, mentions that it was not unusual in late Ch'ing Shaohsing for commoners to demonstrate peacefully outside a yamen to induce the local official to reduce taxes or otherwise alleviate their plight. The participants would each hold a stick of incense and would all kneel in orderly fashion in front of the yamen. The term for such a demonstration was *kuei-hsiang*, "kneeling with incense."[99] Chou tells us that on one such occasion the Shaohsing prefect, a cruel man named Ch'eng, dispersed the demonstrators "with vicious methods." Chou does not elaborate, but to understand what he means consider the following account published in the progressive newspaper, *Hang-chou pai-hua pao* (The Hangchow Plain Speaker), in May, 1902.

Shaohsing prefecture in recent years has not had one year of good harvests. The present price of rice is an exorbitant 7000 cash per picul [tan]. At that rate, how can the average impoverished person eat? There simply is no way. The only thing for them to do was to go, men and women together, to the house of the gentryman named Hu who was in charge of grain storage, and plead with him to distribute the grain. Gentryman Hu gave merely $5 worth to the beggar headman [kai-t'ou, a minor functionary[100] for him to distribute. Who would know that the beggar headman appropriated it all for himself? The next day the same group of men and women thronged to Hu's house. The beggar headman and the constable [ti-pao] were unable to maintain order. The crowd grew. Gentryman Hu, sensing what was in the offing, informed the prefectural and district yamens. Prefect Hsiung Tsai-ch'ing and Shan-yin Magistrate Yao Tzu-ch'i arrived with troops at Hu's house. Pitifully, the commoners, who were really extremely law-abiding, dared not move when they saw the officials approach. They only said, 'Because of the bad harvests and the high price of rice, we wanted to ask gentryman Hu to distribute the stored grain and save our lives.' The local officials heard this speech and exhorted them for awhile, whereupon they began to disperse. Oh, these common folk! How well behaved they are! Who would think that there would be violence? Unexpectedly, at 2 P.M., the Kuei-chi magistrate suddenly arrived. He lined up his troops, all with rifles in hand – completely different from Prefect Hsiung and Magistrate Yao. From the main hall of the Hu residence he delivered an angry cursing, saying, 'You troublemakers! I'll kill a few of you right off! See if that doesn't scare you!' The commoners heard and were terrified. They thought it over and still didn't dare start anything. In the front row someone was jabbed by a bayonet and began bleeding. Then a soldier fired. Rather than await certain death, the people charged. The Kuei-chi magistrate escaped out the back. Gentryman Hu's house was vandalized. It is said that two people were later arrested and executed. Just

before they were executed the two cried out loudly
for justice. It is said that one was a barber; the
other was also an artisan. Both still had old
mothers and wives at home. Oh, the pity of it!
The common people sought to have relief aid distributed. That wasn't any crime. They ran into a bad
local official, and a small incident became big.
Innocent people were unjustly killed. Although that
Kuei-chi magistrate is being transferred, transferral
is small punishment for murder. I don't know whether that magistrate is remorseful or not, ashamed or
not. But if he isn't, he should be the sworn enemy
of all us commoners.[101]

The need for a systematic relief effort to prevent
disaster in years of bad harvest was recognized in Shaohsing. The strengths and weaknesses of this effort inevitably reflected the society which produced it. There is in
the Institute of Oriental Culture at Tokyo University a
document entitled "Financial Report of Grain Sold at Discount in Shaohsing Prefecture" *(Shao-chün p'ing-t'iao cheng-
hsin-lu)*. Despite its title, the report, and the relief
project which it documents, covered only Shan-yin and
Kuei-chi, the counties in which the prefectural capital was
located. The document's preface, dated 1898, was written
by none other than Ts'ai Yüan-p'ei, future chancellor of
Peking University and a native of Shan-yin. In this preface Ts'ai states frankly that the purpose of the relief project was to forestall social unrest. In the spring of 1898
the price of rice in Shaohsing city rose to between 5500 and
5600 cash per picul, because of the poor autumn harvest.
Steps had to be taken to make rice available more cheaply.
Note that this was not a give-away, but rather a price-re-
ducing project. The officials asked the gentry to cooperate. They did; the names of seventeen "gentry-managers" *(shen-tung)* and one "gentleman-merchant" *(shen-
shang)* are listed at the very beginning of the document,
following the names of the participating officials.
It is worth noting that in addition to the names of the
participating prefect and magistrates, the document also
lists the names of participating subofficials such as assistant magistrates *(hsien-ch'eng)*, tax collectors *(shui-k'o
ta-shih)*, county jail wardens *(tien-shih)*, commissaries of
the seal *(chao-mo)*, and commissaries of records *(ching-
li)*. Indeed, it seems plausible that as conditions deterio-
rated toward the end of the dynasty and relief programs

became increasingly necessary, the importance of local subofficials to the harried magistrates and prefects must have
increased. The trend towards greater gentry power must
also have induced magistrates to make more use of their subofficials, in order to reduce dependence on the gentry.
Similarly, attempts to implement the late Ch'ing reforms
after the Boxer Rebellion must have given subofficials much
more to do. We know that during the late Ch'ing, branch
tax depositories *(fen-kuei)* were established in some of the
major market towns of Shan-yin and Kuei-chi so that taxpayers would not have to travel all the way to the county
seat.[102] It is highly probable that assistant or subcounty
magistrates were stationed in these market towns, if not
permanently at least when taxes were due. And, significantly, the 1898 document reveals that an assistant magistrate was sent to Hunan to buy rice for the relief project.[103]

   The 1898 rice relief project in Shaohsing was "a joint
official-gentry undertaking" *(kuan-shen ho-pan).*[104] Management of the project at the actual distribution level was
in the hands of the gentry. The managers of the rice sale
branch offices opened by the relief project were overwhelmingly gentry, although the document does record a few
cases of offices run by a rice shop, a spirit money shop, a
pawnshop, and even a shoemaker's shop. These establishments may well have been owned by gentry or "gentleman-
merchants." Clearly there was room for corruption. But
we know from other sources that the leader of the gentry
participants, a man named Hsü Shu-lan, was both a good
friend of Ts'ai Yüan-p'ei[105] (thus Ts'ai's preface) and an
honest, reform-minded gentryman. As we shall see, Hsü
established, at considerable expense to himself, one of the
earliest semi-modern schools in Shaohsing and a public
library as well. Thus it would be unfair to assume a priori
that this particular relief project was other than honest.

   The role of the "gentleman-merchant" Wang Ch'in was
to serve as external purchasing agent, buying rice in Wu-i
(Chin-hua), Lan-ch'i (Chin-hua), Hankow, Shanghai, and
elsewhere. He was aided by the assistant magistrate mentioned above. A recurring problem was that rice purchased
outside Shaohsing was often not allowed by local officials to
leave the place of purchase. In Shanghai, where rice for
Shaohsing's use was bought from as far away as Saigon, the
circuit intendant *(tao-t'ai)* decided to forbid shipment even
as the boat was being loaded. In Hankow, after Shaohsing

representatives purchased 8000 piculs, the price of rice on the local market rose as a result of the decreased supply, and the governor-general of Liang Hu forbade shipment. This crisis was finessed by Hsü Yu-lan, Shu-lan's brother, who "borrowed a passport" from a Ningpo friend and with this new identity managed to ship 5000 piculs back to Shao-hsing. The remaining 3000 were sold in Hankow by the assistant magistrate at the original purchase price (apparently to avoid further antagonizing the governor-general).[106]

Details on the location of the rice sale branch offices indicate that they were overwhelmingly urban. There were twenty-two branch offices in the Shan-yin half of Shaohsing city, each in a different ward *(fang)*, but only two in all of Shan-yin's villages. In Kuei-chi the pattern is the same: sixteen urban ward branches within Shaohsing city but only one in a village.[107] Thus the relief program was virtually limited to the population of Shaohsing city. This urban focus is understandable on several counts. First, since the purpose of the project was to prevent rice riots, the prefect naturally wanted to protect his immediate environs, the prefectural capital. Second, the leading gentry whose cooperation made the project work probably lived in the city, as upper gentry tended to do, and they too presumably wished to keep the urban populace as peaceful as possible. Third, as mentioned above, the urban population, not growing its own food, was in even greater need of relief than the peasantry. So the decision to concentrate on Shaohsing city was logical, given limited resources.

There is fragmentary evidence that similar discount sales of rice were carried out at different times in other parts of Shaohsing, for example in Chu-chi during the last years of the Ming[108] and, moreover, in Hsin-ch'ang during the Chia-ch'ing and Tao-kuang periods (1796-1850).[109] Doubtless it was common practice.[110] But the degree of corruption was not always as low as it seems to have been in 1898. In 1902, for instance, when the price of the "discount" rice in Shaohsing city actually exceeded the market price, public opinion was outraged, hostile posters appeared, and the prefect was replaced.[111]

But even when they worked perfectly, such relief measures could merely serve as palliatives. Respectable commoners like Jun-tu were still being squeezed dry as a mummy. Little wonder that some sought to survive beyond the law.

CHAPTER THREE
Outlaws and Marginal Elements

"'People should be on their guard against such a turtle's egg. It might be best to order the bailiff not to allow him to live in Weichuang.' But Mr. Chao did not agree, saying that he might bear a grudge, and that in a business like his it was probably a case of 'the eagle does not prey on its own nest': his own village need not worry, and they need only be a little more watchful at night."

(Lu Hsün, "The True Story of Ah Q," *Selected Works*, Vol. One, Peking, 1956, p. 112)

Social outcasts are almost always more interesting than the respectables who ostracize them. Just as the inhabitants of the *Paradiso* are so much more forgettable than those in the *Inferno*, the virtuous and upright statesmen of Chinese history pale before its desperados. Having considered gentry and commoners, we turn now to Shaohsing's dangerous classes, varieties of marginal folk who shared the stigma of being considered beyond the bounds of respectable society.

1. *Salt and Sand*

Although the point has been stressed by Japanese scholars such as Saeki Tomi,[1] the function of salt smuggling as an economic basis of secret societies' survival has not received in the West the attention it deserves. Indeed it has even been argued that technological innovation in the salt-making process resulted in increased secret society activity during the late Ch'ing, specifically in eastern Chekiang.[2] In contrast to the traditional method of producing salt by boiling brine in large vats, a new process called "the board-drying technique" (*pan-shai-fa*) was developed, based on solar evaporation. The new process is said to have been invented during the Chia-ch'ing period (1796-1820) on the island of Tai-shan in Ting-hai, Ningpo prefecture. Yü-yao had already become a major center of illegal salt production based on this new method by 1863.[3] This date is confirmed by another source which states that large numbers of people from Shan-yin and Kuei-chi escaped the fall of Shaohsing city to the Taipings by fleeing out onto the sand bars of Yü-yao, where they survived by drying salt on boards, using the Tai-shan method.[4] Moreover, as of 1910 Tai-shan and Yü-yao were still the two major producers of board-dried salt in Chekiang.[5] In contrast to Yü-yao, Hsiao-shan's salt was not suitable for board drying, so local variation cannot be overlooked.

The new board-drying process was much more economical since there was no need for firewood to boil the brine. Thus did illicit salt production become economically feasible for greater numbers of coastal dwellers, and smuggled salt became even cheaper and more popular. If the government-run salt works had switched to the new method, they too could have reduced expenses. But bureaucratic and occupational inertia and the previous capital investment in the boiling method made official salt production much less flexible than illicit, private production. Thus the price gap between official and smuggled salt increased, and secret societies which did the smuggling flourished. As the official salt monopoly became increasingly impossible to enforce, official salt works went into decline and some of the sites even began to revert to agriculture.[6] The government's loss of salt tax revenue can well be imagined.

In 1880 the prefect of Shaohsing issued a proclamation, preserved in his collected works, addressed to the producers of board-dried salt. This proclamation was written in Mandarin vernacular rather than in the literary language, apparently to increase its readership. It reads in part as follows:

You say that without board-dried salt you wouldn't have rice to eat, and that you're hard up. . . . But the Che-hsi salt region has been hit hard by your smuggled salt and [the official salt-makers there] also don't have rice to eat, so they're hard

up too. Surely you know this. At present helping
the authorized salt-makers *(tsao-hu)* means hurting
the board-dried salt-makers *(pan-hu)*, and helping
board-dried salt-makers means that authorized salt-
makers suffer a loss. It's really a predicament.
The Governor [of Chekiang] recognizes that both
groups among you are commoners *(pai-hsing)*. He
wants to survey the board-dried salt produced in
Tai-shan, Yü-yao, and Sung-chiang [in Kiangsu]
and come up with accurate figures on annual salt
sales in order to help you all out. This is why we
have had to do a survey of drying boards. Recently there have been those who don't know what
they're talking about who say the survey is to count
adult males for conscription. This is laughable.
The Taipings rebelled for so many years, and we
never conscripted anybody. . . . What the Governor has in mind is, for example: In every family
you always figure how many mouths you have to
feed, and just as you are to your families, so is the
Governor to the populace of the whole province. If
there is one person in one family without rice to eat,
the Governor has no peace of mind, just as you
wouldn't if one of your children went hungry. This
is why we have had to do a population survey. Recently smuggling has increased. Smugglers speak
only of helping the poor; they don't understand that
what they do is illegal. If official [salt] permits
aren't sold, we have to carry out coastal patrols,
confiscate the illegal salt, and burn the smugglers'
boats. These brutish smugglers don't know their
own best interests. They even put up a fight,
holding their own lives cheap. Some are killed by
our guns, others fall into the sea. The Governor
has heard that you commonly deal in smuggled salt
in order to make a living. He has also heard that
many of you have been killed. What a shame! At
present the only method to help you is to have the
[official salt] merchants prepare 300,000 cash and
buy the salt from you at an average local price of
four cash per catty. This is called transforming
private [i.e., smuggled] salt into official, and will
save many lives among you smugglers and lawbreak-
ers. This is why merchants are coming to receive
your salt. Your Prefect has been much concerned
with handling this matter. . . . In the coming days
I shall personally visit each coastal island to speak

with you. I shall bring no personal servants or yamen runners, no one to extort money . . . . [De-
tails of the plan to control production of board-dried
salt are as follows.] You are forbidden to sell or
[otherwise] deal in smuggled salt. Formerly when
you sold your salt to smugglers they forced the
price down and didn't have ready cash. Sometimes
you ran into storms on the sea or were arrested by
soldiers, so you were penniless and wasted your
energy. From now on I shall instruct the merchants
to come and collect your salt three times a month.
. . . They will pay cash on the barrel, and you
won't have the other troubles. Today's board-dried
salt will become tomorrow's cash. So you will have
rice to eat. [A dire prediction of what will happen
if they don't comply is omitted here.] You are
forbidden to increase the number of drying boards.
Your Prefect has counted them and recorded the
figures. . . . There may be those among you who
think, 'With our present number of boards we have
just enough to eat. If we added a few more, we
could save some money and gradually get rich.'
Such thinking is common. But you don't realize that
this makes problems for the Governor. It certainly
isn't that he doesn't want you to get rich; but he's
afraid that in the future there will be a problem of
overproduction. If that should happen, the boards
won't make money for you. Then not only will you
fail to become rich, you'll have to go hungry. The
Governor is thinking in long-range terms on your
behalf, considering things you never considered. So
there have to be limits. . . . Everyone who
respects these provisions will be a good commoner,
and the Governor's mind will be set at ease. Afterwards, if a re-check reveals no illegal increase [in
boards], no illegal sales, and no smuggling, your
Prefect's mind will also be set at ease. . . .
Henceforth salt drying and collection will proceed
peacefully and without incident, and you too can
completely put your minds at ease. You should
recognize the Governor's benevolence and pay no
attention to what bad people say. Let everyone look
out for himself and his family, with no disobeying of
this special proclamation.[7]

Apart from its colloquial style, this proclamation is
perhaps most striking for its rather benign tone, much less

hostile than we might expect in an official proclamation concerning violation of the salt monopoly. Yet the Ch'ing Code was more sophisticated in its treatment of contraband salt production than is sometimes realized. Specific provisions of the Code go far in explaining the Shaohsing prefect's assumption that the smugglers could still be reintegrated into respectable society. The Code does not forbid the production of unlicensed salt, only its sale.[8] Thus a family could legally produce salt for its own use. Even more important, the Code specifically permits "soldiers and people suffering from poverty to transport on their backs [i.e., in modest amounts] unauthorized salt and exchange it for rice in order to live."[9] It was probably because his audience, makers of board-dried salt, fell within this last category that the Prefect at one point refers to them, together with the licensed salt-makers, as "commoners," i.e., not criminals. What was illegal, however, was their selling of unlicensed salt by the boatload rather than by the backpack. It was this quantitative difference which made them liable to prosecution.

The proclamation is also notable for its indication that the producers of board-dried salt living along the coast of Yü-yao sold their product to professional smugglers, who exploited them by paying late and at reduced prices. The salt-makers were in no position to resist the smugglers directly, so they took to smuggling their salt themselves in an attempt to increase their income.

Shaohsing's coast dwellers, including these salt-makers and also marginal farmers, were known collectively as "the sand people" (*sha-min*). In the late eighteenth century Wang Hui-tsu described these "sand people" in Yü-yao and Shang-yü as "drifters" and "unemployed."[10] This was before the board-drying technique gave them an income. They inhabited the sand bars and new alluvial deposits that stretched beyond the sixty miles of continuous sea walls and dikes separating the Shaohsing plain from the tidal waters of Hangchow Bay.[11] Chiang Monlin, who was a native of Yü-yao, has described the ecological process involved in creating the habitat of the "sand people."

> The village of the Chiangs was one among many spread - with intervening spaces of one or two miles of luxuriant rice fields - over the alluvial plain by the Chien-tang river. . . . Down the valley, through the centuries, the river slowly laid its rich earth, building its shores farther and farther into Hangchow Bay. On the newly formed shores people

erected temporary enclosures to hold the brine from which common salt is made. A large quantity of salt was produced each year, supplying the needs of many millions. After a number of years, as the shores were further extended, the salt would begin to exhaust itself and dikes would be built along the drying land at some distance from the water. The embanked land was now ready for pasturing. After a long period it was capable of growing cotton[12] to feed the domestic looms or mulberry trees to nourish silkworms. It was still another half century before it could be turned into rice fields.[13]

A nineteenth-century source records that in some parts of Shaohsing the alluvial land "increased by several tens of li [perhaps ten miles] over a thirty year period."[14]

In addition to the problems posed by the board-dried salt-makers, there was a constant struggle between two other groups of "sand people," the marginal farmers and the authorized salt-makers.[15] One Kuei-chi literatus wrote an essay arguing that disputed land should go to the peasants, since "rice is in shorter supply than salt."[16] But in Shang-yü an official resolved the conflict conversely by ruling that all land beyond the dikes be reserved for the authorized salt-makers.[17] Shaohsing's "sand people" gave the government innumerable headaches, due ultimately to their marginal economic situation. Since they could not grow much rice on the sandbars, they were hard hit by its spiralling market price. The result was an armed uprising in 1900.[18] Again in 1907, *Tung-fang tsa-chih* contains a brief notice that "The sand people of Yü-yao county, Chekiang, are making trouble."[19] Since the boundaries of the sand bars were constantly shifting, with new ones always being formed, litigation over their ownership was unceasing.[20] Here we find an ecological factor helping to mold Shaohsing's heritage of legal expertise.

When ownership of alluvial land was impossible to determine even through litigation, the government itself took title, thus becoming landlord for many of the "sand people."[21] In 1904 the Governor dispatched an official to Hsiao-shan to collect "the government's rent" *(kuan-tsu)* on a permanent basis, a move designed "to kill two birds with one stone, benefitting the provincial treasury and ending litigation among the people [over the private ownership of alluvial land]."[22] This policy succeeded only in turning rent resistance directly against the government. In 1912 several thousand "sand people" in Hsiao-shan staged a rent revolt, and troops had to be sent in to put them down.23

2. *Bandits*

Competition and feuding among rival gangs of bandits, often salt smugglers, contributed to the generally violent atmosphere in the last years of the Ch'ing. One sample among many, a 1903 newspaper report from Shang-yü county: "[T]wo bands of smugglers *(hsiao-fei)* clashed, with two killed and eighteen wounded. The tao-t'ai is said to have already dispatched troops to suppress them."24 An account from 1910 describes a fight between two rival gangs in western Ch'eng-hsien who ran into each other at the gambling which accompanied performances of local opera, and set to with knives and guns.25

Appendix A contains evidence of secret society intervention in an interlineage vendetta in Ch'eng-hsien. Such vendettas, chronic in Shaohsing's periphery, presuppose a population trained to fight. Clearly this training could be put to use outside the lineage context, especially by those for whom lineage ties were not sufficiently rewarding. Moreover, the ecology of the periphery encouraged smuggling by secret societies: In coastal areas of Shaohsing there was some overlap between the producers of unlicensed, board-dried salt and the smugglers, as we have seen. At times the producers did their own smuggling. But in Ch'eng-hsien and Hsin-ch'ang, backwoods counties with no coastline, conditions induced a division of labor. For there smuggling was both more difficult and more profitable. All the salt consumed had to be imported. It is no coincidence that of all Shaohsing's counties, it was in Ch'eng-hsien and Hsin-ch'ang - furthest from the source of salt, furthest from the government troops garrisoned in the core (the prefectural capital), and with a tradition of militarization - that bandits were most active.26

Many of the bandits who terrorized Shaohsing's periphery were from T'ai-chou prefecture, which was known for the unruliness of its population. An account from 1910 describes an attack on a town in Hsin-ch'ang by "over two hundred" T'ai-chou bandits armed with rifles, who then headed back to T'ai-chou with their booty.27 Of course Hsin-ch'ang and Ch'eng-hsien produced bandits of their own, some of whom operated in Shanghai during the 1920s, as we shall see, giving Ch'eng-hsien a bad reputation there. Around 1894 there was a gang of banditti from Ch'eng-hsien active in Hsin-ch'ang and Chu-chi. Identifiable by the black waistbands which were their insignia and said to number in the thousands, they were not stopped until the order was given to shoot first and ask questions later. But within a few years Chu-chi was again beset by a new band, known this time for the distinctive silver coins which adorned their clothes.[28]

One aspect of banditry which has gone relatively unnoticed is the relationship between bandits and yamen personnel. The difficulty of bringing bandits to justice was increased by collusion within the yamen. A 1910 newspaper report notes that in the triangle where Hsin-ch'ang, Ch'eng-hsien, and Feng-hua meet, at least one bandit "arranged things" with yamen clerks so that his arrest, although ordered, was "postponed."[29]

Collusion between bandits and yamen clerks was obviously facilitated by the fact that clerks and runners were, to an unknown extent, members of the bandits' own secret societies. A newspaper account from the second month of 1911 states that "the evil depredations of the Sharp Sword Society *(Chien-tao tang)* of Hu-t'ang village in Shan-yin have reached an extreme." Several attempts to arrest its leader, Wei A-ch'eng, proved fruitless. "Wei has been in communication with the county yamen runners [comparable to policemen], and he escaped after getting advance warning." Another member of the same secret society named Sun moved to Hangchow and, Shan-yin native that he was, got a job as a clerk in the yamen of the provincial financial commissioner. Sun's cronies back in Shan-yin then terrified the local people into joining their society by warning, "If you don't, in the future you'll never escape our grasp."[30] For this bandit operating in Shaohsing's core, penetration of the bureaucracy, rather than military prowess, served as the vehicle for his extortions.

Although the revolutionary potential of secret societies, and their role in the fall of the Ch'ing, are important topics, they will not be treated here. For Mary Rankin has already given us a fine political history of the interaction between secret societies in Shaohsing (and elsewhere in Chekiang) and the anti-Manchu revolutionaries of the Restoration Society *(Kuang-fu hui)*. From the perspective of social history, the point to be made is that while a handful of young Shaohsing revolutionaries from privileged families such as Ch'iu Chin[31] and Hsü Hsi-lin considered secret societies as potential allies against the Ch'ing state, the vast majority of Shaohsing's population encountered secret societies all too often as criminal exploiters. Indeed, the very attempts by the Restoration Society to enroll local secret society bandits in its anti-Manchu cause may even reflect this would-be revolutionary organization's lack of concern for the plight of the common people: A group of bandits allied with the Restoration Society "alienated the populace by plundering," and, as Rankin observes, "One is struck by the general aloofness of the Restoration Society revolutionaries [in Shaohsing] from the economic discontent sweeping the lower classes...."[32]   There is no escaping the conclusion that during the late Ch'ing, Shaohsing's masses were infinitely more concerned with economic survival – in Lu Hsün's metaphor, trying to avoid being eaten – than with anti-Manchu revolution.

Moreover, the fact that secret society gangsters continued their depredations unabated even after the 1911 Revolution indicates that the anti-Manchu cause was not their *raison d'être*.   According to Chou Tso-jen, the more important of Shaohsing city's gangsters belonged to the Red and Green Gangs.[33]   This same charge was made in November, 1912, by the local correspondent for the *North-China Herald.*

> Rumor has it that many of these robbers [active in and around Shaohsing city] belong to a society known here as the 'Tsing pang' or 'the Greens.' This and another society known as the 'Hong fong' or 'the Reds' have been regarded both by the masses and by the authorities with suspicion.   An order came from the provincial capital to suppress the Greens, but they anticipated the order and amalgamated with the Reds.   The amalgamated society has assumed a new name and is said to have as many as 20,000 members. . . .[34]

The treatment of bandits in recent scholarship has presented them either as heroic embodiments of the popular will or as essentially criminal gangs.[35]   I would argue that the second characterization fits more of the Shaohsing evidence than does the first.   If, as I have suggested, respectable commoners had fewer organizational options in the periphery than in the core, the decision to opt out of respectable society and into banditry would also be made more often in the periphery than in the core.   But the result of banditry was only increased economic distress, and more banditry.   Thus was established a vicious circle of self-perpetuating criminality.   We know that trade in Hsinch'ang county was suffering in 1900 from bandit raids along regional transport routes.[36]   Such disruptions of marketing patterns could only result in inflation, as merchants raised prices to cover their losses. It is likely that even the social banditry involving expropriation from the rich ultimately victimized the poor, for the rich were not powerless. What they lost to bands of ex-peasants they could regain from the peasants still under their control. Thus whereas class competition in the core, e.g., landlord-tenant struggles, could result in victories for commoners (provoking landlords to lament that good tenants were scarcer than good land), banditry in the periphery actually helped to inhibit class struggle. Observing the principle of geographical avoidance and operating outside their native place - "the eagle does not prey on its own nest" - bandits victimized alien commoners and elites alike. Disfunctional to cooperation along class lines, banditry served to reduce commoners' ability to compete successfully against elites in the periphery.

3. *The Déclassé*

Finally, at the very bottom of the social hierarchy, the déclassé. One fascinating aspect of local society in all eight counties of Shaohsing prefecture, plus part of Ningpo, was the hereditary group of demeaned people, *chien-min,* known in Shaohsing as the *to-min* (literally "fallen people"). The homophone character *to* meaning "lazy" was also used. An alternate name for the Shaohsing to-min was *kai-hu,* "beggar households." The terms are used interchangably in gazetteer descriptions, and it is clear that, at least in Shaohsing, "beggar households" were not necessarily beggars.[37]

The Shaohsing to-min, and others like them throughout China such as the "musician households" of Shansi and Shensi, the Tanka (boat people) of Kwangtung, and the "shed people" of Fukien, to name a few,[38] were ethnically Han Chinese but had been relegated for reasons unknown to the very bottom of the social order. Barred from participation in the examinations, registered separately from respectable commoners *(liang-min),* their women forbidden from gaining status by binding their feet, indeed constituting a virtual caste, the déclassé were an exception, albeit statistically insignificant, to the general pattern of fluid social mobility characteristic of the late imperial period.

Limiting our discussion to the Shaohsing to-min, there are basically two traditional explanations for their debasement, neither of which can be taken at face value. One is that they were punished because their ancestor, a Northern Sung general, treasonously surrendered to the invading Chin army. The second is that they were punished for resisting Chu Yüan-chang at the beginning of the Ming. By the end of the Ming, the to-min's origins had already become obscure.[39]

As to their numbers, Shan-yin county alone was reputed to have contained "tens of thousands" of to-min as of the Chia-ch'ing period (1796-1820).[40] More reliable statistics for Chu-chi county in the 1920s reveal over 820 to-min households divided among forty villages in eight separate districts *(ch'ü)*. In all, as many as seventeen different common surnames were used by Chu-chi's to-min population. In nine of the forty villages, the surname of the resident to-min was part of the village's name, as in the case of "Li family" village, where there were over 100 families of to-min Lis. But other villages had ten or fewer to-min families. Of the thirty-eight villages in Chu-chi for which statistics are provided (two are "unknown"), twenty-three (61 percent) had fewer than twenty to-min families.[41]

The Shaohsing to-min, like déclassé groups elsewhere, were emancipated from legal discrimination by the Yung-cheng Emperor in 1723, but de facto social discrimination continued unabated into the twentieth century.[42] In fact there is evidence that to-min were barred from engaging in commerce and farming in parts of Shaohsing as late as 1945.[43] The phenomenon of social discrimination against a minority group continuing for centuries after its legal emancipation is of course hardly unique to Chinese culture.

To help understand anti-to-min sentiment in Shaohsing, consider Fan Yin, a literatus from Kuei-chi. Fan's exact dates are unknown, but he lived during the mid- and late nineteenth century.[44] As an examination candidate, he had only moderate success, failing to win the chü-jen degree but making the supplementary list *(fu-pang)*. While in his twenties Fan served for a while as a mu-yu, presumably after his setback in the examinations. Chou Tso-jen tells us that he was Fan's neighbor as a child and respected him.[45] Most important to us, Fan is the only Shaohsing native known to have published an essay on the to-min.[46] His *Yüeh yen*, a glossary of Shaohsing patois published around 1878, contains not only literary phrases but also actual street language. Fan came as close to conducting anthropological field work as any traditional Chinese scholar, inducing local children to sing their songs for him to transcribe and rewarding these "informants" with candy.[47] Thus we might expect Fan to show some sympathy for

Shaohsing's déclassé. But his essay on the to-min proves otherwise.

The essay begins, "Among all men there are the respected and the base, the noble and the mean, the great and the little, the gentleman and the small man." This hierarchy is the natural law of the universe. Respect it and there will be good order; flaunt it and there will be anarchy. Although it is doubtless desirable to "look on all with the same benevolence," this does not mean that distinctions can be ignored or categories mixed together. "Mencius' theory that human nature is good," continued Fan, "was a balm for the bitterness of the Warring States period. It is not the last word on the subject. However, Han Yü's explanation that there are three grades of human nature is definitive. How admirable!"

Fan then relates how the prefect of Yen-chou, Chekiang, had quite recently, during the T'ung-chih period, tried without success to assimilate the local déclassé element there. The women remained prostitutes. Fan draws the conclusion, "This is what Sacred Confucius meant when he said, 'By their practice men get to be wide apart' and 'The stupid of the lowest class cannot be changed.'[48] This is what Han Yü meant when he said some humans' nature is evil. How could it be uniformly good?" To what extent Fan's intellectual predilections were typical of his time and place is not known. But it is easy to imagine that thoughtful persons living during the late Ch'ing would find Mencius' assessment of human nature unduly optimistic. Fan's approach is hardheaded. Among the déclassé, "the men do not plow nor the women weave. . . . Even if you wanted to assimilate them, there is no place to begin."

A few segregated schools were established for to-min children during the last years of the Ch'ing. There was one in Shaohsing city called the To-min Farming and Trade School (*Nung-kung to-hu hsüeh-tang*). Around 1906 this school's name was changed to the Shared Benevolence School (*T'ung-jen hsüeh-t'ang*).[49] Most of its students were actors, a common to-min profession. The school did not last long, for financial reasons: Funds for educating the déclassé being rather tight, financing consisted largely of "squeeze" (*lou-kuei*) diverted from the yamen clerks. Angered by this loss of income, the clerks made it their business to get the school closed.[50]

Some accounts claim that the to-min's lot improved marginally after the 1911 Revolution. A nationwide law was passed after the Revolution giving all déclassé groups the rights of regular citizens,[51] thus in effect repeating Yung-cheng's emancipation proclamation. Lu Hsün has left a description of the to-min in a short essay written in 1933, stating in part

> [T]he Tomins in Shaohsing are a sort of freed slaves, who were probably freed during the Yung Cheng period. They therefore all have trades, which are naturally low ones. The men collect junk, sell chicken-feathers, catch frogs, or perform in operas, while the women call on their patrons [chu-jen] during festivals to offer congratulations, and help in marriages and funerals. Here, then, is a trace of their former servitude. But as they leave as soon as the job is done, and are well tipped for it, they are obviously freed.
>
> All Tomins have definite patrons and cannot just go to any house. When the mother-in-law dies, the daughter-in-law takes her place, and so the relationship is handed down from generation to generation like a family heirloom. Only when a Tomin family is so poor that they [sic] have to sell the right, are they separated from their former masters [i.e., patrons]. If some patron, for no reason, tells a Tomin not to come again, it is a serious insult. I remember after the 1911 Revolution my mother said to a Tomin woman: "In the future we shall all be equal, so you needn't come here any more." But the woman was very angry, and answered indignantly: "Whatever are you saying?. . . . [ellipsis in original] We shall go on coming here for thousands of years."
>
> So for a few tips they are not only content to be slaves, but want to find more masters and pay to buy the right to servitude. I dare say this is something inconceivable to free men outside the Tomin caste.[52]

Thus the to-min supported themselves by various hereditary occupations which they were unwilling to abandon even after their successive "emancipations" of 1723 and 1912.[53] Lu Hsün finds their desire to maintain these disesteemed occupations perplexing. But perhaps the to-min's lukewarm response to the economic consequences of their "emancipation" is really not so bizarre or irrational. After all, their déclassé status guaranteed them control of various hereditary occupations which liang-min commoners shunned. Nor was to-min income from these occupations necessarily less than the non-gentry liang-min's income from *their* hereditary occupations. If "emancipation" were to entail abandoning their hereditary occupations, to-min would be at a severe disadvantage in the labor market: They would be forced to compete against the rest of the local population in occupations new to them, for which they had no expertise, and which, moreover, had long since been claimed as hereditary by other segments of the labor force. Anti-to-min discrimination would hardly be likely to diminish under such circumstances of unprecedented competition between to-min and liang-min. In short, the to-min's evident desire to perpetuate the occupational status quo even after their 1912 "emancipation" makes good sense in terms of both economic survival and social harmony.

Lu Hsün's list of to-min occupations is incomplete. Other sources tell us that the women were known as hairdressers, bridal attendants, and matchmakers for families of regular commoners, and also as prostitutes. Thus the to-min were not untouchables in the Indian sense, nor perhaps even as segregated as the Japanese *burakumin*. The men were opera singers, musicians, and banquet attendants - it was apparently very chic to hire them as wine-pourers - as well as fortunetellers, funeral attendants, frog catchers (frogs' legs were a delicacy in eastern Chekiang),[54] sweetmeat sellers, sculptors of clay idols, and yamen runners.[55]

It was in this last capacity that the to-min most affected the lives of the respectable populace. That yamen runners were, by statute, déclassé is well known.[56] But the reverse formulation has not been sufficiently explored. Were yamen runners déclassé because the déclassé became yamen runners? One wonders if historically the position of yamen runner was innately so repellent to decent folk that it became a monopoly of the déclassé by default, or if conversely the statutory déclassé status of yamen runners is merely an ex post facto acknowledgment that déclassé elements were monopolizing the position. In short, is it not possible that yamen runners were despised both socially and legally not only because they were considered incorrigibly corrupt and ruthless, but also because the occupation of yamen runner was hereditary among a caste which was already despised? Perhaps the yamen runner-déclassé relationship became a self-perpetuating vicious circle, with déclassé becoming runners and runners déclassé. It makes sense psychologically that yamen runners, with negative status but considerable de facto power, would become ruthless: Denied prestige by society at large, they compen-

sated by using their power to take revenge. Their social
stigma must have become a self-fufilling prophecy.

To take our speculation one step further, a locale like
Shaohsing with a comparatively large déclassé population
would also be a locale where the percentage of yamen runners from déclassé families would be unusually high (since
not *all* runners necessarily came from déclassé families). In
such a locale, the respectable population would be especially
motivated to assist the magistrate in controlling his yamen
runners. As early as the 1587 edition of the Shaohsing
prefectural gazetteer we find complaints, repeated in later
editions, concerning the abuses perpetrated by to-min serving as yamen runners.[57] Now it is a fact that control of
the yamen runners was one of the mu-yu's major responsibilities.[58] Could it be that Shaohsing's mu-yu heritage
originated in the need to protect the good people of Shaohsing from the to-min who were afflicting them as yamen
runners?

Like all minority groups suffering from discrimination,
the to-min engaged in a certain amount of "passing." This
was especially true of the more prosperous ones, for they
were not all poor.[59] During the Wan-li period (1573-1619),
there was a physician living in Peking who was a Shaohsing
to-min. He prospered and purchased an official position.
Thereupon other officials exposed his shameful origins; he
lost his post and became a physician once again.[60] Another
prosperous Shaohsing to-min purchased a Central Board
clerkship, also during the late Ming.[61] For these to-min
who became wealthy, corruption was socially functional,
opening doors that would otherwise have remained closed.
Likewise, social mobility for to-min was made possible by
geographical mobility, i.e., emigration. After the Yung-
cheng emancipation, some to-min left Shaohsing to avoid
persisting social discrimination. Of these, a few are said
to have managed to become gentry in their new locales.[62]
Such successful "passing" infuriated Fan Yin. "I have
heard of a to-min living in the Three Street section of
Shaohsing city who opened a shop, became moderately successful, and then travelled to Hui-chou and Yang-chou on
business and slipped into the ranks of regular commoners."[63]

Until 1911 at the very earliest and probably long
after, intermarriage between to-min and self-respecting commoners was unthinkable, at least to the latter.[64] But just
as some to-min succeeded in "passing" by moving elsewhere, there is evidence that at least one to-min was so

bold as to attempt to change his registration category and occupation while remaining in Shaohsing - both of which the Yung-cheng emancipation edict gave him every right to do - and even to attempt to marry his daughter into a respectable family. The lineage which suffered this brazen affront, the Chungs of Chu-chi, made their outrage perfectly clear in a proclamation, included in their genealogy, titled "An Open Prohibition of Marriage between the Respectable and the Déclassé."[65] Dated 1883, this document allows us an extremely rare glimpse behind the scissors-and-paste stereotypes of to-min typical of other sources such as gazetteers.

The Chung lineage's proclamation begins by laying a legal groundwork for its opposition to the outrageous marriage proposal. It cites a precedent *(li)* of 1771 which states that between the time a member of any déclassé group applies to change his status and the time when his family members shall be permited to take the examinations, a probationary period of three generations must elapse (counting the applicant as the first generation). During this probationary period the family must be "pure," i.e., not engaged in a déclassé occupation. A period of less than three generations, or persistence in a "vulgar occupation," disqualifies the application. The lineage's proclamation then notes that "Our county has a to-min named Ch'en from Chu Village who, the year before last [1881], petitioned the magistrate, wishing to change his occupation and be counted among the respectables."[66] Whereupon the magistrate issued an edict stating that "local bullies and sticks will no longer be allowed to oppress and insult"[67] Ch'en and his family, a clear indication of the treatment which to-min usually received at the hands of local rednecks. "But," added the magistrate, "the designation to-min shall be retained," presumably until the three generations' probationary period had passed.

Ch'en's petition and the magistrate's response instantly became "the prime topic of conversation. Who would have expected it?!" But that was only the beginning. "A member of our lineage . . . whose personal name is Pang-hua is the local village idiot." He was persuaded by a matchmaker to marry the to-min's daughter. His family and lineage were appalled. They did everything possible to prevent the match. The head of the lineage ordered the engagement terminated, and not only found another fiancée for Pang-hua from a suitable family, but even offered him 5000 cash as an inducement. But Pang-hua persisted. An emergency meeting of "lineage [branch] heads from the various villages" was held and decided to take the case to court. There the magistrate ruled that "The State's law need not accord with human feelings" *(kuo-fa pu shun jen-ch'ing)*. When the two conflict, the law must prevail. From Yung-cheng's emancipation edict on, the law had prescribed that to-min were not be treated differently from other commoners. To forbid the marriage would be both illegal and also "in the final analysis, no remedy for cleansing away the old stain" of discrimination. "The marriage shall go through. Case dismissed."

With the law demanding one course of action and social custom the opposite, a more perfect test of the relative weight of Confucian *li* (proper decorum) versus Legalist *fa* (codified law) in the mind of a late Ch'ing magistrate can hardly be imagined. Nor can a more breathtakingly Legalist verdict. The lineage's description of its reaction is a model of diplomacy: "Likewise the lineage branch heads from the various villages had only to hear the verdict and they were prostrate." Whether their prostration signified submission or shock is moot.

But the lineage's gentry were not helpless. They still had means to mitigate the effects of state coercion. In retribution for the irreparable damage which the marriage, now unavoidable, would do to the lineage's hitherto spotless reputation, Pang-hua and his future progeny were ostracized, stricken from the lineage's genealogy. "We officials and literati [of the lineage] wish to advance upward. How can we be willing to associate with some one who voluntarily cohabits with a member of the déclassé?" Only by resorting to ostracism "can we face our ancestors and set an example for our descendants."

Although we do not usually think of Ch'ing society in such terms, what the unfortunates at the bottom of Shaohsing's social order were up against resembled nothing so much as a caste system. With competition as fierce as it was in late Ch'ing Shaohsing, it must have been comforting for respectable commoners near the bottom of the hierarchy to know that there would always be a minority group even lower.

PART TWO

Survival Through Cooperation:
The Shaohsing Network
in the Ch'ing State

A riddle:

半幅經綸
Half baked.

全憑刀筆餬口
Completely relies on scribbling
to fill his mouth.

處處認同鄉
Knows fellow natives
everywhere.

半月住西邊,半月
住東邊
Each half month takes
opposite sides.

一條光棍
A hired gun.

到底不成人
The bottom line: not quite
a man.

What is being described here?   The answer is in the Notes.

In Part One we examined competition, the law of the
jungle that was Shaohsing.   In Part Two we shall examine
cooperation, the key to Shaohsing natives' survival outside
their native place.   To be sure, intra-prefectural competition cannot have been entirely absent even abroad: Shan-
yin and Kuei-chi natives especially must have provoked jeal-
ousy among the natives of Shaohsing's other counties, for
as we shall see, Shan-yin and Kuei-chi led the way in
Shaohsing's production of government functionaries.   But
since a united front generally proved advantageous to all
Shaohsing natives abroad in the struggle against natives of
other locales, minimizing internal discord made good sense.

73

When Shaohsing natives were far away from home, intra-prefectural tension became, as it were, a minor contradiction, kept within bounds by the threat posed by the more immediate, major contradiction between Shaohsing and the rest of China.

Chapter Four surveys the exodus of Shaohsing natives throughout the Ch'ing empire. Chapters Five and Six proceed to analyze in some detail how Shaohsing's gentry, braving the taunts of competing outsiders such as the riddle recorded above, strove to ensure their survival as gentry by maximizing their representation in the Ch'ing bureaucracy. In short, Part Two examines Shaohsing natives' success in cooperating to survive, and even prosper, in the larger world of the Ch'ing state.

CHAPTER FOUR
Shaohsing's Emigrant Tradition

In their constant struggle for survival and, if they were fortunate, prosperity, Shaohsing natives settled throughout China. Geographical mobility was of course a common phenomenon in no way limited to natives of Shaohsing: Both the law of avoidance barring officials from serving in their home provinces and the merchants' practice of making their profits outside their native place ensured that geographical mobility - resulting in mutual exploitation among locales[1] - would be widespread. But just as Shaohsing was known for mu-yu although it had in fact no monopoly on them, so too were Shaohsing natives proverbial for their tendency to travel. "Three things are to be found everywhere," ran the proverb, "beancurd, sparrows, and Shaohsing natives."[2] In 1875 an English missionary expressed the hope that the wide scattering of Shaohsing natives all over China would promote the spread of Christianity, if only Shaohsing itself could be converted.[3] In order to understand Shaohsing's impact on the Ch'ing state, it is necessary first to survey this exodus of Shaohsing natives and their resettlement throughout China. After making a rapid *tour d'horizon*, we shall then consider in detail the single most significant pattern of emigration from Shaohsing during the Ch'ing: north to Chihli's Shun-t'ien prefecture.

The engine of the exodus was relative overpopulation. Obviously Shaohsing was not alone in this regard. But it has been hypothesized that during the last years of the Yüan dynasty (1270-1368), the fighting between the would-be dynasts Chu Yüan-chang and Chang Shih-ch'eng reduced the population of the Che-hsi region, while leaving

Che-tung unscathed. Thus, the argument runs, Shaohsing was overpopulated in comparison to Che-hsi, and proportionately more Shaohsing natives left home to make a living elsewhere.[4] Although such estimates can never be precise, it has even been claimed that "By the mid-16th century, half of the residents from Ningpo, Shaohsing, Chin-hua, and Ch'u-chou earned their living in other regions throughout China."[5]

Likewise, in the mid-nineteenth century Che-hsi suffered rather worse from the carnage of the Taiping Rebellion than did Che-tung, with the result that once the fighting stopped, peasants from Shaohsing and Ningpo flocked into Chia-hsing prefecture and other accessible regions of Che-hsi containing unclaimed land:

> After the Taiping war northern Chekiang as a whole, and its rich alluvium in particular, immediately attracted immigrants from overcrowded Ningpo and Shaohsing prefectures. Land-hungry peasants from other coastal prefectures, T'ai-chou and Wen-chou, soon joined ranks with Ningpo and Shaohsing peasants and settled first in the delta of Chia-hsing prefecture and then in the valleys and low hills of Hang-chou and Hu-chou prefectures.[6]

So many emigrant peasants had settled in Lin-an county (Hangchow prefecture) by 1900 that Ts'ai Yüan-p'ei worked to establish an elementary school there for them. And of a total of 28,499 immigrants living in Yü-hang county (also in Hangchow prefecture) as of 1898, fully 50 percent (14,336) were from Shaohsing.[7]

Even more intriguing are the statistics on numbers of persons per immigrant household (hu): The emigrants into Yü-hang from everywhere except Shaohsing and Ningpo averaged three to four persons per household; but those from Ningpo prefecture averaged twenty-one persons (4321 immigrants in 203 households), and those from Shaohsing prefecture averaged forty-six persons per household (14,336 immigrants in 309 households).[8] There is no ready explanation for these enormous immigrant households from Shaohsing and, to a lesser extent, Ningpo. Clearly they cannot represent nuclear families. Nor is it likely that these immigrants were gentry living in extended families. Nevertheless, it seems that Ning-Shao "households" were emigrating into Yü-hang as more complex, or at least much larger, family units than were immigrants from elsewhere.

Manner of emigration aside, the cause of this emigration seems to have been refected in population density statistics. The 1933 census found Shaohsing county (composed of the former Shan-yin and Kuei-chi counties) to have the densest population in all Chekiang, which was itself one of the most densely settled provinces in China. For purposes of comparison, the population density of Hanghsien (in the former Hangchow prefecture) in 1933 was 146 persons per square li (one li equalling about a third of a mile), and of Yin-hsien (in the former Ningpo prefecture) 178. That of Shaohsing county (formerly Shan-yin and Kuei-chi) was 212, with a total county population of 1,225,458. The 1933 densities for the remaining counties of the former Shaohsing prefecture are as follows, in descending order (with that year's population in parentheses): Hsiao-shan 177 (499,321), Yü-yao 143 (637,700), Shang-yü 104 (293,291), Chu-chi 83 (527,822), Ch'eng-hsien 72 (422,016), and Hsin-ch'ang 62 (238,169).[9] An American missionary estimated the 1903 population of Shaohsing's prefectural capital at 200-300,000,[10] almost certainly an overcount: A gazetteer gives the capital's population in 1910 as 112,402.[11]

Once a Shaohsing native emigrated, he tended not to return.[12] A case in point is a lineage in Hsiao-shan in which only 40 to 50 percent of those members leaving to escape the Taiping Rebellion returned home afterwards.[13] This percentage is especially low when we consider that the initial motive for emigration in this case was not the usual one of long-term economic advancement but rather self-preservation from a temporary danger. One would have expected a larger percentage of the lineage to have returned to Hsiao-shan once the danger had passed, but they chose to remain in Shanghai.

One way to trace the migrations of Shaohsing natives throughout China is by their establishment of *hui-kuan* (native-place associations, *landsmannschaften*). Ho Ping-ti's study of these associations greatly facilitates this task. By the late Ch'ing five of Shaohsing's eight counties had established hui-kuan in Peking: Shan-yin, Kuei-chi, Hsiao-shan, Yü-yao, and Shang-yü.[14] Note that all five were located on Shaohsing's alluvial plain and were precisely those counties that seem to have had the prefecture's highest population densities during the late Ch'ing. In addition there was one hui-kuan representing all of Shaohsing prefecture.[15] There had been a Shaohsing hui-kuan, the Chi-shan hui-kuan, in Peking built during the Ming's Chia-ching or Lung-ch'ing reign periods (1522-1572). It seems to have been one of Ming Peking's earliest hui-kuan.[16]

One source not available to Ho Ping-ti, a rare manuscript in the collection of the Institute of Oriental Culture (Tōyō bunka kenkyūjo) at Tokyo University, lists a total of 598 hui-kuan or other native-place associations (such as temples) in Peking at some unspecified date between 1912 and 1944. Of these 598 there are 41 from Chekiang, including seven from Shaohsing: Shaohsing hui-kuan, Yao-chiang hui-kuan, Hsiao-shan hui-kuan, Shang-yü hui-kuan, Shan-Kuei i-kuan, Yü-yao hui-kuan, and Che-Shao hsiang-ts'u.[17] Note the close correspondence between this list and Ho's cited above: The same five of Shao-hsing's eight counties appear on both lists. But also note the two organizations not listed by Ho and thus presumably established after 1911: a temple serving natives of all of the former Shaohsing prefecture and a second Yü-yao hui-kuan. Did factionalism within the original Yü-yao hui-kuan require the founding of an additional institution? The answer is unknown.

By the late Ch'ing and early Republic additional Shaohsing hui-kuan could be found (and the list is neces-sarily incomplete) in Hankow, Chiu-chiang, Wu-hu, Nanking (the Che-tung hui-kuan), Soochow, Hangchow, Tientsin, Tsinan (the Che-Shao hsiang-ts'u), Sian (as of 1940), and Shanghai, in addition to the Ning-Shao occupational guilds in Shanghai, of which Ho discovered "too many to cite."[18] There were joint Ning-Shao hui-kuan in smaller towns.[19]

Tsinan's Shaohsing temple, included in the above list, represents another form that native-place associations could take. Serving Shaohsing officials and private secretaries in that part of Shantung, it was flourishing during the Hsien-feng reign, when a literatus from Kuei-chi included a des-cription of it in his collected writings, noting ironically that on his first trip through Tsinan he was ignorant of the tem-ple's existence and learnt of it only later, upon perusing the Shantung provincial gazetteer.[20] Canton had a Ning-Shao charity graveyard as early as the 1620s.[21] And Jehol had a temple and burial ground especially for resident Shao-hsing private secretaries and clerks from the early Ch'ing.[22] A major center of Shaohsing natives in north China was Pao-ting.[23] There were many private secretar-ies from Pao-ting, usually of Shaohsing ancestry.[24] Profes-sor Yang Lien-sheng's forebears are a case in point.[25] There is a story in the *Ch'ing-pai lei-ch'ao*, a collection of Ch'ing stories and anecdotes, about a Shaohsing mu-yu who became an official but then resigned from office and decided to resume his career as a private secretary. He lived in Pao-ting while awaiting employment, presumably because Pao-ting was a good market for mu-yu.[26]

Of all its émigré settlements, Shaohsing's clique in Shanghai was probably the largest. Ningpo and Shaohsing people dominated Shanghai native banks *(ch'ien-chuang,* "money shops") in the second half of the nineteenth and early twentieth centuries. There is disagreement as to exactly when this dominance began, some scholars citing the Sino-French War (1883-1885),[27] other suggesting a somewhat earlier date.[28] Indeed, according to oral tradition, Shanghai's first ch'ien-chuang was founded by a charcoal merchant from Shaohsing sometime in the eighteenth century.[29]

In his autobiography the educator Chiang Monlin (who replaced Ts'ai Yüan-p'ei as chancellor of Peking University and, not incidentally, was a native of Shaohsing's Yü-yao county) recounts how his family's participation in Shanghai banking began. "My grandfather [became] the manager of a Shanghai bank. During the time of the Taiping Rebellion (1851-1864) he [had] put up a money stand in the native city of Shanghai [to which he had presumably moved to avoid the rebels]. This grew later into a small money exchange shop which in turn developed into a native bank. . . ."[30] So many Shaohsing natives fled to Shanghai to escape the Taipings that special relief centers had to be established for them, funded by gentry and merchant contributions in the name of native-place (t'ung-hsiang) solidarity.[31] It seems reasonable to assume that Chiang Monlin's grandfather was not alone among the Shaohsing natives for whom what began as a temporary exile in Shanghai developed into a lucrative career. It has been estimated that there were 20,000 Shaohsing merchants of all kinds in Shanghai as of 1908.[32]

Virtually all the Shaohsing financiers in Shanghai were natives of Yü-yao and Shang-yü counties.[33] Portions of both counties (especially Yü-yao) were economically oriented towards Ningpo. Although the Ningpo clique in Shanghai was perhaps the more famous among Westerners, there is evidence that Shaohsing native banks in Shanghai exceeded their Ningpo counterparts in both capitalization and number of banking establishments.[34] In fact a Japanese source dated 1908 claims that the majority of Shanghai's native banks were run by Shaohsing natives alone, wielding enormous financial power.[35] And the Shaohsing correpondent for the *North-China Herald* reported in 1916 that "The local banks have proved a great training ground for managers and accountants. I suppose most of the Chinese banks in Shanghai are run by them, and even the foreign banks keep a goodly number of Shaohsing accountants."[36] The cooperation between the Shaohsing and Ningpo factions was close; they were usually mentioned together as the Ning-Shao clique *(Ning-Shao pang)*.[37] During the Republican period fully 80 percent of the capitalization of Shanghai's native banks was controlled by the Ning-Shao clique.[38]

A dramatic Shanghai example of the Shaohsing clique's cooperation with its neighbors from Ningpo was the establishment in 1908 of the Ningpo-Shaohsing Steamship Navigation Company. The trial run of the company's flagship, named inevitably the "Ning-Shao," proved a gala event:

> Indeed the whole of the Chinese Bund and all the jetties in the neighborhood were packed with enthusiastic Chinese. . . . Her course down the Huangpu partook of the nature of a triumphal progress. . . . Mr. Yu Ya-ching, Manager of the Company. . . said that trade between Shanghai and Ningpo was on the increase, and it had therefore been decided at an influential meeting of Chinese merchants to start the present enterprise.[39]

The Shaohsing population in Shanghai did not, however, consist solely of enterprising businessmen. The working class was also represented. For example, women from mountainous Ch'eng-hsien flooded into Shanghai to work in the spinning mills. In this way Ch'eng-hsien's peasant opera, sung by women, reached Shanghai. At first the women sang for their own enjoyment, but before long their labor bosses *(pao-kung-t'ou)* were having them sing and pass the hat in tea houses. By the 1920s Ch'eng-hsien opera had become extremely popular in Shanghai. To gain respectability it advertised itself as Shaohsing or Yüeh opera; bandits specializing in kidnapping for ransom had also arrived in Shanghai from Ch'eng-hsien, giving their native place so bad a reputation that respectable Ch'eng-hsien natives in Shanghai began referring to themselves as Shaohsing natives, even though, as we have seen, Shaohsing's reputation itself was not impeccable.[40]

Hangchow too had a large Shaohsing population. In the early 1920s Hangchow was even being called "a colony of Shaohsing natives."[41]

> The noises in the [Hangchow] marketplace are all Shaohsing noises. And when you enter people's

houses, the gatekeepers, chefs, hairdressers, and seamstresses come from Shaohsing without exception. The wetnurses also are Shaohsing women. With Shaohsing natives in such abundance, what you hear all around is naturally Shaohsing dialect.[42]

We know that around 1925 when a person from Shaohsing's Chu-chi county would emigrate to make a living, he was more likely to head for Hangchow than anywhere else. Chu-chi's surplus tailors and barbers especially gravitated there, while her bamboo and wood craftsmen headed for Chia-hsing and Hu-chou.[43] Such definite patterns strongly suggest the existence of specialized Chu-chi craft guilds in each of these cities.

You would think you were in Shaohsing rather than Hangchow. . . . The officials' private secretaries, clerks *(hsü-t'u)*, tutors, merchants, peddlars, artisans, servants, and odd jobbers *(tsa-i)* are mostly Shaohsing people. . . . From cradle to grave there's not a day when we Hangchowers don't come into contact with people from Shaohsing.[44]

Communication between the two groups was almost always in Hangchow dialect, since Hangchow people rarely knew more than a phrase or two of the Shaohsing vernacular.[45]
There is evidence that Shaohsing outlaws were active in Hangchow prefecture during the last years of the Ch'ing. After they were mustered out of the Hunan Army, some ex-braves became "Yellow Taoists" *(Huang tao-shih)* settling on Kuan-shan in Hsin-ch'eng county. There they terrorized the local populace, trying to incite them to seize grain when it became expensive, and burned a Catholic church. One of the outlaw chiefs named Tu Te-sheng, "a Shaohsing native," was captured in 1906. He confessed to organizing gangs totaling over 2000 men in several counties of Hangchow prefecture. Among the items captured with him were two yellow flags and a seal inscribed with a common dissident slogan, "Enact the Way for Heaven."[46]
Soochow, a major commercial center in Kiangsu province, also had a large Shaohsing contingent. It was active in Soochow's soysauce trade as of 1873, as well as in the rice trade there as of 1878.[47] All of Soochow's cloth dyers are said to have been from Shaohsing, "owing to their superiority in capital and technique."[48] This "Shaohsing clique" *(Shao-pang)* in Soochow made its weight felt in 1902, when the arrest of the cloth dye workers' foreman led

the workers, several hundred strong, to shut down.[49] Two years later, in 1904, there were other strikes by Shaohsing workers in Soochow. The dye workers went out again, for higher wages, spreading word of their strike by handbills.[50] And the candle makers also struck for higher wages, returning home to Shaohsing to strengthen their bargaining position.[51]

When the gentry of Sheng-tse, a town in Wu-chiang county, Soochow prefecture, were organizing their local self-government assembly in the ninth month of 1911, they decided to use a vacant temple as their meeting hall. Some unscrupulous Shaohsing natives resident in the town claimed that the building had previously served as the local Ning-Shao hui-kuan before it had become a temple. They even went so far as to attach a sign to the building reading "erected by Ning-Shao natives" to lend authenticity to their claim, which became accepted by the local Ning-Shao community. When the local gentry protested to the magistrate, and he decided in favor of the self-government assembly, the local Ning-Shao community went on strike. This strike had considerable effect, since the resident Shaohsing colony alone accounted for most of the town's calenderers, silk boilers, and dyers, not to mention the money-changers. The local private letter-delivery service was also a Ning-Shao monopoly.[52] To make matters worse, 40 to 50 percent of the town's restaurants, teahouses, and wineshops were Ning-Shao owned and operated. With several dozen enforcers putting pressure on the holdouts, these establishments were all shut down. How the affair ended is unknown, but at last word, after the strike had been going for three days, the local self-government assembly, "at its wit's end," was considering resigning en masse.[53]

The survey presented above should be sufficient to illustrate our theme: Shaohsing natives' exodus throughout China. But for an even more striking example of the power exercised by Shaohsing natives away from home, we must look north to Chihli province. The single most significant pattern of Shaohsing emigration during the Ch'ing involved Chihli's Shun-t'ien perfecture, which included within its borders the imperial capital, Peking. There is considerable evidence, as we shall see, that it was common for Shaohsing natives not only to emigrate to Shun-t'ien but also to register as natives of Shun-t'ien. The term for registration in one's native place was *yüan-chi*. Registering as a native of one's new abode was called *chi-chi*. By statute both locales were covered by the law of avoidance: An official could serve in neither.[54]   Attached to the statute setting forth this stipulation was the following significant note: "For example, in the case of a native of Chekiang with a chi-chi in Shun-t'ien, both provinces, Chekiang and Chihli, are covered by the law of avoidance."[55]

A person could not simply register as a native of his new abode immediately upon arrival.   To become a native of any locale either his family must have lived there for three generations or he himself must have lived there for sixty years.   If, however, he purchased property in his new abode, the term of residence was cut to twenty years.[56] In 1806, in a decision that seems to have remained definitive for the rest of the dynasty, the Chia-ch'ing Emperor ruled that after twenty years' residence a person could request to be registered locally, but permission to take the examinations as a native of that locale would not be granted until after a period of sixty years' peaceful residence.[57]

Given the length of these time periods, there is little wonder that a practice arose known as *mao-chi* (concealing one's actual native place by false registration).   Perhaps the most common motive for false registration was to make oneself eligible for a more favorable examination quota in another locale.   Shaohsing natives were obviously not the only, nor even the majority of, offenders.[58]   Nor did Shaohsing natives limit their false registration to Shun-t'ien: We know of a Shaohsing mu-yu serving in Szechwan province who registered as a native there for examination purposes.[59]   But the pattern of Shaohsing natives registering illegally in Shun-t'ien was frequent during the Ming and even more so during the Ch'ing.[60]

Perhaps the earliest documented case of a Shaohsing native falsely registering in Shun-t'ien occurred in the Chia-ching period (1522-1566) involving one Chang Li from Kuei-chi.   What leads one to believe that this was one of the earliest cases, if not the earliest, is that it not only stirred opposition, but also prompted the Emperor to inquire what the term mao-chi meant.[61]

Another early case, during the Wan-li period (1572-1619), involved one Wang Ssu-jen from Shan-yin: Wang tried to use the fact that his family owned a burial plot west of Peking in Wan-p'ing county (where his granduncle was interred) to justify his registration there for the sheng-yüan examination.   But "a law proscribed an outsider from competing for a vacancy reserved by quota for the natives of the area, and it was strictly enforced by imperial order when Wang arrived in Peking in 1588."   Consequently, "at the examination of 1589 fellow students were

outraged by his presence and approached him threaten-
ingly. He was saved from bodily harm by the magistrate. .
. ."[62] Given the ruthless competition inherent in the Ming-
Ch'ing examination system, little wonder that, when discovered, outsiders attempting to beat the system were slapped down.

The Board of Civil Office issued a strict prohibition
against falsification of native place by clerks serving in
Shun-t'ien. This prohibition, undated but issued no later
than 1626, noted that the problem of mao-chi was more
severe in Shun-t'ien that elsewhere, and demanded meticu-
lous inspections to halt it, "although those who falsify their
native place almost always cover their tracks."[63]   (Shaohsing natives were not specifically mentioned.)

What, we may ask, were Shaohsing natives doing in
Peking? Besides serving as officials, taking examinations to
become chü-jen and chin-shih, serving as clerks in the
central government's Six Boards and as minor functionaries
in the county administrations of metropolitan Peking (on all
of which topics, more below), Shaohsing natives left tantalizing evidence of their business activities. An inscription
discovered in Peking reveals the existence there of a colony
of Shaohsing (or rather, Ning-Shao)[64] gold- and silver-
smelters and moneylenders, the "Southern Silver Office"
(*Nan yin-chü*). It flourished during the K'ang-hsi reign
(1662-1722), began to decline during the Tao-kuang period
(1821-1850), and disappeared by late Ch'ing, replaced by
Chihli natives, for reasons unknown.[65]

Also in Peking was the Shaohsing hui-kuan that rented
rooms to Lu Hsün beginning in 1912: "For some years I
stayed here, copying ancient inscriptions."[66]   This was
the *Shan-Kuei i-kuan*, later called the *Shaohsing hsien-
kuan*.[67] As both these names indicate, its premises actually were open only to natives of Shan-yin and Kuei-chi,
and then only with restrictions. A history of the same
hui-kuan, entitled "Records of the Shaohsing County Hostel
[in Peking]" (*Shaohsing hsien-kuan chi-lüeh*), is another
treasure in the collection of the Institute of Oriental
Culture at Tokyo University. Perhaps the most important
portion of this document is its enumeration of the rules by
which the hui-kuan was run: It was administered by a
committee of Shan-yin and Kuei-chi natives serving as
officials in Peking,[68] and residence in the hui-kuan was
limited to those Shan-yin and Kuei-chi natives who held at
least the status of candidate for the provincial-level examination degree (chü-jen).[69]   Natives expressly forbidden
residence privileges included candidates for the much less

prestigious status of t'ung-sheng, "would-be private secretaries," "those employed at the Boards" (i.e., Central Board clerks), medical doctors, fortunetellers, and "vaudeville performers" *(tsa-chi jen)*.[70] "Scribes hired by candidates for the chü-jen or chin-shih degrees to copy poetry or prose will not be admitted to the hui-kuan even if they are natives."[71] And "as for candidates for the military chin-shih degree and military functionaries, they shall be refused residence, in keeping with the practice in other hui-kuan."[72]

Luckily for Lu Hsün, who could never claim the status of chü-jen candidate, the traditional examination system had been abolished only seven years before he moved to Peking. Otherwise, there would have been no room at the inn.

CHAPTER FIVE
Subofficials

When crowds vie to squeeze through the front door, it is convenient to hold a key to the rear. Let us search for that key and examine the doors which it opened: the institutional domains - the spheres of influence - which Shaohsing natives claimed within the Ch'ing polity, protected with great tenacity, and perpetuated generation after generation. In short, let us investigate the survival strategies of the Shaohsing gentry.

If not the missing link in our knowledge of Ch'ing local administration, the subofficial *(tso-tsa)* is certainly an understudied link. If when analyzing Ch'ing administration one conceives of the interaction between locale and center as including not merely the locale being administered but also the locales producing the administrators, the possibility arises that a study of subofficials might reveal patterns of considerable significance that would otherwise escape our attention. Indeed, such is the case with Shaohsing. It is simplistic to identify local officials merely as representatives of the central government: Their native-place affiliations and loyalties remained active even as they served their emperor. Although we have long recognized the influence of such particularistic cliques within the bureaucracy at the level of court politics, native-place allegiances at lower levels within the bureaucracy have not attracted the attention they deserve. This oversight must now be rectified. For such allegiances were absolutely crucial to the Shaohsing gentry's successful survival as gentry, generation after generation, despite keen competition from the natives of other locales for the limited number of bureaucratic posts. In short, we shall be measuring the extent to which

Shaohsing natives perpetuated themselves within the Ch'ing bureaucracy.

Ho Ping-ti has provided an excellent description of Shaohsing natives' emigration to Shun-t'ien prefecture, and especially to those two of its counties which together comprised the city of Peking, Wan-p'ing and Ta-hsing.

> By late Ming and Ch'ing times so many Shaohsing people had gone out that Shaohsing shih-yeh, subofficials, or members of officials' private staffs who had expert knowledge of fiscal and legal matters, were to be met almost everywhere in the country. Those who served in various central government agencies often chose to settle permanently in the metropolitan counties of Wan-p'ing and Ta-hsing near Peking in order that their profession could be handed on from one generation to another. A sampling of Ming-Ch'ing chin-shih lists reveals that dozens of chin-shih of these two metropolitan counties were of Shaohsing descent.[1]

And again:

> [B]y far the greatest contributors to Hopei's [i.e., Chihli's] better than average academic success were the metropolitan counties of Wan-p'ing and Ta-hsing, where the families of central officials, subofficials, and clerks of various government organs congregated. While they were from practically everywhere in the empire, many of them came from the highly cultured and mobile area of Shaohsing prefecture in Chekiang.[2]

1. *Subofficials in Shun-t'ien*

Evidence not cited by Ho Ping-ti fully corroborates his contention as to the importance of Shaohsing natives in the Peking area. This new evidence consists of records stretching from the beginning of the Ch'ing into the 1880s giving the names and native places of subofficials (tso-tsa) serving in Shun-t'ien. (Subofficials were those officials subordinate to the official in charge at each level of the local administration - e.g., subordinate to the county magistrate at the county level or to the prefect at the prefectural level - but ranking above, and clearly distinguished from, the yamen clerks.) The source of these records is the 1885 edition of the Shun-t'ien prefectural gazetteer. From these records I have compiled the statistical tables on the following pages.

Let us first, for purposes of comparison, consider data on the percentages of department (chou) and county (hsien) magistrates in Shun-t'ien prefecture who were natives of Shaohsing. Obviously the magistrate was more important than any of his subofficials in terms of power. So we can expect the safeguards in the distribution of magistracies to have been tighter - and thus the percentage of magistrates native to any one locale (such as Shaohsing) to be closer to a random distribution - than in the case of subofficial posts. As we shall see, the data in Table 1 confirm this expectation.

After presenting Table 1's figures on magistrates from Shaohsing serving in Shun-t'ien prefecture, we then present the data on the various kinds of subofficials from Shaohsing serving there. The mechanics of Tables 2 through 8 are the same as in Table 1. (Readers not wishing to pursue the statistical data in these tables may proceed directly to the summary on page 97.)

TABLE 1

CHOU AND HSIEN MAGISTRATES SERVING IN SHUN-T'IEN PREFECTURE

Included in the total are all magistrates whose native fu or hsien (or, in case of Bannermen, banner) are recorded, plus those whose native province (but not fu or hsien) is recorded, if that province is not Chekiang. Omitted are those for whom no native place information is given, and those cited only as "natives of Chekiang" (*Che-chiang jen*) with no indication of fu or hsien, since it is impossible to determine whether such Chekiang natives are or are not from Shaohsing. Fortunately, these last cases are usually statistically insignificant, as the appropriate column below indicates. In Tables 1 to 8 a blank space signifies zero. A dash signifies no data.

Reign Period	No. of "Chekiang natives" (not included in Total)	TOTAL	Of Total, number of "Shaohsing natives" (no hsien given)	The Eight Counties of Shaohsing Prefecture								Fraction and percent of Shaohsing in Total
				From SY*	KC	HS	CC	YY	SYü	C	HC	
Shun-chih	3	126		2	1			1	1			5/126 (4%)
K'ang-hsi	3	208	2	2	1			1				6/208 (3%)
Yung-cheng		32	1									1/32 (3%)
Ch'ien-lung	2	154		4	3	1						8/154 (5%)
Chia-ch'ing		67		5				1				6/67 (9%)
Tao-kuang	1	272		6	4	1	2	1	3			17/272 (6%)
Hsien-feng		97		1		1						2/97 (2%)
T'ung-chih		108		2	2		5			1		10/108 (9%)
Kuang-hsü (through KH 9 only)		36			1							1/36 (3%)
TOTAL BY HSIEN				22	12	3	7	4	4	1		Overall fraction and percent for all reign periods 56/1100 (5%)

Compiled from *Kuang-hsü Shun-t'ien fu-chih*, chüan 81 and 82. * SY=Shan-yin, KC=Kuei-chi, HS=Hsiao-shan, CC=Chu-chi, YY=Yü-yao, SYü=Shang-yü, C=Ch'eng-hsien, HC=Hsin-ch'ang

TABLE 2

ASSISTANT COUNTY MAGISTRATES (*hsien-ch'eng*), RANKED 7A.
SERVING IN SHUN-T'IEN PREFECTURE

Reign Period	"Chekiang natives"	TOTAL	"Shao-hsing natives"	SY	KC	HS	CC	YY	SYü	C	HC	Frac. and Percent
Shun-chih	3	11	1	1			1	1				4/11 (36%)
K'ang-hsi	1	28		1	1		1					3/28 (11%)
Yung-cheng		23		1	1							2/23 (9%)
Ch'ien-lung		108		6	1		1	4	1			13/108 (12%)
Chia-ch'ing		47		2		1						3/47 (6%)
Tao-kuang	1	72		2	3	1						6/72 (8%)
Hsien-feng		52		4	3		1					8/52 (15%)
T'ung-chih		57		7	5	2	1	1				16/57 (28%)
Kuang-hsü (though KH 9 only)		24		1	2							3/24 (13%)
TOTAL BY HSIEN				25	16	4	5	6	1			Overall fraction and percent for all reign periods 58/422 (14%)

Compiled from *Kuang-hsü Shun-t'ien fu-chih*, chüan 83.

TABLE 3

SECOND-CLASS ASSISTANT CHOU MAGISTRATES (*chou-p'an*), RANKED 7B, SERVING IN SHUN-T'IEN PREFECTURE

Reign Period	"Chekiang natives"	TOTAL	"Shao-hsing natives"									Frac. and Percent
			SY	KC	HS	CC	YY	SYü	C	HC		
Shun-chih	3	8									0/8 (0%)
K'ang-hsi	1	20	3	1							4/20 (20%)
Yung-cheng		8		1							1/8 (13%)
Ch'ien-lung	2	70			1		1				2/70 (3%)
Chia-ch'ing		30									0/30 (0%)
Tao-kuang		33	2	1	1						4/33 (12%)
Hsien-feng		13			1		1				2/13 (15%)
T'ung-chih		13	.					1			1/13 (8%)
Kuang-hsü (though KH 9 only)		4									0/4 (0%)
TOTAL BY HSIEN			5	3	3		2	1			Overall fraction and percent for all reign periods 14/199 (7%)

Compiled from *Kuang-hsü Shun-t'ien fu-chih*, chüan 83.

TABLE 4

COUNTY REGISTRARS (*chu-pu*), RANKED 9A, SERVING IN SHUN-T'IEN PREFECTURE

Reign Period	"Chekiang natives"	TOTAL	"Shao-hsing natives"	SY	KC	HS	CC	YY	SYü	C	HC	Frac. and Percent
Shun-chih	1	12		1	1							2/12 (17%)
K'ang-hsi	3	12		3					1			4/12 (33%)
Yung-cheng		23		1	1	1		1				9/23 (17%)
Ch'ien-lung	1	94		3	1	2		1	1			0/14 (0%)
Chia-ch'ing	1	14			1		1					3/20 (15%)
Tao-kuang		20		2								4/10 (40%)
Hsien-feng		10		4								4/16 (25%)
T'ung-chih		16		2	2							0/5 (0%)
Kuang-hsü (though KH 9 only)		5										
TOTAL BY HSIEN			16	6	3	1	2	2				Overall fraction and percent for all reign periods 30/206 (15%)

Compiled from *Kuang-hsü Shun-t'ien fu-chih*, chüan 85.

TABLE 5

SUBCOUNTY MAGISTRATES (*hsün-chien*), RANKED 9B,
SERVING IN SHUN-T'IEN

Reign Period	"Chekiang natives"	TOTAL	"Shao-hsing natives"	SY	KC	HS	CC	YY	SYü	C	HC	Frac. and Percent
Shun-chih		—										no data
K'ang-hsi	2	5		1					1			2/5 (40%)
Yung-cheng		8										0/8 (0%)
Ch'ien-lung		32		2	2	1			1			6/32 (19%)
Chia-ch'ing		14			1			1				2/14 (14%)
Tao-kuang	3	56		5	1			2				8/56 (14%)
Hsien-feng	1	21		3				1				4/21 (19%)
T'ung-chih		17		1	1							2/17 (12%)
Kuang-hsü (though KH 9 only)	4	12		2	1				1			4/12 (33%)
TOTAL BY HSIEN				14	6	1		4	3			Overall fraction and percent for all reign periods 28/165 (17%)

Compiled from *Kuang-hsü Shun-t'ien fu-chih*, chüan 87.
(For more on the hsün-chien, see Jonathan K. Ocko, *Bureaucratic Reform in Provincial China*, p. 142.)

TABLE 6

CHOU JAIL WARDENS (*li-mu*), RANKED 9B, AND COUNTY JAIL WARDENS (*tien-shih*), UNRANKED, SERVING IN SHUN-T'IEN PREFECTURE

Reign Period	"Chekiang natives"	TOTAL	"Shao-hsing natives"	SY	KC	HS	CC	YY	SYü	C	HC	Frac. and Percent
Shun-chih	18	48	9	4	11				1			14/48 (29%)
K'ang-hsi	19	150	11	14	1	1			2		1	40/150 (27%)
Yung-cheng	2	23		2	6							3/23 (13%)
Ch'ien-lung	2	124		13	1	1	1					21/124 (17%)
Chia-ch'ing		34		3								5/34 (15%)
Tao-kuang	1	116		15	11	1		1	1			29/116 (25%)
Hsien-feng	1	43		11	3			1				16/43 (37%)
T'ung-chih	5	58		11	1			2				15/58 (26%)
Kuang-hsü (though KH 9 only)	1	34		1	5			2			1	8/34 (24%)
TOTAL BY HSIEN				74	39	3	1	8	4		2	Overall fraction and percent for all reign periods 151/630 (24%)

Compiled from *Kuang-hsü Shun-t'ien fu-chih*, chüan 86.

TABLE 7

JAILKEEPERS (*ssu-yü*), RANKED 9B, SERVING IN SHUN-T'IEN PREFECTURE

Reign Period	"Chekiang natives" TOTAL	"Shao-hsing natives" SY	KC	HS	CC	YY	SYü	C	HC	Frac. and Percent
Shun-chih	—									no data
K'ang-hsi	—									no data
Yung-cheng	1	1								1/1 (100%)
Ch'ien-lung	4	2								2/4 (50%)
Chia-ch'ing	—									no data
Tao-kuang	—									no data
Hsien-feng	2									no data
T'ung-chih	16	3	2	1						6/16 (38%)
Kuang-hsü (cutoff year not given)	10	2	1				1			4/10 (40%)
TOTAL BY HSIEN		8	3	1			1			Overall fraction and percent for all reign periods 13/33 (39%)

Compiled from *Kuang-hsü Shun-t'ien fu-chih*, chüan 87.

TABLE 8

POSTMASTERS (*t-ch'eng*), UNRANKED, SERVING IN SHUN-T'IEN PREFECTURE

Reign Period	"Chekiang natives"	TOTAL	"Shao-hsing natives"	SY	KC	HS	CC	YY	SYü	C	HC	Frac. and Percent
Shun-chih	1	–										no data
K'ang-hsi		27	2	3	4							10/27 (37%)
Yung-cheng		9		1				1				1/9 (11%)
Ch'ien-lung		13		1	1		1					3/13 (23%)
Chia-ch'ing		–										no data
Tao-kuang		–										no data
Hsien-feng		3				1						1/3 (33%)
T'ung-chih		5		2	1						3/5	(60%)
Kuang-hsü (cutoff year not given)		–										no data
TOTAL BY HSIEN				7	6	1	1	1				Overall fraction and percent for all reign periods 18/57 (32%)

Compiled from *Kuang-hsü Shun-t'ien fu-chih*, chüan 87.

To summarize briefly the main points which the tables reveal, the extent to which Shaohsing natives dominate a given post clearly tends to increase as the rank of that post decreases: Compare, for example, Table 1 (chou and hsien magistrates) with Table 8 (postmasters). Moreover, the extent to which Shaohsing natives were able to perpetuate their overrepresentation in these posts throughout the course of the dynasty is striking. The question of when Shaohsing natives began to become overrepresented among subofficials in Shun-t'ien prefecture is impossible to answer definitively. My best guess is sometime between 1600 and 1644. A rare and valuable source on local government in Wan-p'ing county (Shun-t'ien prefecture) published in 1593 demonstrates that, while far from unrepresented, Shaohsing natives had not yet established the dominant position as subofficials which the Ch'ing data document. (The position of county registrar, chu-pu, is a possible exception.) Listing, on the basis of yamen archives, the various subofficials who had held office in Wan-p'ing county from the beginning of the Ming to approximately 1593, this source reveals that, of the assistant county magistrates (hsien-ch'eng) during these years, 7 percent (3/46) had been Shaohsing natives (two from Shan-yin, one from Yü-yao); of the county jail wardens (tien-shih) 6 percent (1/17, one from Yü-yao); and of the county registrars (chu-pu) 16 percent (3/19, one each from Yü-yao, Hsiao-shan, and Shan-yin).[3] These data are not strictly comparable with the Ch'ing data from the Shun-t'ien prefectural gazetteer, since they cover only one county. They do indicate, however, that Shaohsing natives definitely did serve as subofficials in metropolitan Peking prior to the Ch'ing conquest.[4]

A further point revealed by the Shun-t'ien tables is the consistent numerical dominance, within the Shaohsing group as a whole, of Shan-yin and Kuei-chi natives. We should remember that the 1933 census found Shaohsing county, the boundaries of which were exactly coterminous with the former Shan-yin and Kuei-chi, to be the most densely populated in Chekiang. Contrast the tables' paucity of natives from Ch'eng-hsien and Hsin-ch'ang, Shaohsing's outer periphery. The inference is strong that Shaohsing emigrants to Shun-t'ien came primarily from Shaohsing's inner core, its two most urban and densely populated counties.

Moreover, there is no reason to believe that overrepresentation of Shan-yin and Kuei-chi natives in subofficial posts was limited to Shun-t'ien. "During the Ch'ing many of the functionaries such as the assistant county mag-

jail warden were natives of Shan-yin and Kuei-chi. This can be verified by the Complete Register of Ch'ing Officialdom" (Ta Ch'ing chin-shen ch'üan-shu).[5] Note that this geographically unlimited statement, written in the 1920s by Hsü K'o, a Hangchow native with an extremely good knowledge of Shaohsing, mentions precisely those posts in which our Shun-t'ien data reveal an extraordinary overrepresentation of Shan-yin and Kuei-chi natives - a reassuring congruence indeed. But the best verification of Hsü K'o's statement would be to do exactly what its author suggests, examine the "Complete Register of Ch'ing Officialdom," which is the most authoritative source of information on holders of official Ch'ing provincial and local posts. This I have done, examining all China at two points in time, 1892 and 1904.

2. Subofficials Throughout China

I have used the "Complete Register" to calculate the percentage of Shaohsing natives among all the provincial- and local-level government subofficials serving in the Eighteen Provinces as of 1892. The results are presented in Table 9, which reveals that 7 percent of all the provincial- and local-government subofficials in the Eighteen Provinces during that year were natives of Shaohsing prefecture.

As for the distribution of Shaohsing subofficials by province in Table 9, Chihli's first-place ranking reflects the large number of Shaohsing natives in Shun-t'ien prefecture, a phenomenon already discussed. But Chekiang's high percentage of Shaohsing subofficials requires an explanation, since the law of avoidance barred Shaohsing natives from serving as officials and subofficials in their home provinces.[6] The explanation is that education-related subofficials were exempted from the law of avoidance: They were indeed allowed to serve within their home provinces, although not within their home prefectures. All fifty-three of the Shaohsing natives serving as subofficials in Chekiang held education-related posts: Twenty-eight were county subdirectors of studies (hsün-tao and fu-she hsün-tao), twenty-three were county directors of studies (chiao-yü and fu-she chiao-yü), one was a departmental director of studies (hsüeh-cheng), and one was a prefectural director of studies (chiao-shou). These education-related posts held by the Shaohsing suboffcials in Chekiang were completely different from the posts held by the Shaohsing subofficials

TABLE 9

SHAOHSING NATIVES AS FRACTION AND PERCENTAGE OF ALL PROVINCIAL- AND LOCAL-GOVERNMENT SUBOFFICIALS, BY PROVINCE, 1892

Chihli	101/664	= 15%
Fukien (plus Taiwan)	45/358	13%
Chekiang	53/447	12%
Kiangsi	39/419	9%
Kiangsu	45/504	9%
Kwangtung	41/482	9%
Shansi	23/361	6%
Shantung	28/514	5%
Anhui	15/295	5%
Szechwan	20/438	5%
Shensi	13/285	5%
Hunan	14/323	4%
Kwangsi	13/318	4%
Kansu (plus Sinkiang)	8/237	3%
Hupei	12/357	3%
Honan	13/420	3%
Yunnan	9/315	3%
Kweichow	7/250	3%
TOTAL	499/6987	7%

Compiled from *Ta Ch'ing chin-shen ch'üan-shu*, Fall, Kuang-hsü 18.[7]

istrate, county registrar, subcounty magistrate, and county in the rest of China, as we shall see. The education-related posts were probably less lucrative than the others, but the law of avoidance gave Shaohsing natives no choice.

Unfortunately, it is impossible to determine the native counties of these education-related subofficials, since all are identified merely as "Shaohsing natives." But these subofficials' prior statuses are known: Of the fifty-three, thirty-three (62 percent) were chü-jen, eighteen (34 percent) were *kung-sheng* (holders of an intermediate degree between sheng-yüan and chü-jen), one was a sheng-yüan, and one an unsuccessful candidate for the chü-jen degree cited for honorable mention (fu-pang). As we shall see, these statuses were much higher than the statuses of the Shaohsing natives serving as subofficials in the rest of China, doubtless a reflection of higher qualifications demanded of subofficials serving in education-related posts. (For data on education-related subofficials from other prefectures, indicating that they too were overwhelmingly chü-jen and kung-sheng, see Table 15.)

Our calculations above concluded that as of 1892 7 percent of all the provincial and local subofficials in China's Eighteen Provinces were Shaohsing natives. This figure included, of course, the subofficials (all education-related) serving in Chekiang. But it can be argued that since Chekiang was a special case for Shaohsing natives due to the law of avoidance, Chekiang should be excluded from the reckoning. If Chekiang is excluded, the number of Shaohsing subofficials is reduced from 499 to 446 and the total number of subofficials is reduced from 6987 to 6540, yielding a Shaohsing fraction of 446/6540 or 7 percent. Thus whether Chekiang is included or not, Shaohsing natives as of 1892 still accounted for 7 percent of all the subofficials in China.

Let us now examine the 446 Shaohsing subofficials serving in 1892 in all the provinces of China except Chekiang. First, from which counties within Shaohsing did they come? The results are as follows: Shan-yin 59 percent (261/446), Kuei-chi 27 percent (120/446), Hsiao-shan 7 percent (33/446), Shang-yü 3 percent (13/446), Chu-chi 2 percent (8/446), Yü-yao 1 percent (6/446), Ch'eng-hsien 1 percent (3/446), and Hsin-ch'ang 0 percent (1/446), plus one unknown, 0 percent (1/446). Thus the two counties of Shan-yin and Kuei-chi, which together contained Shaohsing's prefectural capital, produced no fewer than 86 percent of Shaohsing's subofficials, with Shan-yin alone accounting for almost 60 percent.

This rank order of Shaohsing's counties in terms of their absolute production of subofficials assumes that the key statistic is how many subofficials each county produced, regardless of its relative population: The more subofficials produced, the more significant that county's native-place network was in the Ch'ing bureaucracy. I believe this assumption to be valid. The natives of a small county which produced a large number of subofficials per capita would remain less influential in the bureaucracy than the natives of a large county which produced fewer subofficials per capita but many more in absolute terms.

Nevertheless, it is also interesting to know how Shaohsing's counties ranked in per capita production of subofficials, because that ranking would give us a clue to how vigorously the natives of each county pursued the subofficial career strategy. That ranking of Shaohsing's counties is as follows for 1892 (with the numbers after each county indicating its relative per capita production of subofficials)[8]: Hsiao-shan 66.0, Shang-yü 44.3, Chu-chi 15.1, Yü-yao 9.4, Ch'eng-hsien 7.1, and Hsin-ch'ang 4.1. The numbers for both Shan-yin and Kuei-chi[9] are a gigantic 310.9.

These calculations are admittedly imperfect. But my confidence in them is bolstered by the fact that they yield a per capita rank order of Shaohsing's counties which is the same as the absolute rank order presented above. In short, whether we rank Shaohsing's counties by their absolute production of subofficials or by their per capita production of subofficials, the results are the same. Therefore, it seems safe to conclude that as producers of subofficials per capita, Shan-yin and Kuei-chi were indeed far and away in a class by themselves, and that Hsin-ch'ang and Ch'eng-hsien brought up the rear as Shaohsing's lowest producers of subofficials per capita. Once again the contrast between core and periphery is striking.

Next, what were the prior statuses of the 446 Shaohsing subofficials serving outside of Chekiang in 1892? The overwhelming majority (375/446 or 84 percent) were chiensheng, 4 percent (19/446) were regular Central Board clerks *(kung-shih)*, 4 percent (18/446) were Central Board clerks qualified by examination to become subofficials *(li-yüan)*, 4 percent (17/446) were of unknown status, and the remaining 4 percent were miscellaneous.

Finally, what posts did the 446 Shaohsing subofficials serving outside of Chekiang occupy? The six posts held most frequently by these Shaohsing subofficials were county jail warden (tien-shih), held by 37 percent (164/446); subcounty magistrate (hsün-chien), often posted in a town other than the county seat and engaged variously in police work or river or salt administration, 26 percent (114/446); assistant county magistrate (hsien-ch'eng) 8 percent (36/446); chou jail warden (li-mu) 6 percent (25/446); various kinds of tax collector (ta-shih) 5 percent (24/446); and prefectural commissary of records (ching-li) 5 percent (23/446). (For other, less frequently held posts, see Table 16.)

In sum, on the basis of the figures for 1892, the typical Shaohsing native serving as a subofficial in the late Ch'ing was a chien-sheng from Shan-yin serving as a county jail warden. This was a desirable post because a jail warden was in a position to extract money from prisoners and their families. A mu-yu from Kuei-chi named Ch'in Wen-k'uei (1757-1830) wrote an admonition to his eldest son, who had purchased the office of county jail warden in Shansi. Dating from around 1810, this admonition warns that the office of county jail warden *(tien-shih i-kuan)* carries the responsibility not to maltreat one's prisoners.[10] "It is impermissible to abuse them." The conditions of confinement should be humane. Lice should be cleaned out of the cells. Sick prisoners should receive medical attention. Prisoners who try to escape should not be starved to death. "Do not twist the law for one's own purposes and accuse people for the sake of profit. Do not entrap people and encourage lawsuits for the sake of wealth." The motivation behind this homily was not merely altruistic, however, for Ch'in believed that evil conduct would have a harmful effect on the fate of one's family and lineage: "Goodness and evil are always recompensed." Yet the very need for such an admonition strongly implies that the Shaohsing natives serving as jail wardens throughout China were hardly as scrupulous in their behavior as Ch'in wished his son to be. Lu Hsün confirms our fears when he notes, "As for prisons of the old type, as these were apparently modelled on the Buddhist hell in addition to the prisoners confined there you have gaolers who torment them. They sometimes also take advantage of their right to bleed the felons' relatives white."[11]

Having demonstrated that Shaohsing natives who were subofficials tended to be county jail wardens, let us turn the question around and ask, How likely was it for a county jail warden to be a Shaohsing native? In other words, what percentage of China's county jail wardens were natives of Shaohsing? As of 1892 the answer is either 14 percent (164/1201) or 15 percent (164/1130), depending on whether the county jail wardens serving in Chekiang are included (none of whom were from Shaohsing due to the law of avoidance). Either way, as of 1892 one out of every seven county jail wardens in China was from Shaohsing prefecture. And one out of every twelve (101/1201 or 8 percent) was from Shan-yin county.[12] The people of Shaohsing, more than any other locale, survived by specializing as China's jailers. This alone would have been enough to make Shaohsing notorious.

The extent of Shaohsing's success as a producer of subofficials cannot be fully appreciated without considering the locales elsewhere in China that also produced substantial numbers of subofficials. From where did Shaohsing's competition come? I have used the 1904 edition of the "Complete Register of Ch'ing Officialdom" to obtain information on the native counties of provincial- and local- government subofficials serving in the Eighteen Provinces during the late Ch'ing. Using this source I counted how many subofficials serving in 1904 were natives of each county, and compiled the following list of the top twenty subofficial-producing counties. The total number of subofficials counted in the 1904 edition is 3422. Omitted from this total are (a) those subofficials for whom no name or native county (or banner, in the case of Bannermen) is given, and (b) the education-related subofficials (e.g., chiao-yü and hsün-tao) since, as explained above, their assignment to office within their native province made them a special case among the subofficials. Moreover, it should be noted that (unlike the statistics for 1892) no data from Taiwan are included, since Taiwan was of course not administered by the Ch'ing in 1904.

The top twenty subofficial-producing counties are listed in Table 10 in descending order, with the name of each county's prefecture and province in parentheses, followed by the number of subofficials native to that county who were serving in office in 1904.

The figures in Table 10 virtually speak for themselves. But four points should be made explicit. First, over half of the top twenty subofficial-producing counties are located in the core of the lower Yangtze macroregion.[14] Second, Shaohsing is the only prefecture to place as many as three of its counties among the top twenty. Third, it is impossible to know how many of the 269 subofficials listed as natives of Ta-hsing and Wan-p'ing were actually émigrés from other locales, including Shaohsing. Fourth, the 201

TABLE 10

THE TOP TWENTY SUBOFFICAL-PRODUCING COUNTIES
IN 1904

Rank Order	County	Number of Subofficials
1.	Ta-hsing (Shun-t'ien, Chihli)	217
2.	Shan-yin (Shaohsing, Chekiang)	201
3.	Kuei-chi (Shaohsing, Chekiang)	89
4.	Ch'ien-t'ang (Hangchow, Chekiang)	57
5.	Wan-p'ing (Shun-t'ien, Chihli)	52
6.	Shang-yüan (Chiang-ning, Kiangsu)	49
7.	Kuei-an (Hu-chou, Chekiang)	46
	T'ung-ch'eng (An-ch'ing, Anhui)	46
9.	Ch'ang-sha (Ch'ang-sha, Hunan)	44
10.	Wu-chin (Ch'ang-chou, Kiangsu)	40
11.	Jen-ho (Hangchow, Chekiang)	37
12.	Hua-yang (Ch'eng-tu, Szechwan)	33
	Shan-hua (Ch'ang-sha, Hunan)	33
14.	Chiang-ning (Chiang-ning, Kiangsu)	32
	Yang-hu (Ch'ang-chou, Kiangsu)	32
16.	Ch'eng-tu (Ch'eng-tu, Szechwan)	31
	Huai-ning (An-ch'ing, Anhui)	31
18.	Ching-hsien (Ning-kuo, Anhui)	27
19.	Wu-hsien (Soochow, Kiangsu)	26
20.	Hsiao-shan (Shaohsing, Chekiang)	25

Compiled from *Ta Ch'ing chin-shen ch'üan-shu,*
Kuang-hsü 30.[13]

subofficials native to Shan-yin amount to 6 percent of the empire-wide total of 3422. The numbers of subofficials native to the other counties in Shaohsing prefecture are as follows: Kuei-chi 89, Hsiao-shan 25, Yü-yao 15, Shang-yü 14, Chu-chi 4, Ch'eng-hsien 1, and Hsin-ch'ang 1. Thus the total number of subofficials native to Shaohsing in 1904 is 350, fully 10 percent of the empire-wide total of 3422.[15]

What accounts for Shaohsing's startling overrepresentation among the locales producing subofficials, testimony to Shaohsing natives' success in penetrating this level of the Ch'ing bureaucracy?

CHAPTER SIX

Central-Government Clerks and Private Secretaries

"At the end of the Han dynasty Yu Fan praised my native place; but that after all was too long ago, for later this district gave birth to the notorious 'Shaohsing pettifoggers' [shih-yeh]. Of course not all of us - old and young, men and women - are pettifoggers in Shaohsing."

(Lu Hsün, "Reminiscences,"
Selected Works, Vol. One,
Peking, 1956, p. 380)

How did Shaohsing natives achieve their considerable overrepresentation among China's subofficials? To answer this question we must begin with the effects of overpopulation, which had different repercussions on different social strata. For tenants, overpopulation meant an adverse manland ratio, and thus a weakened bargaining position with landlords. But for examination candidates and would-be officials, overpopulation meant an adverse examination pass quota. Shaohsing's quota for the sheng-yüan degree (granted at the prefectural level) was especially adverse,[1] and the most probable answer to why Shaohsing produced so many subofficials begins, but obviously does not end, with this simple fact.

There is some evidence that the literacy rate may have been higher in Shaohsing than elsewhere, at least during the late Ming, when career patterns for Shaohsing natives were established that lasted throughout the Ch'ing. It seems that the egalitarian influence of the philosopher Wang Yang-ming (1472-1528), who was of course a native of Yü-

106

yao county, was especially strong in Shaohsing during the late Ming. According to the 1586 edition of the Shaohsing prefectural gazetteer, "Nowadays even the very poor would be ashamed if they did not instruct their sons in the classics. From tradesmen to local-government runners there are very few who cannot read or punctuate. . . . Our local people are generally arrogant and the distinction between officials and commoners is rather blurred. . . . Lately people have been influenced by Wang Yang-ming. . . ."[2] One may venture to speculate that this apparent egalitarianism in late Ming Shaohsing both influnced Wang's philosophy and was in turn influenced by it. His even more radically egalitarian disciple, Wang Chi (Lung-hsi, 1498-1583), who taught that any man could become a sage, was a native of Shan-yin.[3]

Although Shaohsing's putative heritage of above-average literacy is not beyond doubt, clearly its sheng-yüan quota did prove a serious bottleneck to upward mobility through the examination system. Lu Hsün's younger brother Chou Tso-jen reports that during the Kuang-hsü period Kuei-chi's sheng-yüan pass quota was 40 per examination out of over 500 candidates, less than 8 percent at this, the lowest level.[4] Previously the quota must have been even lower, since Shan-yin's sheng-yüan quota as of 1858 was only 25 per examination.[5] It has even been claimed that to pass the sheng-yüan exam in Shaohsing prefecture was harder than to pass the chü-jen exam in one of the less literate provinces.[6] As early as the mid-eighteenth century novel, *The Scholars (Ju-lin wai-shih)*, we find the following suggestion that passing the sheng-yüan exam in Shaohsing was unusually prestigious.

> Well, the imperial examiner will soon be coming to Shaohsing, and there is a man called Chin Tung-yeh who has been a clerk in the Board of Civil Office for a number of years who wants his son to take the examinations. But his son Chin Yao is an absolute idiot. So now, with the examination coming, his father wants to find a substitute. The trouble is that this examiner is very strict: we shall have to think out a new way. That's why I've come to talk it over with you.
>
> How much is he prepared to pay?
>
> To pass the examination in Shaohsing is worth a cool thousand taels.[7]

What happened to those candidates whom fortune did not favor in the prefectural examination sheds but who still aspired to an official career?

'K'ung I-chi, do you really know how to read?' When K'ung looked as if such a question were beneath contempt, they would continue: 'How is it you never passed even the lowest official examination?'
At that K'ung would look disconsolate and ill at ease. His face would turn pale and his lips move, but only to utter those unintelligible classical expressions. Then everybody would laugh heartily again, and the whole tavern would be merry.[8]

To circumvent the sheng-yüan examination bottleneck - and the fate of Lu Hsün's K'ung I-chi, which Chou Tso-jen explicitly relates to Shaohsing's low sheng-yuan quota[9] - many Shaohsing candidates traveled to Peking. There they purchased the chien-sheng degree, and took the examination for the chü-jen degree (the *hsiang-shih*) in Shun-t'ien, since that examination was not limited to natives of Chihli. The chü-jen examination in Shun-t'ien was unique in that it was open to all kung-sheng and chien-sheng, even those from outside the province of Chihli, as well as to kung-sheng, chien-sheng, and sheng-yuan from Chihli. Non-Chihli sheng-yüan were barred. Southerners who succeeded in the chü-jen exam in Shun-t'ien were called "chü-jen on the northern list of passers" (*pei-pang chü-jen*). [10] What made participation in the Shung-t'ien chü-jen exam especially attractive for Shaohsing natives was not only the disadvantageously low pass quota of their own native place but also the advantageously high quota in Shun-t'ien.

At Shun-t'ien-fu there was a separate quota for the admission of chien-sheng and kung-sheng to chü-jen degrees. This meant that these chien-sheng and kung-sheng did not have to compete on equal terms with the sheng-yüan. Judging from the different proportion of number of candidates to the quota, those chien-sheng and kung-sheng participating at Shun-t'ien-fu had a much better chance of success.[11]

For evidence that many Shaohsing natives did in fact play the percentages and take the chü-jen examination in Shun-t'ien (metropolitan Peking) rather than their provincial capital of Hangchow, we have only to return to that history of the Shaohsing hui-kuan in Peking, the *Shaohsing hsien-kuan chi-lüeh*. Therein we find that, as has been noted above, residence privileges in this hui-kuan were explicitly limited to candidates for the chü-jen degree and above.[12] We also find in this source a twenty-page list naming those natives of Shan-yin and Kuei-chi who passed the chü-jen examination during the course of the Ch'ing. Since there is no reason to believe that this list is limited to those who passed in Shun-t'ien, and since moreover some of the names are tagged *pei-pang* ("northern pass list") while others are not, the most prudent assumption is that the list is composed of those Shan-yin and Kuei-chi natives who passed the examination for the chü-jen degree either in Shun-t'ien or in Hangchow.

Unfortunately, there is evidence that not all those who passed in Shun-t'ien are labeled *pei-pang*. So the list is not reliable as the basis for determining the proportion of Shun-t'ien passers to Hangchow passers. But the list does provide a total number of passers, which in turn can give us some indirect indication of the number of candidates (passers and non-passers) involved. The breakdown of passers by reign period is presented in Table 11. (A distinction between Shan-yin and Kuei-chi natives is not made in the list.)

The figures in Table 11 indicate a remarkable long-term continuity in the average numbers of Shan-yin and Kuei-chi natives who succeeded in becoming chü-jen during the course of the Ch'ing. Perhaps most startling of all is the grand total of 1989, especially when we remember that this is the total number of Shan-yin and Kuei-chi natives (plus a trivial number of Shaohsing natives from counties other than these two or registered outside of Shaohsing) who actually succeeded in passing the chü-jen exam. Moreover, since the hui-kuan under whose auspices this list was printed limited its membership to natives of Shan-yin and Kuei-chi, there is no reason to believe that the list is anywhere near complete for Shaohsing natives of counties other than Shan-yin or Kuei-chi or for Shaohsing natives who registered falsely as natives of other locales.

One is tempted by the large grand total to believe that this figure might perhaps represent the total number of candidates rather than passers, but internal evidence leaves little doubt that the list contains passers only. With almost two thousand Shan-yin and Kuei-chi natives passing the chü-jen exam during the course of the Ch'ing, the total number of candidates for the chü-jen degree from Shaohsing

TABLE 11

SHAN-YIN AND KUEI-CHI NATIVES PASSING THE CHÜ-JEN EXAMINATION IN EITHER SHUN-T'IEN OR HANGCHOW

Reign Period	Total Number	Years in Reign Period	Average per Year
Shun-chih	97	18	5.4
K'ang-hsi	232	61	3.8
Yung-cheng	95	13	7.3
Ch'ien-lung	477	60	8.0
Chia-ch'ing	240	25	9.6
Tao-kuang	388	30	12.9
Hsien-feng	109	11	9.9
T'ung-chih	114	13	8.8
Kuang-hsü (to KH 29)	237	29	8.2
GRAND TOTAL	1989		

Compiled from Ting Ts'ai-san, ed., *Shaohsing hsien-kuan chi-lüeh*, pp. 21B-31B.

prefecture as a whole must clearly have totaled in the tens of thousands: During the Ch'ing the pass rate in the chü-jen examination was approximately one in twenty.[13]

Since an indeterminate but substantial fraction of this ocean of candidates can be assumed to have taken the exam in Shun-t'ien rather than in Hangchow, there can be no doubt that there was a steady stream of Shan-yin and Kuei-chi candidates from well-to-do families who bypassed Shaohsing's sheng-yüan bottleneck by traveling to Peking to purchase the chien-sheng degree and taking advantage of Shun-t'ien's more favorable chü-jen exam quota.[14]

1. *Central-Government Clerks*

Given the long odds, it was inevitable that most of these hopefuls would nevertheless fail the chü-jen examination. Many of these failures, unwilling to return home emptyhanded, would seek their livelihood in Peking.[15] This phenomenon is reflected in the "Records of the Shaohsing County Hostel [in Peking]," which includes among its house rules the following:

> Kung-sheng and chien-sheng taking the chü-jen examination [in Shun-t'ien] are not as well known as are the candidates for the chin-shih. . . . They must be guaranteed by a capital official from their native place *(t'ung-hsiang ching-kuan)* before being allowed to join the hui-kuan. If after the chü-jen examination they change their occupation [due to failure], they are to vacate the premises.[16]

During the early Ch'ing, within decades of the dynasty's founding, the statutory quotas for clerks in the Six Central Boards were providing insufficient to meet the work load. (These quotas were Civil Office 81, Revenue 244, Rites 71, War 73, Punishments 98, and Public Works 85.)[17] As a result, Shaohsing exam failures in Peking found little difficulty in being hired as clerks' assistants, exempt from the quota restrictions. These assistants received no salary but made a meager living by sharing the gifts presented by provincial officials visiting the capital.[18] To cite the outstanding example, in spite of the Board of Revenue's statutory quota of 244 clerks, that Board employed in fact over 1000[19] (presumably including the clerks' assistants).

These unquotaed assistants entered into master-disciple relationships with veteran clerks and spent an arduous apprenticeship lasting ten years or more[20] in a guild-like arrangement, learning the statutes and precedents as well as the documentary formulae, so that when vacancies occurred among the regular clerks, they would be appointed to replace them. This situation naturally promoted the development of native-place alliances. It has even been claimed that by the Yung-cheng and Ch'ien-lung reigns, the regular clerkships in *all* Six Boards had become the speciality of failed examination candidates from Shan-yin and Kuei-chi.[21] But this is doubtless an exaggeration.

No one knows for sure how Shaohsing natives first established their dominant position among Central Board clerks (especially in the Board of Revenue and, by the late Ch'ing, the Board of Civil Office). One suggestion, offered by the outstanding modern authority on Ming clerks, Professor Miao Ch'üan-chi of National Taiwan University, is that Shaohsing natives acquired exceptional expertise in mathematics which originally gave them the inside track for clerkships in the Board of Revenue. This expertise allowed them to avoid the Ming ban on natives of Chekiang (one of the major revenue-producing provinces) from serving in that Board. His evidence, a quotation to this effect by Shen Te-fu (1578-1642), a native of Chia-hsing, Chekiang, is suggestive though not conclusive: "But the clerks in the Board of Revenue are all great scoundrels from eastern Chekiang *(chin Che-tung chü chien)*. They infest it. In the transmission of documents upwards and downwards in the Board's bureaucracy, everything emanates from their hands. Furthermore, they have a skilled grasp of mathematics. They look upon their official superiors as dummies" *(mu-ou)*.[22]

We know too that there was a flourishing of popular treatises on practical mathematics for business purposes (including the use of the abacus) beginning in the southern Sung and reaching a peak during the Ming. Many of these treatises were published in Hangchow.[23] It is of course possible that Shaohsing natives were involved in the Hangchow publications. But there is at present no evidence to this effect.

Another possible expertise which Shaohsing natives may have used to gain control of the Central Boards' clerkships was seduction: Ningpo and Shaohsing were known for their male prostitutes *(nan-se)* in Peking during the Ming. "At first they were all people from Ning-Shao in Chekiang. But recently [i.e., late Wan-li], half are from Lin-ch'ing [in Shantung]."[24]

According to the Manchu essayist Chao-lien (1776-1829), "The clerks in each of the Central Boards have all been Shaohsing natives, beginning with the tenure of Chu Keng. That was the starting point, and the situation has not yet been stopped."[25]   Chu Keng (1535-1608) was a native of Shan-yin.[26]   He served as Senior Grand Secretary from 1606 to 1608.[27]   Chu Keng's career was closely associated with that of his predecessor as Senior Grand Secretary, Shen I-kuan, a native of Yin-hsien, Ningpo.   The Ning-Shao connection between the two was a significant factor in their relationship.[28]   Chao-lien has provided a clue, but the details of the Shaohsing clique's rise to power within the Boards' clerkships remain obscure.

As we have seen, the "Record of the Shaohsing County Hostel [in Peking]" specifically denied hui-kuan residence privileges to "those employed at the Boards."[29] Many of these clerks registered themselves as natives of Wan-p'ing and Ta-hsing counties "for the sake of occupational convenience,"[30] presumably to avoid being known as natives of Shaohsing.   False registration in Shun-t'ien was a very common practice among Central Board clerks in general as early as the Wan-li period and in particular among Shaohsing clerks in the Central Boards at least as early as the Yung-cheng period (1723-1735).[32]

It is said that Shaohsing natives' positions as shih-yeh (here meaning Central Board clerks rather than private secretaries) passed from father to son.   Once this hereditary pattern had been established, most of them lost both any desire to return to Shaohsing and any interest in taking the examinations,[33] although the clerk mentioned in *The Scholars* is evidence, albeit fictional, to the contrary.   Nor was the hereditary nature of clerkships limited to the Central Boards.   There is intriguing evidence of a Shaohsing native living in Wan-p'ing county, Shun-t'ien prefecture during the Chia-ch'ing period (1796-1820) who served as a clerk in the yamens of subofficials, themselves perhaps Shaohsing natives, as we have seen.   It was accepted practice that such a clerkship was literally the family property of the clerk filling the post: He could bequeath it to his son, or sell it, and even repossess it if the buyer defaulted.   "Lin Ch'ing's father had originally come from Shaohsing prefecture in Chekiang province and had moved to the Peking area where he had held at least two positions in local governmental offices: first as a clerk in the yamen of the Sub-district Deputy-Magistrate for Wan-p'ing hsien, and then as a clerk in the Sub-prefectural yamen for the Southern district of the capital area." When Lin Ch'ing's father died,

> his mother had arranged for his post as clerk in the Southern-district Sub-prefect's office to be filled by a person who paid her a substantial sum for the privilege. This man had eventually become impatient with the arrangement, and had refused to pay her further. Mrs. Lin, undaunted, filed a charge against him in the very yamen where he worked, asserting her family's right to the post and requesting that it be given to her son instead. Her petition was approved, and thus Lin Ch'ing was able to give up his job as night watchman and take over his father's clerkship.[34]

Thus did Lin Ch'ing use his Shaohsing connection to fill his ricebowl (before going on to lead the Eight Trigrams Rebellion of 1813!). One imagines that control of Central Board clerkships was maintained with equal tenacity.

The clerks in the Central Boards knew the voluminous legal precedents better than the Boards' officials, and even compiled secret guides to these precedents for their own use. As Thomas Metzger has argued, the conception of Confucian officials as purely amateurs with no specialized competence is overdrawn.[35] Nevertheless, there are degrees of specialization, levels of thoroughness, as Metzger himself points out.[36] Especially in a task as timeconsuming as learning the precedents, it would be difficult to demonstrate that officials acquired the high level of competence required of Central Board clerks.[37] This gap in expertise was even wider in the case of newly appointed provincial officials. In fact, it was common for newly appointed provincial officials setting out from Peking to hire well-versed clerks from the Boards of Revenue and Punishments to serve as their private secretaries.[38] We usually think of clerks as having much lower status than private secretaries, and this conception is correct for clerks in local yamens. But the status of Central Board clerks was much higher than that of local clerks.[39] For, unlike provincial officials, officials in the Central Boards were not allowed to hire private secretaries, so the Six Boards' clerks also filled this function for them.[40] Thus the ambiguity in the term shih-yeh.

The extent to which Shaohsing natives dominated the Central Board clerkships is impossible to determine statistically. There exists no comprehensive register of Central

Board clerks indicating native place. So our only recourse is to as many qualitative sources as possible. A late Ming author, Hsieh Chao-chih *(chin-shih* 1592), wrote that "At present all the clerks in the thirteen sections of the Board of Revenue are natives of Kiangsu and Chekiang *(Wu Yüeh)."*[41] When the famous seventeenth-century scholar Ku Yen-wu cited this assertion in his *Jih chih lu*, he changed "Kiangsu and Chekiang" to "Shaohsing,"[42] and it is this amended version that became famous. Ch'ü T'ung-tsu, for one, considers Ku's amendation to be a slip of memory, in short, a mistake. Ch'ü writes, "Much confusion has been caused by this erroneous quotation."[43] There is no doubt that Ku's quotation contributed to the fame, or infamy, of Shaohsing clerks and helped shape the popular image of Shaohsing which we have already discussed. But was Ku's version a misrepresentation of the actual state of affairs in the Board of Revenue? I think not. Ch'ü T'ung-tsu is overly hasty in dismissing Ku's statement as a mere misquote with no grounding in fact. The most that can be said against Ku's version is that he did misquote Hsieh and that probably not "all" the clerks in the Board of Revenue were from Shaohsing. When the rhetorical "all" is discounted, Ku's statement is not farfetched. Consider the following, written by Shen Te-fu (1578-1642), very nearly Ku's contemporary.

> When you enter the yamens of the Central Boards you are surrounded by Shaohsing people. The officials in charge are like puppets *(kuei-lei)* on a string. Whatever the clerks propose is accepted. If among the officials nominally in control there should be a relentless faultfinder who wishes to take charge personally, then the clerks intentionally bring up spurious cases that are hard to understand. They cite obscure legal precedents, and throw him into confusion.[44]

Another indication that Ku Yen-wu knew whereof he spoke when he emphasized Shaohsing natives as Central Board clerks comes from the late Ming official Ch'en Lung-cheng (1585-1645), a native of Chia-shan (Chia-hsing), Chekiang: "Whether the Empire is administered well or ill depends on the Six Boards, and the clerks in the Six Boards are all Shaohsing natives. So the touchstone of the Empire's administration is Shaohsing." Ch'en Lung-cheng provides another telling indication that Shaohsing natives serving as yamen clerks in Peking had already acquired a formidable reputation by the end of the Ming. He writes, "Shan-yin is generally called hard to govern. I am afraid that a straightforward, honest official would have difficulty controlling it. There is a joke about the natives of Shan-yin and Kuei-chi: The sly ones are all clerks at the ya-mens in the capital. The honest ones all stay home in Shaohsing!"[45]

An even earlier account, written no later than 1597 by Wang Shih-hsing, an official from Lin-hai (T'ai-chou), Chekiang, states that there was a colony of Shaohsing natives from Shan-yin, Kuei-chi, and Yü-yao living in the southwest corner of Peking. Driven from Shaohsing because of "insufficient land" (i.e., overpopulation), they had "entered the capital and were serving as government clerks" (hsü) throughout the central bureaucracy. Those not clever enough to become clerks became merchants.[46]

Furthermore, Shaohsing clerks in the Board of Revenue survived the Ming-Ch'ing transition in fine form, their power unabated. In a passage contemporaneous with Ku Yen-wu, the Ch'ing shih-lu informs us that as early as 1651 customs officials (kuan-shui kuan) setting out for their posts from Peking would each take along "several tens" of clerks. These clerks are described as "Shaohsing thugs" (Shaohsing kun-t'u) who "having conspired to fill the clerkship posts, compete for self-advantage by any and all means, collecting bribes even before they pass beyond the capital's gates," and then proceeding to "raise havoc along the road, whipping the courier stationmasters and press-ganging villagers."[47]

Little wonder then that Shaohsing natives serving as Central Board clerks "caused northerners to have a bad feeling toward Shaohsing people,"[48] or that Ku Yen-wu called attention to them. Nor were the activities of these Shaohsing clerks limited to the late Ming and early Ch'ing. There is evidence indicating their importance, and the chicanery in which they engaged, during the mid-nineteenth century: The reform-minded official Feng Kuei-fen, discussing the vast amount of corruption among Central Board clerks at that time, states that he arrived at his estimates "after consulting with a Shaohsing native."[49]

Finally, having discussed both subofficials and Central Board clerks, we are in a position to understand why so many of the Shaohsing natives serving as subofficials were chien-sheng. For besides avoiding the sheng-yüan bottle-neck while permitting participation in the chü-jen examination, purchase of the chien-sheng degree brought an additional advantage: It permitted its holder to purchase an official post. During the Ch'ing the sale of posts *(chüan-na)* was limited to kung-sheng, chien-sheng, and higher degree holders.[50] Thus a Shaohsing chien-sheng who failed the chü-jen examination and did not wish to become a Central Board clerk could purchase a post instead. This must be the reason why the overwhelming majority of Shao-hsing natives serving in the various subofficial posts were, as we have seen, chien-sheng. Of course, the purchase of such posts was in no way limited to Shaohsing natives. But during the nineteenth century, with the price of such posts dropping steadily[51] as the central government desperately tried to increase revenues by attracting an even larger number of purchasers, there must have been an increasing competition among purchasers for the limited number of posts available. Purchase of a post was of course preferable to the corresponding titular rank, since it gave the purchaser a chance to recoup the cost of the post and more. It was the Board of Revenue that handled the sale of these posts.[52] Since that Board was, as we have seen, dominated by Shaohsing clerks, their fellows seem to have proved unusually successful in "flying across the sea"[53] of less fortunate aspirants.

The extent of this success is revealed by the fact that Shaohsing's chien-sheng did not limit their purchases to posts as subofficials. They also purchased a comparatively large number of positions as departmental and county magistrates, according to statistics compiled by Kondō Hideki from the "Complete Register of Ch'ing Officialdom." Kondō's statistics cover twenty-one selected years between 1724 and 1910. Thus his figures do not provide the total number of chien-sheng holding positions as magistrates between 1724 and 1910, but rather merely the totals for the twenty-one years selected by him. Nonetheless, so long as we recognize that his totals have value not as absolute figures but rather as a basis for comparison, Kondō's results are highly significant: Chien-sheng from Shan-yin and Kuei-chi outstripped their counterparts from other locales in Chekiang, purchasing 227 and 157 magistracies respectively. The figures for the rest of Shaohsing are Hsiao-shan 38, Shang-yü 18, Chu-chi 15, Yü-yao 13, Ch'eng-hsien 8, and Hsin-ch'ang 0, giving Shaohsing's chien-sheng a total of 476 magistracies purchased during Kondō's selected years. Shan-yin and Kuei-chi's closest competition within Chekiang came from the chien-sheng of Jen-ho county (in Hangchow prefecture), who purchased 136, Ch'ien-t'ang (also in Hangchow), who purchased 128, and Kuei-an (in Hu-chou prefecture), who purchased 125. The total number of magistracies purchased by Chekiang's chien-sheng amounted to 1127, of which 22 were purchasers whose native county within Chekiang is unknown. Thus Shaohsing chien-sheng's purchases accounted for fully 43 percent (476/1105) of the identifiable Chekiang total. Indeed Shan-yin and Kuei-chi chien-sheng alone accounted for 35 percent (384/1105) of the Chekiang total. Comparable statistics for chien-sheng of other provinces are provided by Kondō only for Hunan and Shansi: The largest magistracy purchase figure from any county in Hunan is a mere 96, in Shansi a trivial 21.[54]

Thus, by purchasing subofficial and also magisterial positions from the clerks in the Board of Revenue who were their fellow natives, Shaohsing's chien-sheng forged a crucial link in the empire-wide network of vertical alliances that constituted the Shaohsing clique. Shaohsing's prospective purchasers of office were not necessarily any richer than their competitors from other locales. But their native-place tie to the clerks who handled the sale of these offices was a priceless asset in their struggle for survival as gentry.

2. Private Secretaries

In addition to subofficials and Central Board clerks, Shaohsing produced, of course, mu-yu (officials' personally-hired private secretaries, expert in the law).[55] It was in fact these legal experts who made Shaohsing famous.

For many hundreds of years Shaohsing men were to be found in almost all the yamens of China. They were the guides and counsellors of Viceroys and Governors as well as the humbler District Magistrates in all matters appertaining to Chinese law and the collection of taxes. The ubiquity of these men gave rise to the saying - 'If without a Shaohsing man, then it is not a yamen.'[56]

As noted above, the production of mu-yu was closely related to the production of Central Board clerks, in that some of these clerks were hired as mu-yu. But it would be a mistake to assume that all Shaohsing mu-yu were ex-clerks. Many were examination candidates, would-be officials. Ironically, the most influential mu-yu of all, Wang Hui-tsu from Hsiao-shan county (1731-1807), decided to become a mu-yu only after repeatedly failing the chü-jen examination; he continued to sit for the exams even after taking up employment as a mu-yu,[57] and eventually gained the chin-shih degree. Wang remarks that it was very common for failed examination candidates from Shaohsing *(yeh-ju wu-ch'eng)* to become mu-yu.[58] Another Shaohsing mu-yu writing during the Tao-kuang period (1821-1850) says the same about his fellow natives: "When they study for the examinations without success and hardship is imminent, they have no recourse but to fend off poverty by becoming mu-yu. But although my fellow natives who are engaged in this occupation are myriad, how many can keep warm and well fed?"[59]

A late nineteenth-century collection of Shaohsing proverbs and patois says of mu-yu, "Many Shaohsing literati fending off poverty engage in this occupation."[60] Lu Hsün recalled that in the mid-1890s, after his grandfather's arrest and his father's illness, it. was expected that he would become either a mu-yu or a merchant, "the two roads usually taken by the sons of down-at-the-heels literati families in my locale [Kuei-chi]."[61]

It is precisely the potential tension between mu-yu as ex-clerks and mu-yu as would-be officials that makes them so fascinating, especially since the tension had a potential intellectual dimension - specialized expertise on one hand, Confucian moral values on the other. The mu-yu, expert in law and taxation, was at the same time supposed to be a Confucian gentleman. "If you are not in accord [with your employer]," counseled Wang Hui-tsu, "then leave" *(pu ho tse ch'ü).* [62] Do not sacrifice your principles. The gentleman, as Confucius said, is not a tool. Yet Wang Hui-tsu also wrote an essay titled "The Need for Specialization" *(Tso-shih hsü chuan)* in which he argues in favor of concentrating one's intellectual resources. "If you invest a thousand gold pieces worth of capital in one business, the interest you will receive must needs be great. If you split that capital among a hundred businesses, not only will there be no interest, you will lose your capital investment. Such is also the case with man's intellectual powers."[63] That Wang's argument for specialization is couched in the language of the marketplace is noteworthy. For what was the purpose of specialization, we may ask, if not to acquire a competitive advantage in the labor market?

Wang Hui-tsu's fame insured that his advice would be read, and not only in Shaohsing. But even if we can assume that Wang's advice helped shape the Shaohsing mentality to some indeterminate degree, is there any evidence that his message was in turn influenced by his Shaohsing milieu? In short, was Wang's advice to specialize a cause or an effect? It was of course both, but let us for the mo-

ment concentrate on the latter.   For Shaohsing was producing mu-yu, who were by definition specialists, before Wang
Hui-tsu was born.   The fact that he himself became a mu-
yu indicates that influence of his environment.   Yet the
course of his intellectual development might conceivably
have been unique.   So we must ask, did the Shaohsing
environment influence others along the same intellectual
lines?   The answer is yes.   Consider Chang Hsüeh-ch'eng
(1738-1801) from Kuei-chi, Wang's contemporary and
friend.   As David Nivison's biography of Chang makes
clear, "Chang Hsueh-ch'eng had insisted again and again in
his essays on the *tao* that human learning had actually begun as a collection of specialized technical traditions of
government functionaries.   Chang's theories implied a new
conception of the intellectual as a technical specialist, just
that conception which was eventually to require the abolition of the examination system."[64]   Can it possibly be only
a coincidence that the members of Chang's own lineage supported themselves "by raising tree-cotton, brewing wine,
and serving as yamen secretaries"?[65]   Chang's own grandfather was a mu-yu.
    Another striking example of what seems to be the
influence of Shaohsing's heritage of specialized legal
expertise on the intellectual tendencies of its elite can be
found in the famous early Ch'ing thinker Huang Tsung-hsi
(1610-1695), a native of Yü-yao.   To quote Wm. Theodore
de Bary,

> Huang's recognition of the fundamental importance
> of law differentiates him from most Confucianists
> and is of far reaching consequence to his political
> philosophy as a whole. . . .   Before men can govern
> well, Huang says, there must be laws which govern
> well.   Thus he resolves the false dilemma with which
> Confucianists had confronted themselves for centu-
> ries.   The choice is not between men and laws but
> between true law and   the unlawful restrictions of
> the ruler.[66]

To be sure, Huang was not presenting a brief for mu-yu
and clerks: He wanted to *simplify* laws, not defend those
who profited from legal complexity.   Yet one is struck by
his rejection of the notion that law *(fa)* is inherently evil,
and of the standard dichotomy between good government by
men and bad government by law.
    There is no way to prove conclusively that Shaohsing's
mu-yu heritage produced a local milieu which placed a high

value on specialized legal expertise as an intellectual orientation suitable for the gentry, but the inference is strong enough to serve as a working hypothesis. Of course all officials, whether from Shaohsing or not, had to acquire specialized knowledge once they took office; if they stayed in the same post long enough, they acquired quite a lot of expertise. But this is different from a situation in which a high regard for specialized expertise is acquired early, long before one becomes (or fails to become) an official - as part, as it were, of one's socialization.

This heritage of legal expertise had its effect on the general environment of Shaohsing, in addition to its influence on elite intellectual tendencies described above. The local ethos emphasized widespread knowledge of the law. A Shan-yin lineage genealogy includes the following among its "family instructions," apparently written during the eighteenth century.[67] "The statutes *(lü)* must be read. Having read the statutes, you will know how to behave yourself. Consequently, transgressions of the law will naturally be fewer, and the sins that you commit will also be reduced. Thus does a gentleman keep in mind the sanctions of the law" *(huai-hsing).*[68]

It is significant that this instruction admonishes lineage members to read the statutes but makes no mention of the much more voluminous precedents, which only a mu-yu or clerk could master after arduous effort. Thus the quotation clearly seems to be addressed to the whole lineage, not merely its mu-yu and clerk members. Most important is the rationale offered for reading the statutes - that one will better be able to observe the law. Expressed here is the same assumption found in Huang Tsung-hsi, that law is not necessarily evil. It is only by mastering the law that one can be lawful.

Mastery of the law, however, did not *necessarily* result in lawful behavior. It was a double-edged sword. That local officials in general often had difficulty controlling local gentry is well known. In Shaohsing, where local officials had to meet mu-yu and clerks on their home ground, their tribulations can well be imagined. We do not have to rely on our imaginations, however, for the evidence is explicit. A 1904 newspaper story reports that since the Shaohsing local gentry *(hsiang hsien-sheng)* are so well-versed in legal matters, a run-of-the-mill magistrate would have no chance of gaining control.[69] Nor was this merely a late Ch'ing phenomenon. Virtually the same description can be found in a Yung-cheng period memorial dated 1727, discussing the appointment of a new prefect in Shaohsing:

> Although Shaohsing prefecture is not harder to govern than Hangchow, Chia-hsing, or Hu-chou, it is likewise a complicated, strenuous locale *(fan-chü chih ch'ü)*. At the moment its perverse tendencies have abated somewhat. But widespread among its populace is a rough familiarity with the statutes and precedents. An official of little talent, lacking prudence and veteran experience, will be insufficient to quell its penchant for incidents *[hao-shih*, i.e., love of litigation].[70]

From such remarks we may surmise that the legal expertise common in Shaohsing was used as often to subvert the law as to obey it.

It can be argued that expertise is by its very nature amoral. The technician has no need for personal moral standards so long as his skill is indispensable. Thus Confucianism, that celebration of government by moral suasion, has always distrusted the professional, the expert, far preferring the gentlemanly amateur. Such at least is the conventional wisdom. Yet both Wang Hui-tsu and Chang Hsüeh-ch'eng would certainly have insisted that they were good Confucians. Wang's specialist mu-yu was not to be devoid of moral principle: "If not in accord, then leave." There was more to Confucianism than the amateur ideal: A specialist could avoid being labeled a tool so long as he kept in mind ends as well as means. The Confucian universe was broad enough to include gentleman-specialists, both morally pure and expert.

In short, despite the potential for tension evident to us, there is no evidence that the Shaohsing gentry were in fact conscious of any necessary contradiction between their mu-yu heritage and their Confucian identity, at least before the late eighteenth century. Up until the mid-Ch'ien-lung period mu-yu behaved, we are told, like the Confucian gentleman they were. They were gentlemen-specialists. After that time they became increasingly corrupt (taking bribes, etc.) and so could no longer be considered gentlemen-specialists, only specialists. Shaohsing mu-yu in the nineteenth and twentieth centuries were reputed to have had a cynical, worldly-wise outlook. A local tale recorded there in 1933 describes how one mu-yu outwitted another, and ends with the loser's lament, "I wanted to manipulate him, but he ended up manipulating me."[71] It has even been suggested that Lu Hsün's use of sarcasm and ridicule is in this (debased) Shaohsing mu-yu tradition.[72]

Wang Hui-tsu himself described this loss of virtue among his colleagues:

Alas! It is difficult to speak about the principles of the private secretary's profession. Formerly, when I was twenty-two or twenty-three (i.e. 1752 or 1753) and was first studying to be a private secretary, those who took positions as judicial aides or tax accountants conducted themselves with dignity as would a guest or a teacher in another's house. From dawn to dusk they would stay at their tables handling documents, not amusing themselves with dice and chess or wasting money drinking with one another. Whenever there was some public business, they would cite the law and talk the matter over, and if some higher official disagreed with them they would have the courage to defend their opinions. Their superiors treated them respectfully, and followed their advice with trust. If they were treated disrespectfully or had any of their advice rejected by their superiors, they would resign. If there chanced to be one or two who lacked self-respect, all the others would point them out in ridicule; there were never any flatterers. When I reached the age of thirty-seven or thirty-eight (i.e. 1767-1768) it was still like this; but shortly thereafter, people became slightly more flexible and compromising. A few years later, a man who remained personally upright was regarded as unrealistic and impractical. It is difficult to swim against the current. Finally it became so bad that they made a trade of their influence and business was arranged by bribery, and men formed cliques and alliances to protect one another. Not even two or three out of ten behaved uprightly. New men entering this profession would usually pick up these evil ways from their mentors and would not know any better.[73]

To Wang Hui-tsu, himself the gentlemen-specialist par excellence, it was their behavior, not their specialty, nor even the fact of their specialization, that branded his colleagues as corrupt. There was to him still no necessary contradiction between the mu-yu heritage and Confucian identity. By the nineteenth century, however, it was widely assumed, not without cause, that mu-yu were corrupt bribetakers, and a contradiction did develop between being a mu-yu and being a gentleman.

What complicates matters, however, is that by the late eighteenth and, a fortiori, the nineteenth century, there were also many "Confucian" scholar-officials who were not gentlemen: The fundamental Confucian unity of personal morality and service to the state became unraveled. As we have seen, subofficial posts were dominated by holders of the purchased chien-sheng degree, whose Confucian credentials were dubious at best. And even the posts of departmental and county magistrate, the crucial "father and mother officials" *(fu-mu kuan)* whose impact on the people was unrivaled, were up for sale in quantities that began increasing during the T'ung-chih period (1862-1874).[74] Thus, if private secretaries were corrupt, they were not alone in their corruption. Rather, they reflected the society in which they lived, a society in which an idealistic Confucian moralist would find little solace.

Instead of defining Confucian orthodoxy in terms of morality, let us limit our definition to the more amenable notion of career paths. As long as a man possesses the right credentials, passes the right examinations, we must - and the Ch'ing did - apply the right label, "orthodox Confucian." Yet here too we must avoid oversimplification. For to picture Shaohsing as *merely* a hotbed of questionable, even Legalist-tinged, career paths would be a half-truth. Let us consider some specific career histories, culled from lineage genealogies.

To illustrate how Shaohsing natives' penetration of the Ch'ing bureaucracy worked at the family level, consider first the P'angs of Shan-yin. P'ang I-chün, born 1680, held the chien-sheng degree. No occupation is listed.[75] He married the daughter of a sheng-yüan, and his own daughters married a county director of studies *(ju-hsüeh)*, a sheng-yüan, and a county jail warden. His son Chao-hsiao, born 1710, began as a Central Board clerk (li-yüan) who rose via examination[76] to hold a subofficial position as local postmaster in Kansu and Shansi before becoming county jail warden *(hsien-wei)*[77] in Hupei. Chao-hsiao's daughters married two chien-sheng, a kung-sheng, and a sheng-yüan. Chao-hsiao's eldest son, Chung-i, born 1733, held the chien-sheng degree and purchased the post of granary supervisor *(ts'ang ta-shih)* in Shensi. He subsequently served in several other subofficial posts, including the local postmaster and county submagistrate in Honan, before ending his career as county jail warden in Kwangtung. Chao-hsiao's second son, I, born 1736, took the examination route. A sheng-yüan, he passed the chü-jen examination in 1780 and was appointed as an expectant county magistrate *(hou-hsüan chih-hsien)*. Chao-hsiao's third son, Chung-pi, born 1739, held the chien-sheng degree and purchased the subofficial post of county jail warden in Kiangsi. The fourth son, Chung-fu, born 1740, also held the chien-sheng degree and purchased an unranked subofficial position *(chüan wei-ju-liu)*, e.g., local postmaster or county jail warden. The fifth son, Chung-ts'iu, born 1746, also held the chien-sheng degree and purchased an unranked subofficial position. The subofficial-by-purchase career strategy pursued by this Shan-yin family is obvious. But note that the higher-prestige examination route was also pursued successfully.

The Ch'in lineage of Kuei-chi provides another example of how Shaohsing natives' penetration of the Ch'ing bureaucracy worked at the family level. The Ch'in lineage genealogy includes the case of a father and son both "training in the profession of Shen [Pu-hai] and Han [Fei-tzu]" *(hsi Shen-Han yeh)* and "serving as mu-yu in Chihli" during the Ch'ien-lung and Chia-ch'ing periods. Another father, born 1778, also "trained in the profession of Shen and Han" and served as a mu-yu in Honan, while his son served as a departmental jail warden in Shensi and married the daughter of a county jail warden.[78] It seems that in Shan-yin and Kuei-chi from at least the late eighteenth century on, it was considered perfectly respectable to study the writings of the Legalists, especially if one were preparing for a career as a mu-yu. "Studying the Legalists' writings" and "training in the profession of Shen [Pu-hai] and Han [Fei-tzu]," apparently meaning Legalism as the art of public adminstration rather than in a pejorative sense, are phrases which occur without any apology in sources from these two counties.[79] Whether the respectability which was seemingly accorded to the study of Legalist philosophy in this part of Ch'ing Shaohsing was an attitude shared in other parts of China prior to the late nineteenth century is as yet unknown.

This Ch'in lineage of Kuei-chi produced subofficials as well as mu-yu. In fact, the lineage included a family which produced subofficials for at least four consecutive generations in two of the family's branches: Wen-k'uei, born 1757, "trained in the profession of Shen and Han" and served as a mu-yu in Honan before achieving the rank of first-class assistant departmental magistrate (chou-t'ung). His second son, T'ao, born 1794, was an expectant departmental jail warden in Shansi, later becoming a lieutenant in charge of a grain station *(wei ch'ien-tsung)*. T'ao's three daughters married a county jail warden from Shan-yin serving in Shantung, a kung-sheng, and a local jailkeeper *(t'ing ssu-yü)* in Kiangsu. T'ao's son, Shou-jen, born 1811, was both a county and departmental jail warden in Kiangsu. Shou-jen's son, I-hui, born 1835, was both a subcounty magistrate (hsün-chien) and a county jail warden in Fukien. In the other branch of the family, Wen-k'uei's eldest son, P'u (T'ao's elder brother), born 1782, was county jail warden in Shansi. His son, Chi-lung, born 1801, "trained in the profession of Shen and Han" and served twice as a subprefect (t'ung-chih and t'ung-p'an) in Shantung. Chi-lung's daughters married an expectant jailkeeper in the Honan judicial commissioner's yamen and an expectant county magistrate. Chi-lung's son, Tseng-lang, born 1818, served first as subcounty magistrate and then was transferred to jailkeeper (ssu-yü) in the Honan judicial commissioner's yamen - probably with his brother-in-law's help - before being promoted to assistant county magistrate (hsien-ch'eng), also in Honan, and finally to county magistrate in Honan and Shansi.

Like the P'angs of Shan-yin, the Ch'ins of Kuei-chi seem to have produced more than their share of subofficials. (Those cited above from each lineage are merely a sampling.) Yet neither lineage foreswore the examination route to office. The P'angs produced a chü-jen, as we have seen, and the Ch'ins produced a chin-shih: Chin-chien, born 1807, the second son of P'u and the younger brother of Chi-lung. Chin-chien passed the chü-jen examination in Shun-t'ien in 1834 and the chin-shih examination in 1840.[80] He served first as a county magistrate in Shantung, then rose to be a prefect and circuit intendant (tao-t'ai) in Fukien. One of his daughters married the governor-general of Fukien and Chekiang, a match more glorious than any of his relatives achieved. As subofficials, they were lower gentry. As a chin-shih and tao-t'ai, he was upper.

For actually Shaohsing was also a bulwark of orthodox careerism, a prolific producer of high degree holders in the examination system. During the Ming, Shaohsing produced more chin-shih (977) than any other prefecture in China save one, Chi-an, Kiangsi. During the Ch'ing it produced 505, ranking sixth. Moreover, of these 505 fully 55 percent (277) were from Shan-yin or Kuei-chi.[81] Thus not only did Shaohsing occupy an extremely distinguished position during both the Ming and the Ch'ing as a hothouse of Confucian orthodoxy (as measured by number of chin-shih), even within Shaohsing itself the same two counties that produced most of her mu-yu,[82] subofficials, and Central Board clerks also produced most of her chin-shih. And lest one consider that Shaohsing's drop in chin-shih production from Ming to Ch'ing implies any weakening of commitment to, and investment in, the orthodox path, Ho Ping-ti considers on the contrary that "It was indeed remarkable for Shaohsing to be able to produce 505 chin-shih in Ch'ing times who were strictly under Shaohsing residential registration."[83] Indeed, of the 266 chin-shih produced by Shaohsing prefecture between 1644 and 1784 no fewer than 102 (38 percent) were registered outside of, and thus not credited to, Shaohsing - 13 in other parts of Chekiang, especially Hangchow, 57 in Ta-hsing and Wan-p'ing (in Shun-t'ien), 16 in other parts of Chihli, and 16 in other provinces.[84]

In sum, Shaohsing was noteworthy for producing not only administrative specialists of varying statuses (mu-yu, Central Board clerks, and subofficials) but also chin-shih and thus, presumably, officials. The two tracks were not considered contradictory. Apparently everyone wanted to become a chin-shih if he could. But some, realizing the odds, never tried, and when the others were derailed sooner or later, as almost all such candidates inevitably were, they had available other viable options. Perhaps the difference between Shaohsing and other locales was not only that more of its native sons did make it to the very top of the examination heap, but more important, that those who dropped off along the way were saved with some regularity from falling to the very bottom. The extent to which the examination system mass-produced rejects and failures, profligately wasting talent, is underappreciated. A locale like Shaohsing which could provide a multiplicity of acceptable alternative careers for those unfortunates among its populace would, by salvaging their individual talents, maximize its own human resources and thus its own competitive advantage over other locales. Sons from Shaohsing's upper gentry families who had no luck in the examinations had at least the security of being able to purchase positions as subofficials. They and their descendants could thus survive as lower gentry, saved by the safety net of the Shaohsing connection from sinking into the oblivion of the laboring classes. As for the unfortunates who fell through the net, Lu Hsün's "K'ung I-chi" dramatizes what could happen to a failed examination candidate who did not take advantage of the Shaohsing connection for a career in government. To a native of Shaohsing, K'ung I-chi must have seemed especially pathetic.

As in the case of the Central Board clerks, there are no statistics on the origins, either social or geographical, of mu-yu. Hired privately by officials, mu-yu were not themselves officials and thus were not included in the "Complete Register of Ch'ing Officialdom." Moreover, like the clerks they were loath to leave a systematic public record of their activities.[85]   So we must rely on qualitative sources:

A special class of *mu-fu* personnel, and the ones which tended to monopolize the positions at the lower levels of the provincial bureaucracy,[86] were the people from Shaohsing Prefecture in Chekiang. For them being in a mu-fu [i.e., serving as a mu-yu] was an hereditary occupation, and it was as natural for a Shaohsing man to be in a mu-fu as it was for a Shansi man to be a banker. For this group, their technical knowledge was their only means of livelihood, and they tried to keep 'as secret as possible the forms of correspondence, the inner wheel of the accounts, and the bribery ledgers, and formed such a powerful combination that it was almost hopeless for a mandarin of merely average ability to work except under their guidance.'[87]

The father of the modern scholar T'ao Hsi-sheng was a magistrate in Honan during the late Ch'ing, and T'ao grew up in his yamen. He notes from personal observation that the majority of judicial and tax mu-yu *(hsing-ming* and *ch'ien-ku)* serving in Honan at that time were from Shaohsing.[88]   The largest concentration of Shaohsing judicial mu-yu in any one yamen during the nineteenth century is said to have been in the yamen of the Chihli judicial commissioner *(Chih-li an-ch'a-ssu shu).*[89]   In contrast, Tseng Kuo-fan's staff of mu-yu totaled 67 persons, not one of whom was from Shaohsing.[90]   It is perhaps not surprising that an unusually upright official such as Tseng steered clear of Shaohsing mu-yu, given their reputation.[91]

The only other locale comparable to Shaohsing for production of mu-yu was Ch'ang-chou prefecture in Kiangsu, especially the two counties of Wu-chin and Yang-hu, but only during the T'ung-chih and Kuang-hsü periods.[92]   Interestingly, Wu-chin and Yang-hu stand in exactly the same relation to Ch'ang-chou as Shan-yin and Kuei-chi do to Shaohsing: In each case they are the counties which include within their boundaries the prefectual capital.[93]   We may hypothesize that large-scale production of mu-yu, like subofficials, occurred in cores - and especially in the cores of core macroregions like the lower Yangtze - not in peripheries.

The mu-yu of high provincial officials made protégés of young men from their native place, trained them as specialists in the penal code and taxation procedures, and found jobs for them with local officials.[94] Thus were vertical alliances among mu-yu created.[95] Such alliances stretched from the county level all the way to the Central Boards.[96] Once these vertical alliances were established, officials were eager to hire Shaohsing natives as mu-yu in order to take advantage of their good connections.[97] By the Yung-cheng period Shaohsing's production of mu-yu, fueled by overpopulation, was already well underway: In 1726 the governor of Chekiang noted in a memorial that Shaohsing's oversupply of talent was resulting in large-scale emigration;[98] and by then Shaohsing mu-yu could be found in every province.[99]

A native of Foochow living during the Tao-kuang period commented that although the ability of Shaohsing mu-yu is overrated, "It really seems that there is a secret transmission" of judicial and tax mu-yu positions among Shaohsing natives, otherwise there is no way to explain how they are able to "overrun *every* province."[100] Similarily the Hangchow native Hsü K'o's *Ch'ing-pai lei-ch'ao*, a compendium of Ch'ing stories and anecdotes, comments that Shaohsing shih-yeh (meaning, in this case, mu-yu) "don't necessarily surpass others in talent or knowledge. Yet they are in all yamens, from the governors-general down to the counties. They all speak the same dialect, communicating readily among themselves. So they are able to entrench themselves. . . . The reason why officials must use them is their ability to deal with higher level yamens."[101]

This testimony that as individuals Shaohsing mu-yu were not more talented than other mu-yu is significant. For it indicates that their secret of success was not aptitude or genetic endowment,[102] but better organization. The true test of organizational effectiveness comes when quality of personnel is not a factor. There is even evidence in a memorial dated 1894 that since judicial and tax mu-yu positions in every province were usually "hereditary among Chekiang's Shaohsing natives" (*Che-Shao jen wei shih-yeh*), a Shaohsing mu-yu might not even be fully competent when he first entered the profession.[103] The only explanation of why any official would be willing to hire a novice Shaohsing mu-yu is the organizational advantage which he would automatically bring with him - the Shaohsing connection.

Toward Survival as a Nation:
Local Reform in
Late Ch'ing Shaohsing

"The people of a weak and backward country, however strong and healthy they may be, can only
serve to be made examples of. . . . The most
important thing, therefore, was to change their
spirit. . . ."

> (Lu Hsün, "Preface to 'Call to
> Arms'," *Selected Works*, Vol. One,
> Peking, 1956, p. 3)

During the last years of the Ch'ing, attempts were
made, both at the center and in many locales, to strengthen
China against the encroachments of foreign imperialism,
which was ready to "carve it up like a melon" after China's
defeat by Japan in 1895. Long inured to the constant
struggle for survival at the levels of lineage and locale,
thoughtful Chinese were now becoming aware of the need
for cooperation at a higher level, the nation, in order for
China to compete in the international arena. For the Chinese, nationalism was a concept which was rooted in the
familiar strategy of survival through cooperation, but which
demanded such cooperation at an unprecedented level - not
the lineage, not the locale, but the nation. As suggested
in the Introduction, the growth of a national consciousness
during the late Ch'ing can be seen as an evolutionary
application of an age-old strategy: coping with a competitive threat at one level by cooperating against it at the
next lower level. Only as a strong nation, it was increasingly felt by the end of the nineteenth century, could

China survive in a world dominated by the Powers red in tooth and claw.

"Improvement of social customs" *(feng-su kai-liang)* was the goal of those who tried - with mixed results, at best - to make nation-strengthening reforms work in late Ch'ing Shaohsing. To be sure, "improvement of social customs" did not involve any radical reshaping of the social structure. Revolution was certainly not what these members of the local elite had in mind. Rather, the emphasis was often as not on what had been the perennial topics of Confucian reformers: diligence, loyalty and sincerity, frugality, injunctions against superstition and assorted vices.

Yet such classic concerns did not exhaust the repertoire of these nationalistic reformers: Self-cultivation alone was not expected to solve China's problems. A strong and prosperous Chinese nation was to be built upon institutional innovation as well as upon moral rededication. Let us now examine three such attempted institutional innovations in Shaohsing - judicial reform, modernized education, and local self-government. Since the pre-nationalist ancien régime - the Ch'ing polity - had in some respects been good to Shaohsing, attempts to reform the ancien régime were fraught with difficulty there. But when change came to be considered inevitable, Shaohsing natives once again demonstrated their skill at self-advancement, making the best of a new situation.

1. *Judicial Reform*

Of all the modernization projects planned in the last years of the Ch'ing, perhaps the most traumatic for Shaohsing natives would have been the inauguration of a Western-style legal system with an independent judiciary.[1] Despite Shaohsing's heritage of legal expertise, the emergence of the lawyer as a legitimate professional - the transition from *sung-shih* to *lü-shih* - was a twentieth-century phenomenon. A native of Chin-hua, Chekiang born in 1900, Ts'ao Chü-jen, states that "In my childhood it was still the era of the pettifogger (sung-shih). By the time I was a young man, it was already the era of the lawyer (lü-shih)."[2] Let us trace the transition from pettifogger to lawyer in Shaohsing. Before the twentieth century the lawyer's function was performed by mu-yu, whose clientele was of course limited to officials, and by "litigation masters" (sung-shih) or "litigation thugs" (sung-kun) - pettifoggers, whose clientele was the general public. However, unlike mu-yu, pettifoggers were illegal throughout the Ch'ing, and local officials were supposed to suppress them.[3] Yet their existence was continuous and widespread (although apparently most numerous in Kiangsu and Chekiang).[4] For pettifoggers filled a need: to advise those involved in litigation.

Most pettifoggers seem to have been moonlighting or former clerks, sheng-yüan, and the less reputable among the mu-yu,[5] especially, one imagines, those retired or unemployed. In the undated "family instructions" of a Shang-yü lineage we read, "Sheng-yüan are not to serve as pettifoggers, giving rise to conflicts and inducing enmity – an utterly vicious mentality."[6] *Sung-shih hua* ("pettifogger talk") was synonymous with deceit. During the Ch'ing pettifoggers were not allowed to appear in court to represent their clients, since they were, after all, illegal. After the 1911 Revolution they gained the right to appear in court, a major step in upgrading their status to that of modern lawyers.[7]

Shaohsing's reputation as a producer of pettifoggers dates from at least mid-Ch'ien-lung, the same era that Wang Hui-tsu cites as the beginning of mu-yu corruption. In a biographical sketch of the man who served as Shaohsing's prefect in 1761, a Yü-yao literatus who was the prefect's contemporary wrote that "The Shaohsing locale has many evil people habitually proficient as corrupt clerks" (*tao-pi*) who make a talent of their inclination for litigation. They "quote copiously from the precedents in their legal briefs." The upright prefect carefully examined these briefs one by one and ordered that the authors of the most flagrantly cooked-up presentations be flogged.[8]

An official report on litigation in Chekiang written in the 1870s notes that among the local constables (ti-pao) and the clerk-scribes who drew up petitions for litigants (*tai-shu*), those in Ningpo and Shaohsing prefectures were especially corrupt, with the worst conditions existing in Shan-yin, Kuei-chi, Chu-chi, and Hsiao-shan counties, all of course in Shaohsing. The Shan-yin magistrate was unable to improve the situation in his county despite exiling some of the worst offenders.[9]

There is evidence from Hai-yen county (Chia-hsing, Chekiang) that as of 1910 pettifoggers were actively instigating discord among potential litigants in order to increase their business.[10] Contemporaneous evidence from Shang-yü in Shaohsing offers an interesting contrast. Unlike Hai-yen, the problem in Shang-yü was not that pettifoggers were drumming up unnecessary business, but rather that private parties were themselves resorting frequently to pettifoggery even without encouragement.[11]   This difference may well reflect Shaohsing's greater proclivity for litigation, a result of its heritage of legal expertise.

In 1910 or shortly before, a progressive member of the Shang-yü gentry delivered a lecture "warning against fondness for litigation":

> For spending time and money and creating enmity, nothing compares with litigation. Whenever litigation flourishes, you know that conditions are unsettled. When two sides don't get along, there are veteran hack pettifoggers to stir up endless mischief, lying and slandering, making the hatred on both sides deeper by the day. Eventually even relatives and good friends are helpless to mediate. A little over ten years ago, with the situation in the local yamen very black, there was a case that cost two or three thousand pieces of gold even before it got to trial. It had cost over a thousand even before the petition was presented. If the litigants instead had taken those two or three thousand gold pieces and distributed them in their neighborhood as charity for orphans and paupers, such an act of benevolence would have become known to all, and everyone would have sung their praises. How wonderful that would have been! . . . Once a family gets involved in litigation, the men have no mind for running their businesses, and the women have no heart for spinning and weaving. Relatives and friends ask how things are going, and the neighbors get frightened. . . . The case drags on for months and years with no end in sight. . . .[12]

Since litigation presupposes discord, an ideology such as Confucianism which idealized harmony and like-mindedness above all else necessarily considered "litigation masters" anathema. But "litigation masters" were anathema also to advocates of national strength: At a time when unity and cooperation were considered essential to "save the nation," legal eagles could be considered not merely unethical but even unpatriotic. To the extent that Shaohsing clerks and mu-yu functioned as pettifoggers, they were tarred with the same brush. A former Kuei-chi magistrate writes, "Now [1904] all judicial and tax mu-yu are officials' pettifoggers"; and in the words of Chin-hua's Ts'ao Chü-jen, "Pettifoggers and Shaohsing shih-yeh were foxes in the

same den, their techniques extremely similar."13   In so far
as they profited from setting Chinese against Chinese, Shaohsing's legal experts were dangerously out of step with the
new drumbeat of nationalism.

Nor were ideological trends the only new problem
facing Shaohsing's legal experts.   During the Kuang-hsü
period the scope of the judicial and tax mu-yu's responsibilities expanded to include supervision of local modernization projects on behalf of the officials whom they served.
This represented if anything an increase in mu-yu power.
But this trend did not continue indefinitely.   On the contrary, the very last years of the Ch'ing and the early
Republican period confronted mu-yu with new, indeed
unprecedented, challenges.   Efforts at judicial reform
inevitably threatened those who profited from the status
quo.   In 1910 the *Ta Ch'ing hsien-hsing hsing-lü*, a new
edition of the Ch'ing Code, went into effect.   It remained in
force until 1929 as China's civil code.   Criminal law was
reformed even more extensively than civil.   In 1912 Yüan
Shih-k'ai promulgated the *Chan-hsing hsing-lü*, which replaced the criminal (but not the civil) sections of the recent *Ta Ch'ing hsien-hsing hsing-lü* and remained in force
until 1928.   Thus within the space of three years (1910-
1912), a revised civil code and an entirely new criminal
code became law.14   The civil code retained much from the
old Ch'ing Code, to be sure, but since judicial mu-yu dealt
mainly with the criminal code, they still had much "retool-
ing" to do to prevent their expertise from becoming obsolete.   In fact, the biography of a mu-yu from Kuei-chi
explicitly blames the implementation of the new criminal code
for his profession's demise.15

Equally distressing, the 1911 Revolution itself resulted
in the wholesale dismissal of Ch'ing officials and thus cost
Shaohsing mu-yu their jobs, at least temporarily.   According to a dispatch from the Shaohsing correspondent for
the *North-China Herald* published in September, 1915,

> The Revolution of 1911 brought back to Shaohsing
> some thousands of yamen secretaries and other offi-
> cials who had been compelled to relinquish their po-
> sitions in the provinces affected by that upheaval.
> Some of the towns on the Shaohsing plain had as
> many as one hundred of these men who were thrown
> out of employment. . . . The Revolution has dealt a
> blow to their monopoly of the office of secretary or
> advisor to the magistrates of China.16

When the dynasty collapsed, the already shifting balance of power between the center and the locales tipped precipitously in favor of the latter. Outsiders, especially those representing the authority of the central government, were expelled. The local elites were now unchallenged in their power. Since penetration of the Ch'ing administrative system was crucial to the survival strategies of Shaohsing's gentry, the fall of the dynasty must have been a traumatic blow indeed. All over China local elites no longer had to tolerate the presence of meddling outsiders such as those from Shaohsing.

But Shaohsing natives were nothing if not resourceful. The resultant eclipse of Shaohsing legal expertise proved temporary: Thrown off balance by the dynasty's collapse but not vanquished, Shaohsing mu-yu within a few years recovered, reappearing in modern garb, as we shall see. The mu-yu system as it had existed under the Ch'ing was, however, doomed. What proved fatal to the mu-yu system was warlordism. Unconcerned with such niceties as legal precedents and impatient with overrefined tax accounting, the warlords administered a rough and ready justice that made the mu-yu's arduous legal training unnecessary.[17] After all, if a warlord overlooked a precedent when he judged a case, who would take him to task? The minimal accountability of warlords made mu-yu a luxury rather than a necessity.

How did mu-yu survive after their profession became obsolete? In a word, they modernized it. Many Shaohsing mu-yu transformed themselves into modern-style lawyers (lü-shih) during the late Ch'ing and Republican periods. As with all the late Ch'ing reforms, judicial reform was plagued by a shortage of competent personnel. There simply were not enough modern-trained lawyers and judges to go around. This situation encouraged judicial mu-yu to retrain, and there were those who urged strongly that their experience should not be wasted: Some argued rather defensively that, after all, corruption was not limited to mu-yu.[18]

Beginning in the last decade of the Ch'ing the sons of mu-yu, who in an earlier generation would have inherited their fathers' positions, flocked to the new "schools of law and administration" (fa-cheng hsüeh-t'ang) which were being established all over China under both public and (beginning in 1910) private auspices.[19] Several of these schools were founded in Shaohsing. The January 21, 1910 issue of the Shanghai newspaper *Shih pao* contains an advertisement by one of these privately established schools,

apparently located in Shaohsing city, recruiting its first
class of a hundred students between the ages of 20 and 40
sui, "without regard to your native place so long as you
can understand the national language" (*kuo-wen*) - an indication that the courses were taught in Mandarin. Tuition
per term was six Mexican dollars, room and board eighteen,
with graduation after three terms.[20]
     The mu-yu themselves were reemerging as lawyers and
"law officials" (i.e., the newly created judges). This opportunity for mu-yu to enter the ranks of officialdom was
apparently too good to miss. As of 1910 such large numbers of judicial mu-yu, not only from Shaohsing, were
taking the new examination to become law officials (*fa-
kuan*) that the need for a quota was suggested;[21] 1910 was
the first year that this nationwide examination was given,
and a list of that year's passers has survived.[22] It reveals
that there were 566 who passed, of whom the native places
of 513 are recorded. Of this 513, 25 (5 percent) were natives of Shaohsing. Furthermore, for these 25 passers from
Shaohsing the breakdown by county is as follows: Kuei-chi
8, Shan-yin 7, Hsiao-shan 4, Chu-chi 2, Ch'eng-hsien 2,
Shang-yü 1, Hsin-ch'ang 1, and Yü-yao 0. No major dis-
continuity here.
     But when we examine the backgrounds of these 25
passers from Shaohsing, we find that 13 (52 percent) were
graduates of the new schools of law and administration (including one graduate of Tokyo's Meiji University law
school), 7 (28 percent) were judicial mu-yu (*hsing-mu*), 4
(16 percent) were kung-sheng, and 1 (4 percent) was a
chü-jen, indicating that while over one-fourth of the new
law officials from Shaohsing were former mu-yu, over one-
half had taken the new academic route to office. Moreover,
there is no overlap between the passers who were mu-yu
and the passers who were graduates of the schools of law
and administration, suggesting that although Shaohsing mu-
yu were actively seeking to take advantage of the law reform and become law officials, they were attempting to do
so by taking the 1910 examination directly, rather than by
first graduating from a school of law and administration.
As for the geographical distribution of the seven Shaohsing
mu-yu passers, continuity triumphed: Four were from
Kuei-chi and the remaining three from Shan-yin. But there
was a much more even distribution among the thirteen Shaohsing passers who were graduates of schools of law and
administration: Shan-yin 3, Kuei-chi 2, Chu-chi 2, Hsiao-
shan 2, Ch'eng-hsien 2, Shang-yü 1, Hsin-ch'ang 1, and
Yü-yao 0.

Pursuing our investigation of Shaohsing's legal experts into the Republican period, an examination of the biographies included in the tenth anniversary volume published in 1924 by the Hang-hsien Lawyers Association *(Hang-hsien lü-shih kung-hui)* in what had been Hangchow prefecture reveals that many of the association's members were former mu-yu. Moreover, of the 336 persons who joined the association between its founding in 1915 and 1924, 31 percent (104) were natives of what had been Shaohsing prefecture.[23] As we might expect, the majority of these members were from Shaohsing county (the former Shan-yin and Kuei-chi).

In contrast, an examination of the membership list of the Shanghai Lawyers Association, published in 1933, reveals only 5 percent (51 of 950) among the practicing lawyers in Shanghai were from what had been Shaohsing prefecture.[24] We may tentatively conclude that Shaohsing's lawyers, although strong within Chekiang, had much less of a nationwide impact than did their mu-yu predecessors.

There is suggestive evidence, however, that those Shaohsing natives who were nationally prominent during the Republican period were significantly more oriented towards legal expertise than were their non-Shaohsing peers. This evidence is contained in the fifth edition of *Who's Who In China,* published in 1936 by The China Weekly Review (Shanghai). When we examine all the persons included in this *Who's Who,* we find that 3 percent (45/1381) were natives of what had been Shaohsing prefecture. But when we focus specifically on the law-related persons in the *Who's Who* (i.e., persons identified as law school graduates, practicing lawyers, judges, law professors, government officials involved in the administration of justice, and authors of legal treatises), we find that 6 percent (12/190) were Shaohsing natives.[25] Moreover, the total of 190 law-related persons (both Shaohsing and non-Shaohsing) is 14 percent of all 1381 persons in the *Who's Who;* but the percentage of law-related Shaohsing persons among all the Shaohsing persons in the *Who's Who* is 27 percent (12/45). In short, Shaohsing natives enjoying national prominence during the Republican period (as measured by inclusion in the 1936 edition of *Who's Who In China)* were nearly twice as likely to have law-related careers as were all Chinese enjoying national prominence during the same period.

Moreover, tallying the native counties of the twelve law-related persons from Shaohsing reveals a strong historical continuity: Exactly two-thirds (8/12) are from Shaohsing county, with the remainder divided among Yü-yao

(2/12), Hsiao-shan (1/12), and Ch'eng-hsien (1/12). These significant disparities are inexplicable without reference to Shaohsing's long and continuing tradition of legal expertise.

In 1930 Ku Chien-ch'en, a playwright from Shaohsing county, published "The Gentry" *(Shen-tung)*, a drama in three acts set contemporaneously in "a large port," apparently Shanghai. The central character is a lawyer, and the role of law in society is one of the play's major themes.

> Only after the world establishes its laws can it become such a mess as this. Alas! Law! Law! Those dead laws, used by living men to punish the innocent. You only know law as the protector of human rights. You don't know that law is really the invader, the ruination of human rights. You only know law as the mainstay of public order. You don't know that law always upsets public order. To speak plainly, law is the bastard of money. Whoever has money can manipulate the law. Whoever has money *is* the law.[26]

Just as Wang Hui-tsu had bemoaned the corruption of mu-yu, over a century later Ku Chien-ch'en now bemoans the corruption of lawyers. Little wonder that Lu Hsün was urging his fellow countrymen to "change their spirit."

In short, judicial reform had proved disappointing as a means to national salvation. Was educational reform any more successful?

2. *Modernized Education*

During the late Ch'ing the scope of education was beginning to expand beyond the responsibility of the family and the lineage. The eventual existence of an educated general public was becoming conceivable as a prerequisite for a strong China.

Ironically, any hope for the success of modernized education in Shaohsing depended upon the support of the same social stratum that had identified most closely with the ancien régime. Yet the behavior of individual literati was not without its surprises: Among Shaohsing's progressive gentry in the late Ch'ing, one of the most distinguished was Hsü Shu-lan (also known as Hsü Chung-fan), an immensely wealthy literatus from Kuei-chi who received his chü-jen degree in 1876 in Shun-t'ien. Hsü apparently never received the chin-shih degree, but ranked, probably by purchase, as both a supplementary circuit attendant *(pu-yung tao)* and expectant prefect *(hou-hsüan chih-fu).*[27] Among his friends was the famous gentry reformer from Nan-t'ung, Kiangsu, Chang Chien.[28] Hsü Shu-lan's activities on behalf of his native place included managing the apparently honest 1898 rice price-control project already described, plus two even more outstanding works of philanthropy: establishing in 1897 both one of the very first semi-modern schools in Shaohsing, the Sino-Occidental School *(Chung-hsi hsüeh-t'ang),*[29] and also the Shaohsing Library *(Ku Yüeh ts'ang-shu-lou),* one of the very first public libraries in China.[30]

The library's stated policy was quintessentially moderate: both to "preserve the old" *(ts'un-ku)* and to "reveal the new" *(k'ai-hsin).* "The mistake of past scholars has been to study the past carefully while slighting the present. The mistake of contemporary scholars is a tendency to esteem the present over the past. The policy of this library is to strike a balance. . . ."[31] Quite a bit of information on the Shaohsing Library has survived, including its catalogue and regulations, which were both published in 1904. The catalogue lists both classical and Western texts, the latter including works in the natural and social sciences. Moreover, "the study of natural science requires equipment and specimens. Therefore this library also collects apparatus for physics and chemistry, and specimens animals, mineral, and vegetable as an aid to textual research."

The library catalogue's table of contents gives further evidence of cosmopolitan concerns: In addition to the traditional categories of classical scholarship, we find such new headings as "General Principles of Eastern and Western Medicine," "Eastern and Western Physics," "Astronomical Mathematics: Chinese, Western, and Sino-Western Techniques," "Christianity," "Various Schools of Chinese and Foreign Philosophy," "Eastern and Western Legalists" *(Tung-hsi yang fa-chia chih hsüeh),* "Eastern and Western Strategists," "Specialized Histories of Countries in Europe, Africa, the Americas, and Australia," "Eastern and Western School Regulations and Pedagogy," "Eastern and Western Armies and Navies," "Eastern and Western Law Codes," "General Principles of Eastern and Western Agronomy," "Western Writing Machines" (i.e., typewriters), "Western Methods of Painting and Photography," "Eastern and Western Fiction," etc.

Located in the western part of Shaohsing city, the library contained over 70,000 volumes as of 1903, with a staff of eight and a main reading room seating sixty. Hours were 9-11 A.M. and 1-5 P.M. Books were not allowed to circulate outside the main reading room. There was a separate reading room for newspapers. "In keeping with the practice of libraries in the East and the West, this library has no residence facilities"; readers coming from a distance "are requested to make their own arrangements for lodging. . . . This library depends entirely on the resources of Mr. Hsü Chung-fan and thus is subject to financial limitations. Any contributions will be gratefully accepted." Indeed, Hsü is reported to have spent 32,000 taels on the library: over 8600 for the purchase of the land and construction of a four-story library building, and over 23,000 more for books and staff salaries.

In an essay dated 1902, Hsü explains why he decided to establish the Shaohsing Library. The rationale for his philanthropy is couched in the Social Darwinist language of national survival that Yen Fu was then making so popular. Arguing essentially that knowledge is power, Hsü describes in some detail the famous libraries of the Western Powers: the Bibliothèque Nationale with its 2,072,000 volumes, the British Museum with its 1,120,000 volumes, plus the great libraries of St. Petersburg, Munich, Vienna, Copenhagen, Washington, and Brussels. The Meiji's establishment of the Ueno Library in Tokyo (forerunner of the National Diet Library) also attracts Hsü's attention. Given his expressed belief in "natural evolution through struggle" (*t'ien-yen wu-ching*) and "survival of the fittest" (*yu-sheng lieh-pai*), Hsü evidently felt that foreign superiority even in librarianship was not to be taken lightly.[32]

As Benjamin Schwartz has stated, "*T'ien-yen lun* (On Evolution) was to be Yen Fu's most resounding success. Not only did it cause a stir among Yen Fu's contemporaries in the ranks of the literati, but a whole literature of memoirs and reminiscences testifies to its resounding impact on the youth of the dawning twentieth century."[33] According to William Lyell, "It probably would be difficult to overestimate the influence of Yen Fu on the young Lu Hsün, who was so taken with the *Evolution and Ethics* that he committed large chunks of it to memory."[34]

That Social Darwinism had become popular among Shaohsing's progressives by the early 1900s is further suggested by an essay contributed to *Tung-fang tsa-chih* in 1906 by a reader from Shan-yin. Entitled "A Personal Proposal to Forbid Gambling," it argues against gambling in terms of national survival: "These days the Empire is beset by a poison more harmful than tigers and leopards but without their claws and teeth, more deadly than spears and lances but without their sharp blades. . . ." The most

popular forms of gambling are mahjong and private lotter-
ies. Even worse, the government itself runs public lotter-
ies. Gambling not only wastes money; would-be students
also waste precious hours at the gambling boards. Gambling obviously damages public morality. Furthermore, given
a world of "nations *(min-tsu)* competing with one another,
how can [a nation of such wastrels] avoid failure? So now
if we wish to preserve the race *(pao-chung)*, we must begin by banning gambling."[35]
    The alacrity with which the language of Social
Darwinism was taken up in the late Ch'ing should not be
surprising. The struggle for survival between lineages and
between locales had long been part of the Chinese experience. Consciousness of China as a nation among other
nations was new, to be sure, but the realpolitik involved
was easily understood from domestic models.

    Hsü Shu-lan's second contribution to educational
modernization in Shaohsing was the Chung-hsi hsüeh-t'ang.
Chiang Monlin, who was a student at this school in 1898,
the year after its founding, describes its mixed curriculum:

> The Sino-Occidental School, as its name implies,
> offered not only Chinese studies but also courses in
> Occidental subjects. This was a new departure in
> Chinese education. Here my mind began to come in-
> to contact with Western knowledge, however poorly
> explained and superficial. . . . The first and most
> surprising thing I learned in this school was that
> the earth is round like a ball. . . . In elementary
> physics I learned how rain is formed. It made me
> give up the idea that a gigantic dragon showers it
> from his mouth. . . . The major part of the cur-
> riculum, however, still consisted of literary studies:
> Chinese literature, classics, and history. . . .
> Foreign languages were divided into three sections:
> English, French, and Japanese.[36]

Chiang compares the school unfavorably with Hangchow's
Chekiang College, where "the courses were more advanced,
more various, and better taught, with less sheer memory
work."[37] Lu Hsün also notes that his dissatisfaction with
the limited curriculum at the Sino-Occidental School contributed to his decision to enroll instead at the Nanking Naval
Academy in 1898.[38]

In 1898 Hsu Shü-lan hired his friend Ts'ai Yüan-p'ei as the school's principal.[39] Taking up the post in 1899, Ts'ai lasted only a year: A faculty dispute soon broke out between the conservatives and two progressives. One of the latter, Ma Yung-hsi, advocated "people's rights" *(min-ch'üan)* and "women's rights" *(nü-ch'üan)*.[40] The other progressive, Tu Ya-ch'üan, who taught science, advocated evolution and the survival of the fittest.[41] (A native of Shaohsing, Tu went on to become one of the first editors of *Tung-fang tsa-chih*.)[42] Ts'ai sided with the two progressive teachers, and the conservative majority forced his resignation.[43] It is doubtful how much of the school's Western curriculum survived the next few years of local conservative backlash. After the failure of the 1898 Reform Movement, the school had changed its name to "the Shaohsing Prefectural School" *(Shaohsing fu hsüeh-t'ang)*, prudently omitting the word "Occidental"; and in the wake of the anti-foreign Boxer Rebellion in 1900, the school even temporarily closed its doors for one year.[44]

Yet 1900 also witnessed in Shaohsing an educational innovation of considerable boldness: A "charity school" *(i-shu)*, privately funded by gentry, was established in that year for children of peasant and worker families. It served northern Shan-yin and northern Kuei-chi, and by 1904 had taught over 200 students. The curriculum included translation first from classical Chinese into colloquial, and then vice-versa. "Generally a completely illiterate person is able to form sentences and write short letters after six months." Arithmetic (including use of the abacus) was also taught. Although its curriculum was hardly "modern" or "Westernized," this school was arguably even more progressive than the hsüeh-t'ang, for it was devoted to mass education, and at no expense to the common people.[45]

In 1903 the central government promulgated a Modern School Charter establishing - on paper - a nationwide modern educational system crowned by a university in Peking.[46] A "Shaohsing Educational Association" was organized in this same year to promote the founding of new schools. In addition to the Association's headquarters in the prefectural capital, there were to be branches in each of Shaohsing's counties as well as in the major communities of Shaohsing natives living in other provinces.[47]

The end of the traditional examination system in 1905 provided an enormous impetus for the establishment of new schools, as the gentry sought new channels of social mobility. The biography of Madam Wu demonstrates that at least some members of Shaohsing's gentry reacted immediately, and pragmatically, to the end of the traditional examination system: "This year [1905] the various governors-general and governors are memorializing that the examination system be halted. All literati would lack a means of advancement were it not for the modernized schools. Madam is concerned."[48] Her stepson, together with several other members of the local elite, began planning to convert a *shu-yüan* (an old-style academy) into a modern elementary school. Madam Wu contributed $3000 Mexican dollars and several other families lesser amounts, bringing the total to $6500. This sum proved insufficient, so various tea and silk merchants in Madam Wu's locale, eastern Kuei-chi, were approached for contributions. The Nine Lotuses Temple was "borrowed" to serve as the school's dormitory. Purchase of books and equipment was completed, a faculty was hired, and the school was opened in the second month of 1906, less than a year after the beginning of the project. Since the government made it clear that the new schools would have to be funded locally, it was inevitable that the impetus should lie with the gentry.

Given this relative dependence upon the private sector to fund educational innovation, it is not surprising that lineages in late Ch'ing Shaohsing continued to play a vital role in education, as they had in earlier periods (see Appendix A). For lineages remained concerned about cultivating talent even after the end of the traditional examination system. In Hsiao-shan, to pick one well-documented county, there are literally dozens of examples of elementary schools *(hsiao hsüeh-hsiao)* established by lineages in the last years of the Ch'ing. Following a pattern centuries old, these new schools were usually located in the lineage temple and were commonly funded by rents from lineage-owned land. In several cases it is noted that the lineages already had charity schools (i-shu), which the new elementary schools presumably replaced.[49] Information from Ch'eng-hsien and Yü-yao confirms that it was very common for schools (hsiao hsüeh-t'ang and hsüeh-hsiao) established after 1905 to be located in lineage temples.[50] Clearly lineages considered it highly desirable to maintain their commitment to education even when the content of that education was being modified to suit changing circumstances.

How many students did the new-style schools attract? Statistics compiled by the new Ministry of Education from questionnaires which it distributed allow us to trace the number of students enrolled in hsüeh-t'ang in each of Shaohsing's counties during the years 1907 through 1909. (Unfortunately comparable statistics are apparently not

available for other years in the late Ch'ing.)   Table 12
indicates that, overall, student enrollments in Shaohsing's
hsüeh-t'ang doubled between 1907 and 1909. Enrollments in
Shan-yin, Kuei-chi, Yü-yao, Shang-yü, and Hsin-ch'ang
approximate this general trend.   Yet the county-by-county
figures also reveal some interesting anomalies, the reasons
for which remain unclear.   What, for example, caused the
phenomenal rise in enrollments in Chu-chi?   Why, conversely, was Hsiao-shan's increase in enrollments so modest?
And why were enrollments in Ch'eng-hsien initially so
impressive but unsustained through time?   On these questions, unfortunately, the available sources are mute.   But
we *are* told that in Chu-chi the initial enthusiastic blos-
soming of hsüeh-t'ang was followed by their wilting on the
vine due to lack of funds, trained teachers, and experi-
enced administrators.[52]

In short, despite the doubling of student enrollments
between 1907 and 1909, the hsüeh-t'ang experiment in Shaohsing, as in China generally, was very far from an unqual-
ified success.   Most schools were financed privately, some
from public funds.   These latter resulted in higher taxes,
further burdening that segment of the population least likely to benefit from the new schools, the common people.
There is no doubt but that the hsüeh-t'ang thus helped
contribute to the mass uprisings and banditry endemic to
the late Ch'ing, and were in turn the victims of peasant
violence.   There are many accounts of peasant destruction
of these modernized schools and other symbols of the late
Ch'ing reforms in Shaohsing, motivated not so much by a
blindly reactionary mentality as by the peasants' unwill-
ingness to submit to increased exploitation without compen-
sating benefits.   In the words of the *North-China Herald's* Shaohsing correspondent, "The people hate these [new]
schools and those who manage them, because of the heavy
taxation and in some instances illicit taxation."[53]   We know
that this basically financial (i.e., anti-tax) motivation was
typical of mass destruction of hsüeh-t'ang throughout China
during the last years of the Ch'ing.[54]   Western scholarship
has emphasized the sterile formalism of traditional Chinese
elementary education (rote memorization and the like).   But
Japanese scholars have pointed out that the semi-Western-
ized curriculum offered by the hsüeh-t'ang was not a whit
more relevant to the peasants' daily lives, and it was the
peasants who by their taxes and rent were being forced to
foot the bill.[55]

Inseparable from the problem of curriculum was the
problem of educational quality: The lack of teachers train-

TABLE 12

**NUMBER OF STUDENTS ENROLLED IN SHAOHSING'S
HSÜEH-T'ANG IN THE YEARS 1907, 1908, AND 1909**

Geographical Scope of Hsüeh-t'ang	1907	Year 1908	1909
Prefecture-wide	162	182	235
Shan-yin	1102+	1334+	2178+
Kuei-chi	678	1011	1401
Hsiao-shan	1053	1313+	1398+
Chu-chi	746+	2812	3957+
Yü-yao	923	879+	1626+
Shang-yü	462	501	1175+
Ch'eng-hsien	1803	1447+	1646+
Hsin-ch'ang	300	386	624
TOTAL	7238+	9865+	14,240+

For sources, see note 51.

ed in the new subjects resulted in standards so mediocre that in 1903 one Shaohsing progressive went so far as to suggest, with considerable chagrin, that to abolish the examination system before drastically upgrading the existing hsüeh-t'ang would be a mistake.[56] Equally damaging was the fact that unscrupulous members of the gentry were not above making a pretense of establishing hsüeh-t'ang in order to induce the local government to grant them property by eminent domain. Buddhist monastaries were especially vulnerable to such fraud, since they could be attacked as dens of superstition and immorality. (The behavior of some monks and nuns apparently did nothing to forestall such criticism.) That the expropriation of Buddhist property under the guise of local reform was in no way limited to Shaohsing is obvious from a 1904 article in *Tung-fang tsa-chih* condemning the practice generally.[57] Thus was the reformers' reputation damaged, their motives impugned. Nor were Shaohsing's hsüeh-t'ang, once established, immune from the corruption endemic to the society at large.

There is evidence of anti-hsüeh-t'ang collusion between "evil gentry," bandits, and ruffians in Yü-yao during 1910-1911. When the people of rural Yü-yao held a religious festival in 1910 to placate the "General of the Locusts," "secret society bandits and thugs" took the opportunity to demolish the several hsüeh-t'ang in Lin-shan-wei, along with a gentryman's house there. It was common knowledge in the vicinity that the mastermind behind these "ignorant rustics" was the "evil gentryman" *(lieh-shen)* and local tyrant Hsieh Keng-hsien. A reoccurrence the following year was feared.[58] Incipient local reform in Yü-yao thereby suffered a serious reversal.

On the other hand, the Ch'iu Chin affair in July, 1907 proved to be less of a setback to the cause of local reform in Shaohsing than one might have suspected. Ch'iu Chin and her colleagues in the revolutionary Restoration Society (Kuang-fu hui) established the Ta-t'ung Normal School just outside Shaohsing city to conceal their preparations for an armed anti-dynastic uprising. This ruse was successful for a while, since schools were permitted to store guns to teach military drill. Although her capture and execution made Ch'iu Chin a martyr - ironically because she was widely believed to be merely an innocent schoolteacher - the affair provided local reactionaries with just the excuse they needed to demand a crackdown on all local hsüeh-t'ang.[59] Yet, as noted above, Table 12 reveals that in Shan-yin and Kuei-chi, the locus of the Ch'iu Chin affair, student enrollments in hsüeh-t'ang doubled from 1907 to 1909, paralleling the prefecture-wide trend. Thus, in purely quantitative terms, the repercussions of the Ch'iu Chin affair did not deter students from attending the new-style schools in increasing numbers.

In assessing the significance of local educational reform in late Ch'ing Shaohsing, quantification tells only part of the story: It is necessary not only to count heads but also to attempt to peek inside them. Consider the following report in the *North-China Herald* of January, 1907.

> There was a rebellion during the summer [of 1906] in the fu [i.e., prefectural middle] school [the former Sino-Occidental School].[60] Complaints were made about the food provided. Some [students] were expelled and the rest left. The school is now being done up and hopes to reopen next (Chinese) year. The government schools in the city, one for each of the two hsien, cannot be said to be flourishing. Less than thirty pupils in one, and forty or so in the other. From this it is clear that the mass of the people are not taking at all kindly to the new learning, and one might fairly describe the results of the government efforts at modern education in Shaohsing as a complete failure. I understand that the teaching and curriculum in the fu school is practically the same as in the hsien schools [although it was supposed to be more advanced], and that there is such difficulty in getting scholars for any of these schools, that all who are willing to come are accepted, raw pupils being taken, and gladly, in the fu school, just as much as in the hsien schools. Chinese friends tell me, though their judgment is of course not entirely unprejudiced, that the boys in these schools lose their respect for their elders, and become overbearing and conceited, and impatient of restraint. My personal belief is that the government, at least our local government, has no heart in the matter, and that the heart of the vast mass of the people, common people and scholars alike, is dead against it.[61]

In all fairness it should be noted that the prefectural middle school's curriculum had expanded impressively from the rather limited offerings with which its predecessor, the Sino-Occidental School, had failed to attract the young Lu Hsün in 1898. As of 1906-1907 the prefectural middle school, by then the leading educational institution in Shao-

hsing, was offering thirteen courses to its 116 students:
moral self-cultivation, Confucian Classics, Chinese language, English language, Chinese and world history, Chinese
and world geography, mathematics, biology, physics and
chemistry, law and finance, painting and drawing, singing,
and physical training.[62]

Despite such educational advances certain behavioral
continuities persisted. One cause of student unrest at the
prefectural middle school during these years was "serious
factionalism stemming from a native-place mentality": To
wit, the boys from Shan-yin and Kuei-chi came to blows
with the boys from Ch'eng-hsien and Chu-chi. When the
scions of the metropolitan counties found the lads from the
prefecture's rugged periphery to be more than they could
handle, they hired tinfoil beaters (skilled in strongarm
tactics - see Appendix C) to provide the requisite mus-
cle.[63]

Yet student unrest in late Ch'ing Shaohsing was not
limited to institutional food and native-place factionalism.
The scent of political revolution was in the air, far more
heady than anything advocated by local reformers. In 1908
a teacher at the prefectural middle school who is said to
have belonged to the T'ung-meng hui covertly organized an
anti-Ch'ing student group called "The Shaohsing Society" *(Yüeh she).*[64] In January 1911 a wave of queue-cutting, symbolic treason, broke out at the school.[65] As
chance would have it, Lu Hsün happened to be serving as
director of studies there at the time,[66] and was thus placed
in an awkward position. For he had cut off his own queue
two years earlier, in 1909, after returning from seven years
in Japan. Moreover, he had refused to buy a false
queue,[67] as many revolutionaries with second thoughts had
done, and the Shaohsing prefect was accordingly keeping a
close eye on him.[68] After struggling with his conscience,
Lu Hsün decided to risk the label of hypocrite and coun-
selled his students to do as he said, not as he did: He
advised them, for their own safety, to cease their queue-
cutting.[69]

When the news reached Shaohsing that on November 5
Hangchow had gone over to the Revolution, Lu Hsün organized an armed student militia which strove to keep people
calm and prevent reactionaries from spreading rumors or engaging in counter-revolutionary violence. The participating
students were apparently not members of any revolutionary
party, but they were definitely sympathetic and wanted to
help.[70] With students at Shaohsing's leading modernized
school rallying to the side of the Revolution, it was clear

that from the government's perspective, local educational modernization had become, in a word, counterproductive. Reform was producing instability, not national strength. Nowhere was this unhappy fact clearer than in the realm of "local self-government."

3. *Local Self-Government*

"Local self-government" *(ti-fang tzu-chih)* was an officially sponsored attempt to enhance the dynasty's chances of survival by establishing assemblies to increase formal, consultative participation in government by the gentry. It was seen as a step towards an eventual constitutional monarchy, which was to re-cement the gentry's allegiance to the Throne (shaken by the end of the examination system in 1905), while yielding to the gentry as little additional power as possible.[71]

From the dynasty's perspective, local self-government would restore the symbiotic relationship between the center and the locales by providing a new and inexpensive institution to coöpt the talent of the gentry, as the examination system had done. But from the gentry's perspective, such "self-government," while in one sense a sham because of its purely consultative nature, did represent a step towards true home rule, symbolized by abolition of the law of avoidance. The gentry wanted the right to hold office in their home locales, and after the Ch'ing fell, they got it. Of course, home rule by the gentry hardly served to advance the cause of national unity.

Late Ch'ing "local self-government" should not be confused with truly representative government or democracy in any meaningful sense. For commoners were excluded from participation: In the words of Philip Kuhn, "[N]one of the preeminent goals of local self-government proponents really required a democratic theoretical basis. The development of wealth and power, the modernization of the local economy, and statecraft programs for bridling the power of local elites could all proceed very well without any basis in democratic theory. And it was essentially devoid of such a body of theory that the idea of local self-government entered twentieth-century politics."[72]

Nor was this turn of events unforeseen. Indeed, a perceptive commentary published in 1906 argues that the proposed local self-government programme is insufficiently democratic, and criticizes the gentry for threatening to perpetuate in local self-government the authoritarian practices of the past. Success of local self-government is crucial to the success of constitutional government, this argument continues, but if "self-government" turns out in practice to be closed and despotic, then the power of the gentry will become antithetical to constitutionalism.[73] Such caveats were of course entirely appropriate, both at the time and long thereafter.

How widespread was Shaohsing gentry participation in "local self-government"? Surviving statistics from Hsiao-shan[74] indicate that, beginning in 1910, assembly-men *(i-yüan)* were selected from twenty-six rural townships *(hsiang)* within the county, plus the county seat. The number of hsiang assemblymen was 310, plus the county seat's 20. Thus the average number of assemblymen per rural township was 12 (the range being from 8 to 18). Compare the statistics on assemblymen from Shan-yin and Kuei-chi counties during 1910, which was, as in Hsiao-shan, their first year of activity: In Shan-yin and Kuei-chi counties combined, the sixty-seven rural townships provided 720 assemblymen, the four urban townships *(chen)*[75] provided 83, and Shaohsing city (the prefectural capital, straddling the county line) provided 32.[76] Thus in Shan-yin and Kuei-chi the average number of assemblymen per rural township was 11 (the range being from 8 to 18), and per urban township 21 (the range being from 20 to 21). The substantial number of assemblymen involved (a total of 1165 from Shan-yin, Kuei-chi, and Hsiao-shan) suggests that in practice "local self-government" in these three counties seems to have fulfilled the central government's objective of providing a mechanism for maximizing gentry representation in (and, it was hoped, coöption by) officially approved local assemblies. Comparable data for the rest of Shaohsing prefecture are unfortunately lacking.

Information on local self-government in late Ch'ing Shaohsing is extremely scant. Indeed, not enough is known about the assemblies there to evaluate their impact on local society during the brief time they existed before the dynasty fell. But it does seem that a local elite composed of degree holders and rich merchants dominated them,[77] the peasantry opposed them[78] (as another excuse for raising taxes), and the yamen clerks feared them (as a threat to their de facto hegemony over local administration). Kuhn's generalization holds true for Shaohsing: "[T]he familiar struggle between the local elite and the clerk-runner group over the control of local resources was played out in a new context of self-government."[79] Indeed, a first-hand account tells of a direct confrontation between yamen clerks and local elite in Shan-yin and Kuei-chi when the 1911 Revolution removed the local officials as a factor in the power balance: The clerks were ordered by the gentry-dominated provisional government to hand over the yamen archives. The clerks resisted, surrendering only worthless files. The gentry finally managed to oust these clerks and install new ones, presumably more malleable.[80] In Chu-chi the county archives, dating back "several hundred years," were deliberately burned in 1912 at the suggestion of the tax mu-yu in order to destroy incriminating evidence, "without one word of opposition from the gentry."[81] Control of the yamen archives, and particularly the tax records, must have been a major goal of the gentry at this time of dynastic collapse and resultant political uncertainty. By destroying such tax records, the gentry would profit from the dynasty's demise, and tilt the balance of power even more drastically in the direction of localism.

Like judicial reform and modernized education, "local self-government" hardly proved, in practice, to be a guarantee of dynastic survival, much less national strength. The evidence from Shaohsing leads us to conclude that, at least during the late Ch'ing, these three institutional innovations failed to foster a rich and strong nation. In the end the center did not hold, and before long mere anarchy was indeed loosed upon the Chinese world.

Conclusion

For Shaohsing, China's transition from Empire to Republic merely added another chronological link to a chain of depressing continuities. The 1911 Revolution was not a watershed in Shaohsing's social history. Class relations did not change. Peasants continued to stagger under an unalleviated burden of rent and taxes. Merchants too remained saddled with likin. If anything, tax collection under the "Republic" was even more ruthless than under the Ch'ing.

But that is a separate story. We have found Shaohsing to be, in effect, a rather paradoxical place. In its relationship to the rest of China, it was highly successful, producing far more than its share of chin-shih examination passers and subofficials (and, if the statistics were known, probably far more than its share of private secretaries and central-government clerks as well). By their participation in the administration of the Ch'ing state, Shaohsing's fame was spread far and wide. The Shaohsing connection worked so well that it drew charges of corruption from natives of less successful locales. No doubt these charges were often justified. The struggle for survival that preoccupied China's locales was Social Darwinism in all but name. In this jungle Shaohsing flourished.

Yet when we turn to Shaohsing's own society, we find that the same struggle for survival which produced a cliquish cooperation among Shaohsing natives abroad also produced a fierce competition among them at home. As we saw in Part One, Shaohsing during the late Ch'ing was racked by internal discord: tenant against landlord, commoner against official, commoner against commoner, elite against elite, respectables against déclassé, ad infinitum. Shaohsing's society could hardly have been more severely cracked and fissured. For all its production of high examination passers, the locale does not seem to have maintained a particularly high moral standard. For all their well-cultivated legal expertise, Shaohsing's people do not seem to have been particularly law-abiding. The ultimate irony, of course, is that the apparent respectability of Legalist philosophy in Shaohsing's local culture does not mean that Shaohsing natives were good Legalists, compliant to the will of the state.

On the contrary, as we saw in Part Two, Shaohsing's gentry carved out spheres of influence within the state's bureaucracy, making it serve their own particularistic ends. By pursuing a strategy of purchasing first the chien-sheng degree and then a subofficial post from fellow-native clerks in the Board of Revenue, Shaohsing natives could effectively bypass the examination route to office and thus shortcircuit one of the key mechanisms by which the central government sought to control local elites. All those who purchased positions as jail wardens, for example, swelled the ranks of the lower gentry, hardly Confucian gentlemen yet able to lord it over the common folk back home. Shaohsing simply contained too many people who knew too much about how to manipulate the levers of government for private advantage. In sum, Shaohsing natives survived by competing at home and cooperating abroad. The strategy that guided their actions might well be termed "Feng-chien wei t'i, chün-hsien wei yung": Centralism at the service of localism.

Beginning at the very end of the nineteenth century, however, progressive gentry in Shaohsing attempted to reverse this formula and create a reformed locale to serve a reformed center, a nation. Implicit in this attempt was the recognition that the old struggle for survival among China's parts was now inimical to China as a whole. For how could a nation survive in the international arena if its citizens were setting their sights too low, cooperating among themselves only in order to vanquish "foreigners" from other locales, other provinces? Given the real foreign threat from the imperialist Powers, no Chinese could benefit from this self-inflicted policy of divide and be conquered.

By the time the dynasty fell, Shaohsing's native-place network - the secret of its success in penetrating the Ch'ing bureaucracy - could be criticized not merely as parochial and corrupt but even as unpatriotic. Ironically, Shaohsing's survival strategy had itself survived long enough to be judged, and found wanting, by the standards of the new nationalism.   But the history of the Chinese Republic would demonstrate how difficult was the transition from native place to nation.

APPENDIX A
Lineages

"In a small village the guest of one family is virtually the guest of the whole community. We were all about the same age, but when it came to determining seniority, many were at least my uncles or grand-uncles, since everybody in the village had the same family name and belonged to one clan."

(Lu Hsün, "Village Opera,"
Selected Works, Vol. One,
Peking, 1956, p. 140)

Competition at the level of the locale implied cooperation at the level of the lineage (t'ung-tsu). Shaohsing natives were highly conscious of the important role that lineages played in their locale. One Kuei-chi genealogy's preface, written in 1911, refers explicitly to "our Shaohsing heritage of emphasizing lineages."[1] Likewise, a survey of Chu-chi county published in 1925 states that "Down to the present Chu-chi is still a lineage society."[2] Of course consanguineal activities did not stop at the county line. There is evidence that higher-order lineages incorporating Shaohsing lineages operated at the inter-prefectural, and even inter-provincial, levels: A genealogy from Kuei-chi reveals that around 1919 its lineage, one branch of a higher-order lineage with headquarters in Yinhsien, Ningpo prefecture, participated in the establishment of an association for members from both Ningpo and Shaohsing who had emigrated to Shanghai to do business. The name of this association was "The Ning-Shao All-Shanghai Association for Strengthening Our Lineage." The purpose

of this group was to counteract a perceived decline in
"lineage consciousness" *(tsung-tsu kuan-nien)* among the
Shanghai membership, who "exist as separate families (chia)
but fail to coalesce." Thus did at least one higher-order
lineage rally its membership in an attempt to forestall the
disrupting effects of Shanghai's hyper-urban, Westernized
environment.[3]

Given this link between Shaohsing and Ningpo in terms
of lineage organization, it is perhaps not amiss to quote
here a description of Ningpo's lineages by Shiba Yoshinobu
and to suggest that his characterization is not irrelevant to
the situation in Shaohsing.

The Ningpo region was one of the few in China
where most of the countryside was dominated by
strong lineages. Single-lineage villages were not
uncommon, and marketing communities and other
intervillage systems were often dominated by one or
two powerful lineages. The precise nature of the
interrelation between lineage strength and the fact
that the region developed in the shadow of Ningpo
qua entrepôt is obscure, but one may conjecture
that lineages benefiting from commercial opportunities
were enabled to mobilize the capital and manpower
needed to build irrigation works and reclaim land.
At any rate, well-endowed lineages in the Ningpo region early mobilized their resources to educate their
brightest young men to compete in the imperial examinations. However, since fewer than one in twenty passed any given examination, successful lineages
inevitably had to contend with many failures. In a
developing economy such as that in the immediate
hinterland of Ningpo, many thwarted scholars turned
to business.[4]

We know that Lu Hsün's own lineage was tightly knit.
It consisted of three branches. Lu Hsün's branch, consist-
ing of several dozen people, lived together in one compound; the other two branches lived close by in separate
compounds. Each branch consisted of several sub-branch-
es *(fang)*, each probably a group of families.[5] This pattern was of course in no way unique to Shaohsing, being
common among those elite families which could afford it.
There is, however, a bit of highly provocative evidence
concerning the unusually large extended (joint) family of
what seems to be a Shaohsing mu-yu, contained in the
autobiography of a Shantung servant woman:

My new master Ch'ien Lao-yeh had passed his examinations and was qualified to be a district magistrate
himself. He had the rank, but as yet had never
been given an official seal of his own. He was
called a "Waiting to Re-place District Magistrate."
Meantime he worked as an assistant to the district
magistrate of P'englai [in Shantung]. He worked up
most of the lawsuits. He had no salary but got his
share of what is paid by those who go to law.[6] His
father had been a prefect. They came from an old
family of famous lawyers. No court in China was
considered complete without a Ch'ien of Hsiao Hsing
[Shaohsing?].

The clan family *[sic]* had not divided the property
for seventeen generations. There were over two
hundred rooms in the house in Hsiao Hsing. When
the family went to meals there were between two and
three hundred people fed at every meal. A gong
was beaten and they all went. The house was open
to any member of the family [i.e., lineage?] at any
time, and he could stay as long as he wished.[7]

How common this phenomenon was in Shaohsing is unknown.[8]

We *are* told, however, that in the majority of eastern
Chekiang's villages, lineages formed the basis of society.[9]
Furthermore, the phenomenon of single-lineage villages
definitely existed in Shaohsing. A missionary writing in
1878 described the situation in Chu-chi's "Great Valley" as
follows: "[T]hese villages consist mostly of families with the
same surname, and all are connected by birth."[10] Lu Hsün
describes his mother's natal village in Kuei-chi in similar
terms, as we have seen. The size of single-lineage villages
in Hsiao-shan county, for which data exist, varied from
twenty to over one thousand households, with those in the
two- or three-hundred range most frequent.[11] Determining
the percentage of single-lineage villages remains, however,
a difficult problem: For example, extant lists of villages in
Hsiao-shan and Hsin-ch'ang counties contain a high percentage with a surname as part of the village name, but it is
impossible to determine how many of these were truly single-lineage villages.[12]

The tendency of people in rural Shaohsing to live near
relatives facilitated a well-developed local system of education, funded privately not only by individual families but

also by lineages. In Shaohsing, as elsewhere in China, a lineage would commonly use the rent from a portion of its real estate to support its lineage school. For the education of its members was one of the best long-term investments that a lineage could make. Those who worked with their minds, to paraphrase Mencius' famous dictum, ruled those who worked with their hands. Just as Shaohsing produced more than its fair share of mind-workers and profited thereby, lineages within Shaohsing that produced more than their fair share of mind-workers could expect to profit at the expense of less well educated competitors. From the viewpoint of the lineage's long-term viability, the educational function of the lineage was probably the most important which it performed. In traditional Chinese society, which was more nearly a meritocracy for a longer period of time than any other society on record, knowledge was power.

Reading the regulations governing lineage schools in Shaohsing, one is immediately struck by the strong emphasis on achievement. Nor is there any reason to think that Shaohsing was unusual in this regard.[13] No lineage, in Shaohsing or elsewhere, wished to waste its resources by cultivating deadwood. And although the evidence is only impressionistic, within Shaohsing the emphasis on achievement seems to have been most strongly expressed precisely in those counties where academic competition was the keenest, namely, the metropolitan counties of Shan-yin and Kuei-chi. The Hu lineage of Kuei-chi, for example, includes the following stipulation among its school's regulations (written in 1882).[14] A "course register" *(k'o-ch'eng-po i-pen)* is to be kept by the lineage school's teacher, in order to record every student's age, his family residence for the past three generations, the books he has already read, how many lines of text he is reading per day, and the quality of his daily performance. Any absence from school, whether excused or not, is also to be recorded. Moreover, "If there are outstanding students whose parents wish them to change their plans [i.e., quit school for economic reasons], the lineage, after ascertaining the facts, will provide financial aid in order to strengthen these students' resolve." Conversely, as for students older than fifteen sui [fourteen by Western count] who fail to make progress, "their parents shall be informed that they should make other plans."

The Hsüs of Shan-yin laid down the following rules (dated 1856) for their lineage school.[15] Lineage sons aged eight sui and above who lack the financial resources to attend school shall be selected by their father and/or elder brother and reported to the manager of the lineage's charity estate, who will provide money for their schooling by a teacher near to their home. Later, the manager will test these students to determine if such aid should be continued or terminated. Students aged thirteen sui and above who have already "finished reading the Classics" and who are "bright and ambitious" shall be allowed to enter the lineage school for a probationary period of one year. Those who fail to do well during that year shall be "sent home to make other career plans [i.e., not the examination path]. Let there be no favoritism or concealment of unworthy students." The size of classes in this lineage school was to be limited to six students each. Students who could afford to were expected to pay for their own food; the others were to be subsidized by the lineage. And of course the lineage bore the cost of instruction. Moreover, this lineage (like many others) helped to defray expenses for those of its members taking the official examinations. (That this Shan-yin lineage also produced mu-yu is clear from a brief reference to their receipt of financial aid from the lineage.)[16]

The Weis of Yü-yao went so far as to bar well-to-do students from their lineage school, in order to maximize the number of deserving but indigent lineage sons who could receive an education: "Those whose family property exceeds thirty mou [approximately five acres] presumably are able to pursue studies on their own resources and shall not be registered in the lineage school."[17] Unlike the Shan-yin Hsüs, who as we have seen subsidized the elementary education of promising lineage lads under thirteen sui but actually provided facilities only for more advanced training, the Yü-yao Weis' lineage school engaged in both elementary and more advanced instruction: It provided two elementary teachers *(ch'i-meng-shih)*, each with a maximum quota of sixteen students (all to be at least seven sui old), one classics-and-history teacher *(ching-shih-shih)* with eight students, and a belles lettres teacher *(wen-i-shih)*, also with eight students, for a total of forty-eight students. Students were forbidden to willfully destroy school property or to use classrooms for nonacademic purposes.

As one might expect in such a highly competitive society, Shaohsing's lineages did not limit their search for the best possible teachers to blood relatives. In fact at least two lineages (one in Shan-yin, the other in Kuei-chi) made it a point to choose their school teachers from members of other lineages.[18] This had obvious advantages, for nepotism at the sub-lineage level would undermine the lineage's attempt to commit the most resources to its most promising and deserving students. Since it was in the line-age's interest to evaluate talent objectively and to maximize the cultivation of that talent, a poor member of a rich lineage was clearly more likely to receive an education than a poor member of a poor lineage. For example, most promi-nent in Hsiao-shan were the Lai lineage of Ch'ang-ho village and the Lou lineage of Lou-chia-t'a village, of whom there was a saying, "No Lais fail to place in the examinations, no Lous but are selected."[19] Behind this rhetoric is the sug-gestion that examination success correlates with lineage strength, which in turn correlates with control of a locale's resources. It is no surprise that the Lais of Hsiao-shan had a well-established lineage school.[20]

But not only did rich lineages produce more officials than poor lineages, the more officials and other elite mem-bers a lineage produced the richer it became. Nor was this result merely a matter of indirect or ad hoc support. Line-ages in Shaohsing - and there is absolutely no reason to think them unique in this regard - were quite systematic in soliciting contributions from their elite members. In fact, Chang Chung-li has discovered that a detailed, graduated income "tax" schedule was used by one Kuei-chi lineage as of 1841, specifying the assessment of its elite: A chin-shih, for example, was expected to contribute 8000 copper cash annually to the lineage, a chü-jen 4000, and a sheng-yüan 1000, while an official of the seventh rank (the level of a county magistrate) was expected to contribute 20,000, fifth rank 40,000, etc.[21] Thus the fortunes of a lineage varied in a very literal sense with the fortunes of its elite members.

Of course a lineage could not tap the fortunes of its members if it did not keep track of who and where its mem-bers were. Further indication of the importance of lineages in Shaohsing's society is the fact that Shaohsing was pro-lific in its production of that celebration of lineage cohesiveness and continuity, the genealogy. By my own count, among the 816 genealogies held in the Tōyō Bunko's collection in Tokyo, 18 percent (150) are from Shaohsing. There is no way of knowing whether this percentage is an accurate indication of Shaohsing's proportion of all Chinese genealogies, or whether for some unknown reason the Tōyō Bunko's holdings of Shaohsing genealogies are dispropor-tionately rich. Yet it is intriguing that among the Har-vard-Yenching Library's 125 genealogies, virtually the same percentage (19 percent, 24 of 125) are from Shaohsing.[22]

We know that in late Ch'ing and early Republican Chu-chi county there were printers called *p'u-chiang* who specialized in publishing genealogies.[23]   The existence of such a specialization further reflects the large number of genealogies produced in the locale. Since at least one Shaohsing lineage banned its members from lending copies of their genealogies to outsiders,[24] it is unlikely that the overrepresentation of Shaohsing genealogies in the Tōyō Bunko and Harvard-Yenching collections resulted from sale on the open market.

     Taga Akigorō notes that Shaohsing was one of several locales in China which produced a large number of genealogies and suggests in passing that perhaps the "Shaohsing School" of scholars, presumably Huang Tsung-hsi, Chang Hsüeh-ch'eng, and Wang Hui-tsu, had something to do with the phenomenon.[25]   It is highly probable, moreover, that Shaohsing's emigrant tradition also played a significant role: One Kuei-chi genealogy has a preface dated 1911 which specifically states that the motive for producing genealogies was to keep track of relatives who had emigrated.[26]   Significantly, the same preface reveals that this lineage produced mu-yu, almost all of whom were of course employed outside of Shaohsing.

     Given the struggle for survival, Shaohsing's emphasis on strong lineages also had its violent consequences. One aspect of lineage activity which we usually associate with Kwangtung and Fukien but which also flourished in Shaohsing was the vendetta.[27]   Given the tendency of Shaohsing lineages to occupy discrete areas (a phenomenon dramatically represented by single-lineage villages), it is hardly surprising that disputes over water control should result in lineage vendettas. Injunctions against vendettas can be found in a few Shaohsing genealogies,[28] but seem to have been rather rare.

     Water control was an obvious area where the private interests of elite members in different lineages could easily come into conflict, since water control was directly related to their lineages' survival. Ku Yen-wu (1613-1682) comments in his *T'ien-hsia chun-kuo li-ping shu* ("The Assets and Defects of the Empire's Territories"), an encyclopedic study of economic and physical geography, that control of the lakes serving as reservoirs in Shaohsing gave rise to disputes *(cheng-shui)* "or even fatal vendettas," especially during the summer months.[29]   To Shaohsing's farmers a reliable water supply was life itself.[30]

Periods of dynastic collapse, or at least weakened governmental control over local society, seem to have been especially prone to vendettas. The mid-seventeenth century, in which Ku lived, was one such period. Another was the first three decades of the twentieth century. In the peripheral county of Ch'eng-hsien vendettas between villages were frequent, and local officials declined to interfere.[31] *Tung-fang tsa-chih* records a vendetta in progress during the seventh and eighth months of 1910 between the Lungs and the Ts'aos, both of Ch'eng-hsien, a conflict which attracted official attention only when a well-known secret society chief began to intervene actively on the side of the Ts'aos, tipping the balance. It is specifically stated that the locale was suffering from drought at the time.[32]

In Ch'eng-hsien the martial arts were highly esteemed, even by the literati,[33] rather like the K'ang-hsi Emperor's description of Fukien (also of course prone to vendettas), where even the "scholars use shield and sword."[34] Nor was Ch'eng-hsien the only part of Shaohsing in which vendettas occurred. We also have detailed information on outbreaks in Chu-chi and Yü-yao, plus an anti-vendetta injunction in a Hsiao-shan genealogy.[35] It was not unknown for lineage vendettas in Chu-chi to involve lawsuits lasting over twenty years.[36] There may well have been a connection between Shaohsing's vendettas and its "litigation masters," for it would obviously serve a lineage's interests to have access to as much legal expertise as possible. But although the argument from silence is dangerous, existing evidence suggests that vendettas were less frequent in the inner core counties of Shan-yin and Kuei-chi, both because the gentry ethos was less martial there than in the periphery and because government troops sufficient to suppress such outbreaks were closer at hand.

In 1943 Niida Noboru interviewed Chou Tso-jen on the subject of lineage vendettas. According to Chou, vendettas in Shaohsing occurred typically between single-lineage villages, with the symbol of victory being the overturning or destruction of the enemy lineage's cooking stoves *(tsao)*, each of which symbolized the hearth god. It was considered very shameful to have one's stove destroyed during a vendetta, and the losing side would soon seek revenge against the victors.[37] From Chou's account it seems that, despite the economic motivations which commonly underlay vendettas, these struggles were not lacking in ritual.

In Yü-yao a reform-minded member of the gentry in 1910, or slightly before, compared participants in the locale's vendettas to "uncivilized savages." Moreover, he noted a connection between vendettas and gambling: A winning gambler could hardly go to the authorities to help him collect on his debts, since gambling, though widespread, was illegal. Since litigation was thus impossible, gamblers would frequently resort to vendettas. Moreover, claimed the would-be reformer, the personality of habitual gamblers made them prone to seek violent solutions, with fatal results. "Vendettas always become capital cases."[38]

Even if secret society bandits did not become involved in a vendetta (as we saw did in fact happen in Ch'eng-hsien), the village anti-bandit militia itself had a dangerous potential for involvement,[39] given the strength of lineage ties and the large number of single-lineage villages. With so much potential for violence, it is understandable that lineages should at least pay lip service to the Confucian virtue of harmony: A Hsiao-shan genealogy published in 1878 exhorted, "Forget private hatreds."[40] But when vendettas did erupt, lineage temples served as command posts.[41] Confucianism's anti-military bias could be outweighed by its even stronger emphasis on kinship solidarity.

A rare, modern-style history of Chu-chi in the collection of Tokyo's National Diet Library contains fascinating detail on vendettas in that peripheral county. The local officials there were clearly no more able to stop the feuding than their counterparts elsewhere. In fact, this source specifically states that during the first years of the Republic, Chu-chi's local officials were weak and incompetent,[42] a situation which certainly must have suited the local elite. For vendettas are symptomatic of the government's loss of control over local society, just as they are symptomatic of the tension and animosity among members of the local elite themselves. As late as 1923, inter-lineage vendettas over water rights were still common in Chu-chi, not only between lineages but even between alliances of lineages, as the following example indicates.[43] When the Yangs undertook to repair a long-broken reservoir dike, the Chaos became fearful that their own water supply would suffer. So they stepped in to stop the repair work, and the vendetta was on. Several attempts at mediation proved futile. The Chaos began stockpiling guns and ammunition and "united neighboring villages in preparation for battle." But the Yangs, a lineage of "several thousand families," famous for their martial valor and hitherto unequaled, remained unperturbed. The Chaos then made a secret

alliance with the Kus, who were "grinding their teeth in
anger at the insults to which they were commonly subjected
at the hands of the Yangs." In fact, just the previous
year (1922) the Kus had suffered an attack by "several
thousand" Yangs. Needless to say, they were ready for
revenge. This alliance with the Kus increased the Chao
ranks by some three- to four-hundred men, all armed with
guns. A Yang village was surrounded and flags unfurled.
The Yangs, having complacently allowed matters to reach
this state, now hurried to mobilize their kinsmen from other
villages. A rescue party over four-hundred strong quickly
arrived at the besieged village. The Chao flagbearer was
felled with one shot, and the ensuing melee lasted for three
hours before the Chaos (and presumably the Kus) were
forced to withdraw.

When the battle began, the local police had sent a
frantic message to the county magistrate, who led a force of
ninety men to suppress the fighting. Fortunately for the
outnumbered magistrate, the battle was almost over before
he arrived on the scene. It did resume for a while even
after the magistrate's arrival, as the younger warriors,
"with courage to spare," tried for a clear-cut victory. But
finally the shooting stopped. In view of the fire power
assembled, casualties were amazingly light; on each side
were one dead and a dozen or so wounded.[44] The next
day the magistrate called together the gentry on both
sides. It was agreed that the Chaos would pay a moderate
indemnity and stand the expense of a banquet. In return
the Yangs would build a new dike that would leave undis-
turbed the Chaos' access to water.

This depiction of a lineage vendetta in Shaohsing might
suggest that the locale's lineages were perpetrators of
uncivilized, antisocial behavior. Such an interpretation,
while not without some merit, would be distinctly unfair.
For although the basic motivation of lineage behavior was
certainly a search for wealth, power and prestige – a competitive "inter-lineage imperialism"[45] – these goals could be
gained, at least in part, by more acceptably civilized
behavior. Artistic patronage was one such means by which
a lineage could exhibit and enhance its stature. Indeed,
lineage celebrations provided the context for the development of theater in Shaohsing. Major festivals were occa-
sions for performances. We have seen that one wealthy
member financed the reconstruction of his lineage's ancestral
hall *(tsung-ts'e)* to provide more room for the stage and

audience. Performances under lineage auspices were extremely popular in Shaohsing, and although injunctions
against them can be found in some genealogies, such stric-
tures were widely ignored throughout the Ch'ing.[46] The
fact that the genealogies themselves contain open references
to their respective lineages' dramatic productions clearly
demonstrates that the prohibitions had become meaningless.

Tanaka Issei, a specialist on the social history of
Chinese drama, has written a fascinating article on "Performances of Lineage Drama in the Early Ch'ing."[47] It is in
fact based heavily on data from Shaohsing genealogies,
although he does not make this point explicit. Shaohsing's
tradition of strong, rich lineages, plus the easy availability
of professional actors among the locale's hereditary déclassé
minority *(to-min,* discussed in Chapter Three) are probably
sufficient to explain the flourishing of lineage-sponsored
drama there. From the Shaohsing data assembled by
Tanaka it is clear that drama was used to enhance lineage
solidarity. As suggested above, performances were sched-
uled to coincide with major festivals; for example, in
Ch'eng-hsien around 1870 "the large lineages had plays performed on festival days."[48] These festivals fell mainly
during the agricultural off-seasons, so peasants too were
able to enjoy the plays staged by their lineage,[49] a literally
dramatic benefit of consanguineal unity.

Conversely, a common penalty for those who broke
lineage rules was the financing of a play as an act of pen-
ance. When this play was performed the miscreant would
publically reaffirm his commitment to obeying lineage regulations in the future.[50] Normally, however, responsibility
for financing the performances rotated among the branches
of the lineage. A variant practice made place of residence
rather than lineage branch the basis for financing. But
since, as we have already noted, Shaohsing's villages were
often inhabited by lineages or lineage segments, the result
was very often the same. In one case, the financing of
lineage drama was institutionalized to the point of specific
lineage land being set aside as "drama land" *(hsi-t'ien).*
Tanaka has discovered only one instance of such a formal
arrangement; significantly, it was in Shaohsing's Shan-yin
county.[51]

Information on the content of lineage-sponsored drama
is unfortunately extremely sparse, but we do know that a
distinction was made between plays honoring lineage heroes,
ancestors, and spirits *(nei-shen,* "inner gods") and those
honoring their non-lineage counterparts *(wai-shen,* "outer
gods").[52] Among the wai-shen included were the local god

of the soil *(t'u-ti-shen)*, the god of war *(Kuan-ti)*, and the god of civil examinations *(Wen-ch'ang-ti)*. If plays honoring them could insure good harvests, victory in vendettas, and a host of examination passers, the lineage would indeed be blessed. Tanaka observes that even the wai-shen were honored by performances sponsored on a lineage rather than a local-place basis,[53] but as we have seen, in Shaohsing this was often a distinction without a difference. Plays honoring the two sets of spirits were often performed on the same day, those for wai-shen in the morning, those for nei-shen in the evening, when the audience was presumably larger.

In sum, although not all lineages were strong, a strong lineage functioned as a virtual mini-state. It kept a detailed census in the form of regularly updated genealogies; elicited periodic financial (quasi-tax) contributions from its population to support its functions; provided "public" educational facilities for those who could most benefit from them (and whose education could in turn most benefit the lineage community); created an ideology in the form of a dramatized mythology celebrating internally generated heroes; formed external alliances; and even waged war both to protect its vital interests and (one suspects) to strengthen in-group solidarity. As for the administration of justice, the final hallmark of a polity, it would be most surprising if intra-lineage disputes were not settled by lineage leaders, as was the norm in South China. A Shan-yin genealogy published in 1919 states explicitly that a member who bypasses arbitration by the lineage and resorts directly to litigation would be punished by the lineage.[54] The existence of single-lineage villages in Shaohsing makes the lineage's judicial function all the more probable. In short, Shaohsing's lineages attempted to do everything they could to insure their functional integrity, and thus their survival, in a context of fierce competition.

Yet if strong lineages functioned as mini-states, there is no reason to assume that these microcosms achieved perfect equity for their members any more sucessfully than did the dynastic macrocosm. Exploitation of the poor by the rich, of the relatively powerless by the relatively powerful, certainly occurred within both strong and weak lineages, as it did throughout the Ch'ing state as a whole. Nevertheless, the poor and powerless could derive real benefits from lineage membership. Maurice Freedman's generalization rings true for Shaohsing when he writes:

While it makes good sense to speak of some lineages being richer or stronger than others, the richer and the stronger the lineage the more it was likely to be differentiated into rich and poor, strong and weak. . . . [A] poor family in a powerful lineage was inferior and exploitable at home yet in a privileged position against the wider world. The riches, renown, and power that from one point of view were the prerogative of the lineage elite were from another the property of the lineage as a whole, all its members sharing in it. Whom the elite might oppress at home they might protect abroad. They might effectively rob the poor of their rightful share in the lineage estates and rig the rules about ritual privileges so as to monopolize them, but in his transactions with the members of other lineages the poor man in a strong lineage could stand with powerful co-members behind him.[55]

In this "Eat people" society, a poor man in a weak lineage was likely to end up as someone else's fish and meat, unless (more likely in the periphery) he turned to banditry or (more likely in the core) he sought protection through ties of class.

Comparative Production
of Subofficials by
Ch'ang-chou, Soochow, Hangchow,
and Shaohsing Prefectures, 1892

In order to put Shaohsing's production of subofficials in greater comparative perspective, I have examined three other prominent prefectures (all of which contained counties ranking among the top twenty producers of subofficials, listed in Table 10) to discover how their production of subofficials compared with Shaohsing's. The results are as follows.

TABLE 13

NATIVES OF CH'ANG-CHOU, SOOCHOW, HANGCHOW, AND SHAOHSING PREFECTURES AS PERCENTAGE OF ALL PROVINCIAL- AND LOCAL-GOVERNMENT SUBOFFICIALS, BY PROVINCE, 1892

	CH'ANG-CHOU NATIVES	SOOCHOW NATIVES	HANGCHOW NATIVES	SHAOHSING NATIVES	TOTAL SUBOFFICIALS SERVING IN EACH PROVINCE
Chihli	17=3%(17/664)	6=1%	13=2%	101=15%	664
Fukien (plus Taiwan)	9=3%	2=1%	15=4%	45=13%	358
Chekiang	25=6%	39=9%	34=8%*	53=12%*	447
Kiangsi	14=3%	5=1%	18=4%	39=9%	419
Kiangsu	27=5%*	23=5%*	23=5%	45=9%	504
Kwangtung	3=1%	9=2%	13=3%	41=9%	482
Shansi	2=1%	2=1%	2=1%	23=6%	361
Shantung	8=2%	2=0%	4=1%	28=5%	514
Anhui	6=2%	6=2%	5=2%	15=5%	295
Szechwan	7=2%	3=1%	8=2%	20=5%	438
Shensi	3=1%	1=0%	5=2%	13=5%	285
Hunan	6=2%	5=2%	4=1%	14=4%	323
Kwangsi	1=0%	2=1%	1=0%	13=4%	318
Kansu (plus Sinkiang)	3=1%	0=0%	2=1%	8=3%	237
Hupei	16=4%	6=2%	9=3%	12=3%	357
Honan	6=1%	5=1%	2=0%	13=3%	420
Yunnan	1=0%	0=0%	1=0%	9=3%	315
Kweichow	2=1%	0=0%	4=2%	7=3%	250
NATIVES OF PREFECTURE AS PERCENT OF GRAND TOTAL OF SUBOFFICIALS	156=2%(156/ 6987)	116=2%	163=2%	499=7%	6987 GRAND TOTAL OF SUBOFFICIALS

* All holding education-related posts, due to the law of avoidance

Compiled from *Ta Ch'ing chin-shen ch'üan-shu*, Fall, Kuang-hsü 18.

TABLE 14

NATIVES OF CH'ANG-CHOU, SOOCHOW, HANGCHOW, AND SHAOHSING PREFECTURES
SERVING AS SUBOFFICIALS OUTSIDE THEIR NATIVE PROVINCE, BY STATUS, 1892

	CH'ANG-CHOU NATIVES	SOOCHOW NATIVES	HANGCHOW NATIVES	SHAOHSING NATIVES
chien-sheng	119=92% (119/129)	71=76%	102=79%	375=84%
kung-sheng	3=2%	6=6%	8=6%	
sheng-yüan		5=5%	4=3%	
chü-jen			2=2%	
t'ung-sheng			2=2%	
kung-shih*				19=4%
li-yüan#				18=4%
miscellaneous	3=2%	4=4%	5=4%	17=4%
no status recorded	4=3%	7=8%	6=5%	17=4%
TOTAL SUB-OFFICIALS, BY NATIVE PREFECTURE	129=99%	93=99%	129=101%	446=100%

(Some columns do not total 100%, due to rounding.)

* Clerks in the Imperial Clan Court, the Grand Secretariat, and the Hanlin Academy[1]

\# Central Board clerks qualified by examination to become subofficials[2]

Compiled from *Ta Ch'ing chin-shen ch'üan-shu*, Fall, Kuang-hsü 18.

TABLE 15

**NATIVES OF CH'ANG-CHOU, SOOCHOW, HANGCHOW, AND SHAOHSING PREFECTURES
SERVING AS SUBOFFICIALS (ALL EDUCATION-RELATED) WITHIN THEIR
NATIVE PROVINCE, BY STATUS, 1892**

	CH'ANG-CHOU NATIVES	SOOCHOW NATIVES	HANGCHOW NATIVES	SHAOHSING NATIVES
kung-sheng	13=48% (13/27)	8=35%	15=44%	18=34%
chü-jen	12=44%	13=57%	17=50%	33=62%
chin-shih		2=9%	2=6%	
sheng-yüan	1=4%			1=2%
fu-pang*	1=4%			1=2%
TOTAL SUB-OFFICIALS, BY NATIVE PREFECTURE	27=100%	23=101%	34=100%	53=100%

(One column does not total 100%, due to rounding.)

* Unsuccessful candidate for chü-jen degree cited for honorable mention

Compiled from *Ta Ch'ing chin-shen ch'üan-shu*, Fall, Kuang-hsü 18.

TABLE 16

NATIVES OF CH'ANG-CHOU, SOOCHOW, HANGCHOW, AND SHAOHSING PREFECTURES SERVING AS SUBOFFICIALS OUTSIDE THEIR NATIVE PROVINCE, BY TYPE OF POST, 1892

	CH'ANG-CHOU NATIVES	SOOCHOW NATIVES	HANGCHOW NATIVES	SHAOHSING NATIVES
county jail warden (tien-shih)	51=40% (51/129)	27=29%	29=22%	164=37%
sub-county magistrate (hsün-chien)	26=20%	25=27%	31=24%	114=26%
assistant county magistrate (hsien-ch'eng)	'9=7%	8=9%	18=14%	36=8%
various tax collectors (ta-shih)	8=6%	6=6%	10=8%	24=5%
county registrar (chu-pu)	5=4%	5=5%	2=2%	10=2%
chou jail warden (li-mu)	5=4%	1=1%	3=2%	25=6%
prefectural commissary of records (ching-li)	5=4%	7=8%	7=5%	23=5%
prefectural commissary of the seal (chao-mo)	5=4%	2=2%	2=2%	10=2%
subprefect (t'ung-p'an)	3=2%	4=4%	4=3%	2=0%
subprefect (t'ung-chih)	included in "miscellaneous"	3=3%	6=5%	8=2%
jailkeeper (ssu-yü)	included in "miscellaneous"	4=4%	5=4%	10=2%
miscellaneous	12=9%	1=1%	12=9%	20=5%
TOTAL SUBOFFICIALS, BY NATIVE PREFECTURE	129=100%	93=99%	129=100%	446=100%

(One column does not total 100%, due to rounding.)

Compiled from *Ta Ch'ing chin-shen ch'üan-shu,* Fall, Kuang-hsü 18.

TABLE 17

**NATIVES OF CH'ANG-CHOU, SOOCHOW, HANGCHOW, AND SHAOHSING PREFECTURES
SERVING AS SUBOFFICIALS OUTSIDE THEIR NATIVE PROVINCE, BY NATIVE HSIEN, 1892**

Native Hsien of Subofficials from Ch'ang-chou Prefecture

Omitted: The 27 serving in Kiangsu, all education-related subofficials, since they are
identified only as "Ch'ang-chou natives" *(Ch'ang-chou jen)*.

Yang-hu	51/129	40%	I-hsing	7/129	5%
Wu-chin	37/129	29%	Chiang-yin	6/129	5%
Wu-hsi	14/129	11%	Ching-hsi	3/129	2%
Chin-k'uei	11/129	9%	Ching-chiang	0/129	0%

(Percentages do not total 100%, due to rounding.)

Native Hsien of Subofficials from Soochow Prefecture

Omitted: The 23 serving in Kiangsu, all education-related subofficials, since they are
identified only as "Soochow natives."

Wu-hsien	44/93	47%	Chao-wen	3/93	3%
Yüan-ho	19/93	20%	Chen-tse	2/93	2%
Ch'ang-chou	12/93	13%	Wu-chiang	1/93	1%
Ch'ang-shu	9/93	10%	Hsin-yang	0/93	0%
K'un-shan	3/93	3%	T'ai-hu t'ing	0/93	0%

(Percentages do not total 100%, due to rounding.)

Native Hsien of Subofficials from Hangchow Prefecture

Omitted: The 34 serving in Chekiang, all education-related subofficials, since they are
identified only as "Hangchow natives."

Ch'ien-t'ang	61/129	47%	Lin-an	1/129	1%
Jen-ho	57/129	44%	Fu-yang	0/129	0%
Hai-ning chou	5/129	4%	Yü-ch'ien	0/129	0%
Yü-hang	3/129	2%	Hsin-ch'eng	0/129	0%
Ch'ang-hua	2/129	2%			

Native Hsien of Subofficials from Shaohsing Prefecture

Omitted: The 53 serving in Chekiang, all education-related subofficials, since they are
identified only as "Shaohsing natives."

Shan-yin	261/446	59%	Chu-chi	8/446	2%
Kuei-chi	120/446	27%	Yü-yao	6/446	1%
Hsiao-shan	33/446	7%	Ch'eng-hsien	3/446	1%
Shang-yü	13/446	3%	Hsin-ch'ang	1/446	0%
			unknown	1/446	0%

Compiled from *Ta Ch'ing chin-shen ch'üan-shu*, Fall, Kuang-hsü 18.

Exhaustive analysis of the data in the preceding tables in not possible within the confines of this appendix. However, comparing the subofficials who were Shaohsing natives with subofficials who were natives of Ch'ang-chou, Soochow, and Hangchow, we can reach the following conclusions: First, Shaohsing natives holding posts as subofficials in 1892 outnumbered their Ch'ang-chou counterparts not only in the aggregate (499 to 156) and in percentage of total subofficials (7 percent to 2 percent), but also in the totals for each of the Eighteen Provinces except one, Hupei. Second, in both the Ch'ang-chou and Shaohsing cases, the overwhelming majority of non-education-related subofficials were chien-sheng (84 percent of the Shaohsing total, 92 percent of the Ch'ang-chou total). Third, the three most commonly held subofficial posts were the same in both cases: county jail warden (tien-shih), 37 percent of the Shaohsing total, 40 percent of the Ch'ang-chou total; sub-county magistrate (hs'ün-chien), 26 percent of the Shaohsing total, 20 percent of the Ch'ang-chou total; and assistant county magistrate (hsien-ch'eng), 8 percent of the Shaohsing total, 7 percent of the Ch'ang-chou total. Fourth, the overwhelming majority of Shaohsing and Ch'ang-chou natives serving as education-related subofficials (all within their native province) were either kung-sheng or chü-jen: 96 percent of the total among Shaohsing natives, 92 percent among Ch'ang-chou natives. (The percentages for Soochow and Hangchow natives are comparable: 92 percent and 94 percent respectively.) Fifth and finally, in both Shaohsing and Ch'ang-chou the counties that included the prefectural capital within their boundaries produced the overwhelming majority of the prefecture's subofficials: Shan-yin and Kuei-chi, together producing 86 percent of the Shaohsing total; and Yang-hu and Wu-chin, together producing 69 percent of the Ch'ang-chou total. Note also that since Yang-hu and Wu-chin were outstanding for their production of mu-yu during the second half of the nineteenth century, the positive correlation between production of subofficials and production of mu-yu holds true for Yang-hu and Wu-chin as well as for Shan-yin and Kuei-chi.

Comparing the statistics on subofficials from Soochow with the comparable figures for Shaohsing and Ch'ang-chou, one is struck immediately by the relatively modest number of subofficials from Soochow as of 1892 (116, compared to Ch'ang-chou's 156 and Shaohsing's 499). Like Ch'ang-chou and Hangchow, Soochow produced only 2 percent of all the subofficials serving in the Eighteen Provinces as of Fall 1892, significantly less than Shaohsing's share of 7 per-

cent. Indeed, it is remarkable that the combined total of
Ch'ang-chou, Soochow, and Hangchow natives serving as
subofficials in the Eighteen Provinces in 1892 was less than
the number from Shaohsing alone.

Soochow did produce the same proportion (9 percent)
of all subofficials serving in Chekiang as Shaohsing produced of all subofficials serving in Kiangsu. But this
instance of reciprocity is the sole case in which Soochow
rivalled Shaohsing in the province-by-province comparison.
In other respects the Soochow figures fully confirm the patterns which we have already noted in the Shaohsing and
Ch'ang-chou data: the overwhelming predominance of
chien-sheng among the non-education-related subofficials
(76 percent of the Soochow total); the ranking of county
jail warden (tien-shih), subcounty magistrate (hsün-chien),
and, at a lower order of magnitude, assistant county magistrate (hsien-ch'eng) as the three most commonly held posts
(29 percent, 27 percent, and 9 percent respectively);[3] and
finally, the predominance of the so-called metropolitan
counties (i.e., those which included the prefectural capital
within their boundaries), Wu-hsien producing 47 percent of
Soochow's subofficials, Yüan-ho 20 percent, and Ch'ang-
chou 13 percent,[4] together accounting for 80 percent of the
total. Shaohsing's Shan-yin, Ch'ang-chou's Yang-hu, Soochow's Wu-hsien, and Hangchow's Ch'ien-t'ang each produced no less than 40 percent of its prefecture's total.

The Hangchow figures confirm the by now familiar
patterns: In no province did subofficials native to Hangchow outnumber their counterparts from Shaohsing. Among
the non-education-related subofficials from Hangchow, as
elsewhere, the overwhelming majority were holders of the
purchased chien-sheng degree. The subofficial posts most
commonly occupied in each case were sub-county magistrate
(hsün-chien) and county jail warden (tien-shih), not néces-
sarily in that order, with assistant county magistrate
(hsien-ch'eng) always ranking third. Moreover, the overwhelming majority of subofficials from Hangchow were
natives of the counties in which the prefectural capital was
located (Ch'ien-t'ang and Jen-ho). And in all four prefectures studied, the counties that produced the most subofficials were also the ones that, according to Ho Ping-ti, produced the most chin-shih.[5]

Thus there is a striking positive correlation between a
county's production of subofficials, its production of chin-
shih, and its degree of urbanization relative to other
counties in the prefecture (the assumption being that counties containing the prefectural capital were the most urban

in the prefecture). Whether these correlations hold true for all the other prefectures in Ch'ing China is not yet known. However, the data presented above do suggest that residents of metropolitan counties held a comparative advantage over residents of less urban counties in the competition for a governmental career, regardless of whether that career was pursued via the examination route or by purchasing a degree and becoming a subofficial. Urban residence seems to have been not merely the result of participation in officialdom, but also a factor predisposing towards such participation, at least in the lower Yangtze region.

APPENDIX C
Shaohsing's Wine, Spirit Money, and Earliest Modern Industry

The most famous commodity produced by Shaohsing's workers was undoubtedly its wine. We are told that in the "late Ch'ing" (date unspecified) over 2000 winemaking establishments, both urban and rural, operated in Shaohsing prefecture.[1] Just as Scotch whisky is called "Scotch" *tout court*, Shaohsing wine was "Shaohsing" to its patrons, who found the word "wine" redundant.[2] Shaohsing has been famous for its wine for well over two thousand years. But the wine itself has not remained unchanged: The "Shaohsing" popular in Peking and the cities of the lower Yangtze during the Wan-li period of the Ming (1573-1619), for example, was made from green beans. Later, for reasons unknown, this green bean wine was completely supplanted by the rice wine for which Shaohsing is still famous.[3]

Despite this fame, the amount of information available on the social history of Shaohsing wine - as opposed to the technicalities of its production[4] - is surprisingly meager. The wine's distribution was of course not universal within China: It did not travel well overland, since the jouncing of transport vehicles disturbed the sediment. Thus regions lacking access to water transport remained outside the wine's marketing area.[5] Nevertheless, "Shaohsing" was almost certainly the most widespread wine in China, a fact that must be related to the far-reaching employment of Shaohsing mu-yu. There were wags who compared these two most famous products of Shaohsing, claiming that both were widespread - and overrated.[6] Nonetheless, Tseng Kuo-fan, who steered clear of Shaohsing mu-yu (as we have seen),

177

was not immune to the charms of the wine.[7]   Moreover, it served as a lubricant to the genius of China's greatest novelist, Ts'ao Hsüeh-ch'in (1715?-1763):   "Contemporaries make frequent mention of his heavy drinking and there are references to his obtaining wine on credit or borrowing money to buy it with. . . .   [Hsüeh-ch'in] is reported to have said once, 'If anyone is in a hurry to read my novel, all he's got to do is keep me daily supplied with roast duck and good Shaoxing [Shaohsing] wine, and I'll be happy to oblige him'."[8]   In Lu Hsün's stories - "K'ung I-chi," "In the Wine Shop," etc. - Shaohsing wine has achieved literary immortality.   It has even been claimed that Lu Hsün reveals himself as a Shaohsing native by the number of his stories with wine-drinking scenes.[9]

In Shaohsing knowledge of winemaking was so widespread that "it wasn't considered anything special."[10] When Shaohsing natives emigrated from their native place, they of course took this knowledge with them.   During the early Ch'ing the Tan family of Shaohsing winemakers began production in Shun-te (a county in Kwangtung), with considerable financial success.[11]   In fact, the prosperity of the Shun-te operation led one commentator to conclude that Shaohsing natives' skill at winemaking did not depend on the exceptional purity of their water supply.[12]   It must have been a source of local pride that so-called "Soochow wine" was actually produced in Soochow by Shaohsing natives, specially recruited.[13]   On the other hand, almost all the rice from which Shaohsing wine was made was imported from Kiangsu![14]

Ironically the large market for Shaohsing wine had an adverse effect on the quality of the product available in Shaohsing itself.   Superior wine was reserved for export.[15] But the very best, not commercially available, remained in Shaohsing.   This "little girl wine" *(nü-erh chiu)* was produced by wealthy families at the birth of a daughter, buried in jars to age, and consumed only upon her marriage.[16]

As we might expect, Shaohsing wine far outstripped all other varieties produced in Chekiang, accounting for approximately 169 million of the 186 million *chin* produced in the province as of 1916.[17]

But there was another of Shaohsing's specialities which was of equal importance in the daily lives not only of its own inhabitants but throughout the country.   In his story "Medicine" Lu Hsün describes the mother of a martyred revolutionary "carrying an old, round, red-lacquered basket, with a string of paper money hanging from it. . . .

Old Chuan's wife watched the other woman set out four dishes and a bowl of rice, then stand up to wail and burn the paper money. . . ."[18] Ning-Shao, and especially Shaohsing, was famous all over China for its large-scale production of this "paper money," i.e., tinfoil spirit money.[19] Even at night the "ding ding" of the tinbeaters' hammers would be heard in Shaohsing city.[20] Religious piety was thus a mainstay of the locale's economy.

These tinbeaters played a prominent role in Shaohsing city's criminal underworld. They contributed to the spread of a "gangster atmosphere *(liu-mang feng-ch'i)*. There were innumerable incidents caused by people picking fights, including many workers hired by the owners of tinfoil spirit money shops to beat small, thick pieces of tin into flat tinfoil. . . . These workers were all outsiders, and oppressive types in the city often hired them as strongarm men. This atmosphere influenced the children and gave rise to violence-prone tempers."[21] As of 1932-33, unfortunately the earliest years for which we have detailed statistics, Shaohsing county (formerly Shan-yin and Kuei-chi) contained no fewer than 106 tinfoil workshops, mostly within Shaohsing city, employing 2167 workers to pound out the tinfoil.[22] Literally tens of thousands of urban and rural women and children, working in their homes, pasted this tinfoil onto its distinctive yellow paper backing to produce the spirit money.[23] Lu Hsün begins his story "Soap" with a reference to this typical Shaohsing byemployment: "With her back to the north window in the slanting sunlight, Ssumin's wife was pasting paper money for the dead with her eight-year old daughter . . . ."[24]

With the exception of spirit money, useful information on urban artisans and the handful of factory workers in late Ch'ing Shaohsing is extremely sketchy. No reliable statistics on wages in Shaohsing are available for the Ch'ing, but some idea of the general situation can perhaps be inferred from an account dated 1898 which states that the wage rate in Shaohsing's earliest silk mills was half that paid in Shanghai.[25] And as we have pointed out, urban artisans and workers were extremely vulnerable to inflated prices for commodities, especially food.

Among Shaohsing's earliest modern factories were the *Ho-i-ho sao-ssu-ch'ang,* a silk mill established in 1895, and the *T'ung-hui kung—sha-ch'ang,* a cotton mill established in 1899.[26] Both these mills were in Hsiao-shan, and both were founded by the same man, Lou Ching-hui, who held the rank of expectant sub-prefect *(hou-hsüan t'ung-*

chih). [27]   The T'ung-hui cotton mill began with 10,192
spindles and added 2184 more in 1910.[28]   Thus it was a
small operation: Mills with several times that number of
spindles were being opened in Shanghai and elsewhere
during the same period.[29]   In 1905 another cotton mill,
the Hou-sheng fang-chih kung-ssu, was established, also in
Hsiao-shan, in the town of Lin-p'u.   Its founder is described as a member of the "gentry" (shen).[30]   The quality
of this mill's printed cotton towels was said to be equal to
any foreign competition.[31]   The following year (1906)
another gentryman established a cotton mill, the Te-ch'ang-
sheng kung-ssu, which was apparently located in or near
Shaohsing city, since it was built on land rented from the
prefectural school (fu-hsüeh).   This mill too was reported
to be planning to specialize in towels.[32]

The fact that these mills were founded by gentry
indicates once again the importance of mercantile interests
among Shaohsing's local elite.   But during the late Ch'ing
such harbingers of modern industry played only a trivial
role on the local scene, far less important to the local
economy than the wine and spirit money for which Shaohsing had long been famous.

Abbreviations
Used in the Notes

CCKK   Chu-chi min-pao she, ed., *Chu-chi kai-kuan* [Chu-chi: An Overview], 1925.

LHCC   Lu Hsün, *Lu Hsün ch'üan-chi* [Complete Works of Lu Hsün], Peking, 1957-58.

NCH   *North-China Herald*, Shanghai.

SHTL   *Shaohsing hsien-chih tzu-liao ti-i-chi* [Materials for a Gazetteer of Shaohsing County, First Collection], 1937.

SWLH   Lu Hsün, *Selected Works of Lu Hsün*, Peking, 1956-60.

TFTC   *Tung-fang tsa-chih* [The Eastern Miscellany], Shanghai.

181

Notes

As in the bibliography, "Taga number" refers to the catalogue of Japanese-held genealogies in Taga Akigorō, *Sōfu no kenkyū: shiryō hen* (Tokyo, 1960).

Introduction

1. I am of course referring to Hilary J. Beattie, *Land and Lineage in China: A Study of T'ung-ch'eng County, Anhwei, in the Ming and Ch'ing Dynasties* (Cambridge, England, 1979); Philip A. Kuhn, *Rebellion and Its Enemies in Late Imperial China: Militarization and Social Structure, 1796-1864* (Cambridge, 1970); Johanna Menzell Meskill, *A Chinese Pioneer Family: The Lins of Wu-feng,Taiwan 1729-1895* (Princeton, 1979); Susan Naquin, *Millenarian Rebellion in China: The Eight Trigrams Uprising of 1813* (New Haven, 1976) and *Shantung Rebellion: The Wang Lun Uprising of 1774* (New Haven, 1981); Elizabeth J. Perry, *Rebels and Revolutionaries in North China, 1845-1945* (Stanford, 1980); Evelyn Sakakida Rawski, *Agricultural Change and the Peasant Economy of South China* (Cambridge, 1972); R. Keith Schoppa, *Chinese Elites and Political Change: Zhejiang Province in the Early Twentieth Century* (Cambridge, 1982); and Frederic Wakeman, Jr., *Strangers at the Gate: Social Disorder in South China, 1839-1861* (Berkeley, 1966).

2. Chou Tso-jen, *Chih-t'ang hui-hsiang lu*, pp. 304-305. Lu Hsün was far from the only person of note produced by Shaohsing prefecture. Indeed, one of the intriguing facts about Shaohsing is the substantial number of famous people native to the locale. Among those well known to students of Chinese history are Wang Ch'ung (author of the *Lun Heng*), Lu Yu, Wang Yang-ming, Wang Chi (Lung-hsi), Hsü Wei, Ch'en Hung-shou, Liu Tsung-chou, Huang Tsung-hsi, Chang Hsüeh-ch'eng, Wang Hui-tsu, Ts'ai Yüan-p'ei, Ch'iu Chin, Chou Tso-jen, Chu Tzu-ch'ing (born in Kiangsu of Shaohsing parents), Chiang Monlin, Lo Chen-yü (born in Kiangsu), Liu Ta-pai, Lo Chia-lun (born in Kiangsi), Fan Wen-lan, Shao Li-tzu, Wang Ching-wei (born in Canton), Chou En-lai (born in Anhui), and Yao Wen-yüan.

3. Here as elsewhere my debt to G. William Skinner's conceptualizations is obvious. In this instance see his "Regional Urbanization in Nineteenth-Century China" (especially Maps 1 and 2, pp. 214-215) in G. William Skinner, ed., *The City in Late Imperial China*.

4. Shaohsing city, the seat of the prefectural administration, contained also the yamens (offices) of the Shan-yin and Kuei-chi county magistrates. The boundary between these two counties

ran down the center of the city. This expedient, which was common during the Ch'ing dynasty, efficiently ensconced three yamens within a single city wall. The 1911 Revolution resulted in the abolition of prefectures as administrative units. Shan-yin and Kuei-chi counties were combined, and the name "Shaohsing" was transferred to this new county. For a convenient, though somewhat sanitized and idealized, sketch of Shaohsing's history, see Chu Min et al., *Lu Hsün tsai Shaohsing*, pp. 1-18. A recent overview by the historical geographer Ch'en Ch'iao-i is *Shaohsing shih hua*, especially useful for its history of water control and for its discussion of famous Shaohsing natives through the Sung period.

5. The preeminent work of core-periphery analysis treating all regions of China is of course G. William Skinner's *The City in Late Imperial China*. Recently Keith Schoppa, using the criteria of population density and degree of commercialization (the latter measured by postal rank and number of financial institutions per capita), has focused on Chekiang. He divides Chekiang's seventy-five counties into four "social ecological zones": inner core, outer core, inner periphery, and outer periphery. Schoppa includes among Chekiang's "inner core" counties Shaohsing (i.e., Shan-yin and Kuei-chi), Yü-yao, Hsiao-shan, and Shang-yü. He includes among Chekiang's "outer core" counties Ch'eng (i.e., Cheng-hsien), Chu-chi, and Hsin-ch'ang. My own research confirms Schoppa's classification of Shaohsing's eight counties, and indeed I have appropriated his "inner core, outer periphery" terminology. But I have decided to forego his distinction between "outer core" and "inner periphery": Four categories for seventy-five counties are not excessive, but four categories for eight counties would be. One great merit of Schoppa's typology is that it helps to set Shaohsing within its Chekiang context: It must be constantly borne in mind that the counties which were peripheral in the context of Shaohsing prefecture - viz., Hsin-ch'ang, Ch'eng-hsien, and Chu-chi - were still relatively core (Schoppa's "outer core") in the context of Chekiang as a whole. Conversely, it must be remembered that those of Shaohsing's counties which rank as "inner core" in the context of Chekiang as a whole, e.g., Yü-yao, Hsiao-shan, and Shang-yü, do not necessarily rank as "inner core" in the more exclusive context of Shaohsing prefecture. In sum, Schoppa's typology serves to remind us that Shaohsing prefecture *as a whole* was relatively core. See R. Keith Schoppa, *Chinese Elites and Political Change: Zhejiang Province in the Early Twentieth Century*, Chapter 2, especially p. 18.

6. *Shaohsing fu-chih*, preface 1792, 13/pp. 33B-34B.
7. Ko Sui-ch'eng, ed., *Che-chiang (fen-sheng ti-chih)*, pp. 64-65. For the 1933 population figures by county, see Chapter Four below.
8. *Shaohsing fu-chih*, preface 1586, 14/pp. 5A-5B.
9. *Shaohsing fu-chih*, 1683, 14/pp. 7B-8A.
10. Shaohsing prefecture's population per square kilometer in 1820 was 579.55, surpassed only by Soochow (1073.21), Chia-hsing (719.26), and Sung-chiang (626.57). See Liang Fang-chung, comp., *Chung-kuo li-tai hu-k'ou, t'ien-ti, t'ien-fu t'ung-chi*, pp. 273-279.
11. E.H. Parker, "A Journey in Chekiang," *Journal of the China Branch of the Royal Asiatic Society*, new series, 19 #1 (1884), p. 44.
12. For necessary amplification of this oversimple generalization, see Benjamin Elman, "Ch'ing Dynasty 'Schools' of Scholarship," *Ch'ing-shih wen-t'i* 4 #6 (December 1981).
13. See for example Li Tz'u-ming, *Yüeh-man-t'ang wen-chi*, 2/p. 12B.

14. *Su pao*, Kuang-hsü 29 (1903), lunar 2nd month, 14th day, p. 80 of the 1965 Taiwan photoreprint.
15. "Now [1904] all judicial and tax mu-yu are officials' pettifoggers" *(kuan sung-shih)*. The man who penned these lines, Sun Ting-lieh, had previously served as magistrate of Kuei-chi. Sun Ting-lieh, *Ssu-hsi-chai chüeh-shih*, author's preface, p. 2A.
16. Neither late Ch'ing revolutionaries nor reformers spoke kindly of mu-yu. See for example Chang Ping-lin's denunciation of them in *Min pao* #8 (October 1906), pp. 22-23. See also the reformist memorial discussing the faults of mu-yu in *Kuang-hsü ch'ao Tung-hua lu*, Kuang-hsü 20 (1894), lunar 9th month, "chi hai," p. 3482 of the 1958 Peking edition.
17. Hsü K'o comp., *Ch'ing-pai lei-ch'ao*, 27/pp. 119-121.
18. Ibid., 27/p. 121, states that not only from the Hsien-feng period (1851-1861) did the sale of offices increase, moreover many of the purchasers were natives of Wu-chin, Yang-hu (both in Ch'ang-chou, Kiangsu), Shan-yin, and Kuei-chi.
19. Lu Hsün, *LHCC*, vol. 3, p. 495, note 7. The *tao* referred to the use of a knife as an eraser. "[T]he pettifogger or litigation trickster [:] Described in a [Ch'ing] Penal Code commentary as anyone who 'taught the unknowing to make a plaint and induced the reluctant to submit a plaint,' the tricksters included scribes who falsified petitions, exacerbators of nearly mediated minor suits, and appeals specialists who took advantage of magistrates' carelessly worded decisions" (Jonathan K. Ocko, *Bureaucratic Reform in Provincial China*, p. 70). For more on pettifoggers, see Huang Liu-hung, *A Complete Book Concerning Happiness and Benevolence, Fu-hui ch'üan-shu: A Manual for Local Magistrates in Seventeenth-Century China*, pp. 258-262 and Na Ssu-lu, *Ch'ing-tai chou-hsien ya-men shen-p'an chih-tu*, pp. 53-55.
20. Liu Ta-pai, *Ku-shih ti t'an-tzu*, p. 210. This page also includes an interesting list of epithets attached to natives of other locales.
21. Miao Ch'üan-chi, "Ch'ing-tai mu-fu chih-tu chih yen-chiu," M. A. thesis in Political Science, National Taiwan University, 1962, p. 419 and Hsieh Te-hsi, *Lu Hsün tso-p'in chung ti Shaohsing fang-yen chu-shih*, p. 28.
22. See for example Hsu K'o, comp., *Ch'ing-pai lei-ch'ao*, 28/p. 2.
23. For translation of shih-yeh as pettifogger see Lu Hsün, *SWLH*, vol. 1, p. 380. For paraphrase of shih-yeh as *hsü-li* (i.e., clerk) see Niida Noboru, *Chūgoku hōseishi kenkyū*, vol. 4, p. 722. For use of the term shih-yeh to mean Central Board clerk and pettifogger as well as mu-yu see Ts'ao Chü-jen, *Wan-li hsing-chi*, pp. 240-242. Shih-yeh is also used to refer to both Central Board clerks and mu-yu in the important article by Wang Chieh-mou, "Ch'ing-tai ti Shaohsing shih-yeh," *Che-chiang yüeh-k'an* 2 #2 (January 1970), pp. 18-19.
24. Lu Hsün, "Wu chang," or Life-Is-Transient," *SWLH*, vol. 1, p. 380, and "A Slap-Dash Diary Continued," in ibid, vol. 2, p. 282. See also Lu Hsün, *LHCC*, vol. 3, p. 495, note 7.
25. Martino Martini, *Novus atlas sinensis* . . ., p. 143; Abbé [Jean-Baptiste] Grosier, *A General Description of China* . . ., vol. 1, p. 68.
26. Miao Ch'üan-chi, *Ch'ing-tai mu-fu jen-shih chih-tu*, p. 19, note 17.
27. See page 3 of Chou Tso-jen's preface to Chang Tai, *T'ao-an meng-i*.
28. Hsü K'o, *K'o yen*, 10/p. 9B in Hsü Hsin-liu, ed., *Tien-su-ko ts'ung-kan erh-chi*.
29. Jacques Gernet, *Daily Life in China on the Eve of the Mongol Invasion*, pp. 248-249.

30. Although pursuit of this point falls beyond the bounds of the present study, it should be noted in passing that one function which nationalism serves is to provide a common ideology facilitating cooperation at this new, higher level. The concern for ideological cohesion which both the Kuomintang and the Chinese Communists have long displayed indicates that, as nationalists, they fully appreciate the necessity for a common ideology, a "unified will" or "comradeship" *(t'ung-chih)*. But although other t'ung ties such as t'ung-tsu and t'ung-hsiang are ascribed characteristics, t'ung-chih must be achieved, and thus is rarer.

Part One: Introduction

1. Johanna Menzel Meskill, *The Lins of Wu-feng, Taiwan 1729-1895*, p. 261.

Chapter One

1. Chou Hsia-shou, *Lu Hsün hsiao-shuo li ti jen-wu*, pp. 84-85. The author is Lu Hsün's brother Tso-jen.
2. Ch'iao-feng, *Lüeh-chiang kuan-yü Lu Hsün ti shih-ch'ing*, p. 24. The author is Lu Hsün's brother Chien-jen.
3. See Ho Ping-ti, *The Ladder of Success in Imperial China*, pp. 34-37; Chang Chung-li, *The Chinese Gentry*, pp. 6-9; and Sakai Tadao, *Chūgoku zensho no kenkyū*, p. 82.
4. *CCKK*, section "Chu-chi she-hui hsien-hsiang," p. 2.
5. This case of a peasant-led anti-Taiping resistance movement is examined in my monograph, *The People Versus the Taipings: Bao Lisheng's "Righteous Army of Dongan"* (Berkeley, 1981).
6. Sakai Tadao, *Chūgoku zensho no kenkyū*, pp. 137-139. For an excellent general description of the early Ch'ing's success in stifling sheng-yuan activism (and thus in effect adopting Ming T'ai-tsu's attitude), see Ono Kazuko, "Shusho no shiso tosei o megutte," *Tōyōshi kenkyū* 18 #3 (December 1959), pp. 99-123.
7. For a summary and analysis of Ku Yen-wu's essay in the *Jih chih lu*, see Makino Tatsumi, "Ko Enbu no seiinron," in Hayashi Tomoharu, ed., *Kinsei Chūgoku kyōikushi kenkyū*, pp. 219-229.
8. Ibid., p. 223.
9. Ku Chien-ch'en, *Shen-tung*, p. 47.
10. Ch'ü T'ung-tsu, *Local Government in China under the Ch'ing*, pp. 189-190.
11. Sun Ting-lieh, *Ssu-hsi-chai chüeh-shih*, 1/pp. 15A-15B. However, as we have seen, control over the local constables (ti-pao) by the magistrate was in practice not so straightforward as Sun's statement implies.
12. An injunction against sheng-yüan activism issued early in the Ch'ing (1652) was, if anything, even stricter than Ming T'ai-tsu's version. See Ōmura Kyōdo, "Shinchō kyōiku shisōshi ni okeru 'Seiyu kōkun' no chii ni tsuite," in Hayashi Tomoharu, ed., *Kinsei Chūgoku kyōikushi kenkyū*, pp. 242-246.
13. See Sasaki Masaya's superb monograph-length study, "Kanpō ninen Yinken no kōryō bakudō," in Tōyō Bunko kindai Chūgoku kenkyū iinkai, ed., *Kindai Chūgoku kenkyū dai go shū* (1963), p. 273.
14. Ibid.
15. *Chu-chi hsien-chih*, 1905, 17/p. 7A. Many years previous there had been in Chu-chi just such an upright magistrate to rectify corruption in the yamen: During the early Tao-kuang period he managed to fire over 500 yamen clerks and runners, shaking up the status quo to such an extent that runners were afraid to

186   *Notes to pages 20-26*

accept gifts from villagers (*CCKK*, section "Chu-chi she-hui hsien-hsiang," p. 98).

16. *CCKK*, ibid., p. 96.
17. Ch'ü T'ung-tsu, *Local Government*, p. 182.
18. *Min li pao*, January 11, 1911, p. 4.
19. *TFTC* 2 #4, Kuang-hsü 31 (1905), lunar 4th month, section "tsa tsu," p. 44.
20. *Shinkoku jihō* #2 (April 10, Meiji 38 (1905)), pp. 1-2 and #3 (May 20, Meiji 38 (1905)), p. 1.
21. Yen Chung-p'ing et al., eds., *Chung-kuo chin-tai ching-chi shih t'ung-chi tzu-liao hsüan-chi*, p. 223.
22. Ch'ü Ying-kuang, *Ch'ü hsün-an-shih hsün-shih ch'üan-Che wen-kao*, 1/p. 72A. For a brief historical sketch of water control in Che-tung see Cheng Chao-ching, *Chung-kuo shui-li shih*, pp. 246-248.
23. John Meskill, *Ch'oe Pu's Diary: A Record of Drifting Across the Sea*, p. 76.
24. Li Tz'u-ming, *Yüeh-man-t'ang p'ien-t'i wen*, 2/p. 39B in Li Tz'u-ming, *Yüeh-man-t'ang wen-chi*.
25. Ch'ü T'ung-tsu, *Local Government*, p. 327, note 94.
26. The San-chiang-cha system was originally constructed by the prefect of Shaohsing in 1537 (Pu T'ung, pseud., "Chien-hu ho Chi-shan," *Che-chiang yüeh-k'an* #3 (September 1968), p. 13).
27. Sun Ting-lieh, *Ssu-hsi-chai chüeh-shih*, 3/pp. 8A, 11A, 23A.
28. Satō Taketoshi, "Min-Shin jidai Settō ni okeru suiri jigyō: Sankō kō o chūshin ni," *Shūkan Tōyōgaku* #20 (October 1968), pp. 93-109.
29. Tuan Kuang-ch'ing, *Ching-hu tzu-chuan nien-p'u*, pp. 208-212.
30. Ibid., p. 209.
31. Ibid., p. 210.
32. Ibid., p. 211.
33. Tung Chin-chien, *Wu T'ai-fu-jen nien-p'u*, section "hsia," pp. 19A-19B.
34. Fujii Hiroshi, "Hsin-an shōnin no kenkyū," *Tōyō gakuhō* 36 #4 (March 1954), especially pp. 115-132. Evelyn Rawski, *Agricultural Change and the Peasant Economy of South China*, pp. 88-94.
35. Thomas Metzger, "The State and Commerce in Imperial China," *Asian and African Studies* #6 (1970), p. 25.
36. See for example Richard Howard, "K'ang Yu-wei (1858-1927): His Intellectual Background and Early Thought," in Arthur F. Wright and Denis Twitchett, eds., *Confucian Personalities*, p. 297.
37. Chou Hsia-shou, *Lu Hsün ti ku-chia*, p. 210.
38. Yokoyama Himitsu, "Ro Jin nōto: 'Kokyō' o chūshin ni shite," *Yamaguchi daigaku bungakukai shi* 16 #1 (1965), p. 34. Yokoyama's source is Chou Hsia-shou, *Lu Hsün ti ku-chia*, pp. 207-209.
39. See Marie-Claire Bergère, *La Bourgeoisie chinoise et la révolution de 1911*, pp. 33, 35; the same author's article, "The Role of the Bourgeoisie," in Mary Wright, ed., *China in Revolution: The First Phase, 1900-1913*, pp. 239-241; and R. Keith Schoppa, *Chinese Elites and Political Change*, p. 60.
40. *Shao-chün p'ing-t'iao cheng-hsin lu*, section "t'i-ming," p. 2B.
41. Marianne Bastid, *Aspects de la réforme d'enseignement en Chine au debut de 20e siècle, d'après des écrits de Zhang Jian*, p. 20.
42. Chou Hsia-shou, *Lu Hsün ti ku-chia*, p. 280. For a detailed but anecdotal account of Lu Hsün's early schooling in Shaohsing, see Chu Min et al., *Lu Hsün tsai Shaohsing*, pp. 68-100.

43. Tung Chin-chien, *Wu T'ai-fu-jen nien-p'u*, in Tung Chin-chien, ed., *Tung-shih ts'ung-shu*. The account below is based on this biography. For a biography of Chin-chien himself see *SHTL*, section "jen-wu lieh-chüan," p. 196B. According to a nineteenth-century diary account written during the T'ung-chih period, "In Shaohsing it is customary for all the officials *(chin-shen)* to be also engaged in commerce." See Chao Lieh-wen, "Neng ching chü-shih jih-chi" in T'ai-p'ing t'ien-kuo li-shih po-wu-kuan, ed., *T'ai-p'ing t'ien-kuo shih-liao ts'ung-pien chien-chi*, vol. 3, p. 239.
44. Tung Chin-chien, *Wu T'ai-fu-jen nien-p'u*, section "shang," p. 9A.
45. Ibid., section "shang," p. 17A.
46. Compare the entrepreneurship of a Shaohsing native named Lu. While serving in Peking in an unspecified governmental capacity *(kung-chih ching-shih)* during the Tao-kuang period (1821-1850), he noticed that the demand for satin garments in Peking far exceeded the supply. He thereupon returned to Shaohsing, set up shop in Hsia-fang-ch'iao in Shan-yin, and manufactured the cloth, which he proceeded to ship to Peking and sell at great profit. Thus did Shaohsing's production of satin begin (Chien-she wei-yüan-hui ching-chi tiao-ch'a-so t'ung-chi-k'o, ed., *Shaohsing ti ssu-ch'ou*, p. 32).
47. His brother had also purchased the same rank.
48. See Denis Twitchett's exemplary study, "The Fan Clan's Charitable Estate, 1050-1760," in David S. Nivison and Arthur F. Wright, eds., *Confucianism in Action*, pp. 97-133. In an essay entitled "I liang-li shan-tsu" ("One Should Exert Himself To Support His Lineage") Wang Hui-tsu also argued that, given the inevitability of both rich and poor within any given lineage, the Fans' charity estate should be emulated as a model *(Shuang-chieh-t'ang yung-hsün*, 3/p. 24A in Wang Hui-tsu, *Wang Lung-chuang i-shu)*.
49. Tung Chin-chien, *Wu T'ai-fu-jen nien-p'u*, section "chung," p. 3B.
50. Ibid., p. 12A.
51. Ibid., p. 9A.

Chapter Two

1. Sasaki Masaya, "Kanpō ninen Yinken no kōryō bakudō," in *Kindai Chūgoku kenkyū dai go shū*, p. 214.
2. Ibid., p. 209.
3. For a description of British operations in Ningpo prefecture during the Opium War, see Arthur Waley, *The Opium War Through Chinese Eyes* (London, 1958).
4. *Shang-yü hsien-chih*, 1890, 34/p. 9B.
5. Ibid.
6. Ibid.
7. Imabori Seiji, *Chūgoku kindaishi kenkyū josetsu*, pp. 91-132.
8. Northeastern Yü-yao had already witnessed rent resistance uprisings in 1841-43 and 1845 (Kojima Shinji, "Taihei tenkoku kakumei," in *Iwanami kōza sekai rekishi*, vol. 21, p. 283).
9. *Shang-yü hsien-chih*, 1890, 35/p. 14A.
10. *Chung-wai hsin-pao* 1 #1, Hsien-feng 8 (1858), lunar 11th month, 15th day, p. 4A. The text is not clear as to whether the "several tens of thousands of mou" were the corporate property of the Hsieh lineage or the total amount held by the lineage's individual families.

11. Denis Twitchett, "The Fan Clan's Charitable Estate, 1050-1760," p.111.
12. Taga Akigorō, *Sōfu no kenkyū*, p. 554. For an example (from Nan-ch'ang, Kiangsi) of the damaging tensions produced by the opposite strategy, whereby a lineage encouraged its landlord members to engage tenants who were also members of that same lineage, see Philip Kuhn, *Rebellion and Its Enemies*, pp. 159-160.
13. For one example among many, see the lists of lineage tenants in *Hsiao-shan Hsi-ho Ch'an-shih tsung-p'u*, 16/pp. 10A, 12A. Taga number 851. For a rather rare example of a lineage which rented much, although by no means all, of its land to tenants with the same surname (presumably members of the lineage), see the list of tenants in *Kuei-chi T'ao-shih tsu-p'u*, 25/pp. 17B-22B. Taga number 794.
14. See the English summary of Muramatsu's research on Kiangnan landlordism, with references to his original articles in Japanese: Muramatsu Yūji, "A Documentary Study of Chinese Landlordism in Late Ch'ing and Early Republican China," *Bulletin of the School of Oriental and African Studies* 29 #3 (1966), especially p. 589.
15. Taga Akigorō, *Sōfu no kenkyū*, p. 554.
16. Another source states that the tenants demanded a 25 percent rent reduction (Kojima Shinji, "Taihei tenkoku kakumei," p. 299). The characteristic goal of such tenant rebellions was not the abolition of rent, merely its reduction.
17. *Chung-wai hsin-pao* 2 #1, Hsien-feng 9 (1859), lunar 3rd month, 1st day, pp. 3A-3B.
18. Kojima Shinji, "Taihei tenkoku kakumei," p. 299.
19. Lo Erh-kang, "Che-tung ch'i-i tien-nung ts'an-chia T'ai-p'ing t'ien-kuo," *Li-shih yen-chiu* #4 (April 1956), p. 90. Lo quotes from a contemporaneous gentryman's account of the rent resistance. The account indicates that the tenants led by Wang came from at least three different lineages. I am assuming that Wang Ch'un-sheng and Huang Ch'un-sheng are the same person. See note 21 below.
20. In his translation of this passage Hsiao Kung-chuan places quotation marks around the following words: tenant bandits, big families, and bandits. But Li Tz'u-ming's original text provides no justification for Hsiao's implication that Li used these words with reservation. So the quotation marks have been removed.
21. Notice that the tenants' leader in the first-cited account was named Wang Ch'un-sheng, and in this account Huang Ch'un-sheng. They are almost certainly the same person. Probably as news of the incident spread by word of mouth the surnames Wang and Huang became confused.
22. Hsiao Kung-chuan, *Rural China*, p. 429, translated from Li Tz'u-ming, *Yüeh-man-t'ang jih-chi-pu*, Hsien-feng 9 (1859), lunar 1st month, 26th day, in ts'e 6, "chi chi," p. 6A. Hsiao's translation has been checked against Li's original text. English words in brackets were inserted by Hsiao.
23. Ch'iao-feng, *Lüeh-chiang kuan-yu Lu Hsün ti shih-ch'ing*, pp. 10, 23. Cf. Shiga Masatoshi, "Ro Jin to minkan bungei (jō)," *Tenri daigaku gakuhō* #30 (December 1959), p. 61. The parish opera described by Lu Hsün was sponsored jointly by at least two villages (Lu Hsün, "Village Opera," *SWLH*, vol. 1, p. 141). On the *she* as a spatial unit in Shaohsing, "corresponding to a village in area," see Hsieh Te-hsi, *Lu Hsün tso-pin chung ti Shaohsing fang-yen chu-shih*, p. 13.
24. Sun Ting-lieh, *Ssu-hsi-chai chüeh-shih*, 2/p. 48A.
25. There is a tantalizing reference to a Kuei-chi native's organization of a militia force (t'uan) numbering "several tens of

thousands" of people from thirty-six she to protect against the Taiping threat *(SHTL,* section "jen-wu lieh-chüan," p. 105B). And in 1852 the "several tens of thousands" of peasants participating in a tax resistance demonstration in Yin-hsien, Ningpo prefecture, marched in separate groups, each carrying banners which displayed the image of its temple god *(miao-shen-ch'i)* and which proclaimed the parish to which that group belonged (Kwang-Ching Liu, "Wan-Ch'ing ti-fang-kuan tzu-shu chih shih-liao chia-chih," *Chung-yang yen-chiu-yüan ch'eng-li wu-shih chou-nien chi-nien lun-wen chi,* p. 355, citing chüan 29 of the *Hsien-feng Yin-hsien chih).*

26. Ch'üan Tsu-wang, *Chieh-ch'i-t'ing chi wai-pien,* 48/pp. 15B-17A.
27. In other sources the tenants fighting the Hsiehs are said to have grouped themselves into eighteen "bureaus" (chü), the organizational principles of which are unfortunately not revealed (Lo Erh-kang, "Che-tung ch'i-i tien-nung ts'an-chia T'ai-p'ing t'ien-kuo," p. 90, and Kojima Shinji, "Taihei tenkoku kakumei," p. 299). The number of peasants involved was in the "tens of thousands" according to the gazetteer quoted by Kojima.
28. *Chung-wai hsin-pao* 2 #1, Hsien-feng 9 (1859), lunar 3rd month, 1st day, pp. 2A-3A.
29. *Hsiao-shan hsien-chih kao,* 1935, 4/p. 35A.
30. Ibid.
31. Franz Michael, ed., *The Taiping Rebellion: History and Documents,* vol. 3, p. 1260.
32. *Hsiao-shan hsien-chih kao,* 1935, 4/p. 35A.
33. The two passages cited are both from ibid.
34. Such seems to have been the case in Chu-chi, where rents were very low immediately after the Taipings were driven out but rose steadily in succeeding decades, along with population pressure *(CCKK,* p. 51).
35. *Hsiao-shan hsien-chih kao,* 1935, 4/p. 35A.
36. Imabori Seiji, *Chūgoku kindaishi kenkyū josetsu,* p. 130. Imabori's source is Sun Ting-lieh, *Ssu-hsi-chai chüeh-shih,* 1/p. 4B.
37. Quoted in Imabori, ibid., from Sun, *Ssu-hsi-chai chüeh shih,* 1/p.36B.
38. Imabori Seiji, "Shindai no kōso ni tsuite," *Shigaku zasshi* 76 #9 (September 1967), p. 49. Imabori's source is Sun, *Ssu-hsi-chai chüeh-shih,* 1/pp. 1A-1B.
39. Li Wen-chih, ed., *Chung-kuo chin-tai nung-yeh shih tzu-liao ti-i-chi (1840-1911),* pp. 185-186.
40. George Jamieson et al., "Tenure of Land in China and the Condition of the Rural Population," *Journal of the China Branch of the Royal Asiatic Society,* new series, 23 #2 (1888), p. 105.
41. Takeuchi Yoshimi, *Ro Jin,* p. 25. Chu Min et al., *Lu Hsün tsai Shaohsing,* pp. 138-140, confirms Lu Hsün's family's 40-50 mou, but notes that the family's fortunes were on the decline during Lu Hsün's early years, even before his grandfather's arrest for corruption in 1893. In any case the average peasant landowner in Shaohsing certainly held less land than did Lu Hsün's family.
42. George Jamison et al., "Tenure of Land in China and the Condition of the Rural Population," pp. 105-106.
43. E.H. Parker, "A Journey in Chekiang," p. 45.
44. Ch'ü T'ung-tsu, *Local Government,* p. 332, note 132.
45. Ch'ü, ibid., p. 186 makes this point for China as a whole.
46. Wang Yeh-chien, *Land Taxation in Imperial China, 1750-1911,* pp. 38-39.
47. Tso Tsung-t'ang, *Tso Wen-hsiang-kung ch'üan-chi,* section "tso kao," 8/pp. 69A-70B. Tso's memorial is dated T'ung-chih 3 (1864), lunar 3rd month, 27th day.

48. Nor was this mere rhetoric. In another memorial also dated 1864, describing conditions in Ningpo prefecture, Tso wrote that tax abuses there were bad, "But not as bad as in Shaohsing." Ibid., 9/p. 62A.
49. For detailed evidence that tax overcollection in Shaohsing during the T'ung-chih period (1862-1874) was by no means limited to these three counties but was also practiced in Chu-chi, Shang-yü, and Yü-yao, see Sasaki Masaya, "Kanpō ninen Yinken no kōryo bakudō," pp. 229-235.
50. Tso Tsung-t'ang, Tso Wen-hsiang-kung ch'üan-chi, section "tso-kao," 8/p. 71A.
51. Ch'ü T'ung-tsu, Local Government, p. 332, note 132.
52. SHTL, section "tien-fu," pp. 33A-33B.
53. T'ung-wen Hu-pao, Kuang-hsü 30 (1904), lunar 2nd month, 27th day, unpaginated (Hangchow section).
54. Ibid. For an analysis that confirms these conclusions regarding Tso's memorial and the inequities of the late Ch'ing tax system, see Kobayashi Yukio, "Shinmatsu no Sekkō ni okeru fuzei kaikaku to sessen nōzei ni tsuite," Tōyō gakuhō 58 #1-#2 (December 1976), pp. 49-85.
55. Sasaki Masaya, "Kanpō ninen Yinken no kōryō bakudō," p. 196.
56. Ibid., p. 273.
57. Li Wen-chih, ed., Chung-kuo chin-tai nung-yeh, p. 963. On this same page are descibed similar incidents of anti-likin violence in Yü-yao and Hsiao-shan. Cf. NCH, June 13, 1898, p. 1020.
58. E.H. Parker, "A Journey in Chekiang," p. 45.
59. Chu-chi hsien-chih, 1905, 15/p. 22B.
60. Hsin-ch'ang hsien-chih, 1918, 1/p. 61A.
61. NCH, September 3, 1902, p. 474.
62. Min li pao, August 30, 1911, p. 4.
63. Takahashi Kōsuke, "Shinmatsu ni okeru rikin shūdatsu to shōnōmin keiei," Rekishigaku kenkyū #392 (January 1973), pp. 20-30. Cf. Takahashi Kosuke, "Jūkyūseiki chūyō no Chūgoku ni okeru zei shūdatsu taisei no saihen katei: rikin kenkyū josetsu," Rekishigaku kenkyū #383 (April 1972), pp. 48-59 and Kobayashi Kazumi, "Chūgoku hanshokuminchika no keizei katei to minshū no tatakai: rikin o megutte, jūkyūseiki kōhan," Rekishigaku kenkyū #369 (February 1971), pp. 1-18.
64. Takahashi Kōsuke, "Shinmatsu," pp. 21-22.
65. A work which touches on the relationship between foreign imperialism and rural exploitation (not specifically in Shaohsing) is Bannō Ryōkichi, "Kindai Chūgoku ni okeru nōgyō henkaku," Rekishi hyōron #279 (August 1973), especially pp. 9-10. Banno's treatment, while overly schematic rather than empirical, is useful as a starting point. He argues that imperialism did not transform the preexisting hierarchy of rural exploitation; it merely added another layer at the top, providing new capital to fuel the process.
66. Takahashi Kōsuke, "Shinmatsu," p. 28.
67. We know that the imposition of a heavy likin tax severely curtailed Shaohsing's export of cocoons from 1883 on (Li Wen-chih, ed., Chung-kuo chin-tai nung-yeh, p. 376 and Kobayashi Kazumi, "Chūgoku hanshokuminchika," p. 6).
68. Kobayashi, ibid., pp. 3, 6.
69. See Wang Chieh-mou, "Shaohsing hsi-po kuan ch'üan-kuo," Che-chiang yüeh-k'an 2 #4 (April 1970), p. 19 and Anonymous, "Shaohsing po-yeh kai-k'uang," Kung-shang pan-yüeh-k'an 4 #11 (June 1932), section "kuo-nei ching-chi," p. 3. For more on spirit money see Appendix C.

70. Takahashi Kōsuke, "Shinmatsu," pp. 26-27.
71. *T'ung-wen Hu-pao*, Kuang-hsü 27 (1901), lunar 2nd month, 6th day, p. 2.
72. Kobayashi Kazumi, "Chūgoku hanshokuminchika," p. 8.
73. See Hata Korehito, "Yōmu undō jiki no minshū undō: Kō-Setsu no kōen tōsō o chūshin to shite," *Rekishi hyōron* #282 (November 1973), p. 57; Ōtani Toshio, *Chūgoku kindai seijikeizaishi nyūmon*, p. 87; and Kobayashi Kazumi, "Chūgoku hanshokuminchika," p. 14.
74. Kobayashi, ibid., p. 2.
75. Ibid., p. 3.
76. Ibid., pp. 11-12. Kobayashi's gunboat figure apparently refers to the 1880s.
77. Lo Yü-tung, *Chung-kuo li-chin shih*, p. 257.
78. Ch'ü T'ung-tsu, *Local Government*, p. 284, note 2.
79. Ramon Myers, review of books by Ch'üan Han-sheng, *Journal of Asian Studies* 33 #1 (November 1973), p. 108.
80. Tung Chin-chien, *Wu T'ai-fu-jen nien-p'u*, section "shang," p. 14A.
81. Hsü K'o, *K'o yen*, 14/pp. 7A-7B. Hsü seems to be referring here to the lower Yangtze in general, including Shaohsing.
82. Yeh-chien Wang, "The Secular Trend of Prices during the Ch'ing Period (1644-1911)," *Journal of the Institute of Chinese Studies* 5 #2 (December 1972), pp. 360-361.
83. Shiba Yoshinobu, *Commerce and Society in Sung China*, p. 59.
84. Li Wen-chih, ed., *Chung-kuo chin-tai nung-yeh*, p. 524.
85. E.g., Sun Ting-lieh, *Ssu-hsi-chai chüeh-shih*, 1/p. 39A.
86. *NCH*, March 22, 1907, p. 611.
87. Ibid., October 7, 1911, p. 26.
88. The widespread rice shortages of 1907 seem to have been especially severe, judging from various newspaper accounts.
89. *Kuei-chi Chung-shih tsu-p'u*, 3/p. 77A. Taga number 1131.
90. Ch'iao-feng, *Lüeh-chiang kuan-yü Lu Hsün ti shih-ch'ing*, p. 17 and Chu Min et al., *Lu Hsün tsai Shaohsing*, p. 18. "Chuang ta-chia" has also been described as destroying rice shops when the price of rice rose too high (Chang Neng-keng, *Lu Hsün tsao-ch'i shi-chi pieh-lu*, p. 11).
91. *Shih pao*, May 18, 1911, p. 3.
92. *TFTC* 4 #2, Kuang-hsü 33 (1907), lunar 2nd month, section "tsa tsu," p. 8. For brief quotations from Chou Tso-jen's unpublished diary describing similar attacks on rice shops, see Chu Min et al., *Lu Hsün tsai Shaohsing*, p. 18.
93. Ibid., 4 #6, Kuang-hsü 33 (1907), lunar 6th month, section "tsa tsu," p. 8.
94. *Hsiao-shan hsien-chih kao*, 1935, 5/p. 6B.
95. *Shih pao*, May 18, 1911, p. 3.
96. Chou Hsia-shou, *Lu Hsün ti ku-chia*, p. 243.
97. *CCKK*, section "Chu-chi kai-kuan," p. 111.
98. Lu Hsün, "The True Story of Ah Q," *SWLH*, vol. 1, pp. 86-87.
99. Ch'iao-feng, *Lüeh-chiang kuan-yü Lu Hsün ti shih-ch'ing*, pp. 18-19.
100. For discussions of the *kai-t'ou*, see Rinji Taiwan kyūkan chōsakai, ed., *Shinkoku gyōseihō*, vol. 2, p. 106 and especially Kiyama Hideo, "Settō 'damin' kō," *Shakaishi kenkyū* #4 (April 1984), pp. 104-105.
101. *Hang-chou pai-hua pao* #31, Kuang-hsü 28 (1902), lunar 4th month, 5th day, pp. 1B-3A.
102. *Che-chiang-sheng ts'ai-cheng yüeh-k'an*, July 1934, pp. 254-255.
103. *Shao-chün p'ing-t'iao cheng-hsin lu*, section "wen-an," p. 5B.
104. Ibid., p. 6A.

105. T'ao Ying-hui, *Ts'ai Yüan-p'ei nien-p'u (shang)*, pp. 40, 69.
106. *Shao-chün p'ing-t'iao cheng-hsin lu*, section "chu-p'i ts'ai-pan," p. 12B.
107. Figures on Shan-yin computed from ibid., section "chu-jih t'iao-mai," pp. 1A-29B. Figures on Kuei-chi computed from ibid., pp. 29B-49A.
108. William S. Atwell, "Ch'en Tzu-lung (1608-1647): A Scholar-Official of the Late Ming Dynasty," Ph.D. thesis in East Asian Studies, Princeton University, 1974, p. 107.
109. *Hsin-ch'ang hsien-chih*, 1918, 1/pp. 44A-44B.
110. Compare a similar rice distribution program carried out in the forty wards (fang) of Shaohsing city in 1900 as a result of mass rioting over the high cost of rice *(SHTL*, section "jen-wu lieh-chüan," p. 177A).
111. *T'ung-wen Hu-pao*, Kuang-hsü 28 (1902), lunar 6th month, 11th day, p. 3.

Chapter Three

1. Saeki Tomi, *Shindai ensei no kenkyū*, p. 158 and Kotake Fumio et al., *Tōa no kindaika*, p. 93 (in chapter 5, written by Saeki Tomi). Cf. Watanabe Atsushi, "Shinmatsu Yōsukō karyūiki ni okeru shien shūdan," *Shakai bunka shigaku* #6 (August 1970), p. 1.
2. See Watanabe Atsushi, "Bansaihō no taitō to sono eikyō: Shinmatsu Ryōsetsu engyō no ichisokumen," *Tōyōshi kenkyū* 21 #1 (June 1962), pp. 54-75 and Watanabe Atsushi, "Shinmatsu enkai shoenjō ni okeru seien gijutsu no tenkan to sono igi: senhō kara saihō e no ikō o chūshin to shite," in *Yamazaki sensei taikan kinenkai*, ed., *Yamazaki sensei taikan kinen tōyōshigaku ronshū*, pp. 515-527.
3. Watanabe Atsushi, "Bansaihō," pp. 62, 63, 71.
4. Fan Yin, *Yüeh yen*, section "hsia," p. 26A.
5. *Che-chiang ch'ing-li ts'ai-cheng chü*, ed., *Che-chiang ch'ing-li ts'ai-cheng shuo-ming shu*, unpaginated ("shang-pien," section "shou-k'uan yen-k'o shui-li," subsection "kuan-pan Shang-hai tsu-chieh chien-li," 6th page).
6. Watanabe Atsushi, "Bansaihō," p. 72.
7. Fu Tse-hung, *Pao-i-t'ang wen-ts'un* 1/11A-14A.
8. Guy Boulais, *Manuel du code chinois*, p. 330.
9. Ibid., p. 332.
10. Wang Hui-tsu, *Meng-hen lu-yü*, p. 38B in Wang Hui-tsu, *Wang Lung-chuang i-shu*.
11. *NCH*, March 21, 1925, p. 473.
12. Evidence of the large amount of cotton grown on Yü-yao's alluvial land from the late Ch'ien-lung period through the 1930s is cited in Amano Motonosuke, *Chūgoku nōgyōshi kenkyū*, p. 570. Indeed, according to Amano, Yü-yao continued thereafter to produce more cotton than any other county in Chekiang.
13. Chiang Monlin, *Tides from the West*, p. 8.
14. Fan Yin, *Yüeh yen*, section "hsia," p. 26A.
15. Ibid., p. 26B.
16. Ibid., p. 27A.
17. *Shang-yü hsien-chih chiao-hsü*, 1898, 5/p. 26A.
18. Li Wen-chih, ed., *Chung-kuo chin-tai nung-yeh*, p. 420.
19. *TFTC*, 4 #3, Kuang-hsü 33 (1907), lunar 3rd month, section "tsa tsu," p. 9. For mention of a rice riot by the *sha-min* of Shan-yin in August 1911, see *Min li pao*, August 30, 1911, p. 4.
20. *Che-chiang ch'ing-li ts'ai-cheng chü*, ed., *Che-chiang ch'ing-li ts'ai-cheng shuo-ming shu*, unpaginated ("shang-pien," penulti-

mate page of section "shou-k'uan t'ien-fu"). For Ku Yen-wu's mention of such disputes over alluvial land in Ning-Shao, see Ku Yen-wu, *Tien-hsia chün-kuo li-ping shu* (section "Che-chiang hsia")/ pp. 51B-52A in the Ssu-pu ts'ung-k'an edition. For a Wan-li period reference to "fondness for litigation" along the coastline of Shaohsing, see *Kuang yü t'u*, p. 121 of the 1969 Taiwan photoreprint.

21. For what seems to be the relevant clause of the Ch'ing Code permitting this procedure, see Guy Boulais, *Manuel du code chinois*, p. 224.

22. *T'ung-wen Hu-pao*, Kuang-hsü 30 (1904), lunar 2nd month, 24th day, unpaginated (in Hangchow section).

23. Kojima Yoshio, "Hsinhai kakumeiki no rōnō undō to Chūgoku shakaidō," *Rekishigaku kenkyū*, supplement (October 1971), p. 110.

24. *T'ung-wen Hu-pao*, Kuang-hsü 29 (1903), lunar 5th month, 2nd day, p. 4.

25. *TFTC* 7 #10, Hsüan-t'ung 2 (1910), lunar 10th month, p. 301.

26. For more on bandits in Shaohsing's periphery (especially Hsin-ch'ang and Ch'eng-hsien), see Mary B. Rankin, *Early Chinese Revolutionaries: Radical Intellectuals in Shanghai and Chekiang, 1902-1911*, pp. 134, 175, 221. Cf. Schoppa, *Chinese Elites and Political Change*, pp. 107, 120.

27. On T'ai-chou's reputation for unruliness, see *Hsin-ch'ang hsien-chih*, 1918, 7/p. 40A. Cf. Yamashita Yoneko, "Hsinhai kakumei no jiki no minshū undō: Kō-Setsu chiku no nōmin undō o chūshin to shite," *Tōyō bunka kenkyūjo kiyō* #37 (March 1965), p. 131. On the attack in Hsin-ch'ang see *TFTC* 7 #10, Hsüan-t'ung 2 (1910), lunar 10th month, p. 301.

28. *CCKK*, section "Chu-chi she-hui hsien-hsiang," p. 63.

29. *Min li pao*, October 17, 1910, p. 4.

30. *Shih pao*, February 22, 1911, p. 3.

31. Ch'iu Chin's father was a chü-jen and many of his relatives were subofficials. See Ch'en To, "Ch'iu Chin chia-shih tzu-liao ti hsin fa-hsien," *Hang-chou ta-hsüeh hsüeh-pao* 13 #2 (June 1983), pp. 126-131 (especially the photoreproductions of the newly discovered biographical information on the father).

32. Rankin, *Early Chinese Revolutionaries*, pp. 186, 174-175.

33. Chou Hsia-shou, *Lu Hsün hsiao-shuo li ti jen-wu*, p. 68.

34. *NCH*, November 2, 1912, p. 309.

35. See Thomas Metzger, "Chinese Bandits: The Traditional Perception Re-evaluated," *Journal of Asian Studies* 33 #3 (May 1974), pp. 455-458. For a more recent attempt to make a balanced assessment, see Phil Billingsley, "Bandits, Bosses, and Bare Sticks: Beneath the Surface of Local Control in Early Republican China," *Modern China* 7 #3 (July 1981), especially pp. 283-284.

36. *Chiang-nan shang-wu pao* #33, Kuang-hsü 26 (1900), lunar 11th month, 21st day, section "shang ch'ing," p. 3B.

37. *CCKK*, section "Chu-chi she-hui hsien-hsiang," p. 5. That eastern Chekiang's "beggar households" were not necessarily beggars, nor even necessarily poor, was noted in the Wan-li period (1573-1619) by Shen Te-fu in his *Wan-li yeh-huo pien*, p. 624 of the 1959 Peking edition, and even earlier by Yeh Ch'üan (1522-1578) in his *Hsien po pien*, pp. 187-188 (included in *Ming shih tzu-liao ts'ung-k'an ti-i-chi*, Shanghai, 1981). In fact Yeh states that "early in the Chia-ching period" (1522-1566) a "very wealthy" to-min family in Kuei-chi tried to marry its beautiful daughter into a respectable family. But not even extremely poor commoners would marry the girl, for fear of their neighbors' reaction. As we shall see, the same antipathy towards intermarriage between to-min and respectables was displayed some three

hundred years later, in the late nineteenth century. (I am highly indebted to Prof. Joseph McDermott both for bringing the *Hsien po pien* to my attention and for providing me with the text of the relevant passage.)

38. For a good overview of the various types of chien-min during the Ch'ing, see Rinji Taiwan kyūkan chōsakai, ed., *Shinkoku gyōseihō*, vol. 2, pp. 104-110.

39. Shen Te-fu, writing around 1606, expresses his own bewilderment (*Wan-li yeh-huo pien*, p. 624). A recent scholar has concluded that the true origins of the to-min will never be conclusively known (Feng Erh-k'ang, "Yung-cheng ti hsieh-ch'u Shaohsing ho Ch'ang-shu kai-chi," *Shūkan Tōyōgaku* #44 (October 1980), p. 3). Feng's account is the best overview of the to-min in Chinese. He presents an excellent summary of the various origin theories, and speculates shrewdly as to the reasons for the Yung-cheng liberation edict.

40. Terada Takanobu, "Yōseitei no semmin kaihōrei ni tsuite," *Tōyō-shi kenkyū* 18 #3 (December 1959), p. 129. Terada is ambiguous as to whether this estimate refers to all of Shaohsing prefecture or merely to Shan-yin county. The source which he cites, however, implies the latter (*Chia-ch'ing Shan-yin hsien-chih*, 1803, 11/p. 3B of the "feng-su" section). Terada's citation, which reads chuan 1 rather than 11, is in error.

41. These statistics on Chu-chi's to-min population during the 1920s are compiled from *CCKK*, section "Chu-chi she-hui hsien-hsiang," pp. 6-7.

42. In addition to the article by Feng Erh-k'ang cited above in note 39, see Terada Takanobu, "Yōseitei," p. 127 and Pei Huang, *Autocracy At Work: A Study of the Yung-cheng Period, 1723-1735*, pp. 226-231.

43. Ling Ch'ih,   "Shaohsing ti to-min," *Che-chiang yüeh-k'an* 3 #1 (January 1971), p. 17.

44. A very brief biographical sketch is included in *SHTL*, section "jen-wu lieh-chuan," p. 123A.

45. Chou Tso-jen, "Yüeh yen pa," pp. 1A-1B, in Fan Yin, *Yüeh yen*, 1932 Peking edition.

46. Fan Yin, "Lun to-p'in," in Fan Yin, *Yüeh yen*, section "hsia," pp. 23A-25B of the 1932 Peking edition. To-p'in was a stylized synonym for to-min. Poverty was not necessarily implied. The passages translated below are from this essay.

47. Chou Tso-jen, "Yüeh yen pa," p. 1B.

48. These quotations are of course from *The Analects*. See James Legge, *Confucian Analects*, book XVII, chapters II and III in Legge, *The Chinese Classics*, vol. 1, p. 318. Legge notes in reference to this passage, "The case of the hsia-yü [characters rather than romanization in original] would seem to be inconsistent with the doctrine of the perfect goodness of the moral nature of all men."

49. *CCKK*, section "Chu-chi she-hui hsien-hsiang," p. 3. Another school for to-min was established in Ningpo in 1904 (Rankin, *Early Chinese Revolutionaries*, p. 193).

50. Pi-chih she, ed., *Chung-kuo k'o-ming-tang ta shou-ling Hsü Hsi-lin*, pp. 99, 102.

51. Chang Wei-jen (interviewer), "Ch'ing-chi ti-fang ssu-fa: Ch'en T'ien-hsi hsieng-sheng fang-wen chi (hsia)," *Shih-huo* 1 #7 (October 1971), p. 53. Cf. Ku Shih-chiang, ed., *Hsiao-shan hsiang-t'u-chih*, rev. ed., 1933, p. 83.

52. Lu Hsün, "The 'Tomins'," *SWLH*, vol. 3, p. 286. The Chinese text is in *LHCC*, vol. 5, pp. 176-177.

53. Ku Shih-chiang, ed., *Hsiao-shan hsiang-t'u-chih*, rev. ed., 1933, p. 83.
54. Thomas Goodchild, "Northeastern Chehkiang, China: Notes on Human Adaptation to Environment," *Bulletin of the American Geographical Society* 43 #11 (1911), p. 816.
55. This information on to-min occupations comes from *Shang-yü hsien-chih*, 1890, 38/p. 8A, *Ch'eng-hsien chih*, 1870, 20/p. 12A, *Shan-yin hsien-chih*, 1671, 8/p. 10A, and *Hsin-ch'ang hsien-chih*, 1918, 5/p. 91B.
56. Ch'ü T'ung-tsu, *Local Government*, p. 62.
57. *Shaohsing fu-chih*, 1587, 12/p. 9A.
58. Ch'ü T'ung-tsu, *Local Government*, p. 106.
59. *CCKK*, section "Chu-chi she-hui hsien-hsiang," p. 4 and section "feng-su chih," p. 10.
60. Terada Takanobu, "Yōseitei," pp. 129-130. The locus classicus of this story is Shen Te-fu, *Wan-li yeh-huo pien*, p. 624 of the 1959 Peking edition. Shen's account seems to be highly reliable: He even notes that as a child he was ministered to by this same to-min doctor. Shen uses the story to illustrate his point that no matter how rich a to-min became, he would never be allowed to buy his way into the officialdom.
61. Miao Ch'üan-chi, *Ch'ing-tai mu-fu jen-shih chih-tu*, p. 10.
62. *CCKK*, section "feng-su chih," pp. 10-11.
63. Fan Yin, *Yüeh yen*, section "hsia," p. 25A. On the three-street neighborhood in Shaohsing city where to-min congregated, see Hsieh Te-hsi, *Lu Hsün tso-p'in*, p. 60. The names of the three streets are given in Iikura Shōhei, "Shōkō zatsubun," *(Toritsudai) Jimbun gakuhō* #140 (March 1980), p. 44.
64. Lu Hsün, "Ping-hou tsa-t'an chih yü," *LHCC*, vol. 6, pp. 142-143.
65. *Chu-chi Chung-shih tsung-p'u*, section "chin-li," pp. 1A-2B. The passages below are translated from this document. Taga number 1132.
66. We know from another source that there were over fifty to-min families named Ch'en living in the Chu-chi village of "Chu-chia keng" (presumably "Chu ts'un") as early as the 1920s *(CCKK*, section "Chu-chi she-hui hsien-hsiang," p. 6).
67. The magistrate is here quoting verbatim from the relevant precedent of the Ch'ing Code *(Ta Ch'ing lü li* 8/2/ *li* 6). The text of this precedent, together with the Yung-cheng Emperor's proclamation emancipating the to-min, is reprinted in Rinji Taiwan kyūkan chōsakai, *Taiwan shihō furoku sankōsho*, vol. 2, part 1, pp.132-133, and in Pierre Hoang, *Mélanges sur l'administration*, p. 140.

Part Two

This anonymous riddle dissects, both literally and figuratively, the characters of Shaohsing. Takigawa Masajirō, *Shina hōseishi kenkyū* (Tokyo, 1940), p. 326.

Chapter Four

1. In G. William Skinner's words, "[T]he upwardly mobile Chinese in either the trader or scholar track left his own locality to serve in other local systems, which in turn were plundered for the benefit of his own" ("Chinese Peasants and the Closed Community: An Open and Shut Case," *Comparative Studies in Society and History* 13 #3 (July 1971), p. 277).

2. W. Gilbert Walshe, "The Ancient City of Shaohing," *Journal of the China Branch of the Royal Asiatic Society*, new series, 33 (1900-1901), p. 283. Cf. Fan Yin, *Yüeh yen*, section "shang," p. 9B. An alternate version reads "Mah-jong, beancurd, and Shaohsing natives" (Shih San-ch'ang, *Lun-t'ai tsa-chi*, section "hsia," p. 19B).

3. Arthur E. Moule, *The Story of the Cheh-kiang Mission of the Church Missionary Society*, p. 93, quoting a statement made in 1875 by Bishop Russell (Anglican bishop of North China, 1872-1879).

4. This theory is set forth in Miao Ch'üan-chi, *Ming-tai hsü-li*, p. 199. Miao repeats his theory in *Ch'ing-tai mu-fu jen-shih chih-tu*, p. 10, and in his article "Ch'ing-tai hsing-mu shu-yao" in Hsieh Kuan-sheng and Ch'a Liang-chien, eds., *Chung-kuo fa-chih shih lun-chi*, p. 327.

5. Angela Hsi, "Social and Economic Status of the Merchant Class of the Ming Dynasty: 1368-1644," Ph.D. thesis in History, University of Illinois (Urbana), 1972, p. 145. A late sixteenth-century account by a native of Lin-hai (T'ai-chou), Chekiang states that "the majority" of natives of Ningpo and Shaohsing "earn their living outside their native place" (Wang Shih-hsing, *Kuang-chih i*, 4/ p. 1B). This passage was kindly brought to my attention by Prof. Joseph McDermott.

6. Ho Ping-ti, *Studies on the Population of China, 1368-1953*, p. 156. For more on these immigrants see Li Wen-chih, ed., *Chung-kuo chin-tai nung-yeh*, pp. 167, 170. Shaohsing natives also accounted for the majority of outsiders responsible for clearing new land near K'un-shan, Soochow prefecture, from the 1870s on. See Hsü K'o, *K'o yen*, 1/ p. 6B. And Richthofen found Ning-Shao settlers in "Fan-sui" (Fen-shui?) valley near the Chekiang-Anhui border in the 1870s (Ferdinand von Richthofen, *Baron Richthofen's Letters 1870-1872*, 2nd ed., p. 76).

7. Ts'ai Yüan-p'ei, *Ts'ai Yüan-p'ei tzu-shu*, p. 115. See also Ts'ai Shang-ssu, *Ts'ai Yüan-p'ei hsüeh-shu ssu-hsiang chuan-chi*, p. 50. For the immigrant statistics, see Ho, *Population*, p. 157.

8. Ho, ibid. Ho does not comment on this striking disparity. Having checked Ho's source, I can verify that his citation is accurate. Whether the source itself is accurate is, of course, another matter. I draw attention to this puzzle in the hope that future research will provide a more satisfactory solution. One possibility is that registering several households as one might have resulted in a tax advantage. Hilary Beattie points out that in late fifteenth-century Anhui, a fairly "common method of evasion, especially among the wealthy, was to have many households registered as one so that they might count as one for the performance of labour service" (*Land and Lineage in China*, p. 59). The parallel is hardly exact, due to changes in the tax system since that time, but it is suggestive.

9. The statistics for 1933 are from Ko Sui-ch'eng, ed., *Che-chiang (fen-sheng ti-chih)*, pp. 64-65. Fractions have been rounded to the nearest whole number. I have chosen to use the population figures for 1933, which are admittedly not ideal for the study of late Ch'ing conditions, because what earlier figures gain in contemporaneity they lose both in accuracy and in uniformity of coverage of all Shaohsing (not to mention all Chekiang) at one point in time. In using the 1933 figures I am of course assuming that they would not differ drastically, at least in the density rankings of the various counties, from equally accurate, uniform, and comprehensive late Ch'ing data if the latter existed.

10. Francis Goddard, *Called to Cathay*, p. 94.

11. *SHTL*, ts'e 11, section "hsiang chen," p. 1A.

12. Miao Ch'üan-chi, "Ch'ing-tai hsing-mu shu-yao," p. 327.

13. Taga Akigorō, "Sōzoku no shūfu katei ni tsuite," in Hayashi Tomoharu, ed., *Kinsei Chūgoku kyōikushi kenkyū*, p. 412.

14. Ho Ping-ti, *Chung-kuo hui-kuan shih-lun*, p. 28.

15. Ibid.

16. Ibid., p. 16 and especially Li Hua, "Ming-Ch'ing i-lai Pei-ching ti kung-shang-yeh hang-hui," *Li-shih yen-chiu* #4 (April 1978), p. 69.

17. The title assigned to this anonymous, untitled, undated manuscript (in one chüan) by the Institute of Oriental Culture's catalogue is *Tsai Pei-ching hui-kuan mu-lu*. Although the manuscript's use of the term *Shan-Kuei i-kuan* suggests a pre-1911 date (since Shan-yin and Kuei-chi were combined to form Shaohsing hsien after the fall of the Ch'ing), this hui-kuan's name must have been anachronistic: Proof of the post-1911 provenance of the manuscript is its use of the term *min-kuo* in the name of one of the associations which it lists. A pre-1944 (Showa 19) provenance is demonstrated by the fact that Niida purchased the manuscript in that year (as indicated by Niida's note on the inside cover).

18. Ho Ping-ti, *Chung-kuo hui-kuan shih-lun*, p. 50. On Ning-Shao merchants in Hankow during the nineteenth century, see William T. Rowe, "Urban Society in Late Imperial China: Hankow, 1796-1889," Ph.D. thesis in History, Columbia University, 1980, pp. 425-428 (pp.230-232 of the book version).

19. Ho Ping-ti, *Chung-kuo hui-kuan shih-lun*, p. 65.

20. Tsung Chi-ch'en, *Kung-ch'ih-ch'ai shih-ch'ao wen-ch'ao*, "hou-pien," 5 "hsia"/p. 4A.

21. Ho Ping-ti, *Chung-kuo hui-kuan shih-lun*, p. 40.

22. Ibid., p. 64.

23. Chang Ch'un-ming, "Ch'ing-tai ti mu-chih," *Ling-nan hsüeh-pao* 9 #2 (June 1949), p. 45.

24. Ibid.

25. Personal communication from Professor Yang Lien-sheng, November 1973.

26. Hsü K'o, comp., *Ch'ing-pai lei-ch'ao*, 84/p. 58.

27. Minami Manshū tetsudō kabushikikaisha Shanghai jimusho, ed., *Sekkō zaibatsu*, p. 7.

28. See Susan Mann Jones, "Finance in Ningpo: The 'Ch'ien Chuang,' 1750-1880" in W. E. Willmott, ed., *Economic Organization in Chinese Society*, pp. 47-77.

29. Andrea McElderry, *Shanghai Old-Style Banks (Ch'ien-chuang)*, 1800-1935, p. 63.

30. Chiang Monlin, *Tides from the West*, p. 30.

31. Ching Yüan-shan, *Ch'ü-t'ing chi-shu*, 2/pp. 4A, 5A.

32. Tōa dōbunkai, ed., *Shina keizai zensho*, vol. 7, p. 160. The Ningpo merchant population in Shanghai was estimated by the same source (p. 159) at 50,000. (Both the Shaohsing and Ningpo figures presumably include merchants' family members.) There was also a large nonmerchant population. A 1918 estimate gave the total Shaohsing population in Shanghai as 30,000 and the total Ningpo population there as over 100,000 (Lin Ch'uan-chia, ed., *Ta Chung-hua Che-chiang-sheng ti-li chih*, p. 158). For the texts of eight stele inscriptions concerning the activities of Shaohsing natives in Shanghai during the nineteenth century (especially activities involving the Shaohsing hui-kuan in Shanghai, the *Yung-hsi t'ang*), see Shanghai po-wu kuan t'u-shu tzu-liao shih, ed., *Shang-hai pei-k'o tzu-liao hsüan-chi*, pp. 207-230.

33. Jones, "Finance in Ningpo," p. 58.

34. "In 1921, out of 69 *ch'ien-chuang* in Shanghai, 38 were operated
by the Shaohsing *pang* and 16 by the Ningpo *pang.* . . . Out of
72 *ch'ien-chuang* in 1932, the Shaohsing *pang* had 35 while the
Ningpo *pang* had 17. Figures on capital show that the Shaohsing *ch'ien-chuang* accounted for almost fifty percent of the combined capital of the 72 *ch'ien-chuang.* . . and the Ningpo *ch'ien-
chuang* accounted for almost exactly twenty-five percent. . . ."
(McElderry, *Shanghai Old-Style Banks*, p. 52). Cf. Yamakami
Kaneo, *Sekkō zaibatsu ron*, pp. 106-107, which places Shaohsing-
run ch'ien-chuang ahead in numbers but Ningpo-run
ch'ien-chuang ahead in capitalization.
35. Tōa dōbunkai, ed., *Shina keizai zensho*, vol. 7, p. 160.
36. *NCH*, April 8, 1916, p. 17.
37. For more detail on this cooperation see Nishizato Yoshiyuki,
"Shinmatsu no Nimpō shōnin ni tsuite (jō)," *Tōyōshi kenkyū* 26 #1
(June 1967), p. 22, note 51.
38. Ibid.; McElderry, pp. 52-53, says "over seventy-three percent."
39. *NCH*, July 10, 1909, p. 123. For more on the establishment of
the Ning-Shao Steamship Company, see *Shina keizai hōkokusho* #5
(July 15, 1908), p. 58, and *Min-hu jih-pao*, Hsüan-t'ung 1
(1909), lunar 8th month, 11th day, p. 1.
40. The information in this paragraph comes from Shan-hsi jen
(pseud.), "Ti-ma-pan t'ui-pien wei Shaohsing-hsi ti lai-yu," *Che-
chiang yüeh-k'an* #2 (July 1968), pp. 22-23. For more on the
pao-kung-t'ou system and Ch'eng-hsien peasant opera in
Shanghai, see Ch'iu Chen, "Huai-hsiang i-chiu: Ch'eng-hsien
Ch'ung-jen so chi," *Che-chiang yüeh-k'an* #76 (August 1975), pp.
9-10. For more on musical and theatrical performances in teahouses in late Ch'ing Kiangsu and Chekiang, see Suzuki Tomoo,
"Shinmatsu Kō-Setsu no sakan ni tsuite," in *Rekishi ni okeru
minshū to bunka*, p. 532. (Shaohsing women also accounted for
most of the female tea workers in Ningpo as of 1871, according to
P'eng Tse-i, ed., *Chung-kuo chin-tai shou-kung-yeh shih tzu-liao
(1840-1949)*, vol. 2, p. 272.)
41. Hsü K'o, *Ta-shou-t'ang cha-chi*, 2/ p. 1B in Hsü K'o, *Hsin-yüan
ts'ung-k'o i-chi*.
42. Ibid., 2/pp. 1B-2A.
43. CCKK, p. 111.
44. Hsü K'o, *K'o yen*, 9/p. 6A. The U.S. consul in Hangchow, writing in 1905, adds to the list all of Hangchow's wine merchants,
plus many of its bankers, money changers, and blacksmiths
(Frederick Cloud, *Hangchow the "City of Heaven,"* p. 10).
45. Hsü K'o, ibid. One Shaohsing rice merchant in Hangchow was
called a traitor when in 1911 he sold to foreign countries at a
time of local shortage *(Min li pao*, April 16, 1911, p. 4).
46. *TFTC* 3 #8, Kuang-hsü 32 (1906), lunar 7th month, section "chün
shih," p. 148.
47. Ho Ping-ti, *Chung-kuo hui-kuan shih-lun*, p. 103. For more on
Shaohsing rice merchants operating in Soochow, see Hung Huan-
ch'un, "Lun Ming-Ch'ing Su-chou ti-chu hui-kuan ti hsing-chih
chi ch'i tso-yung," *Chung-kuo shih yen-chiu* #2 (June 1980), pp.
4, 14; for more on Shaohsing soysauce merchants in Soochow, see
ibid., pp 5, 10.
48. Ho Ping-ti, *Chung-kuo hui-kuan shih-lun*, p. 104. Shaohsing
flannel dyers established a guild in Soochow in 1870 (see Hung
Huan-ch'un,"Lun Ming-Ch'ing Su-chou," pp. 9-10). Shaohsing
natives' expertise in cloth dyeing dates from at least the Ming.
An official "weaving and dyeing bureau" *(chih-jan chü)* producing
an annual quota, apparently for Court consumption, was
established in Shaohsing during the Hung-wu reign (1368-1398).

See *Ming-shih, shih-huo-chih,* 82/p. 9B. This item is indexed in Hung Yeh, ed., *Shih-huo-chih shih-wu-chung tsung-ho yin-te,* p. 381.

49. *T'ung-wen Hu-pao,* Kuang-hsü 28 (1902), lunar 7th month, 7th day, p. 3.

50. *T'ung-wen Hu-pao,* Kuang-hsü 30 (1904), lunar 3rd month, 24th day, unpaginated (Soochow section).

51. *T'ung-wen Hu-pao,* Kuang-hsü 30 (1904), lunar 12th month, 3rd day, unpaginated (Soochow section). Shaohsing natives (especially those from Shan-yin and Kuei-chi) dominated both the manufacture and sale of wax candles in Soochow. Their guildhall, the *Tung Yüeh hui-kuan,* was established in Soochow during the Chia-ch'ing period (1796-1820) and rebuilt in 1892. See Hung Huan-ch'un, "Lun Ming-Ch'ing Su-chou," pp. 5, 8, 12 and Lü Tso-hsieh, "Ming–Ch'ing shih-ch'i ti hui-kuan ping fei kung-shang-yeh hang-hui," *Chung-kuo shih yen-chiu* #14 (June 1982), p. 73. (Hung, p. 5, also mentions that Ning-Shao natives occupied a dominant position among Soochow's coal dealers.)

52. *Shih pao,* September 18, 1911, p. 4. China's first private letter agencies, which served as the traditional postal system, are said to have begun during the Ming in the port of Ningpo in order to deliver the prolific correspondence of Shaohsing's mu-yu (Ying-wan Cheng, *Postal Communication in China and its Modernization, 1860-1896,* p. 37).

53. *Shih pao,* September 18, 1911, p. 4.

54. Ho Ping-ti, *Chung-kuo hui-kuan shih-lun,* p. 6. In 1777 (Ch'ien-lung 42), the emperor granted an audience to an official about to be assigned to Shaohsing. But he noticed that the man had a Shaohsing accent, apparently a breach of the law of avoidance. The official had a ready answer: He had lived in Shaohsing as a child for several years while his father had business there (whether official or commercial is not clear), and had picked up the local accent. The emperor was not completely convinced (ibid., pp. 6-7).

55. Ibid., p. 6.

56. Peng Chang, "The Distribution and Relative Strength of the Provincial Merchant Groups in China, 1842-1911," Ph.D. thesis in Economics, University of Washington (Seattle), 1958, pp. 47-48. After three generations' residence, the new abode legally became one's yüan-chi. But in practice there is disagreement among Chinese over the determination of one's native place (ku-hsiang). See Ts'ao Chü-jen, *Wan-li hsing-chi,* p. 281, where the case of Chou En-lai is cited.

57. Guy Boulais, *Manuel du code chinois,* pp. 161-162.

58. For the case of a Chin-hua, Chekiang native who falsely registered in Shun-t'ien for examination purposes during the K'ang-hsi period, see Wu Ch'eng-ch'iao, comp., *Ch'ing-tai li-chih ts'ung-t'an,* 1/ p. 171. For more on "the widespread practice of falsified and dual registration," see William T. Rowe, "Urban Society," p. 446 ff. In a remark that applies perfectly to Shaohsing, Rowe notes, "[F]or natives of such talent-rich areas as Hui-chou and Yangchow to fit into local quotas for the taking and passing of exams it was almost necessary for them to sit for these in a locality other than that of their origin. This meant the establishment of registration elsewhere. . . ." (p. 443; in book version p. 239, with minor stylistic changes).

59. Shih Shan-ch'ang, *Lun-t'ai tsa-chi,* section "hsia," p. 19A.

60. Miao Ch'uan-chi, *Ming-tai hsü-li,* p. 123.

61. Iriya Yoshitaka, ed., *Kinsei suihitsu shū,* p. 210, being a Japanese translation of a passage in Hsieh Chao-chih, *Wu-tsa-tsu,* chüan 14 (pp. 412-413 of the 1959 Peking edition). The original passage has been checked against the translation.

62. L. Carrington Goodrich and Fang Chao-ying, eds., *Dictionary of Ming Biography*, p. 1420.
63. This prohibition is reprinted in a late Ming guide for officials, Wang Shih-mao's *Shih-t'u hsien-ching*, 3/ pp. 29A-29B. For more on Ming policy towards mao-chi, see Shen Te-fu, *Wan-li yeh-huo pien*, 14/ p. 374 of the 1959 Peking edition.
64. On the basis of his own on-site study of Peking guild inscriptions, Niida Noboru corrects Katō by noting that the members of the Nan yin-chu were specifically from Shang-yü county in Shaohsing prefecture and Tz'u-ch'i county in Ningpo prefecture (Saeki Yūichi and Tanaka Issei, eds., *Niida Noboru hakase shu Pekin kōshō girudo shiryo shu (ichi)*, p. 137 and Niida Noboru, *Chūgoku hōseishi*, rev. ed., p. 162).
65. Katō Shigeshi, "Shindai ni okeru Pekin no shōnin kaikan ni tsuite," *Shigaku zasshi* 53 #2 (February 1942), pp. 155-157. This article is reprinted in Katō's *Shina keizaishi kōshō*. Cf. Li Hua, "Ming-Ch'ing i-lai," pp. 66, 70, which testifies to the prominence of Shaohsing moneylenders in Peking during the K'ang-hsi period and dates the founding of their hui-kuan at 1667.
66. Lu Hsün, "Preface to 'A Call to Arms'," *SWLH*, vol. 1, p. 5.
67. Lu Hsün's diary records that he moved into the Shan-Kuei i-kuan on the sixth day of the fifth month, 1912, immediately upon his arrival in Peking (*Lu Hsün jih-chi*, vol. 1, p. 3). For proof that this establishment was the same as the Shaohsing hsien-kuan, see Ting Ts'ai-san, *Shaohsing hsien-kuan chi-lueh*, p. 1A; also Ts'ao Chü-jen, *Lu Hsün p'ing-chuan*, p. 46.
68. Ting Ts'ai-san, ed., *Shaohsing hsien-kuan chi-lüeh*, p. 7B. An inscription written by Niida on the front page of the copy in the Institute of Oriental Culture notes that this item was purchased for him in Peking by Imabori Seiji in 1943.
69. Ibid., p. 6A.
70. Ibid.
71. Ibid., p. 6B.
72. Ibid.

Chapter Five

1. Ho Ping-ti, *The Ladder of Success*, p. 253.
2. Ibid., p. 236.
3. Shen Pang, *Wan-shu tsa-chi*, pp. 24-26.
4. Nor was Shun-t'ien the only locale where Shaohsing natives served as subofficials during the Ming. *SHTL*, section "jen-wu lieh-chuan," provides at least twelve examples of Shan-yin and Kuei-chi natives serving as subofficials outside of Shun-t'ien prefecture during the Ming: five county jail wardens (tien-shih), four registrars (chu-pu), two assistant hsien magistrates (hsien-ch'eng), and one prefectural commissary of records (ching-li). The breakdown by native county for the holders of these twelve posts is six from Shan-yin, three from Kuei-chi, and three from "Shaohsing" (county unspecified). The breakdown by province in which the twelve posts were located is four in Hunan, three in Fukien, and one each in Kiangsu, Kiangsi, Honan, Hupei, and Pei Chih-li. (The biographies from which these data were culled are located on pp. 12A, 12B, 38A, 40B, 44B, 51A, and 63B.) Since *SHTL's* coverage is limited to the former Shan-yin and Kuei-chi counties it does not include subofficials native to other counties in Shaohsing. It does clearly indicate, however, that Shaohsing's production of subofficials began not in the Ch'ing but in the

Ming, and that their service during the Ming was not limited to Shun-t'ien.

5. Hsü K'o, *Ta-shou-t'ang cha-chi*, 3/p. 19A. Hsü also suggests in this passage (p. 19B) that many of these Shan-yin and Kuei-chi natives serving as subofficials were former mu-yu.

6. No law of avoidance was enforced for mu-yu, clerks, and yamen underlings. Nor does the *Ta Ch'ing chin-shen chüan-shu* (or any other known source) include detailed, long-term data on persons serving in these occupations.

7. Omitted are the few subofficials whose names are not provided.

8. In order to rank Shaohsing's counties by per capita production of subofficials, I have taken the number of each county's natives serving as subofficials outside of Chekiang in 1892 (listed above) and divided that number by the county's population in 1933, which is the first year after 1791 for which we have point-in-time population figures for all of Shaohsing's counties. (The 1933 population figures have already been presented above.) I have then arbitrarily multiplied the resulting fraction by 10^6 to eliminate zeros and produce easily comparable index numbers. For example, the resulting index number for Hsiao-shan is 33 divided by 499,321 times 10^6 = 66.0. Obviously this index number does not correlate precisely with Hsiao-shan's production of subofficials per capita in 1892, since the total-population figure (the denominator) is anachronistic by forty-odd years. But if we may assume that the distortion caused by the anachronistic total-population figures is approximately the same for each of Shaohsing's counties, then the resulting index numbers are useful as approximate indicators of production of subofficials per capita in 1892.

9. Unfortunately the 1933 population figures do not allow us to compute separate index numbers for Shan-yin and Kuei-chi, since these two metropolitan counties had already been combined to form "Shaohsing county."

10. The admonition is reprinted in his lineage's genealogy, *Kuei-chi Ch'in-shih tsung-p'u*, 1911, ts'e 2, "Huang-ching chü-shih hsün-tzu pien," pp. 1A-7A. The quotes below are from pp. 5A-6A. For biographical detail on the mu-yu author and his jail warden son, see ibid., p. 2A and ts'e 1, *shih-piao*, p. 17A. Taga number 605.

11. Lu Hsün, "Two or Three Things Chinese," *SWLH*, vol. 4, p. 30. For a description of prison conditions in the early Ch'ing see Huang Liu-hung, *A Complete Book Concerning Happiness and Benevolence, Fu-hui ch'üan-shu: A Manual for Local Magistrates in Seventeenth-Century China*, pp. 307-318.

12. Compiled from *Ta Ch'ing chin-shen ch'üan-shu*, Fall, Kuang-hsü 18 (1892). The percentage of all tien-shih for Kuei-chi was 3 percent (42/1201).

13. Reprinted (with continuous pagination) as volume 130 in the series "Chin-tai Chung-kuo shih-liao ts'ung-k'an," published by Wen-hai, Taipei, 1967. The copy used is held by Sterling Library, Yale. This reprint of the Kuang-hsü 30 edition has been retitled *Chüeh-chih ch'üan-lan*.

14. See the maps on pp. 214-215 of G. William Skinner, ed., *The City in Late Imperial China*.

15. It should also be noted that seventeen of the top twenty subofficial-producing counties in 1904 were metropolitan counties, i.e., those which include the prefectural capital within their boundaries. (This pattern of metropolitan counties being disproportionate producers of subofficials is discussed further in Appendix B.) Among the top twenty counties, the only ones which were not metropolitan counties are Ching-hsien (#18),

Hsiao-shan (#20), and T'ung-ch'eng (#7). The fact that T'ung-ch'eng county, Anhui, was an outstanding producer of subofficials is intriguing. For Hilary Beattie's excellent study of T'ung-ch'eng argues that it was a locale where elite families perpetuated their power through the centuries by emphasizing landholding rather than officeholding: "It is therefore impossible to claim that in T'ung-ch'eng academic degrees and office were the sole precondition of wealth; rather, they were the occasional results of it" *(Land and Lineage in China*, p. 131). Yet the fact that in 1904 T'ung-ch'eng ranked seventh among all the counties in China in production of subofficials suggests that officeholding (at subofficial rather than more exalted levels) may have been more important in the long-term survival strategies of T'ung-ch'eng's gentry than Beattie has realized. Here is but another example of how the study of subofficials might reveal patterns of considerable significance that would otherwise escape our attention.

Chapter Six

1. Kao Yüeh-t'ien, "Shen Ting-i hsien-sheng ti i-sheng (i)," *Che-chiang yüeh-k'an* 4 #4 (April 1972), p. 5. See also the citations in notes 4 and 5 below.
2. Cited by Ho Ping-ti, *The Ladder of Success*, p. 251.
3. See Julia Ching's biography of Wang Chi in L. Carrington Goodrich and Chaoying Fang, eds., *Dictionary of Ming Biography*, pp. 1351-1355.
4. Chou Tso-jen, *Chih-t'ang hui-hsiang lu*, p. 50.
5. Liu Ta-pai, *Ku-shih ti t'an-tzu*, pp. 13-14.
6. Kao Yüeh-t'ien, "Shen Ting-i hsien-sheng ti i-sheng (i)," p. 5.
7. Wu Ching-tzu, *The Scholars*, p. 279. This famous novel also includes a Shaohsing mu-yu, Niu Pu-i, among its characters. Ibid., p. 161.
8. Lu Hsün, "K'ung I-chi," *SWLH*, vol. 1, pp. 24-25.
9. Chou Tso-jen, *Chih-t'ang hui-hsiang lu*, p. 50.
10. On the special conditions of the chü-jen examination in Shun-t'ien, see Liu Ta-pai, *Ku-shih ti t'an-tzu*, p. 59 and Chang Chung-li, *The Chinese Gentry*, p. 22. For examples of Shaohsing natives passing the chü-jen examination in Shun-t'ien, see *Shaohsing fu-chih*, 1792, chüan 33, passim.
11. Chang Chung-li, ibid., p. 22 and p. 167, note 9.
12. Ting Ts'ai-san, ed., *Shaohsing hsien-kuan chi-lüeh*, p. 6A.
13. Frederic Wakeman, Jr., *The Fall of Imperial China*, p. 22.
14. Wang Chieh-mou, "Ch'ing-tai ti Shaohsing shih-yeh," *Che-chiang yüeh-k'an* 2 #2 (January 1970), p. 19.
15. Ibid., pp. 18-19.
16. Ting Ts'ai-san, *Shaohsing hsien-kuan chi-lüeh*, pp. 6A-6B.
17. Miao Ch'uan-chi, *Ming-tai hsü-li*, p. 264. Miao gives as his source the *Ta Ch'ing hui-tien shih-li*, chüan 147.
18. Wang Chieh-mou, "Ch'ing-tai," pp. 18-19.
19. Miao Ch'üan-chi, *Ming-tai hsü-li*, p. 285. Information on actual practice is of course scarcer than on statutory regulations. Thus E-tu Zen Sun's detailed article on "The Board of Revenue in Nineteenth Century China," *Harvard Journal of Asiatic Studies* #24 (1962-1963), based largely on the *Hui-tien*, contains no discussion of the Board's clerks.
20. Hosoi Shōji, "Shinsho no shori," *Shakai keizei shigaku* 14 #6 (September 1944), p. 10.
21. Wang Chieh-mou, "Ch'ing-tai," p. 19. The possibility of an interrelationship between Shaohsing Central Board clerks and

Shaohsing merchants in Peking is speculated on inconclusively in Hosoi Shōji, "Shinsho no shori," p. 9.

22. Miao Ch'üan-chi, *Ch'ing-tai mu-fu jen-shih chih-tu*, p. 11. The Shen Te-fu quote is from his *Wan-li yeh-huo pien, pu-i*, 3/ p. 33 (p. 889 of the 1959 Peking edition). Shen speaks in terms of "eastern Chekiang" *(Che-tung)*, but Miao clearly understands this to refer to Shaohsing.

23. Yabuuchi Kiyoshi, *Chūgoku no sūgaku*, chapter 5. For a detailed study of Chekiang (including Shaohsing) mathematicians, which does not indicate, however, any particularly widespread knowledge of mathematics on the popular level in Shaohsing, see Ch'ien Pao-ts'ung, "Che-chiang ch'ou-jen cho-shu chi," *Wen-lan hsüeh-pao* 3 #1 (January-March 1937), pp. 1597-1608.

24. Hsieh Chao-chih, *Wu tsa tsu*, 8/pp. 4B-5A (p. 209 of the 1959 Peking edition).

25. Chao-lien, *Hsiao-t'ing tsa-lu*, section "Ming-mo feng-su," p. 512 of the 1980 Peking edition. Chao's dates are given as 1780-1833 in Hummel, *Eminent Chinese*, p. 78, but I prefer those given on p. 3 of the punctuator's preface to *Hsiao-t'ing tsa-lu*.

26. Chu Pao-chiung and Hsieh P'ei-lin, comps., *Ming-Ch'ing chin-shih t'i-ming pei-lu so-yin*, p. 760.

27. Goodrich and Fang, eds., *Dictionary of Ming Biography*, p. 328.

28. See Chu Keng's biography in the *Ming Shih*, chüan 219 (p. 2538 of the Taiwan Kuo-fang yen-chiu yüan edition).

29. Ting Ts'ai-san, ed., *Shaohsing hsien-kuan chi-lüeh*, p. 6A.

30. Wang Chieh-mou, "Ch'ing-tai," p. 19.

31. Miao Chüan-chi, *Ch'ing-tai mu-fu jen-shih chih-tu*, p. 10.

32. Miao Ch'üan-chi, *Ming-tai hsü-li*, p. 286.

33. Wang Chieh-mou, "Ch'ing-tai," p. 19.

34. Susan Naquin, "Millenarian Rebellion in China: The Eight Trigrams Uprising of 1813," pp. 89-90. The book version, pp. 72-73, has minor stylistic differences.

35. Thomas Metzger, *The Internal Organization of Ch'ing Bureaucracy*, pp. 149-150.

36. Ibid., p. 149.

37. On the Central Board clerks' expert knowledge of the precedents and the clerks' resultant power, see Miao Ch'üan-chi, "Ch'ing-tai hsü-li shu-kai (hsia)," *Ssu-hsiang yü shih-tai* #129 (April 1965), p. 15. For fascinating detail on how the clerks maintained closely-guarded "secret compilations" of new precedents, keyed to the relevant statutes, in order to perpetuate their legal expertise, see Fan P'u-chai, "Lüeh lun ch'ien-Ch'ing li-hsü," *Kuang-ming jih-pao*, January 1, 1957, p. 3.

38. Wang Chieh-mou, "Ch'ing-tai," p. 19. For more on the use of Central Board clerks as local officials' mu-yu, see also Miyazaki Ichisada, "Shindai no shori to bakuyū," *Tōyōshi kenkyū* 16 #4 (March 1958), p. 9; Miao Ch'üan-chi, *Ch'ing-tai mu-fu jen-shih chih-tu*, p. 11; and Miao Ch'üan-chi, "Ch'ing-tai hsing-mu shu-yao," p. 326.

39. Miao Ch'üan-chi, "Ch'ing-tai hsü-li shu-kai (hsia)," p. 15. Also Miao Ch'üan-chi, *Ming-tai hsü-li*, p. 284.

40. Miao Ch'üan-chi, *Ming-tai hsü-li*, p. 284.

41. Hsieh Chao-chih, *Wu tsa tsu*, 15/p. 5B (p. 426 of the 1959 Peking edition).

42. Ku Yen-wu, *Jih chih lu chi-shih*, 8/pp. 18B-19A, as cited in Ch'ü T'ung-tsu, *Local Government*, pp. 268-269, note 169. Ku's passage has been checked by me against Ch'ü's citation, which is to the Ssu-pu pei-yao edition.

43. Ch'ü, *Local Government*, p. 269, note 169.

44. Shen Te-fu, *Wan-li yeh-huo pien*, 24/p. 610 (Peking edition, 1959). Shen's preface is dated Wan-li 34 (1606).
45. The "Six Boards" statement by Ch'en Lung-cheng is quoted in Mitamura Taisuke, *Min to Shin*, p. 144. I have been unable to check Ch'en's original text. But compare the following paraphrase of this same statement by Ch'en in Ch'ien Mu, *Traditional Government in Imperial China: A Critical Analysis*, p. 107: "The Empire's good government or disorder depends on the Six Ministries and the clerks of the Six Ministries are all Shao-hsing men. . . . When the clerks have changed for the better, the Empire will be well governed." The joke is from Chen's *Chi-t'ing ch'üan-shu*, 44/p. 21A. This passage is in an undated letter, but since Ch'en died in 1645, it presumably reflects late Ming attitudes. (Punctuation was inserted by an earlier reader.)
46. Wang Shih-hsing, *Kuang chih i*, 4/p. 6A. I am grateful to Prof. Joseph McDermott for bringing this passage to my attention.
47. *Ta Ch'ing li-ch'ao shih-lu*, Shun-chih 8, 54/pp. 4B-5A (pp. 628-629 of the Taiwan reprint).
48. Chou Hsia-shou, *Lu Hsün ti ku-chia*, p. 401.
49. Quoted in Ts'ao Chü-jen, *Wan-li hsing-chi*, p. 240. This same quotation is cited in Chang Ch'un-ming, "Ch'ing-tai ti mu-chih," p. 45. Feng's statement (part of an essay entitled "A Proposal to Transform the Clerks") can be found in Sheng K'ang, ed., *Huang-ch'ao ching-shih wen-pien hsü-pien*, 28/p. 38B (p. 2928 of the Taiwan reprint). Nor should we assume that Shaohsing clerks were uniformly admired within Shaohsing itself: One of the undated "family instructions" in a lineage genealogy from either Shan-yin or Kuei-chi reads, "Descendants, do not become clerks" *(li-hsü) (Shaohsing Yu-lin-kuan Chin-shih tsung-p'u*, section "ko fei chang," p. 1A. Taga number 352). Unfortunately it is unclear whether this lineage injunction was directed against Central Board clerks, or those in local Shaohsing yamens, or both. Except for Hangchow and perhaps Shun-t'ien, there is no evidence that Shaohsing natives were prominent as clerks in local officials' yamens outside of Shaohsing.
50. Hsü Ta-ling, *Ch'ing-tai chüan-na chih-tu*, p. 82.
51. Ibid., pp. 111-112.
52. Ibid., plates 2, 3, and 4 are photographs of actual purchased commissions issued by the Board of Revenue.
53. This phrase is used in reference to Shaohsing natives in the late Ming collection of stories *Chin-ku ch'i-kuan*, by Pao-weng lao-jen, pseud., section "Ts'ai hsiao-chieh jen-ju pao-ch'ou." I am indebted to Dr. Ming K. Chan for bringing this reference to my attention. The same phrase, *fei kuo hai*, is also used by the late Ming official Ch'en Lung-cheng *(Chi-t'ing wai-shu*, 4/p. 38A) to describe local yamen clerks who take their ill-gotten gains to Peking in order to buy official posts. Shaohsing is not mentioned specifically.
54. These statistics on purchase of chou and hsien magistracies are from Kondō Hideki, "Shindai no ennō to kanryō shakai no shūmatsu (chū)," *Shirin* 46 #3 (May 1963), pp. 80-81, 84, 95. Kondō compiled his statistics from the *Ta Ch'ing chin-shen ch'üan-shu*.
55. The date of the first appearance of mu-yu as civil officials' private secretaries and legal advisers is the subject of some disagreement. In Fang Chao-ying's opinion, "The system of employing private secretaries by civil officials developed in the early Ch'ing period" (Goodrich and Fang, eds., *Dictionary of Ming Biography*, p. 754). But Ch'ü T'ung-tsu states that "the employment of private secretaries in local government began in the

Ming" *(Local Government*, p. 258, note 8). In addition to the considerable evidence presented by Ch'ü to support his statement, it is clear that as early as 1593 the Wan-p'ing county yamen contained a *mu-t'ing* (mu-yu's office). See Shen Pang, *Wan-shu tsa-chi*, p. 19. Unfortunately there are no sources extant which describe the origins of the judicial and tax mu-yu (hsing-ming and ch'ien-ku). See Miao Ch'üan-chi, *Ch'ing-tai mu-fu jen-shih chih-tu*, p. 282 and Na Ssu-lu, *Ch'ing-tai chou-hsien ya-men shen-p'an chih-tu*, p. 23.

56. *NCH*, September 25, 1915, p. 869.
57. Wang Hui-tsu, *Ping-t'a meng-hen lu*, section "shang," p. 9A, in Wang Hui-tsu, *Wang Lung-chuang i-shu*. Wang's father was a county jail warden (tien-shih) in Honan. See Abe Takeo, *Shindaishi no kenkyū*, p. 579 and Ho Ping-ti, *The Ladder of Success*, p. 292.
58. Wang Hui-tsu, *Shuang-chieh-t'ang yung hsün*, 5/p. 13A, in Wang Hui-tsu, *Wang Lung-chuang i-shu*.
59. Quoted in Miao Ch'üan-chi, *Ch'ing-tai mu-fu jen-shih chih-tu*, p. 257.
60. Fan Yin, *Yüeh yen*, section "chung," p. 12B.
61. Lu Hsün, "Tzu-chuan" (autobiographical sketch dated May 16, 1930), in *Lu Hsün ch'üan-chi*, vol. 20 (Shanghai, 1938), p. 609. Also published as a preface to Wang Yeh-ch'iu, *Min-yüan-chien ti Lu Hsün hsien-sheng*, p. 5. Chou Tso-jen tells us that his (and thus Lu Hsün's) family traditionally considered the mu-yu profession to be a natural one for examination failers and others unable to rise above sheng-yüan status (Chou Hsia-shou, *Lu Hsün ti ku-chia*, p. 210).
62. Wang Hui-tsu, *Tso-chih yao-yen*, p. 1.
63. Wang Hui-tsu, *Shuang-chieh-t'ang yung-hsün*, 5/pp. 15A-15B.
64. David S. Nivison, *The Life and Thought of Chang Hsüeh-ch'eng*, p. 284. For a discussion of the emphasis placed on specialization and practicality by the Eastern Chekiang school of historiography in general, and by Chang Hsüeh-ch'eng in particular, see also Ts'ang Hsiu-liang, "Chang Hsüeh-ch'eng yü Che-tung she-hsueh," *Chung-kuo shih yen-chiu* #9 (March 1981), pp. 116-120.
65. Nivison, *Life and Thought*, pp. 20-21.
66. W.T. de Bary, "Chinese Despotism and the Confucian Ideal: A Seventeenth-Century View," in John K. Fairbank, ed., *Chinese Thought and Institutions*, pp. 172-173.
67. This passage is not dated; but the author of the section of the *chia-hsün* in which the passage appears, "Shih-shih-kung" (i.e., one Hu Jen-chi), flourished during the Yung-cheng and Ch'ien-lung periods, as is clear from the dates of essays by him elsewhere in the genealogy (27/pp. 50B, 51A-51B).
68. *Shan-yin Chang-ch'uan Hu-shih tsung-p'u*, 21/p. 9A. Taga number 474. Compare Confucius in *The Analects* (Legge's translation, Book IV, Chapter XI): "The superior man thinks of the sanctions of the law; the small man thinks of favours which he may receive."
69. *T'ung-wen Hu-pao*, Kuang-hsü 30 (1904), lunar 2nd month, 27th day, unpaginated (Hangchow section).
70. *Yung-cheng chu-pi yü-chih*, memorials of Li Wei, 2/pp. 47A-47B (p. 4340 of the Taiwan photoreprint edition). My attention was called to this passage by Ch'ü T'ung-tsu, *Local Government*, p. 268, note 169.
71. T'u Chien-lu, "Pai-mu shih-yeh ti ku-shih," *Min-chien yüeh-k'an* 2 #9 (September 1933), p. 189.
72. Ts'ao Chü-jen, *Pei-hsing san-yü*, p. 50.

73. Translation by Étienne Balazs in his *Political Theory and Adminis-trative Reality in Traditional China*, pp. 68-69. In regard to the spread of corruption during the mid-Ch'ing, Nivison notes that the dates cited by Wang Hui-tsu in this passage coincide with the rise of Ho-shen, on whom, Nivison argues, Wang was implicitly placing the blame (David S. Nivison, "Ho-shen and His Accusers: Ideology and Political Behavior in the Eighteenth Century," in David S. Nivison and Arthur F. Wright, eds., *Confucianism in Action*, pp. 216-217). It should be noted that Wang's contempor-ary Hung Liang-chi made a similar attack on Ho-shen's corrupting influence. See Suzuki Chūsei, *Shinchō chūkishi kenkyū*, p. 48.

74. For an important statistical study of the sale of chou and hsien magistracies from 1724 to 1910, see Kondō Hideki, "Shindai no ennō to kanryū shakai no shūmatsu," *Shirin* 46 #2, #3, #4 (March, May, July 1963).

75. *Shan-yin P'ang-shih tsung-p'u*, ts'e 4, pp. 47A-50A is the source for my discussion of the P'angs. (This manuscript genealogy is unpaginated. The page numbers indicated are as counted from the beginning of ts'e 4.)

76. Herbert Giles, *A Chinese-English Dictionary* (2nd ed., 1912), p. 880 defines li-yüan as "officials who have gained admission into the public service, by examination, from among the ranks of clerks in the Government Boards, Peking." The P'ang genealogy (ts'e 4, p. 47A) confirms the accuracy of Giles' definition by noting that the position of local postmaster in Kansu held by Chao-hsiao was "conferred after examination" (*hsüan-shou*).

77. Hsien-wei is a synonym for tien-shih, county jail warden. See Morohashi Tetsuji, *Dai Kanwa jiten*, vol. 8, p. 1146 and Ni-Chū minzoku kagaku kenkyūjo, ed., *Chūgoku rekidai shokukan jiten*, p. 82.

78. For the first father-and-son example, see *Kuei-chi Ch'in-shih tsung-p'u*, 1911, ts'e 1, shih-piao, p. 12A. For the second example, see ibid., p. 13A.

79. One mu-yu from Shaohsing (county unknown) during the Yung-cheng period was known to "study the Legalists' writings" (*hsi fa-chia yen*) (Wu Ch'eng-ch'iao, comp., *Ch'ing-tai li-chih ts'ung-t'an*, 1/p. 182); a mu-yu from Kuei-chi during the Kuang-hsü period is described similarly (*SHTL*, section "jen-wu lieh-chüan," p. 210B). Another Kuei-chi native "studied the Legalists' writ-ings" after abandoning the examination path, presumably during the Chia-ch'ing period, and later became a mu-yu (ibid., p. 81B). A Shan-yin native "studied the Legalists' writings as a youth" before serving as mu-yu in Yunnan during the Tao-kuang period (ibid., p. 74B).

80. The information on Chin-chien is from *Kuei-chi Ch'in-shih tsung-p'u*, ts'e 1, shih-piao, pp. 21A-21B, 22B. (See ibid., 17A-17B, 25A-25B for information on the Ch'in's four consecutive genera-tions of subofficials.) For confirmation that Chin-chien did indeed pass the chin-shih examination in 1840 (Tao-kuang 20), see Fang Chao-ying and Tu Lien-che, comps., *Tseng-chiao Ch'ing-ch'ao chin-shih t'i-ming pei-lu fu yin-te*, p. 171, center column, name #25. Like many of his fellow Shaohsing natives, he was registered as a native of Wan-p'ing, Shun-t'ien.

81. The above figures on chin-shih production are from Ho Ping-ti, *The Ladder of Success*, pp. 246, 247, 254.

82. Hsü Ko, *Ta-shou-t'ang cha-chi*, 3/p. 19A.

83. Ho Ping-ti, *The Ladder of Success*, p. 253.

84. Ibid., p. 346, note 33. The percentage was computed from Ho's figures.

85. Miao Ch'üan-chi, *Ch'ing-tai mu-fu jen-shih chih-tu*, p. 282. There is, however, evidence that handbooks containing professional secrets were passed in manuscript from mu-yu father to son. See ibid., p. 157; Miao, "Ch'ing-tai hsing-mu shu-yao," p. 354; and Cheng T'ien-t'ing, "Ch'ing-tai ti mu-fu," *Chung-kuo she-hui k'o-hsüeh* #6 (November 1980), p. 140.

86. For an indication that Shaohsing natives were also well represented among the mu-yu of governors and governors-general (i.e., at the upper level of the provincial bureaucracy), see Hsü K'o, *Ta-shou-t'ang cha-chi*, 3/p. 19A.

87. Kenneth Folsom, *Friends, Guests, and Colleagues: The Mu-fu System in the Late Ch'ing Period*, pp. 46-47. In the final sentence Folsom is quoting Edward H. Parker, *China, Past and Present* (London, 1903), p. 246.

88. T'ao Hsi-sheng, *Ch'ing-tai chou-hsien ya-men hsing-shih shen-p'an chih-tu chi ch'eng-hsü*, p. 10.

89. *Chang-shih hui-p'u*, section "chuan," p. 2A. Taga number 711.

90. Compiled from the chart of Tseng's mu-yu in Miao Ch'üan-chi, *Ch'ing-tai mu-fu jen-shih chih-tu*, p. 311.

91. Jonathan Porter's statement that "Actually, Shao-hsing natives were by no means prevalent in *mu-fu* positions" must be understood in the context of Porter's concentration on Tseng Kuo-fan's mu-yu (Porter, *Tseng Kuo-fan's Private Bureaucracy*, p. 20).

92. Hsü K'o, *Ta-shou-t'ang cha-chi*, 3/p. 19A. See Appendix B for statistics on subofficials from Ch'ang-chou prefecture.

93. G. M. H. Playfair, *The Cities and Towns of China*, 2nd ed., p. 26.

94. For the story of a veteran Shan-yin mu-yu serving in Hunan whose protégés held most of the fu- and hsien-level mu-yu positions in the province, sharing their salaries with their master, see Hsü K'o, comp., *Ch'ing-pai lei-ch'ao*, 82/p. 22. A memorial written in 1894 states that lower-level mu-yu got their jobs through recommendation by higher-level mu-yu and might not even be competent *(Kuang-hsü ch'ao Tung-hua lu* (Peking, 1958), p. 3482).

95. For a brief, general statement (apparently written during the T'ung-chih or early Kuang-hsü periods) deploring the widespread existence of vertical cliques composed of provincial-level mu-yu and their protégés serving as chou- and hsien-level mu-yu, see Ko Shih-chün, ed., *Huang-ch'ao ching-shih-wen hsü-pien*, 23/pp. 2B-3A (first essay by Ho Kuei-fang). Shaohsing natives are not mentioned specifically.

96. Ts'ao Chü-jen, *Wan-li hsing-chi*, p. 241. For more on alliances between local officials' mu-yu and Central Board clerks during the Yung-cheng period, see Miyazaki Ichisada, "Shindai no shori to bakuyū," p. 9.

97. Chang Ch'un-ming, "Ch'ing-tai ti mu-chih," p. 45.

98. Quoted in Hosoi Shōji, "Shinsho no shori," p. 9.

99. Wang Chieh-mou, "Ch'ing-tai," p. 19.

100. Liang Chang-chü, *Lang-chi hsü-t'an*, 4/p. 5B, in Liang Chang-chü, *Liang-shih pi-chi*.

101. Hsü K'o, comp., *Ch'ing-pai lei-ch'ao*, 28/p. 2.

102. A very unconvincing argument for Shaohsing natives' genetic superiority can be found in Ch'üan Tseng-yu, "Ch'ing-tai mu-liao chih-tu lun (hsü)," *Ssu-hsiang yü shih-tai* #32 (March 1944), p. 38. Ch'üan was apparently influenced by P'an Kuang-tan's contemporaneous popularization of eugenics.

103. *Kuang-hsü ch'ao Tung-hua lu*, Kuang-hsü 20 (1894), lunar 9th month, "chi hai" (p. 3482 of the 1958 Peking edition). This pas-

sage was called to my attention by Hatano Yoshihiro, *Chugoku kindai kogyoshi no kenkyū*, p. 65, note 14A.

Epilogue

1. The hope, of course, was that the existence of a Western-style judicial system would undercut the imperialists' case for extraterritoriality. On the central government's plan, conceived in 1905, to establish law schools at the national and provincial levels, see *Shinkoku jihō* #6, July 20, Meiji 38 (1905), p. 35 and #8, September 20, Meiji 38 (1905), p. 41. Chekiang's new system of lawcourts *(shen-p'an-t'ing)* went into effect in 1910 *(Chengchih kuan-pao* #885, Hsüan-t'ung 2 (1910), lunar 3rd month, 9th day, pp. 9–11).

2. Ts'ao Chü-jen, *Wan-li hsing-chi*, p. 242.

3. Rinji Taiwan kyūkan chōsakai, *Shinkoku gyōseiho*, vol. 5, p. 124. For the Ch'ing statute authorizing punishment of pettifoggers, see also Guy Boulais, *Manuel du code chinois*, p. 652. A recent study of pettifoggers is Kawakatsu Mamoru's "Minmatsu Shinsho no shōshi ni tsuite," *Kyūshu daigaku tōyōshi ronshu* #9 (March 1981), pp. 111–129. In this article Kawakatsu cites evidence (not specifically from Shaohsing) demonstrating that pettifoggers (sung-shih) commonly allied with yamen clerks and served as private legal advisers to gentry (pp. 125–126). Yet although Kawakatsu finds that some pettifoggers did indeed exploit the common people, he also cites evidence (p. 128) of "a pettifogger who sided with the masses" and led a popular uprising in Hangchow in 1583 (Wan-li 10). This pettifogger, named Ting Shih-ch'ing, was a native of Shaohsing's Shang-yü county. Kawakatsu concludes that it is not yet possible to offer a definitive evaluation of pettifoggers' politics.

4. Kan Han, ed., *Huang-ch'ao ching-shih-wen hsin-pien hsü-chi*, 4/ p. 27A. Pages 26A–27A contain an interesting anonymous essay comparing and contrasting Chinese pettifoggers and Western lawyers.

5. For clerks see Miao Ch'üan-chi, "Ch'ing-tai hsing-mu shu-yao," p. 326, and Abe Takeo, *Shindaishi no kenkyū*, p. 564. For sheng-yüan see Hattori Unokichi, "Shina chihōkan no shokumu," p. 77 of the appendix to the Tokyo 1966 reprint of Hattori's *Shinkoku tsūkō*, but originally published in Hattori's *Shina kenkyū* (Tokyo, 1916), p. 32. For mu-yu see Sun Ting-lieh, *Ssu-hsi-chai chüeh-shih*, author's preface, p. 2A.

6. *Ku Yü Chang-shih tsung-p'u*, 1/p. 25B. Taga number 629.

7. Chang Wei-jen, interviewer, "Ch'ing-tai ti-fang ssu-fa: Ch'en T'ien-hsi hsien-sheng fang-wen chi (hsia)," *Shih-huo* 1 #7 (October 1971), p. 53.

8. Lu Wen-ch'ao, *Pao-ching-t'ang wen-chi*, 30/p. 2A in Lu Wen-ch'ao, *Pao-ching-t'ang ts'ung-shu*.

9. Che-chiang pu-cheng an-cha-shih shu, *Ch'ing-sung chang-ch'eng*, p. 34A.

10. *Che-chiang feng-su kai-liang ch'ien-shuo*, p. 56B.

11. Ibid., p. 58B.

12. Ibid., pp. 58A–58B. If Shang-yü's inhabitants did not shrink from litigation, Kuei-chi's seem to have thrived on it: According to a magistrate who had served there in 1898, "The people of Kuei-chi county love litigation" *(Kuei-i min-ch'ing hao-sung)* (Sun Ting-lieh, *Ssu-hsi-chai chüeh-shih*, 2/p. 9A).

13. Ts'ao Chü-jen, *Wan-li hsing-chi*, p. 242. For the Kuei-chi magistrate's citation, see my Introduction above, note 15.

14. Shiga Shūzō, "Shinchō no hōsei," in Banno Masataka et al., eds., *Kindai Chūgoku kenkyū nyūmon*, pp. 302-303.
15. *Chang-shih hui-p'u*, section "chuan," pp. 2A-2B. Taga number 711.
16. *NCH*, September 25, 1915, p. 869.
17. Hsü Ch'in-wen, *I-t'an chiu*, p. 130. For further testimony to the disappearance of the mu-yu profession after 1911, see Wang Chieh-mou, "Ch'ing-tai," p. 19.
18. *Pei-hsin tsa-chih*, 30/pp. 25B-27B. Unfortunately the date, place, and author of this source are all unknown. It was perhaps published in 1907, since it is bound with another magazine published in that year. (Held by the Institute of Humanistic Studies, Kyoto.)
19. Sun Fu-yüan, *Fu-yüan yu-chi ti-i-chi*, p. 27, and Yeh Lung-yen, "Ch'ing-mo Min-ch'u chih fa-cheng hsüeh-t'ang (1905-1919)," Ph. D. thesis in History, College of Chinese Culture (Yang-ming Shan, Taiwan), 1974, p. 62. Yeh's is the most complete study of these schools. For a brief account of the reform of legal education in the late Ch'ing, see Joseph Cheng, "Chinese Law in Transition: The Late Ch'ing Law Reform, 1901-1911," Ph. D. thesis in History, Brown University, 1976, pp. 141-154.
20. *Shih pao*, January 21, 1910, unnumbered page of advertisements following page 4. Some of the information cited in the text comes from advertisements in subsequent issues.
21. *Ta Ch'ing Hsüan-t'ung cheng-chi shih-lu*, Hsüan-t'ung 2 (1910), 34/p. 18A.
22. The list is titled *Keng-hsü [1910] k'o ti-i-tz'u k'ao-shih fa-kuan t'ung-nien lu*. No place or date of publication. Held by Harvard-Yenching Library.
23. Statistics compiled from *Hang-hsien lü-shih kung-hui shih-chou chi-nien chi*, section "pen-hui hui-yüan ming-lu," pp. 1-7.
24. Statistics compiled from Shanghai lü-shih kung-hui, ed., *Shanghai lü-shih kung-hui hui-yüan lu*, pp. 1-68.
25. The total number of 1381 excludes approximately 120 persons in the following two categories: (a) persons whose biographies in the *Who's Who* consist of only their name and the citation "government official," since it is thus impossible to ascertain either their native places or whether they were law-related, and (b) a very few law-related persons whose biographies in *Who's Who* fail to indicate their native places.
26. Ku Chien-ch'en, *Shen-tung*, p. 121.
27. Hsü Shu-lan's biography in *SHTL*, section "jen-wu lieh-chuan," p. 163B, identifies him as a native of Shan-yin, but the catalogue of the library which he founded (discussed in the text) leaves no doubt that he was from Kuei-chi. In all probability he lived in Shaohsing city, which contained within its walls portions of both counties. On Hsü's chü-jen degree see Ting Ts'ai-san, ed., *Shaohsing hsien-kuan chi-lüeh*, p. 30B. But Hsü's name is not listed in either of the authoritative guides to Ch'ing chin-shih, *Tseng-chiao Ch'ing-ch'ao chin-shih t'i-ming pei-lu fu yin-te*, compiled by Fang Chao-ying and Tu Lien-che, and *Ming-Ch'ing chin-shih t'i-ming pei-lu so-yin*, compiled by Chu Pao-chiung and Hsieh P'ei-lin. On Hsü's ranks, see Hsü Erh-ku, ed., *Ku Yüeh ts'ang-shu-lou shu-mu*, "shou" (section "nieh p'ien"), p. 1A. Chu Min et al., *Lu Hsün tsai Shaohsing*, p. 147, states that Hsü Shu-lan served as an official in the Board of War and as a prefect before retiring to his home in Shaohsing and engaging in philanthropic activities.
28. Chang Chien contributed a short essay to the *Ku Yüeh ts'ang-shu-lou shu-mu* in which he refers to Hsü Shu-lan as "my friend"

(ibid., "shou" (section "chi"), pp. 1A-1B). In 1898 Shu-lan was also one of the three founders of the Agricultural Study Association (Nung-hsüeh-hui) in Shanghai *(SHTL,* section "jen-wu lieh-chuan," p. 164A).

29. Hsü Erh-ku, ed., *Ku Yüeh ts'ang-shu-lou shu-mu,* "shou" (section "ch'eng"), p. 1A; Lu Hsün, *LHCC,* vol. 2, p. 450, note 2; and Hsieh Te-hsi, *Lu Hsün tso-p'in,* p. 35. For a survey, largely statistical, of modern-style educational enterprises in late Ch'ing and early Republican Chekiang, see Li Kuo-ch'i, "Ch'ing-chi Min-ch'u Che-chiang ti-ch'ü chin-tai-hua yen-chin kuo-ch'eng chung ti chiao-yü yü wen-hua shih-yeh (1895-1916)," *Chung-hua hsüeh-pao* 3 #2 (July 1976), pp. 123-152. In 1893, four years before the establishment of the Sino-Occidental School, gentry in Hsiao-shan added modern-style courses to the curriculum of an existing elementary school; and gentry in peripheral Hsin-ch'ang established a modern-style "New Knowledge School" in 1898, only one year after the Sino-Occidental School (Li Kuo-ch'i, "Ching-chi," p. 124).

30. Anonymous, "'Ku Yüeh ts'ang-shu-lou' tsai Chung-kuo chin-tai t'u-shu-kuan shang ti ti-wei," *Kuang-ming jih-pao,* December 16, 1963, p. 1.

31. Hsü Erh-ku, ed., *Ku Yüeh ts'ang-shu-lou shu-mu,* "shou" (section "chang ch'eng"), pp. 1A-1B is the source of the quotations.

32. The library expenditure figure is from ibid., "shou" (section "kung ch'eng"), p. 1A. The quotation and information on the library's operations are from ibid., "shou" (section "chang ch'eng"), pp. 2A-5A. The Social Darwinist essay is in ibid., Preface, pp. 1A-1B.

33. Benjamin I. Schwartz, *In Search of Wealth and Power: Yen Fu and the West,* p. 99. The most exhaustive study of Social Darwinism's influence on China is James Reeve Pusey, *China and Charles Darwin* (Cambridge, 1983).

34. William A Lyell, Jr., *Lu Hsün's Vision of Reality,* p. 49.

35. Sun Meng-lan, "Chin-tu ssu-i," *TFTC* 3 #11, Kuang-hsü 32 (1906), lunar 10th month, pp. 215-218.

36. Chiang Monlin, *Tides from the West,* pp. 40-41.

37. Ibid., p. 50.

38. Lu Hsün, "Ch'ao-hua hsi-shih," in *LHCC,* vol. 2, p. 265.

39. T'ao Ying-hui, *Ts'ai Yüan-p'ei nien-p'u (shang),* p. 69.

40. Ts'ai Yüan-p'ei, *Ts'ai Yüan-p'ei tzu-shu,* p. 53.

41. Ibid.

42. Wang Tzu-liang, "Ch'ing-mo wu-shih-nien Che-chiang wen-chiao chi-yao," *Che-chiang yüeh-k'an* 3 #4 (April 1971), p. 19. For Tu's biography see *SHTL,* section "jen-wu lieh-chuan," p. 213A.

43. Ts'ai Yüan-p'ei, *Ts'ai Yüan-p'ei tzu-shu,* p. 53.

44. Chu Min et al., *Lu Hsün tsai Shaohsing,* p. 148. Chu, p. 147ff, presents a detailed account of this school and its metamorphoses, citing several rare sources unavailable outside China, including the school's charter and a draft history written on the occasion of the school's fiftieth anniversary.

45. *TFTC* 1 #5, Kuang-hsü 30 (1904), lunar 5th month, "chiao-yü" section, pp. 121-122. The gentry contributors are not named. Of course the establishment of "charity schools" did not begin in the late Ch'ing. (See Evelyn Rawski, *Education and Popular Literacy in Ch'ing China,* p. 37.) But the timing of this particular school's establishment in Shaohsing strongly suggests that a traditional institution was being used for a reformist purpose.

46. Rinji Taiwan kyūkan chōsakai, ed., *Shinkoku gyōseihō,* vol. 3, p. 441. The most convenient collection of such central government-level, late Ch'ing educational documents is Taga Akigorō,

comp., *Kindai Chūgoku kyōikushi shiryō: Shinmatsu hen* (Tokyo, 1972).

47. Li Kuo-ch'i, "Ch'ing-chi Min-ch'u," p. 147.
48. Tung Chin-chien, *Wu T'ai-fu-jen nien-p'u hsü*, p. 2B. The information below on the efforts of Madam Wu's family to establish a new-style school is from ibid., pp. 2B-3A.
49. *Hsiao-shan hsien-chih kao*, 1935, 10 "hsia"/pp. 808-819.
50. *Ch'eng-hsien chih*, 1934, 6/pp. 20B-23A; *Yü-yao liu-ts'ang chih*, 1920, 15/pp. 11B-15B. For more on Chekiang lineages' support of modern-style education see Schoppa, *Chinese Elites and Political Change*, p. 50.
51. Based on Hsüeh-pu tsung-wu ssu, comp., *Ti-i-tz'u chiao-yü t'ung-chi t'u piao, Kuang-hsü 33 nien-fen*, pp. 2-12 of Chekiang section; *Ti-erh-tz'u. . .Kuang-hsü 34 nien-fen*, pp. 3-13 of Chekiang section; and *Ti-san-tz'u. . .Hsüan-t'ung yüan nien-fen*, pp. 2-12 of Chekiang section. I am most grateful to Dr. Mary B. Rankin for bringing these three volumes to my attention. The statistics in Table 12 are my tabulation of the total enrollments in the four categories of hsüeh-t'ang included in the three volumes: "specialized" *(chuan-men)*, "vocational" *(shih-yeh)*, "pedagogical" *(shih-fan)*, and - by far the largest category - "regular" *(p'u-t'ung)*. A plus sign (+) indicates that the enrollment figure is an undercount. The number of hsüeh-t'ang omitted from the statistics for 1907 (Kuang-hsü 33) is as follows: Shan-yin 1 and Chu-chi 1 (see Hsüeh-pu tsung-wu ssu, comp., *Ti-i-tz'u. . .Kuang-hsü 33 nien-fen*, p. 12 of Chekiang section). The number of hsüeh-t'ang omitted from the statistics for 1908 is as follows: Shan-yin 3, Hsiao-shan 1, Yü-yao 2, and Ch'eng-hsien 1 (see ibid., *Ti-erh-tz'u. . . Kuang-hsü 34 nien-fen*, p. 13 of Chekiang section). The number of hsüeh-t'ang omitted from the statistics for 1909 is as follows: Shan-yin 3, Hsiao-shan 2, Chu-chi 1, Yü-yao 1, Shang-yü 1, and Ch'eng-hsien 1 (see ibid., *Ti-san-tz'u... Hsüan-t'ung yüan nien-fen*, p. 11 of Chekiang section). These omissions occurred because these hsueh-t'ang did not return their completed questionnaires in time.
52. *CCKK*, section "Chu-chi she-hui hsien-hsiang," p. 42.
53. *NCH*, July 15, 1910, p. 138. For just a few other accounts among many, see *TFTC* 7 #5, Hsüan-t'ung 2 (1910), lunar 5th month, section "Chung-kuo ta-shih-chi pu-i," p. 27 and *Shih pao*, August 15, 1910, p. 3.
54. Nakamura Tsune, "Shinmatsu gakudō setsuritsu o meguru Kō-Setsu nōson shakai no ichidanmen," *Rekishi kyoikū* 10 #11 (November 1962), p. 79 and Abe Hiroshi, "'Tōhō zasshi' ni mirareru Shinmatsu kyōikushi shiryō ni tsuite (jo)," *Rekishi hyōron* #137 (January 1962), p. 29.
55. E.g., Abe Hiroshi, "Shinmatsu kindai gakkō: Shinmatsu ni okeru gakudō no setsuritsu to unei," in Taga Akigorō, ed., *Kinsei Ajia kyōikushi kenkyū*, p. 799. Joseph Esherick's *Reform and Revolution in China* was one of the very first books in English to emphasize the financially repressive nature of the late Ch'ing reform projects from the viewpoint of the common people.
56. Tu Shih-chen, "Lun Hu-shang chien-she Shaohsing chiao-yü-hui shih," *Hsin shih-chieh tsa-chih* #11, Kuang-hsü 29 (1903), lunar 2nd month, section "Chiao-yu hsueh," pp. 8-9.
57. *TFTC* 1 #9, Kuang-hsü 30 (1904), lunar 9th month, pp. 200-202. Monastaries were sometimes successful in resisting confiscation by appealing to the provincial capital for a favorable ruling. For such a case involving a monastery in Ch'eng-hsien, see *T'ung-wen Hu-pao*, Kuang-hsü 31 (1905), lunar 4th month, 26th day (unpaginated).

58. *Shih pao*, June 4, 1911, p. 4. Much the same account can be found in *Min li pao*, June 4, 1911, p. 4.
59. Pi-che she, ed., *Chung-kuo ko-ming-tang ta shou-ling Hsü Hsi-lin*, pp. 134-137. Cf. Mary Rankin, "The Revolutionary Movement in Chekiang: A Study in the Tenacity of Tradition," p. 358. The Pi-che she account of the repercussions of the Ch'iu Chin affair was written soon after her execution, when local reactionaries were in full cry, and consequently overemphasizes the deleterious impact of the affair upon local hsüeh-t'ang. For more on Ch'iu Chin see Mary Rankin, *Early Chinese Revolutionaries* and the same author's "The Emergence of Women at the End of the Ch'ing: The Case of Ch'iu Chin," in Margery Wolf and Roxane Witke, eds., *Women in Chinese Society*.
60. This school went through several changes of name. It began in 1897 as the Chung-hsi hsueh-t'ang, then in 1899 became the Shaohsing-fu hsüeh-t'ang, next in 1906 the Shaohsing-fu chung-hsüeh-t'ang, and finally, after the 1911 Revolution, the Sheng-li ti-wu chung-hsüeh.
61. *NCH*, January 25, 1907, p. 201.
62. For courses taught, see Chu Min et al., *Lu Hsün tsai Shaohsing*, pp. 149, 158. For student enrollment at the prefectual middle school in 1907, see Hsüeh-pu tsung-wu ssu, comp., *Ti-i-tz'u chiao-yü t'ung-chi t'u piao, Kuang-hsü 33 nien-fen*, p. 8 of Chekiang section.
63. Chu Min et al., *Lu Hsün tsai Shaohsing*, p. 151.
64. Ibid., p. 150, which also notes that a branch of the Yüeh she was established in 1910 among Shaohsing students in Peking.
65. *Min li pao*, January 17, 1911, p. 4. For reports of other student disturbances at this school, see *Min li pao*, November 16, 1910, p. 4; November 18, 1910, p. 4; and September 1, 1911, p. 4.
66. Chou Hsia-shou, *Lu Hsün hsiao-shuo li ti jen-wu*, p. 36 and Hsü Shou-ch'ang, *Wo so jen-shih ti Lu Hsün*, p. 7.
67. Wang Yeh-ch'iu, *Min-yüan-ch'ien ti Lu Hsün hsien-sheng*, p. 115.
68. Wang Shih-ching, *Lu Hsün chuan*, p. 73.
69. Wang Yeh-ch'iu, *Min-yüan-ch'ien ti Lu Hsün hsien-sheng*, pp. 117-118. Compare the account of the school's queue-cutting episode in Chu Min et al., *Lu Hsün tsai Shaohsing*, pp. 152-154, which agrees well with Wang's version.
70. Chou Chien-jen, "Shaohsing kuang-fu-ch'ien Lu Hsün ti i-hsiao-tuan shih-ch'ing," *Jen-min wen-hsüeh* #140-#141 (July-August, 1961), p. 124 and Chou Hsia-shou, *Lu Hsün hsiao-shuo li ti jen-wu*, p. 100.
71. For detailed studies of local self-government see John H. Fincher, "The Chinese Self-Government Movement, 1900-1912," Ph.D. thesis in History, University of Washington (Seattle), 1969 and his more recent *Chinese Democracy: The Self-Government Movement in Local, Provincial and National Politics, 1905-1914*. See also R. Keith Schoppa, "Local Self-Government in Zhejiang, 1909-1927," *Modern China* 2 #4 (October 1976), pp. 503-530 (which contains, however, virtually nothing on Shaohsing) and his *Chinese Elites and Political Change*, which includes additional relevant detail on pp. 81-82.
72. Philip A. Kuhn, "Local Self-Government Under the Republic" in Frederic Wakeman, Jr. and Carolyn Grant, eds., *Conflict and Control in Late Imperial China*, p. 276.
73. *TFTC* 3 #11, Kuang-hsü 32 (1906), lunar 10th month, section "nei-wu," pp. 211-213. For a discussion of various types of local-elite abuses in the conduct of local self-government (not specifically in Shaohsing), see *Shinkoku jiho* #72, January 31, Meiji 44 (1911), pp. 11-13.

74. Statistics compiled from *Hsiao-shan hsien-chih kao*, 7/ section "chu so," pp. 31A-32A (pp. 645-647 of the Taiwan reprint edition).
75. Unlike Shan-yin and Kuei-chi, Hsiao-shan apparently had no category of urban township assemblyman.
76. Statistics compiled from *SHTL*, ts'e 11, section "hsiang-chen," pp. 1A-6A.
77. For the biography of a rich merchant elected first as an assemblyman in Kuei-chi and then as a provincial assemblyman, see *SHTL*, section "jen-wu lieh-chuan," p. 202A.
78. On the destruction in 1910 of a "self-government study office" (tzu-chih yen-chiu so) and a "statistical bureau" (t'ung-chi ch'u) in Shang-yü county, in addition to several new educational institutions, see *Che-chiang tzu-i chü wen-tu*, ts'e 4, p. 63A. To the peasantry statistics implied taxes.
79. Kuhn, "Local Self-Government Under the Republic," p. 279.
80. See Ch'en Hsieh-shu, "Shaohsing kuang-fu shih chien-wen," *Chin-tai shih tzu-liao* #1 (1958), pp. 105-108.
81. *CCKK*, section "she-hui hsien-hsiang," p. 104.

Appendix A

1. *Kuei-chi Ch'in-shih tsung-p'u*, first preface (dated Hsüan-t'ung 3, 7th month), p. 2A. Taga number 605.
2. *CCKK*, section "wei-wen," p. 50.
3. *Chang-shih hui-p'u*, section "fu lu," p. 1A. Taga number 711. Since this source indicates that both the Shaohsing and Ningpo Changs descended from an actual (rather than a fictionalized) common ancestor, I refer to the Changs as a higher-order lineage rather than a clan (following James L. Watson, "Chinese Kinship Reconsidered: Anthropological Perspectives on Historical Research," *China Quarterly* #92 (December 1982), p. 610.
4. Yoshinobu Shiba, "Ningpo and Its Hinterland," in G. William Skinner, ed., *The City in Late Imperial China*, p. 434.
5. Maruyama Noboru, *Ro Jin: Sono bunkagu to kakumei*, p. 9.
6. This arrangement suggests that the man was serving as both mu-yu and pettifogger at the same time. Perhaps the magistrate permitted this in order to avoid having to pay him a mu-yu's salary.
7. Ida Pruitt, *A Daughter of Han*, p. 115.
8. Compare the following description of a rich merchant's compound in nineteenth-century Canton: "[W]e saw the large town residence of the 'Ng', or Howqua family. This mansion consists, in short, of three or four houses. . . . In this large family residence, not less than five hundred souls reside." Quoted in Hugh D. R. Baker, "Extended Kinship in the Traditional City," in G. William Skinner, ed., *The City in Late Imperial China*, p. 502.
9. Ku Shih-chiang, ed., *Hsiao-shan hsiang-t'u-chih*, rev. ed., 1933, p. 52.
10. Arthur E. Moule, *The Story of the Cheh-kiang Mission of the Church Missionary Society*, p. 122.
11. Ku Shih-chiang, ed., *Hsiao-shan hsiang-t'u-chih*, rev. ed., 1933, p. 52.
12. For these lists see *Hsin-ch'ang hsien-chih*, 1918, 1/ pp. 21B-29B and *Hsiao-shan hsiang-hu-chih*, 1925, 8/ pp. 4A-6B.
13. Evelyn Rawski, *Education and Popular Literacy in Ch'ing China*, pp. 28-32.
14. *Hu-shih chia-p'u*, section "chia-yüeh," p. 10A-10B. Taga number 464.
15. *Shan-yin An-ch'ang Hsü-shih tsung-p'u*, section "Hsü-shih i-tsang kuei-t'iao," pp. 3B-4B. Taga number 559.

16. Ibid., p. 4B. Unfortunately no details are provided on the lineage's role in training mu-yu. Such information was a professional secret, too sensitive for publication in either this or other genealogies.

17. *Lan-feng Wei-shih tsung-p'u*, 3("t'iao-kuei")/p. 52B. Taga number 1155.

18. Taga Akigorō, "Kindai Chūgoku ni okeru zokujuku no seikaku," p. 219 in *Kindai Chūgoku kenkyū dai shi shū.* In this article many of Taga's examples of lineage schools come from Shaohsing, although Taga does not comment on this fact.

19. Ku Shih-chiang, ed., *Hsiao-shan hsiang-t'u-chih*, rev. ed., 1933, p. 52.

20. Taga Akigorō, "Kindai Chūgoku ni okeru," p. 209.

21. Chang Chung-li, *The Income of the Chinese Gentry*, p. 28, Table 8.

22. Statistics compiled from the list of Harvard-Yenching genealogical holdings in Lo Hsiang-lin, *Chung-kuo tsu-p'u yen-chiu*, pp. 191-210.

23. *CCKK*, section "feng-su chih," p. 8. See also T'ao Ts'un-chao, "Yao Hai-ch'a hsien-sheng nien-p'u," *Wen-lan hsüeh-pao* 1 #1 (January 1935), p. 17.

24. Taga Akigorō, *Sōfu no kenkyū*, p. 820, item 295 (from a Hsiao-shan genealogy published in 1870).

25. Ibid., p. 63.

26. *Kuei-chi Ch'in-shih tsung-p'u*, first preface (dated Hsüan-t'ung 3, 7th month), p. 1A. Taga number 605.

27. For a general discussion of vendettas, see Harry J. Lamley, "*Hsieh-tou:* The Pathology of Violence in Southeastern China," *Ch'ing-shih wen-t'i* 3 #7 (November 1977), pp. 1-39.

28. See for example the undated injunction in *Hsiao-shan Ch'ung-hua Liu-shih tsung-p'u*, section "ssu-chieh," unpaginated. Taga number 1028.

29. Ku Yen-wu, *T'ien-hsia chün-kuo li-ping shu*, section "Che-chiang hsia"/ p. 41A in the Ssu-pu ts'ung-k'an edition.

30. Ibid.

31. Chao Han-yu, *Ch'eng-hsien ku-hsiang shih-shih chi*, p. 19. For an indication that local officials' reluctance to interfere to stop vendettas was not limited to Ch'eng-hsien, see Niida Noboru, "Shina kinsei dōzoku buraku no kaitō," in *Tōyō nōgyō keizaishi kenkyū*, p. 67.

32. *TFTC* 7 #8, Hsüan-t'ung 2 (1910), lunar 9th month, p. 219 and 7 #9 Hsüan-t'ung 2 (1910), lunar 10th month, p. 250.

33. Chao Han-yu, *Ch'eng-hsien ku-hsiang shih-shih chi*, p. 19. This same source (p. 24) also claims that Ch'eng-hsien produced forty-two graduates of Paoting Military Academy, supposedly more than any other county in China. The case of Ch'eng-hsien supports G. William Skinner's generalization that "there was a tendency for the peripheral counties within a prefecture to produce proportionately more military than civil degree holders" (Skinner, "Mobility Strategies in Late Imperial China: A Regional Systems Analysis," in Carol A. Smith, ed., *Regional Analysis. Volume I: Economic Systems*, p. 355). Cf. Schoppa, *Chinese Elites and Political Change*, pp. 122-124.

34. Jonathan D. Spence, *Emperor of China: Self-portrait of K'ang-hsi*, p. 49.

35. See note 28 above for the reference to the Hsiao-shan injunction.

36. *CCKK*, section "Chu-chi she-hui hsien-hsiang," p. 92.

37. Niida Noboru, "Shina kinsei dōzoku buraku no kaitō," p. 100.

38. *Che-chiang feng-su kai-liang ch'ien-shuo*, p. 59B.

39. Ibid.
40. Taga Akigorō, *Sōfu no kenkyū*, p. 651, item 107.
41. *CCKK*, section "Chu-chi she-hui hsien-hsiang," p. 90.
42. Ibid., section "feng-su chih," p. 12.
43. The account below is taken from ibid., section "Chu-chi she-hui hsien-hsiang," p. 89.
44. Accounts of other Chu-chi vendettas in this same source also indicate that casualties were usually light (e.g., ibid., p. 91).
45. The useful term "interlineage imperialism" was coined by Philip Kuhn in his *Rebellion and Its Enemies in Late Imperial China*, p. 79.
46. Tanaka Issei, "Shindai shoki no sōzoku engeki ni tsuite," *Tōhōgaku* #32 (June 1966), p. 103.
47. Ibid., pp. 102-116.
48. *Ch'eng-hsien chih*, 1870, 20/p. 10A.
49. Tanaka Issei, "Shindai shoki," p. 108.
50. Ibid., p. 109.
51. Ibid., p. 111.
52. Ibid., p. 102.
53. Ibid., pp. 107-108.
54. Hui-chen Wang Liu, *The Traditional Chinese Clan Rules*, pp. 156-157.
55. Maurice Freedman, *The Study of Chinese Society*, pp. 339-340.

Appendix B

1. Esther Morrison, "The Modernization of the Confucian Bureaucracy," p. 91.
2. Herbert Giles, *A Chinese-English Dictionary* (2nd ed., 1912), p. 880.
3. It is worth noting, however, that among natives of Ch'ang-chou and Soochow in 1892, the assistant county magistrate (hsien-ch'eng) post held third place by only the barest of margins, whereas among Hangchow and Shaohsing natives that post was firmly ensconced in third place.
4. County in Soochow prefecture, not to be confused with Ch'ang-chou prefecture. See the Glossary for the different characters.
5. Ho Ping-ti, *The Ladder of Success*, p. 254.

Appendix C

1. P'eng Tse-i, ed., *Chung-kuo chin-tai shou-kung-yeh*, vol. 3, p. 55. Shaohsing's three locales most active in professional wine-making were Tung-p'u, Yüan-she, and K'o-ch'iao (Chien-she wei-yüan-hui, ed., *Che-chiang chih Shao-chiu*, p. 3).
2. *Pi-chi hsiao-shuo ta-kuan hsü-pien*, 5/p. 15 (continuous pagination p. 4485).
3. Lou Tzu-kuang, "Che-chiang chih chiu," *Che-chiang yüeh-k'an* #64 (August 1974), p. 13.
4. For technical information on the making of Shaohsing wine see Che-chiang sheng kung-yeh t'ing, ed., *Shaohsing chiu niang-tsao* (Peking, 1958) and Chien-she wei-yüan hui, ed., *Che-chiang chih Shao-chiu* (Hangchow, 1937).
5. Chien-she wei-yüan hui, ed., *Che-chiang chih Shao-chiu*, p. 31.
6. Liang Chang-chü, *Lang-chi hsü-t'an*, 4/p. 5B. This bon mot is copied in Ch'ai O, *Fan-t'ien-lu ts'ung-lu*, 36/p. 3B.
7. Andrew Hsieh, "Tseng Kuo-fan, A Nineteenth Century Confucian General," Ph.D. thesis in History, Yale University, 1975, p. 175.
8. David Hawkes' introduction to Cao Xueqin [Ts'ao Hsüeh-ch'in], *The Story of the Stone*, vol. 1., p. 23.

9. Ts'ao Chü-jen, *Pei-hsing san-yü*, p. 51.
10. Ling Ch'ih,pseud.,"Shaohsing chiu," *Che-chiang yüeh-k'an* 2 #10 (December 1970), p. 20.
11. Hsü K'o, *K'o yen*, 13/p. 16B and Ch'ai O, *Fan-t'ien-lu ts'ung-lu*, 36/p. 4A. There was also a prefecture in Chihli named Shun-te. It is unclear which was the site of the Tan family's winemaking, although I am inclined towards the Kwangtung locale.
12. Hsü K'o, *K'o yen*, 13/p. 16B. The sole source of water for high-quality wine made in Shaohsing was Ching-hu (also known as Chien-hu), a manmade lake created in the Han dynasty (Che-chiang sheng kung-yeh t'ing, ed., *Shaohsing chiu niang-tsao*, p. 12). "Water is taken from Chien Lake, near the city [of Shao-hsing], which is fed by pure mountain springs and is free from mineral and organic impurities, and therefore particularly suitable for brewing purposes" (Anonymous, "Shaohsing Brewing Indus-try," *Chinese Economic Journal and Bulletin* 18 #6 (June 1936), p. 880).
13. Ling Ch'ih,   "Shaohsing chiu," p. 21. For Shaohsing winemak-ers in Chin-t'an, southern Kiangsu, see P'eng Tse-i, ed., *Chung-kuo chin-tai shou-kung-yeh*, vol. 2, p. 683.
14. Che-chiang sheng kung-yeh t'ing, ed., *Shaohsing chiu niang-tsao*, p. 8.
15. Ch'ai O, *Fan-t'ien-lu ts'ung-lu*, 36/p. 4A and Chien-she wei-yüan hui, ed., *Che-chiang chih Shao-chiu*, p. 31.
16. Liang Chang-chü, *Lang-chi hsü-t'an*, 4/p. 5B and Ch'ai O, *Fan-t'ien-lu ts'ung-lu*, 36/p. 4A.
17. Tōa dōbunkai, ed., *Shina shōbetsu zenshi*, vol. 13 *(Sekkō shō)*, pp. 669-671.
18. Lu Hsün, "Medicine," *SWLH*, vol. 1, p. 37.
19. P'eng Tse-i, ed., *Chung-kuo chin-tai shou-kung-yeh*, vol. 2, p. 293 and Wang Chieh-mou, "Shaohsing hsi-po kuan ch'üan-kuo," p. 19.
20. Anonymous, "Shaohsing po-yeh kai-k'uang," p. 2. This source also reveals that none of the raw materials used in the production of spirit money was native to Shaohsing. The tin came from as far away as Szechwan and Yunnan, and the yellow paper for the backing came from as far away as Kiangsi.
21. Ch'iao-feng, *Lüeh chiang kuan-yü Lu Hsün ti shih-ch'ing*, p. 24.
22. Che-chiang sheng shih-yeh pu kuo-chi mao-i chü, ed., *Chung-kuo shih-yeh chih: Che-chiang sheng*, section 3, p. 66.
23. Anonymous, "Shaohsing po-yeh kai-k'uang," p. 3 and Wang Chieh-mou, "Shaohsing hsi-po kuan ch'üan-kuo," p. 19.
24. Lu Hsün, "Soap," *SWLH*, vol. 1, p. 198.
25. *Nung-hsüeh pao* #20, Kuang-hsü 24 (1898), lunar 1st month, "chung hsün," p. 2B.
26. Wang Ching-yü, ed., *Chung-kuo chin-tai kung-yeh shih tzu-liao ti-erh-chi (1895-1914)*, part two, p. 1094.
27. Yen Chung-p'ing, *Chung-kuo mien-fang-chih shih kao*, p. 139 and Yen Chung-p'ing et al., eds., *Chung-kuo chin-tai ching-chi shih t'ung-chi tzu-liao hsüan-chi*, p. 98. Ku Shih-chiang, ed., *Hsiao-shan hsiang-t'u-chih*, rev. ed., 1933, p. 38 records a dif-ferent founder for the T'ung-hui mill, but implies that he had partners (presumably including Lou).
28. Yen Chung-p'ing, *Chung-kuo mien-fang-chih shih kao*, p. 334.
29. Ibid., p. 328ff.
30. *TFTC* 2 #7, Kuang-hsü 31 (1905), lunar 7th month, section "shih-yeh," p. 129.
31. Ibid. 3 #6, Kuang-hsü 32 (1906), lunar 5th month, section "shih-yeh," p. 135.

32. Ibid. 3 #10, Kuang-hsü 32 (1906), lunar 9th month, section "shih-yeh," p. 197.

Bibliography

As in the Notes, "Taga number" refers to the catalogue of Japanese-held genealogies in Taga Akigorō, *Sōfu no kenkyū: shiryō hen* (Tokyo, 1960). In the case of rare works, a library known to hold the item is indicated.

Abe Hiroshi 阿部洋. "Shinmatsu kindai gakkō: Shinmatsu ni okeru gakudō no setsuritsu to unei" 清末近代学校：清末における学堂の設立と運営. In *Kinsei Ajia kyōikushi kenkyū* 近世アジア教育史研究, edited by Taga Akigorō 多賀秋五郎, pp. 719-816. Tokyo, 1966.

_____. "'Tōhō zasshi' ni mirareru Shinmatsu kyōikushi shiryō ni tsuite (jō)"「東方雜誌」にみられる清末教育史資料について(上). *Rekishi hyōron* 歷史評論 #137 (January 1962), pp. 23-33.

Abe Takeo 安部健夫. *Shindaishi no kenkyū* 清代史の研究. Tokyo, 1971.

Amano Motonosuke 天野元之助. *Chūgoku nōgyōshi kenkyū* 中国農業史研究. Tokyo, 1962.

Anonymous. "'Ku Yüeh ts'ang-shu-lou' tsai Chung-kuo chin-tai t'u-shu-kuan shang ti ti-wei" 古越藏書樓在中國近代圖書館上的地位, *Kuang-ming jih-pao* 光明日報 (December 16, 1963), p. 1.

Anonymous. "Shaohsing Brewing Industry," *Chinese Economic Journal and Bulletin* 18 #6 (June 1936), pp. 878-883.

Anonymous. "Shaohsing po-yeh kai-k'uang" 紹興箔業概況 ,
Kung-shang pan-yüeh-k'an 工商半月刊 4 #11 (June 1932),
section 國內經濟, pp. 2-4.

Atwell, William S. "Ch'en Tzu-lung (1608-1647): A Scholar-Official of
the Late Ming Dynasty." Ph.D. thesis in East Asian Studies,
Princeton University, 1974.

Baker, Hugh D. R. "Extended Kinship in the Traditional City."
In *The City in Late Traditional China*, edited by G. William Skinner,
pp. 499-518. Stanford, 1977.

Balazs, Étienne. *Political Theory and Administrative Reality in
Traditional China*. London, 1965.

Banno Masataka 坂野正高 et al., eds. *Kindai Chūgoku kenkyū
nyūmon* 近代中国研究入門 . Tokyo, 1974.

Banno Ryōkichi 坂野良吉. "Kindai Chūgoku ni okeru nōgyō
henkaku: tochi kakumei no rekishiteki igi ni tsuite" 近代中国にお
ける農業変革：土地革命の歴史的意義について ,
Rekishi hyōron #279 (August 1973), pp. 2-28.

Bastid, Marianne. *Aspects de la réforme d'enseignement en Chine au
début du 20e siècle, d'après des écrits de Zhang Jian*. Paris, 1971.

Beattie, Hilary J. *Land and Lineage in China: A study of T'ung-ch'eng
County, Anhwei, in the Ming and Ch'ing Dynasties*. Cambridge,
England, 1979.

Bergère, Marie-Claire. *La bourgeoisie chinoise et la révolution de
1911*. The Hague, 1968.

_____. "The Role of the Bourgeoisie." In *China in Revolution:
The First Phase, 1900-1913*, edited by Mary C. Wright, pp. 229-295.
New Haven, 1968.

Billingsley, Phil. "Bandits, Bosses, and Bare Sticks: Beneath the Surface of Local Control in Early Republican China," *Modern China* 7 #3 (July 1981), pp. 235-288.

Borthwick, Sally. *Education and Social Change in China: The Beginnings of the Modern Era.* Stanford, 1983.

Boulais, Guy. *Manuel du code chinois.* Shanghai, 1924. Taiwan photoreprint, 1966.

Cao Xueqin [Ts'ao Hsüeh-ch'in]. *The Story of the Stone.* Volume 1. Translated and with an introduction by David Hawkes. Harmondsworth, England, 1974. Also known as *The Dream of the Red Chamber.*

Ch'a Shih-chieh 查時傑. "Ts'ung Yüeh-man-t'ang jih-chi k'an wan-Ch'ing ti ch'ing-i" 從越縵堂日記看晚清的清議 . M.A. thesis in History, National Taiwan University, 1965. Copy held by the Wason Collection, Cornell.

Ch'ai O 柴萼. *Fan-t'ien-lu ts'ung-lu* 梵天廬叢錄. 1925. Held by the Tōyō Bunko. Ch'ai was a native of Tz'u-ch'i, Ningpo.

Chang Ch'un-ming 張純明. "Ch'ing-tai ti mu-chih" 清代的幕制 , *Ling-nan hsüeh-pao* 嶺南學報 9 #2 (June 1949), pp. 29-50.

Chang Chung-li. *The Chinese Gentry: Studies on Their Role in Nineteenth-Century Chinese Society.* Seattle, 1955.

_____. *The Income of the Chinese Gentry.* Seattle, 1962.

Chang Neng-keng 張能耿. *Lu Hsün ti ch'ing-shao-nien shih-tai* 魯迅的青少年時代. Sian, 1982.

_____. *Lu Hsün tsao-ch'i shih-chi pieh-lu* 魯迅早期事迹別錄. Shih-chia-chuang, Hopei, 1981. Based on interviews with Shaohsing natives who were Lu Hsün's contemporaries.

Chang Peng. "The Distribution and Relative Strength of the Provincial Merchant Groups in China, 1842-1911." Ph.D. thesis in Economics, University of Washington (Seattle), 1958.

Chang-shih hui-p'u 章氏會譜 . 1919. The Changs lived in Kuei-chi. Held by the Tōyō Bunko. Taga number 711.

Chang Tai 張岱. *T'ao-an meng-i* 陶奄夢憶. Peiping, 1927. This punctuated edition includes a preface by Chou Tso-jen. Held by the Institute of Humanistic Studies, Kyoto. A native of Shan-yin, Chang lived during the late Ming.

Chang Wei-jen 張偉仁, interviewer. "Ch'ing-chi ti-fang ssu-fa: Ch'en T'ien-hsi hsien-sheng fang-wen chi (hsia)" 清季地方司法: 陳天錫先生訪問記（下）, *Shih-huo* 食貨 1 #7 (October 1971), pp. 46-55. Interview with an octagenarian former mu-yu.

Chao Han-yu 趙寒友. *Ch'eng-hsien ku-hsiang shih-shih chi* 嵊聯故鄉史實記. Taipei, 1965. Held by the Hoover Institution.

Chao Lieh-wen 趙烈文. "Neng ching chü-shih jih-chi" 能靜居士日記. In *T'ai-p'ing t'ien-kuo shih-liao ts'ung-pien chien-chi* 太平天国史料叢編簡輯, volume 3, edited by T'ai-p'ing t'ien-kuo li-shih po-wu-kuan 太平天国歷史博物館. Shanghai, 1962.

Chao-lien 昭槤 . *Hsiao-t'ing tsa-lu* 嘯亭雜錄 . Peking, 1980.

Che-chiang ch'ao 浙江潮. Tokyo, 1903.

Che-chiang ch'ing-li ts'ai-cheng chü 浙江清理財政局 , ed. *Che-chiang ch'ing-li ts'ai-cheng shuo-ming shu* 浙江清理財政說明書. Hangchow?, 1910. Held by the Institute of Oriental Culture, Tokyo University.

Che-chiang ch'üan-sheng yü-t'u ping shui-lu-tao li chi 浙江全省輿圖並水陸道里記 . Hangchow?, 1894.

Che-chiang feng-su kai-liang ch'ien-shuo 浙江風俗改良淺說 . Hangchow?, 1910. Held by the National Diet Library. Contains the texts of sixty-one lectures delivered in Chekiang by reform-minded gentry during the last decade of the Ch'ing. Among the topics covered are footbinding, gambling, geomancy, wedding and funeral expenses, family management, and "civic virtue."

Che-chiang pu-cheng an-ch'a-shih shu 浙江布政按察使署. *Ch'ing-sung chang-ch'eng* 清訟章程. Hangchow?, 1878. Held by the Institute of Oriental Culture, Tokyo University.

Che-chiang sheng kung-yeh t'ing 浙江省工業厅 ,ed. *Shaohsing chiu niang-tsao* 紹興酒釀造 , Peking, 1958.

Che-chiang sheng shih-yeh pu kuo-chi mao-i chü 浙江省實業部國際貿易局 ,ed. *Chung-kuo shih-yeh chih: Che-chiang sheng* 中國實業誌：浙江省 . Shanghai, 1933.

Che-chiang sheng ts'ai-cheng yüeh-k'an 浙江省財政月刊 (July 1934). Special issue on land-tax adjustment.

Che-chiang tzu-i chü wen-tu 浙江諮議局文牘 . Hangchow?, 1910. Held by the Institute of Oriental Culture, Tokyo University.

Ch'en Ch'iao-i 陈桥驿 . *Shaohsing shih hua* 紹興史話. Shanghai, 1982.

_____. *Shaohsing ti-fang wen-hsien k'ao lu* 紹興地方文獻考录. Hangchow, 1983. A comprehensive and fully annotated bibliography of primary sources (genealogies excepted). Includes some items unavailable outside China and thus not seen by me.

Ch'en Ch'ing-chih 陳青之. *Chung-kuo chiao-yü shih* 中國敎育史 . Changsha, 1936. Taiwan photoreprint, 1963.

Ch'en Hsieh-shu 陳爕樞 . "Shaohsing kuang-fu shih chien-wen" 紹興光復時見聞, *Chin-tai shih tzu-liao* 近代史資料 #1 (1958), pp. 105-108.

Ch'en Lung-cheng 陳龍正. *Chi-t'ing ch'üan-shu* 幾亭全書. Published in 1665 by Ch'en's descendants. Held by the Naikaku Bunko.

_____. *Chi-t'ing wai-shu* 幾亭外書. 1631. Harvard-Yenching microfilm of National Central Library (Taipei) original.

Ch'en To 農朵 . "Ch'iu Chin chia-shih tzu-liao ti hsin fa-hsien" 秋瑾家世資料的新发現, *Hang-chou ta-hsüeh hsüeh-pao* 杭州大学学報 13 #2 (June 1983), pp. 126-131.

Cheng Chao-ching 鄭肇經 . *Chung-kuo shui-li shih* 中國水利史 .
Changsha, 1939. Taiwan photoreprint, 1970.

Cheng-chih kuan-pao 政治官報 . Peking, 1907-1911. Taiwan photoreprint, 1965.

Ch'eng-hsien chih 嵊縣志 . 1870 and 1934.

Cheng, Joseph. "Chinese Law in Transition: The Late Ch'ing Law
Reform, 1901-1911." Ph.D. thesis in History, Brown University,
1976.

Cheng T'ien-t'ing 鄭天挺 . "Ch'ing-tai mu-fu chih ti pien-ch'ien"
清代幕府制的变迁 , *Hsüeh-shu yen-chiu* 学术研究 #6 (1980),
pp. 66-68.

————. "Ch'ing-tai ti mu-fu" 清代的幕府 , *Chung-kuo she-hui
k'o-hsüeh* 中国社会科学 #6 (November 1980), pp. 127-147.

————. "Ch'ing-tai ti mu-fu." In *Ming-Ch'ing shih kuo-chi t'ao-
lun hui lun-wen chi* 明清史国际学术讨论会论文集   , edited
by Ming-Ch'ing shih kuo-chi hsüeh-shu t'ao-lun hui mi-shu ch'u lun-
wen tsu 明清史国际学术讨论会秘书处论文组   , pp. 188-
226. Tientsin, 1982.

Cheng Ying-wan. *Postal Communication in China and its Modernization,
1860-1896*. Cambridge, 1970.

Chia-ch'ing Shan-yin hsien-chih 嘉慶山陰縣志 . 1803.

Chiang Monlin. *Tides from the West*. New Haven, 1947.

Chiang-nan shang-wu pao 江南商務報 . Shanghai. The first
thirty-six issues (published in 1900) are held by Tenri University
Library.

Chiang Tao-chang. "The Salt Trade in Ch'ing China," *Modern Asian
Studies* 17 #2 (April 1983), pp. 197-219.

Ch'iao-feng 喬峯 . *Lüeh chiang kuan-yü Lu Hsün ti shih-ch'ing*
略講關于魯迅的事情 . Peking, 1955. The author is Lu
Hsün's youngest brother, better known as Chou Chien-jen
(1887-1984).

Ch'ien Mu. *Traditional Government in Imperial China: A Critical Analysis*. Translated by Chün-tu Hsüeh and George O. Totten. Hong Kong, 1982.

Ch'ien Pao-ts'ung 錢寶琮. "Che-chiang ch'ou-jen chou-shu chi" 浙江疇人著述記 , *Wen-lan hsüeh-pao* 文瀾學報 3 #1 (January-March 1937), pp. 1597-1608.

Chien-she wei-yüan hui ching-chi tiao-ch'a so t'ung-chi k'o 建設委員會經濟調查所統計課 *Che-chiang chih Shao-chiu* 浙江之紹酒 . Hangchow, 1937. Held by the Library of Congress.

————. *Shaohsing chih ssu-ch'ou* 紹興之絲綢 . Hangchow, 1937. Held by the Harvard-Yenching Library.

China Weekly Review, ed. *Who's Who in China*. Fifth edition. Shanghai, 1936.

Ching Yüan-shan 經元善. *Chü-i ch'u-chi* 居易初集 . 1903. Held by the Tōyō Bunko. Ching, born in 1841, was a native of Shang-yü.

————. *Ch'ü-t'ing chi-shu* 趨庭記述 . 1897. Held by Tōyō Bunko.

Ch'iu Chen 裘軫. "Huai-hsiang i-chiu: Ch'eng-hsien Ch'ung-jen so-chi" 懷鄉憶舊：嵊縣崇仁瑣記 , *Che-chiang yüeh-k'an* 浙江月刊 #76 (August 1975), pp. 7-10.

Chou Chien-jen 周建人. "Shaohsing kuang-fu-ch'ien Lu Hsün ti i-hsiao-tuan shih-ch'ing" 紹興光復前魯迅的一小段事情 *Jen-min wen-hsüeh* 人民文學 #140-#141 (July-August 1961), pp. 123-124. The author is Lu Hsün's youngest brother.

Chou Hsia-shou 周遐壽. *Lu Hsün hsiao-shuo li ti jen-wu* 魯迅小說裏的人物. Shanghai, 1954. The author is one of Lu Hsün's younger brothers, better known as Chou Tso-jen (1885-1966).

————. *Lu Hsün ti ku-chia* 魯迅的故家. Shanghai, 1953.

Chou Tso-jen 周作人 . *Chih-t'ang hui-hsiang lu* 知堂回想錄 .
Hong Kong, 1970.

————. "Yüeh yen pa" 越諺跋 . In *Yüeh yen* 越諺 , by
Fan Yin 范寅 . Peiping, 1932.

Chu Min 朱态 , Hsieh Te-hsi 謝德銑 et al. *Lu Hsün tsai Shaohsing*
魯迅在紹興 . Hangchow, 1981.

Chu Pao-chiung 朱保烱 and Hsieh P'ei-lin 謝沛霖 , comps. *Ming-Ch'ing*
chin-shih t'i-ming pei-lu so-yin 明清進士題名碑錄索引 .
Shanghai, 1980.

Ch'ü T'ung-tsu. *Local Government in China under the Ch'ing*.
Cambridge, 1962.

Ch'ü Ying-kuang 屈映光 . *Ch'ü hsün-an-shih hsün-shih ch'üan-Che*
wen-kao 屈巡按使巡視全浙文告 . Hangchow, 1915? Held
by the Institute of Oriental Culture, Tokyo University, and by the
Hoover Institution.

Chu-chi Chung-shih tsung-p'u 諸暨鍾氏宗譜 . 1922. Held by
the Tōyō Bunko. Taga number 1132.

Chu-chi hsien-chih 諸暨縣志. 1905.

Chu-chi min-pao she 諸暨民報社 , ed. *Chu-chi kai-kuan* 諸暨概觀
1925. Held by the National Diet Library. A Xerox copy is in the
Hoover Institution.

Ch'üan Tseng-yu 全增右 . "Ch'ing-tai mu-liao chih-tu lun (hsü)"
清代幕僚制度論(續), *Ssu-hsiang yü shih-tai* 思想與時代
#32 (March 1944), pp. 35-41. Held by the University of Washington
(Seattle).

Ch'üan Tsu-wang 全祖望. *Chieh-chi-t'ing chi wai-pien* 鮚綺亭
集外編. 1804. Held by the Institute of Humanistic Studies,
Kyoto. Ch'üan (1705-1755) was a native of Yin-hsien, Ningpo.

Chung-wai hsin-pao 中外新報 . Originally published in Ningpo,
1858-1861, apparently by missionaries. A Japanese government

reprint of the first twelve issues, undated but pre-1868, is held by Kyoto University Library.

Cloud, Frederick. *Hangchow the "City of Heaven."* Shanghai, 1906. Cloud served as U.S. consul in Hangchow.

Cole, James H. *The People Versus the Taipings: Bao Lisheng's "Righteous Army of Dongan."* Berkeley, 1981.

_____. "Social Discrimination in Traditional China: The To-min of Shaohsing," *Journal of the Economic and Social History of the Orient* 25 #1 (1982), pp. 100-111.

_____. "The Shaoxing Connection: A Vertical Administrative Clique in Late Qing China," *Modern China* 6 #3 (July 1980), pp. 317-326.

de Bary, W.T. "Chinese Despotism and the Confucian Ideal: A Seventeenth-Century View." In *Chinese Thought and Institutions*, edited by John K. Fairbank, pp. 163-203. Chicago, 1957.

Elman, Benjamin. "Ch'ing Dynasty 'Schools' of Scholarship," *Ch'ing-shih wen-t'i* 4 #6 (December 1981), pp. 1-44.

Esherick, Joseph W. *Reform and Revolution in China: The 1911 Revolution in Hunan and Hubei.* Berkeley, 1976.

Fairbank, John K., ed. *Chinese Thought and Institutions.* Chicago, 1957.

Fan P'u-chai 范朴斋. "Lüeh lun ch'ien-Ch'ing li-hsü: tui ch'ien-Ch'ing 'Shaohsing shih-yeh' ho 'shu-pan' ti chieh-shao" 略论前清吏胥：对前清"绍兴师爷"和"书办"的介绍, *Kuang-ming jih-pao* 光明日报 (January 1, 1957), p. 3.

Fan Yin 范寅. *Yüeh yen* 越谚. Author's preface dated 1878. Reprinted with a postface by Chou Tso-jen, Peiping, 1932. Fan was a native of Kuei-chi.

Fang Chao-ying 房兆楹 and Tu Lien-che 杜聯喆, comps. *Tseng-chiao Ch'ing-ch'ao chin-shih t'i-ming pei-lu fu yin-te* 增校清朝進士題名碑錄附引得. Peiping, 1941. Taiwan photoreprint, 1966.

Feng Erh-k'ang 馮爾康. "Yung-cheng ti hsiao-ch'u Shaohsing ho Ch'ang-shu kai-chi" 雍正的削除紹興和常熟丐籍, *Shūkan Tōyōgaku* 集刊東洋学 #44 (October 1980), pp. 1-11.

Feng-shih tsung-p'u 馮氏宗譜. 1892. The Fengs lived in Kuei-chi. Held by the Tōyō Bunko. Taga number 904.

Fincher, John H. *Chinese Democracy: The Self-Government Movement in Local, Provincial and National Politics, 1905-1914.* New York, 1981.

_____. "The Chinese Self-Government Movement, 1900-1912." Ph.D. thesis in History, University of Washington (Seattle), 1969.

Folsom, Kenneth. *Friends, Guests, and Colleagues: The Mu-fu System in the Late Ch'ing Period.* Berkeley, 1968.

Fortune, Robert. *Two Visits to the Tea Countries of China.* London, 1853.

Freedman, Maurice. *The Study of Chinese Society.* Stanford, 1979.

Fu Tse-hung 傅澤鴻. *Pao-i-t'ang wen-ts'un* 寶彝堂文存. 1909. Held by the Tōyō Bunko. A native of Hsiang-hsiang county, Hunan, Fu served as prefect of Shaohsing as of 1880.

Fujii Hiroshi 藤井宏. "Shinan shōnin no kenkyū" 新安商人の研究 (四完)," *Tōyō gakuhō* 東洋學報 36 #4 (March 1954), pp. 115-145.

Gernet, Jacques. *Daily Life in China on the Eve of the Mongol Invasion, 1250-1276.* New York, 1962.

Giles, Herbert A. *A Chinese-English Dictionary.* Second edition. Shanghai, 1912. Taiwan reprint, 1964.

Goddard, Francis. *Called to Cathay.* New York, 1948. Goddard was a medical missionary in Shaohsing city.

Goodchild, Thomas. "Northeastern Chehkiang, China: Notes on Human Adaptation to Environment," *Bulletin of the American Geographical Society* 43 #11 (1911), pp. 801-826.

Goodrich, L. Carrington and Fang Chao-ying, eds. *Dictionary of Ming Biography, 1368-1644.* New York, 1976.

Grosier, Jean-Baptiste. *De la Chine ou description générale de cet empire.* Paris, 1818-1820.

_____. *A General Description of China. . . .* London, 1788.

Hang-chou pai-hua pao 杭州白話報. Hangchow, 1901-1902. Held by the National Diet Library.

Hang-hsien lü-shih kung-hui shih-chou chi-nien chi 杭縣律師公會十週紀念集. 1924?. Held by the Institute of Oriental Culture, Tokyo University.

Hatano Yoshihiro 波多野善大. *Chūgoku kindai kōgyoshi no kenkyū* 中国近代工業史の研究. Kyoto, 1961.

Hata Korehito 秦惟人. "Yōmu undō jiki no minshū undō: Kō-Setsu no kōen tōsō o chūshin to shite" 洋務運動時期の民衆運動：江浙の抗捐闘争を中心として, *Rekishi hyōren* 歴史評論 #282 (November 1973), pp. 45-63.

Hattori Unokichi 服部宇之吉. *Shina kenkyū* 支那研究. Tokyo, 1916.

_____. *Shinkoku tsūkō* 清国通考. Tokyo, 1905. Photoreprint with an appendix, Tokyo, 1966.

Hayashi Tomoharu 林友春, ed. *Kinsei Chūgoku kyōikushi kenkyū* 近世中国教育史研究. Tokyo, 1958.

Ho Ping-ti 何炳棣. *Chung-kuo hui-kuan shih lun* 中國會館史論. Taipei, 1966.

_____. *The Ladder of Success in Imperial China: Aspects of Social Mobility, 1368-1911.* New York, 1962.

_____. *Studies on the Population of China, 1368-1953.* Cambridge, 1959.

Hoang, Pierre. *Mélanges sur l'administration. Variétés sinologiques* #21. Shanghai, 1902.

Hosoi Shoji 細井昌治. "Shinsho no shori" 清初の胥吏, *Shakai keizai shigaku* 社會経濟史學 14 #6 (September 1944), pp. 1-23.

Howard, Richard. "K'ang Yu-wei (1858-1927): His Intellectual Background and Early Thought." In *Confucian Personalities*, edited by Arthur F. Wright and Denis Twitchett, pp. 294-316. Stanford, 1962.

Hsi, Angela. "Social and Economic Status of the Merchant Class of the Ming Dynasty: 1368-1644." Ph.D. thesis in History, University of Illinois at Urbana-Champaign, 1972.

Hsiao Kung-chuan. *Rural China: Imperial Control in the Nineteenth Century.* Seattle, 1960.

Hsiao-shan Ch'ung-hua Liu-shih tsung-p'u 蕭山崇化劉氏宗譜. 1922. Held by the National Diet Library. Taga number 1028.

Hsiao-shan hsiang-hu-chih 蕭山湘湖志. 1925.

Hsiao-shan hsien-chih kao 蕭山縣志稿. 1935. Taiwan photo-reprint, 1970.

Hsiao-shan Hsi-ho Ch'an-shih tsung-p'u 蕭山西河單氏宗譜. Preface dated 1922. Held by the Tōyō Bunko. Taga number 851.

Hsieh, Andrew. "Tseng Kuo-fan, A Nineteenth-Century Confucian General." Ph.D. thesis in History, Yale University, 1975.

Hsieh Chao-chih 謝肇淛. *Wu tsa tsu* 五雜組. First published during the Wan-li period. Punctuated edition, Peking, 1959.

Hsieh Kuan-sheng 謝冠生 and Ch'a Liang-chien 查良鑑, eds. *Chung-kuo fa-chih shih lun-chi* 中國法制史論集. Taipei, 1968.

Hsieh Te-hsi 謝德銑. *Lu Hsün tso-p'in chung ti Shaohsing fang-yen chu-shih* 魯迅作品中的紹興方言注釋 . Hangchow, 1979.

Hsin-ch'ang hsien-chih 新昌縣志. 1918.

Hsü Ch'in-wen 許欽文. *I-t'an chiu* 一罈酒 . Shanghai, 1930. Hsü (born in 1897), a native of Shaohsing hsien, was a protégé of Lu Hsün.

Hsü Erh-ku 徐爾穀, ed. *Ku Yüeh ts'ang-shu-lou shu-mu* 古越藏書樓書目 . Kuei-chi, 1904. Held by the Seikadō and the Harvard-Yenching Library.

Hsü Hsin-liu 徐新六, ed. *T'ien-su-ko ts'ung-k'an erh-chi* 天蘇閣叢刊二集 . Hangchow, 1923. Held by the Institute of Humanistic Studies, Kyoto, and the Hoover Institution.

Hsü K'o 徐珂, comp. *Ch'ing-pai lei-ch'ao* 清稗類鈔 . 1917. Hsü, born in 1869, was a native of Ch'ien-t'ang county, Hangchow.

_____. *Hsin-yüan ts'ung-k'o i-chi* 心園叢刻一集 . 1925. Held by the Osaka Prefectural Library.

_____. *K'o yen* 可言 . In *Tien-su-ko ts'ung-k'an erh-chi* 天蘇閣叢刊二集 , edited by Hsü Hsin-liu 徐新六. Hangchow, 1923.

_____. *Ta-shou-t'ang cha-chi* 大受堂札記 . In *Hsin-yüan ts'ung-k'o i-chi* 心園叢刊一集 , by Hsü K'o. 1925.

Hsü Shou-ch'ang 許壽裳. *Wo so jen-shih ti Lu Hsün* 我所認識的魯迅. Peking, 1952. A native of Shaohsing, Hsü (1887-1948) edited *Che-chiang ch'ao* and was a friend of Lu Hsün.

Hsü Ta-ling 許大齡. *Ch'ing-tai chüan-na chih-tu* 清代捐納制度 Peking, 1950. Hong Kong photoreprint, 1968.

Hsüeh-cheng ch'üan-shu 學政全書 . 1812.

Hsüeh-pu tsung-wu ssu 學部總務司, comp. *Ti-i-tz'u chiao-yü t'ung-chi t'u piao, Kuang-hsü 33 nien-fen* 第一次敎育統計圖表光緒三十三年分 . No place or date of publication. Held by

Harvard-Yenching. Like the following two items, an impressive statistical compilation.

_____. *Ti-erh-tz'u chiao-yü t'ung-chi t'u piao, Kuang-hsü 34 nien-fen* 第二次教育統計圖表，光緒三十四年分 . N.p., n.d.

_____. *Ti-san-tz'u chiao-yü t'ung-chi t'u piao, Hsüan-t'ung yüan nien-fen* 第三次教育統計圖表，宣統元年分 . N.p., n.d.

Hu-shih chia-p'u 胡氏家譜 . 1888. Held by the Tōyō Bunko. Taga number 464. From Kuei-chi.

Huang, Liu-hung. *A Complete Book Concerning Happiness and Benevolence, Fu-hui ch'üan-shu: A Manual for Local Magistrates in Seventeenth-Century China.* Djang Chu, translator and editor. Tucson, 1984.

Huang, Pei. "A Study of the Yung-cheng Period, 1723-1735: The Political Phase." Ph.D. thesis in History, University of Indiana, 1963. Published as *Autocracy At Work: A Study of the Yung-cheng Period, 1723-1735.* Bloomington, Indiana, 1974.

Hung Huan-ch'un 洪煥椿 . "Lun Ming-Ch'ing Su-chou ti-ch'ü hui-kuan ti hsing-chih chi ch'i tso-yung" 论明清苏州地区会馆的性质及其作用 , *Chung-kuo shih yen-chiu* 中国史研究 #2 (June 1980), pp. 3-15.

_____. *Che-chiang ti-fang-chih k'ao lu* 浙江地方志考录 . Peking, 1958. A comprehensive and fully annotated bibliography.

Hung Yeh 洪業 ,ed. *Shih-huo-chih shih-wu-chung tsung-ho yin-te* 食貨志十五種綜合引得 . Peiping, 1938. Taiwan reprint, 1966.

Iikura Shōhei 飯倉照平 . "Shōkō zatsubun" 紹興雜聞 , *(Tōritsudai) Jimbun gakuhō* (都立大)人文學報 #140 (March 1980), pp. 21-46.

Imabori Seiji 今堀誠二 . *Chūgoku kindaishi kenkyū josetsu* 中国近代史研究序説 . Tokyo, 1968.

_____. "Shindai no kōso ni tsuite" 清代の抗租について ,
Shigaku zasshi 史学雑誌 76 #9 (September 1967), pp. 37-61.

Iriya Yoshitaka 入矢義高, ed. *Kinsei suihitsu shū* 近世随筆集 .
Tokyo, 1971.

Jamieson, George et al. "Tenure of Land in China and the Condition of
the Rural Population," *Journal of the China Branch of the Royal
Asiatic Society* (new series) 23 #2 (1888), pp. 59-183.

Jones, Susan Mann. "Finance in Ningpo: The 'Ch'ien Chuang,' 1750-
1880." *In Economic Organization in Chinese Society*, edited by W.
E. Willmott, pp. 47-77. Stanford, 1972.

Kan Han 甘韓 , ed. *Huang-ch'ao ching-shih-wen hsin-pien hsü-chi*
皇朝經世文新編續集 . Shanghai, 1902.

Kao Yüeh-t'ien 高越天. "Shen Ting-i hsien-sheng ti i-sheng (i)"
沈定一先生的一生 (一), *Che-chiang yüeh-k'an* 浙江月刊
4 #4 (April 1972), pp. 5-8.

Katō Shigeshi 加藤繁. *Shina keizaishi kōshō* 支那經濟史考證
Tokyo, 1952. Reprinted Tokyo, 1974.

_____. "Shindai ni okeru Pekin no shōnin kaikan ni tsuite"
清代における北京の商人會館について, *Shigaku zasshi* 史學雜誌
53 #2 (February 1942), pp. 151-181.

Kawakatsu Mamoru 川勝守. "Minmatsu Shinsho no shōshi ni tsuite"
明末清初の訟師について, *Kyūshu daigaku tōyōshi ronshu* 九州
大學東洋史論集 #9 (March 1981), pp. 111-124.

Keng-hsü k'o ti-i-tz'u k'ao-shih fa-kuan t'ung-nien lu 庚戌 [1910]
科第一次考試法官同年錄 . No place or date of publication.
Held by the Harvard-Yenching Library.

Kiyama Hideo 木山英雄 . "Settō 'damin' kō" 浙東"隨民"考 ,
Shakaishi kenkyū 社会史研究 #4 (April 1984), pp. 61-116.

Seen too late to be incorporated into the text.

Ko Shih-chün 葛士濬, ed. *Huang-ch'ao ching-shih-wen hsü-pien* 皇朝經世文續編 . 1888.

Ko Sui-ch'eng 葛綏成, ed. *Che-chiang (fen-sheng ti-chih)* 浙江 (分有地誌). Shanghai, 1939.

Kobayashi Kazumi 小林一美 . "Chūgoku hanshokuminchika no keizai katei to minshū no tatakai: rikin o megutte, jūkyūseiki kōhan" 中国半殖民地化の經濟過程と民衆の闘い：厘金をめぐって，十九世紀後半 , *Rekishigaku kenkyū* 歴史學研究 #369 (February 1971), pp. 1-18.

Kobayashi Yukio 小林幸夫. "Shinmatsu no Sekkō ni okeru fuzei kaikaku to sessen nōzei ni tsuite" 清末の浙江における財税改革と折錢納税について , *Tōyō gakuhō* 東洋學報 58 #1-#2 (December 1976), pp. 49-85.

Kojima Shinji 小島晋治. "Taihei tenkoku kakumei" 太平天国革命 . In *Iwanami kōza sekai rekishi* 岩波講座世界歴史 , volume 21, pp. 281-334. Tokyo, 1971.

Kojima Yoshio 小島淑男. "Shingai kakumeiki no rōnō undō to Chūgoku shakaidō" 辛亥革命期の労農運動と中国の社会党 , *Rekishigaku kenkyū* 歴史學研究 , supplement (October 1971), pp. 106-115.

_____. "Kindai Chūgoku no nōson keizai to tochi shoyū kankei: Shōkōfu Shōzanken no saden chi'iki o chūshin ni" 近代中国の農村経済と土地所有関係：紹興府蕭山県の沙田地域を中心に , *Keizai shūshi* 経済集志 48 #2 (July 1978), pp. 125-141.

Kondō Hideki 近藤秀樹. "Shindai no ennō to kanryū shakai no shūmatsu" 清代の捐納と官僚社会の終末 , *Shirin* 史林 46 #2 (March 1963), pp. 82-110; #3 (May 1963), pp. 77-100; and #4 (July 1963), pp. 60-86.

Kono Takeo hakushi kanreki kinen ronbunshū kankōkai 小野武夫 博士還曆記念論文集刊行会 , ed. *Tōyō nōgyo keizaishi kenkyū* 東洋農業經濟史研究. Tokyo, 1948.

Kotake Fumio 小林文夫 et al. *Tōa no kindaika* 東亞の近代化. Revised edition. Osaka, 1969.

Ku Chien-ch'en 谷劍塵 . *Shen-tung* 紳董 . Shanghai, 1930. A play in three acts by a native of Shaohsing hsien. Held by the Institute of Humanistic Studies, Kyoto.

Ku Shih-chiang 顧士江, ed. *Hsiao-shan hsiang-t'u-chih* 蕭山鄉土誌. Revised edition. Shanghai?, 1933.

Ku Yen-wu 顧炎武 . *Jih chih lu chi-shih* 日知錄集釋 . Ssu-pu pei-yao edition.

_____. *T'ien-hsia chün-kuo li-ping shu* 天下郡國利病書 . Ssu-pu ts'ung-k'an edition.

Ku Yü Chang-shih tsung-p'u 古虞張氏宗譜. 1888. Held by the Tōyō Bunko. Taga number 629.

Kuang-hsü ch'ao Tung-hua lu 光緒朝東華錄. Punctuated edition. Peking, 1958.

Kuang-hsü Shun-t'ien fu-chih 光緒順天府志. 1885. Held by the Hoover Institution.

Kuang yü t'u 廣輿圖. Expanded by Hu Sung 胡松 from Lo Hung-hsien's 羅洪先 original edition. Taiwan photoreprint, 1969, of the 1579 edition.

Kuei-chi Ch'in-shih tsung-p'u 會稽秦氏宗譜 . 1911. Held by the Tōyō Bunko and Harvard-Yenching. Taga number 605.

Kuei-chi Chung-shih tsung-p'u 會稽鍾氏宗譜 . 1923. Held by the Tōyō Bunko. Taga number 1131.

Kuei-chi T'ao-shih tsu-p'u 會稽陶氏族譜 1904. Held by the Tōyō Bunko. Taga number 794.

Kuhn, Philip A. "Local Self-Government under the Republic." In *Conflict and Control in Late Imperial China*, edited by Frederic Wakeman, Jr. and Carolyn Grant, pp. 257-298. Berkeley, 1975.

_____. *Rebellion and Its Enemies in Late Imperial China: Militarization and Social Structure, 1796-1864.* Cambridge, 1970.

Lamley, Harry J. " *Hsieh-tou:* The Pathology of Violence in Southeastern China," *Ch'ing-shih wen-t'i* 3 #7 (December 1977), pp. 1-39.

Legge, James, transl. *The Chinese Classics*. London and Oxford, 1865-1895. Hong Kong reprint, 1961.

Lan-fang Wei-shih tsung-p'u 蘭風魏氏宗譜 . 1878. Held by the Tōyō Bunko. Taga number 1155. From Yü-yao.

Li Hua 李华 . "Ming-Ch'ing i-lai Pei-ching ti kung-shang-yeh hang-hui" 明清以來北京的工商业行会 , *Li-shih yen-chiu* 历史研究 #4 (April 1978), pp. 63-79.

Li Kuo-ch'i 李國祁 . "Ch'ing-chi Min-ch'u Che-chiang ti-ch'ü chin-tai-hua yen-chin kuo-ch'eng chung ti chiao-yü yü wen-hua shih-yeh (1895-1916)" 清季民初浙江地區近代化演進過程中的教育與文化事業 (1895-1916), *Chung-hua hsüeh-pao* 中華學報 3 #2 (July 1976), pp. 123-152.

_____. *Chung-kuo hsien-tai-hua ti ch'ü-yü yen-chiu: Min Che T'ai ti-chü, 1860-1916* 中國現代化的區域研究:閩浙臺地區 , 1860-1916. Taipei, 1982.

Li Tz'u-ming 李慈銘 . *Yüeh-man-t'ang jih-chi pu* 越縵堂日記補.Peiping, 1936. Li (1830-1894) was a native of Kuei-chi.

_____. *Yüeh-man-t'ang p'ien-t'i-wen* 越縵堂駢體文 . In *Yüeh-man-t'ang wen-chi* 越縵堂文集 , by Li Tz'u-ming. Peiping, 1930. Taiwan photoreprint, 1971.

_____. *Yüeh-man-t'ang wen-chi* 越縵堂文集 . Peiping, 1930. Taiwan photoreprint, 1971.

Li Wen-chih 李文治 , ed. *Chung-kuo chin-tai nung-yeh shi tzu-liao ti-i-chi (1840-1911)* 中國近代農業史資料第一集 (1840-1911). Peking, 1957.

Liang Chang-chü 梁章鉅 . *Lang-chi hsü-t'an* 浪跡續談 . In *Liang-shih pi-chi* 梁氏筆記, by Liang Chang-chü. Shanghai, 1918. Liang, a native of Foochow, lived during the Tao-kuang period. Held by Institute of Humanistic Studies, Kyoto.

Liang Fang-chung 梁方仲. *Chung-kuo li-tai hu-k'ou, t'ien-ti, t'ien-fu t'ung-chi* 中国历代户口田地,田賦統計. Shanghai, 1980.

Lin Ch'uan-chia 林傳甲 ,ed. *Ta Chung-hua Che-chiang sheng ti-li chih* 大中華浙江省地理誌 . Hangchow, 1918.

Ling Ch'ih 鈴癡, pseud. "Shaohsing chiu" 紹興酒 , *Che-chiang yüeh-k'an* 浙江月刊 2 #10 (December 1970), pp. 20-21.

————————. "Shaohsing ti to-min" 紹興的惰民, *Che-chiang yüeh-k'an* 3 #1 (January 1971), p. 17.

Liu, Hui-chen Wang. *The Traditional Chinese Clan Rules*. Locust Valley, N.Y., 1959.

Liu Kwang-Ching 劉廣京 . "Wan-Ch'ing ti-fang kuan tzu-shu chih shih-liao chia-chih: Tao-Hsien chih chi kuan-shen kuan-min kuan-hsi ch'u t'an" 晚清地方官自述之史料價值：道咸之際官紳官民關係初探 . In *Chung-yang yen-chiu yüan ch'eng-li wu-shih chou nien chi-nien lun-wen chi* 中央研究院成立五十周年紀念論文集 , pp. 333-364. Taipei, 1978.

Liu Ta-pai 劉大白 . *Ku-shih ti t'an-tzu* 故事的罎子 . Shanghai, 1934. Held by the University of California, Berkeley. Collected stories by Liu (1880-1932), a native of Shaohsing hsien.

Lo Erh-kang 羅爾綱 . "Che-tung ch'i-i tien-nung ts'an-chia T'ai-p'ing t'ien-kuo" 浙東起義佃農參加太平天国 , *Li-shih yen-chiu* 歷史研究 #4 (April 1956), p. 90. The title is misleading, since this very brief article deals with tenants' rent resistance in eastern Chekiang before the Taipings entered the province.

Lo Hsiang-lin 羅香林. *Chung-kuo tsu-p'u yen-chiu* 中國族譜研究. Hong Kong, 1971.

Lo Yü-tung 羅玉東. *Chung-kuo li-chin shih* 中國釐金史. Shanghai, 1936.

Lou Tzu-kuang 婁子匡. "Che-chiang chih chiu" 浙江之酒, *Che-chiang yüeh-k'an* 浙江月刊 #64 (August 1974), pp. 12-13.

Lu Hsün 魯迅 (Chou Shu-jen 周樹人). *Lu Hsün ch'üan-chi* 魯迅全集. Shanghai, 1938.

_____. *Lu Hsün ch'üan-chi* 魯迅全集. Peking, 1957-1958.

_____. *Lu Hsün jih-chi* 魯迅日記. Peking, 1962. This is a typeset, punctuated edition of the original manuscript diary (which covers 1912-1936 and was published by photolithographic reproduction in Peking in the early 1950s). The contents of both editions are identical.

_____. *Selected Works of Lu Hsun.* Peking, 1956-1960.

Lü Tso-hsieh 呂作燮. "Ming-Ch'ing shih-ch'i ti hui-kuan ping fei kung-shang-yeh hang-hui" 明清時期的會館并非工商業行會 *Chung-kuo shih yen-chiu* 中國史研究 #14 (June 1982), pp. 66-79.

Lu Wen-ch'ao 盧文弨. *Pao-ching-t'ang wen-chi* 抱經堂文集. In *Pao-ching-t'ang ts'ung-shu* 抱經堂叢書, edited by Lu Wen-ch'ao. Published in Yü-yao during the Ch'ien-lung period. Lu (born in 1718) was a native of Yü-yao. Held by the Institute of Humanistic Studies, Kyoto.

Lyell, William A., Jr. *Lu Hsün's Vision of Reality.* Berkeley, 1976.

Makino Tatsumi 牧野巽. "Ko Enbu no seiinron" 顧炎武の生員論. In *Kinsei Chūgoku kyōikushi kenkyū* 近世中國教育史研究, edited by Hayashi Tomoharu 林友春, pp. 219-229. Tokyo, 1958.

Martini, Martino. *Novus atlas sinensis.* . . . Amsterdam?, 1663. Maps
   by Blaeu. Text in French.

Maruyama Noboru 丸山昇. *Ro Jin: Sono bungaku to kakumei* 魯迅：
そ の 文学 と 革命. Tokyo, 1965.

Mayers, William F. *The Chinese Government.* Third edition. Shanghai,
   1897. Taiwan photoreprint, 1970.

McElderry, Andrea Lee. *Shanghai Old Style Banks (Ch'ien-chuang),*
   1800-1935. Ann Arbor, 1976.

Meng Yao 孟瑤. *Chung-kuo hsi-ch'ü shih* 中國戲曲史. Taipei, 1965.

Meskill, Johanna Menzel. *A Chinese Pioneer Family: The Lins of*
   Wu-feng, Taiwan 1729-1895. Princeton, 1979.

Meskill, John. *Ch'oe Pu's Diary: A Record of Drifting Across the*
   Sea. Tucson, 1965.

Metzger, Thomas. "Chinese Bandits: The Traditional Perception
   Reevaluated," *Journal of Asian Studies* 33 #3 (May 1974),
   pp. 455-458.

_____. *Escape From Predicament: Neo-Confucianism and China's*
   Evolving Political Culture. New York, 1977.

_____. *The Internal Organization of Ch'ing Bureaucracy: Legal,*
   Normative, and Communication Aspects. Cambridge, 1973.

_____. "The State and Commerce in Imperial China," *Asian and*
   African Studies (Jerusalem) #6 (1970), pp. 23-46.

Miao Ch'üan-chi 繆全吉. "Ch'ing-tai hsing-mu shu-yao" 清代刑幕
述要. In *Chung-kuo fa-chih shih lun-chi* 中國法制史
論集, edited by Hsieh Kuan-sheng 謝冠生 and Ch'a Liang-chien
查良鑑, pp. 317-371. Taipei, 1968.

_____. "Ch'ing-tai hsü-li shu-kai (hsia)" 清代胥吏述概(下).
   Ssu-hsiang yü shih-tai 思想與時代 #129 (April 1965), pp. 14-17.

_____. "Ch'ing-tai mu-fu chih-tu chih yen-chiu" 清代幕府制度之研究. M.A. thesis in Political Science, National Taiwan University, 1962.

_____. *Ch'ing-tai mu-fu jen-shih chih-tu* 清代幕府人事制度. Taipei, 1971.

_____. *Ming-tai hsü-li* 明代胥吏. Taipei, 1969.

Michael, Franz. *The Taiping Rebellion: History and Documents*. Seattle, 1966-1971.

Min-hu jih-pao 民呼日報. Shanghai, 1909. Taiwan photoreprint, 1969.

Min li pao 民立報. Shanghai, 1910-1911. Taiwan photoreprint, 1969.

Min pao 民報. Tokyo, 1905-1910.

Minami Manshū tetsudō kabushiki kaisha Shanghai jimusho 南滿洲鐵道株式會社上海事務所, ed. *Sekkō zaibatsu* 浙江財閥. Dairen, 1929.

Ming shih 明史. Kuo-fang yen-chiu yüan edition. Taipei, 1963.

Mitamura Taisuke 三田村泰助. *Min to Shin* 明と清. Tokyo, 1969.

Miyazaki Ichisada 宮崎市定. "Shindai no shori to bakuyū" 清代の胥吏と幕友, *Tōyōshi kenkyū* 東洋史研究 16 #4 (March 1958), pp. 1-28.

Morohashi Tetsuji 諸橋轍次. *Dai kanwa jiten* 大漢和辞典. Tokyo, 1955-1960.

Morrison, Esther. "The Modernization of the Confucian Bureaucracy: An Historical Study of Public Administration." Ph.D. thesis in History and Far Eastern Languages, Radcliffe College, 1959.

Moule, Arthur E. *The Story of the Cheh-kiang Mission of the Church Missionary Society*. Fourth edition. London, 1891. Reverend Moule was stationed in Ningpo.

Muramatsu Yūji. "A Documentary Study of Chinese Landlordism in Late Ch'ing and Early Republican China," *Bulletin of the School of Oriental and African Studies* 29 #3 (1966), pp. 566-599.

Myers, Ramon. Review of books by Ch'üan Han-sheng, *Journal of Asian Studies* 33 #1 (November 1973), pp. 106-109.

Na Ssu-lu 那思陸 . *Ch'ing-tai chou-hsien ya-men shen-p'an chih-tu* 清代州縣衙門審判制度 . Taipei, 1982.

Nakamura Tsune 中村恒. "Shinmatsu gakudō setsuritsu o meguru Kō-Setsu nōson shakai no ichidanmen" 清末學堂設立をめぐる江浙農村社會の一断面 , *Rekishi kyōiku* 歷史教育 10 #11 (November 1962), pp. 72-85.

Naquin, Susan. "Millenarian Rebellion in China: The Eight Trigrams Uprising of 1813." Ph.D. thesis in History, Yale University, 1974. Published under the same title, New Haven, 1976.

_____. *Shantung Rebellion: The Wang Lun Uprising of 1774.* New Haven, 1981.

Ni-Chū minzoku kagaku kenkyūjo 日中民族科學研究所 , ed. *Chūgoku rekidai shokukan jiten* 中国歷代職官辭典 . Tokyo, 1980.

Niida Noboru 仁井田陞 . *Chūgoku hōseishi* 中国法制史 . Revised edition. Tokyo, 1963.

_____. *Chūgoku hōseishi kenkyū* 中國法制史研究 . Tokyo, 1959-1964.

_____. "Shina kinsei dōzoku buraku no kaitō" 支那近世同族部落の械鬪 . In *Tōyō nōgyo keizaishi kenkyū* 東洋農業經濟史研究, edited by Ono Takeo hakushi kanreki kinen ronbunshū kankōkai 小野武夫博士還曆記念論文集刊行会 , pp. 65-100. Tokyo, 1948.

Nishizato Yoshiyuki 西里喜行 . "Shinmatsu no Nimpō shōnin ni tsuite (jō)" 清末の寧波商人について（上） , *Tōyōshi kenkyū* 東洋史研究 26 #1 (June 1967), pp. 1-89.

Nivison, David S. "Ho-shen and His Accusers: Ideology and Political Behavior in the Eighteenth Century." In *Confucianism in Action*, edited by David S. Nivison and Arthur F. Wright, pp. 209-243. Stanford, 1959.

_____. *The Life and Thought of Chang Hsüeh-ch'eng (1738-1801)*. Stanford, 1966.

North-China Herald. Shanghai.

Nung-hsüeh pao 農學報. Shanghai, 1897-1901. Held by the Tōyō Bunko.

Ocko, Jonathan K. *Bureaucratic Reform in Provincial China: Ting Jih-ch'ang in Restoration Kiangsu, 1867-1870*. Cambridge, 1983.

Ōmura Kyōdō 大村興道. "Shinchō kyōiku shisōshi ni okeru 'Seiyu kokun' no chii ni tsuite" 清朝教育思想に於ける「聖諭廣訓」の地位に就いて. In *Kinsei Chūgoku kyōikushi kenkyū* 近世中國教育史研究, edited by Hayashi Tomoharu 林友春, pp. 231-271. Tokyo, 1958.

Ono Kazuko 小野和子. "Shinsho no shisō tōsei o megutte" 清初の思想統制をめぐって, *Tōyōshi kenkyū* 東洋史研究 18 #3 (December 1959), pp. 99-123.

Ōtani Toshio 大谷敦夫. *Chūgoku kindai seijikeizaishi nyūmon* 中国近代政治経済史入門. Toyko, 1972.

Ou-yang Fan-hai 歐陽凡海. *Lu Hsün ti shu* 魯迅的書. Canton, 1949.

Pao weng lao-jen 抱甕老人 (pseud.), comp. *Chin-ku ch'i-kuan* 今古奇觀. First published during the 1630s-1640s.

Parker, E.H. "A Journey in Chekiang," *Journal of the China Branch of the Royal Asiatic Society* (new series) 19 #1 (1884), pp. 27-53.

Pei hsin tsa-chih 北新雜誌. 1907? Held by the Institute of Humanistic Studies, Kyoto.

P'eng Tse-i 彭澤益 ,ed. *Chung-kuo chin-tai shou-kung-yeh shih tzu-liao (1840-1949)* 中國近代手工業史資料 (1840-1949).
    Peking, 1957.

Perry, Elizabeth J. *Rebels and Revolutionaries in North China, 1845-1945.* Stanford, 1980.

Pi-chi hsiao-shuo ta-kuan hsü-pien 筆記小說大觀續編.
    Taipei, 1962.

Pi-chih she 畢志社 , ed. *Chung-kuo ko-ming-tang ta shou-ling Hsü Hsi-lin* 中國革命黨大首領徐錫麟. Shanghai?, 1907.
    Held by the Tōyō Bunko. A rare source on Hsü Hsi-lin and Ch'iu Chin, published within months of their death.

Playfair, G.M.H. *The Cities and Towns of China.* Second edition.
    Shanghai, 1910. Taiwan photoreprint, 1965.

Porter, Jonathan. *Tseng Kuo-fan's Private Bureaucracy.* Berkeley, 1972.

Pruitt, Ida. *A Daughter of Han: The Autobiography of a Chinese Working Woman.* New Haven, 1945. Reprint with index, Stanford, 1967.

Pu T'ung 不同 , pseud. "Chien-hu ho Chi-shan" 鑑湖和稽山 , *Che-chiang yüeh-k'an* 浙江月刊 1 #3 (September 1968). pp. 12-13.

Pusey, James Reeve. *China and Charles Darwin.* Cambridge, 1983.

Rankin, Mary B. *Early Chinese Revolutionaries: Radical Intellectuals in Shanghai and Chekiang, 1902-1911.* Cambridge, 1971.

_____. "The Emergence of Women at the End of the Ch'ing: The Case of Ch'iu Chin." In *Women in Chinese Society*, edited by Margery Wolf and Roxane Witke, pp. 39-66. Stanford, 1975.

_____. "The Revolutionary Movement in Chekiang: A Study in the Tenacity of Tradition." In *China in Revolution: The First Phase, 1900-1913*, edited by Mary C. Wright, pp. 319-361. New Haven, 1968.

Rawski, Evelyn S. *Agricultural Change and the Peasant Economy of South China*. Cambridge, 1972.

_____. *Education and Popular Literacy in Ch'ing China*. Ann Arbor, 1979.

Richthofen, Ferdinand von. *Baron Richthofen's Letters 1870-1872*. Second edition. Shanghai, 1903.

Rinji Taiwan kyūkan chōsakai 臨時臺灣舊慣調查會 . *Shinkoku gyōseihō* 清國行政法. Tokyo and Kobe, 1910-1914. Photoreprint with a new index, Tokyo, 1972. The best survey of Ch'ing institutions ever written.

Rinji Taiwan kyūkan chōsakai 臨時臺灣舊慣調查會 . *Taiwan shihō furoku sankosho* 臺灣私法附錄參考書. Tokyo and Kobe, 1909-1911.

Rowe, William T. "Urban Society in Late Imperial China: Hankow, 1796-1889." Ph.D. thesis in History, Columbia University, 1980. Published as *Hankow: Commerce and Society in a Chinese City, 1796-1889*. Stanford, 1984.

Saeki Tomi 佐伯富 . *Shindai ensei no kenkyū* 清代鹽政の研究 Second edition. Kyoto, 1962.

Saeki Yūichi 佐伯有一, Tanaka Issei 田仲一成 , et al., eds. *Niida Noboru hakase shū Pekin kōshō girudo shiryo shū (ichi), (roku)* 仁井田陞博士輯北京.工商ギルド資料集 (一)(六) . Tokyo, 1975 and 1983.

Sakai Tadao 酒井忠夫 . *Chūgoku zensho no kenkyū* 中國善書 の研究 . Tokyo, 1960.

Sasaki Masaya 佐々木正哉 . "Kanpō ninen Yinken no kōryō bakudō" 咸豐二年鄞縣の抗糧暴動 . In *Kindai Chūgoku kenkyū dai go shū* 近代中國研究第五輯, edited by the Tōyō Bunko kindai Chūgoku kenkyū iinkai 東洋文庫近代中國研究委員会, pp. 185-299. Toyko, 1963.

Satō Taketoshi 佐藤武敏 . "Min-Shin jidai Settō ni okeru suiri jigyō: Sankōkō o chūshin ni" 明清時代浙東における水利事業:三江

闡を中心に   , *Shūkan Tōyōgaku* 集刊東洋學 #20 (October 1968), pp. 93-109.

Schoppa, R. Keith. *Chinese Elites and Political Change: Zhejiang Province in the Early Twentieth Century.* Cambridge, 1982.

_____. "Local Self-Government in Zhejiang, 1909-1927," *Modern China* 2 #4 (October 1976), pp. 503-530.

Schwartz, Benjamin I. *In Search of Wealth and Power: Yen Fu and the West.* Cambridge, 1964.

Shan-hsi jen 剡溪人 , pseud. "Ti-ma-pan t'ui-pien wei Shaohsing-hsi ti lai-yu" 的篤班蛻變為紹興戲的來由, *Che-chiang yüeh-k'an* 浙江月刊 1 #2 (July 1968), pp. 22-23.

Shan-yin An-ch'ang Hsü-shih tsung-p'u 山陰安昌徐氏宗譜 . 1884. Held by the Tōyō Bunko. Taga number 559.

Shan-yin Chang-chuan Hu-shih tsung-p'u 山陰張川胡氏宗譜 . Preface dated 1886. Held by the Tōyō Bunko. Taga number 474.

Shan-yin hsien-chih 山陰縣志 . 1671.

Shan-yin P'ang-shih tsung-p'u 山陰厖氏宗譜 . Preface dated 1808, but text contains later additions. Unpublished manuscript held by the Harvard-Yenching Library.

Shan-yin Tou-wei Chu-shih tsung-p'u 山陰陡亹朱氏宗譜 . Preface dated 1894. Held by the Tōyō Bunko. Taga number 139.

Shanghai lü-shih kung-hui 上海律師公會 , ed. *Shanghai lü-shih kung-hui hui-yüan lu* 上海律師公會會員錄 . Shanghai, 1933? Held by the Institute of Oriental Culture, Tokyo University.

Shanghai po-wu kuan t'u-shu tzu-liao shih 上海博物館圖書資料室, ed. *Shanghai pei-k'o tzu-liao hsüan-chi* 上海碑刻資料選輯 . Shanghai, 1980.

Shang-yü hsien-chih 上虞縣志 . 1890.

Shang-yü hsien-chih chiao-hsü 上虞縣志校續. 1898.

Shao-chün p'ing-t'iao cheng-hsin lu 紹郡平糶徵信錄 . Preface
(by Ts'ai Yüan-p'ei) dated 1898. Held by the Institute of Oriental
Culture, Tokyo University.

Shaohsing fu-chih 紹興府志 . 1568, 1683, and 1792.

Shaohsing hsien-chih tzu-liao ti-i-chi 紹興縣志資料第一輯 .
1937.

Shaohsing Yü-lin-kuan Chin-shih tsung-p'u 紹興魚臨關金氏宗
譜 . 1931. Held by the National Diet Library. Taga number 352.

Shen Pang 沈榜 . *Wan-shu tsa-chi* 宛署雜記 . First published
1593. Punctuated edition, Peking, 1961. The author, a native of
Hu-Kuang province, served as magistrate of Wan-p'ing hsien beginning in 1590. A rare account of late Ming Peking.

Shen Te-fu 沈德符 . *Wan-li yeh-huo pien* 萬曆野獲編 . Preface
dated 1606. Punctuated edition, Peking, 1959. Shen was a native
of Chia-hsing, Chekiang. Peking edition includes a supplementary
section, "pu-i."

Sheng K'ang 盛康 , ed. *Huang-ch'ao ching-shih wen-pien hsü-pien*
皇朝經世文編續編 . 1898. Taiwan reprint, 1972.

Shiba Yoshinobu. *Commerce and Society in Sung China*. Abridged
translation by Mark Elvin. Ann Arbor, 1970.

_____. "Ningpo and Its Hinterland." In *The City in Late Imperial
China*, edited by G. William Skinner, pp. 391-439. Stanford, 1977.

Shiga Masatoshi 志賀正年 . "Ro Jin to minkan bungei (jō)" 魯迅と
民間文芸（上） , *Tenri daigaku gakuho* 天理大学学報
#30 (December 1959), pp. 52-73.

Shiga Shūzō 滋賀秀三 . "Shinchō no hōsei" 清朝の法制 . In
Kindai Chūgoku kenkyū nyūmon 近代中国研究入門 , edited
by Banno Masataka 坂野正高 et al., pp. 271-318. Tokyo, 1974.

Shih pao 時報 . Shanghai, 1909-1911.

Shih Shan-ch'ang 史善長 . *Lun t'ai tsa-chi* 輪臺雜記 . 1887. Held by Kyoto University Library. Shih was a native of Shan-yin.

Shina keizai hōkokusho 支那經濟報告書 . Published by the Tōa dōbunkai Shina keizai chōsabu 東亞同文會支那經濟調查部 , Tokyo. The Tōyō Bunko contains all but one of the first fifty-one issues (1908-1910).

Shinkoku jihō 清國時報 . A monthly digest of the late Ch'ing press, compiled by the Political Affairs Bureau of the Japanese Foreign Office, Tokyo. The first eighty-four issues (1905-1911) are held by Tenri University Library.

Skinner, G. William. *A Bibliography of Gazetteers Treating the Ning-Shao Region of Chekiang.* Produced in Xerox by the Ning-Shao Project, Stanford University, 1975.

_____. "Chinese Peasants and the Closed Community: An Open and Shut Case," *Comparative Studies in Society and History* 13 #3 (July 1971), pp. 270-281.

_____. "Regional Urbanization in Nineteenth-Century China" and "Introduction: Urban Social Structure in Ch'ing China." Both in *The City in Late Imperial China,* edited by G. William Skinner, pp. 211-249 and 521-553. Stanford, 1977.

_____. "Mobility Strategies in Late Imperial China: A Regional Systems Analysis." In *Regional Analysis, Volume I: Economic Systems,* edited by Carol A. Smith, pp. 327-364. New York, 1976.

Spence, Jonathan D. *Emperor of China: Self-portrait of K'ang-hsi.* New York, 1974.

Ssu-fa hsing-cheng pu 司法行政部, ed. *Chung-kuo min shang hsi-kuan tiao-ch'a pao-kao lu* 中國民商習慣調查報告錄 . Nanking, 1930. Taiwan reprint, 1969.

Su pao 蘇報 . Shanghai, 1902-1903. Taiwan photoreprint, 1965.

Sun, E-tu Zen. "The Board of Revenue in Nineteenth-Century China," *Harvard Journal of Asiatic Studies* #24 (1962-1963), pp. 175-228.

Sun Fu-yüan 孫伏園. *Fu-yüan yu-chi ti-i-chi* 伏園遊記第一集. Shanghai?, 1926. Held by the Institute of Humanistic Studies, Kyoto. A native of Shaohsing, Sun was a close friend of Lu Hsün.

Sun Meng-lan 孫夢蘭. "Chin-tu ssu-i" 禁賭私議, *Tung-fang tsa-chih* 東方雜誌 3 #11 (Kuang-hsü 32 [1906], lunar 10th month), pp. 215-218. Sun was a native of Shan-yin.

Sun Te-tsu 孫德祖. *Chi k'an wen-ts'un tz'u* 寄龕文存詞. 1884. Held by the Seikadō. Sun (1840-1905) was a native of Kuei-chi.

Sun Ting-lieh 孫鼎烈. *Ssu-hsi-chai chüeh-shih* 四西齋決事. 1904. Held by the Institute of Oriental Culture, Tokyo University. A native of Wu-hsi county, Kiangsu, Sun served as magistrate of Kuei-chi in 1897.

Suzuki Chūsei 鈴木中正. *Shinchō chūkishi kenkyū* 清朝中期史研究. Tokyo, 1952. Tokyo photoreprint, 1971.

Suzuki Tomō 鈴木智夫. "Shinmatsu Kō-Setsu no sakan ni tsuite" 清末江浙の茶館について. In *Rekishi ni okeru minshū to bunka* 歴史における民衆と文化, edited by Sakai Tadao sensei koki shukuga kinen no kai 酒井忠夫先生古稀祝賀記念の会, pp. 529-540. Tokyo, 1982.

Ta Ch'ing chin-shen ch'üan-shu 大清搢紳全書. Peking. Published quarterly. Issues used are held by Hoover, Yale, and Harvard-Yenching. An invaluable register of Ch'ing officialdom.

Ta Ch'ing Hsüan-t'ung cheng-chi shih-lu 大清宣統政記實錄. Mukden, 1933. Taiwan photoreprint, 1964. A continuation of the *Ta Ch'ing li-ch'ao shih-lu*.

Ta Ch'ing li-ch'ao shih-lu 大清歷朝實錄. Mukden, 1933. Taiwan photoreprint, 1964.

Ta Ch'ing shih-chi ch'üan-pien 大清仕籍全編 . 1767. Held by the Hoover Institution. A register of officials.

Taga Akigorō 多賀秋五郎 , comp. *Kindai Chūgoku kyōikushi shiryō: Shinmatsu hen* 近代中國教育史資料：清末編 . Tokyo, 1972.

_____. "Kindai Chūgoku ni okeru zokujuku no seikaku" 近代中国における族塾の性格 . In *Kindai Chūgoku kenkyū dai shi shū* 近代中国研究第四輯 , edited by the Tōyō Bunko kindai Chūgoku kenkyū iinkai 東洋文庫近代中国研究委員会 , pp. 207-254. Tokyo, 1960.

_____. *Kinsei Ajia kyōikushi kenkyū* 近世アジア教育史研究. Tokyo, 1966.

_____. *Sōfu no kenkyū: shiryō hen* 家譜の研究：資料編. Tokyo, 1960. Indispensable for the location and study of Chinese genealogies. A revised version of the holding information (without, however, the useful geographical index) is included in volume 2 of Taga's more recent *Chūgoku sōfu no kenkyū* 中国宗譜の研究 (Tokyo, 1981-1982).

_____. "Sōzoku no shūfu katei ni tsuite" 家族の修譜過程について. In *Kinsei Chūgoku kyōikushi kenkyū* 近世中国教育史研究 , edited by Hayashi Tomoharu 林友春 , pp. 329-518. Tokyo, 1958.

Takahashi Kōsuke 高橋孝助 . "Jūkyūseiki chūyō no Chūgoku ni okeru zei shūdatsu taisei no saihen katei: rikin kenkyū josetsu" 19世紀中葉の中国における税収奪体制の再編過程：釐金研究序説 , *Rekishigaku kenkyū* 歴史学研究 #383 (April 1972), pp. 48-59.

_____. "Shinmatsu ni okeru rikin shūdatsu to shōnōmin keiei" 清末における釐金收奪と小農民經營 , *Rekishigaku kenkyū* 歴史学研究 #392 (January 1973), pp. 20-30.

Takeuchi Yoshimi 竹内好. *Ro Jin* 魯迅 . Tokyo, 1948.

Takigawa Masajirō 瀧川政次郎. *Shina hōseishi kenkyū* 支那法制史研究. Tokyo, 1940. Held by Yale.

Tanaka Issei 田仲一成, comp. *Shindai chihōgeki shiryōshū: Kachū Kanan hen* 清代地方劇資料集：華中華南編 . Tokyo, 1968.

_____. "Shindai shoki no sōzoku engeki ni tsuite" 清代初期の宗族演劇について, *Tōhōgaku* 東方學 #32 (June 1966), pp. 102-116.

Tang, Ching-ping. "Mu-fu System [sic] in China under the Ch'ing." M.A. thesis in Asian Studies, Australian National University, 1976. Focuses on Wang Hui-tsu.

T'ao Hsi-sheng 陶希聖 . *Ch'ing-tai chou-hsien ya-men hsing-shih sheng-p'an chih-tu chi ch'eng-hsü* 清代州縣衙門刑事審判制度及程序. Taipei, 1972.

T'ao Ying-hui 陶英惠. *Ts'ai Yüan-p'ei nien-p'u (shang)* 蔡元培年譜(上). Taipei, 1976.

T'ao Ts'un-chao 陶存照. "Yao Hai-ch'a hsien-sheng nien-p'u" 姚海槎先生年譜, *Wen-lan hsüeh-pao* 文瀾學報 1 #1 (January 1935), pp. 1-18.

Terada Takanobu 寺田隆信. "Yōseitei no semmin kaihōrei ni tsuite" 雍正帝の賤民開放令について , *Tōyōshi kenkyū* 東洋史研究 18 #3 (December 1959), pp. 124-141.

Ting Ts'ai-san 丁采三 , ed. *Shaohsing hsien-kuan chi-lüeh* 紹興縣館紀略 . Preface dated 1920. Held by the Institute of Oriental Culture, Tokyo University.

Tōa dōbunkai 東亞同文會 , ed. *Shina keizai zensho* 支那經濟 全書 . Tokyo, 1907-1908.

_____. *Shina shōbetsu zenshi* 支那省別全誌. Volume 13: *Sekkō shō* 浙江省 . Tokyo, 1919.

Tōyō Bunko kindai Chūgoku kenkyū iinkai 東洋文庫近代中国研究 委員会 , ed. *Kindai Chūgoku kenkyū dai go shū* 近代中国研 究第五輯. Tokyo, 1963.

Tsai Pei-ching hui-kuan mu-lu 在北京會館目錄 . Anonymous, originally untitled manuscript held by the Institute of Oriental Culture, Tokyo University. The title was assigned by the Institute's catalogue. Undated but post-1911.

Ts'ai Shang-ssu 蔡尚思 . *Ts'ai Yüan-p'ei hsüeh-shu ssu-hsiang chuan-chi* 蔡元培學術思想傳記. Shanghai, 1950.

Ts'ai Yüan-p'ei 蔡元培. *Ts'ai Yüan-p'ei tzu-shu* 蔡元培自述 . Taipei, 1967. Ts'ai (1868-1940) was a native of Shan-yin.

Ts'ang Hsiu-liang 仓修良 , "Chang Hsüeh-ch'eng yü Che-tung shih-hsüeh" 章学诚与浙东史学, *Chung-kuo shih yen-chiu* 中国 史研究 #9 (March 1981), pp. 111-123.

Ts'ao Chü-jen 曹聚仁. *Lu Hsün p'ing-chuan* 魯迅評傳 . Hong Kong, 1961. Reprinted Hong Kong, 1973. Ts'ao (1900-1972) was a native of Chin-hua, Chekiang.

_____. *Pei hsing san yü* 北行三語 . Hong Kong, 1970.

_____. *Wan li hsing chi* 萬里行記 . Hong Kong, 1970.

Tso Tsung-t'ang 左宗棠 . *Tso Wen-hsiang-kung ch'üan-chi* 左文 襄公全集. Kuang-hsü.

Tsung Chi-ch'en 宗稷辰 . *Kung-ch'ih-chai shih-ch'ao wen-ch'ao* 躬 耻齋詩鈔文鈔 . 1867. Held by the Tōyō Bunko. Tsung was a native of Kuei-chi.

T'u Chien-lu 屠劍廬 . "Pai-mu shih-yeh ti ku-shih" 白木師爺 的故事, *Min-chien yüeh-k'an* 民間月刊 2 #9 (September

1933), pp. 187-189. This folklore journal was published in Shaohsing at the time. Held by the Institute of Humanistic Studies, Kyoto.

Tu Shih-chen 杜士珍 . "Lun Hu-shang chien-she Shaohsing chiao-yü-hui shih" 論滬上建設紹興教育會事 , *Hsin shih-chieh tsa-chih* 新世界雜誌 #11 (Kuang-hsü 29, lunar 2nd month), section 教育學 , pp. 1-11. Held by the National Diet Library.

Tuan Kuang-ch'ing 段光清 . *Ching-hu tzu-chuan nien-p'u* 鏡湖自撰年譜 . Peking, 1960. Tokyo photoreprint, 1968. Autobiography of Tuan (1798-1878), a native of Su-sung hsien, Anhwei, who served as an official in Ning-Shao.

Tung Chin-chien 董金鑑 , ed. *Wu T'ai-fu-jen nien-p'u* 吳太夫人年譜 . Preface dated 1905. In *Tung-shih ts'ung-shu* 董氏叢書 edited by Tung Chin-chien. Kuei-chi, 1906. Held by the Tōyō Bunko.

_____ . *Wu T'ai-fu-jen nien-p'u hsü* 吳太夫人年譜續 . In *Tung-shih ts'ung-shu*. Kuei-chi, 1906.

Tung-fang tsa-chih 東方雜誌 . Shanghai, 1904-1948.

T'ung-wen Hu-pao 同文滬報 . A daily newspaper published by the Tōa dōbunkai, Shanghai. The National Diet Library holds the issues published 1900-1906.

Twitchett, Denis. "The Fan Clan's Charitable Estate, 1050-1760." In *Confucianism in Action*, edited by David S. Nivison and Arthur F. Wright, pp. 97-133. Stanford, 1959.

Wakeman, Frederic, Jr. *The Fall of Imperial China*. New York, 1975.

_____ . *Strangers at the Gate: Social Disorder in South China, 1839-1861*. Berkeley, 1966.

Waley, Arthur. *The Opium War Through Chinese Eyes*. London, 1958. Reprinted Stanford, 1968.

Walshe, W. Gilbert. "The Ancient City of Shaohsing," *Journal of the China Branch of the Royal Asiatic Society* (new series) 33 (1900-1901), pp. 261-283.

Wang Ch'ao-yung 汪兆鏞. *Shan-yin Wang-shih p'u* 山陰汪氏譜. 1947. The genealogy of Wang Ching-wei's lineage, demonstrating that many of Wang's ancestors were mu-yu and a few, subofficials.

Wang Chieh-mou 王杰謀. "Ch'ing-tai ti Shaohsing shih-yeh" 清代的紹興師爺, *Che-chiang yüeh-k'an* 浙江月刊 2 #2 (January 1970), pp. 18-19.

_____. "Shaohsing hsi-po kuan ch'üan-kuo" 紹興錫箔冠全國, *Che-chiang yüeh-k'an* 浙江月刊 2 #4 (April 1970), p. 19.

Wang Ching-yü 汪敬虞, ed. *Chung-kuo chin-tai kung-yeh shih tzu-liao ti-erh-chi (1895-1914)* 中國近代工業史資料第二集 (1895-1914). Peking, 1957.

Wang Hui-tsu 汪輝祖. *Meng-hen lu-yü* 夢痕錄餘. In *Wang Lung-chuang i-shu* 汪龍莊遺書. 1889. Wang (1731-1807), a native of Hsiao-shan, was China's most famous mu-yu.

_____. *Ping-t'a meng-hen lu* 病榻夢痕錄. Author's preface dated 1796. In *Wang Lung-chuang i-shu*. 1889.

_____. *Shuang-chieh-t'ang yung-hsün* 雙節堂庸訓. Author's preface 1794. In *Wang Lung-chuang i-shu*. 1889.

_____. *Tso-chih yao-yen* 佐治藥言. Author's preface dated 1785. Shanghai, 1937. Volume 895 in the Commercial Press Ts'ung-shu chi-ch'eng series.

Wang Shih-ching 王士菁. *Lu Hsün chuan* 魯迅傳. Peking, 1959.

Wang Shih-hsing 王士性. *Kuang chih i* 廣志繹. Author's preface dated 1597. Wang was a chin-shih from Lin-hai, Chekiang.

Wang Shih-mao 王世茂. *Shih-t'u hsien-ching* 仕途懸鏡. 1626. Held by the Naikaku Bunko.

Wang Tzu-liang 王梓良. "Ch'ing-mo wu-shih-nien Che-chiang wen-chiao chi-yao" 清末五十年浙江文敎紀要 , *Che-chiang yüeh-k'an* 3 #4 (April 1971), pp. 18-19.

Wang Yeh-chien. *Land Taxation in Imperial China, 1750-1911.* Cambridge, 1973.

_____. "The Secular Trend of Prices during the Ch'ing Period (1644-1911)," *Journal of the Institute of Chinese Studies* (Chinese University of Hong Kong) 5 #2 (December 1972), pp. 347-368.

Wang Yeh-ch'iu 王冶秋. *Min-yüan-ch'ien ti Lu Hsün hsien-sheng* 民元前的魯迅先生. Shanghai?, 1942.

Watanabe Atsushi 渡辺惇. "Bansaihō no taitō to sono eikyō: Shinmatsu Ryōsetsu engyō no ichisokumen" 板曬法の擡頭とその影響:清末兩浙塩業の一側面 , *Tōyōshi kenkyū* 東洋史研究 21 #1 (June 1962), pp. 54-75.

_____. "Shinmatsu enkai shoenjō ni okeru seien gijutsu no tenkan to sono igi: senhō kara saihō e no ikō o chūshin to shite" 清末沿海諸塩場における製塩技術の転換とその意義:煎法から晒法への移行を中心として. In *Yamazaki sensei taikan kinen tōyōshigaku ronshū* 山崎先生退官記念東洋史学論集, edited by the Yamazaki sensei taikan kinenkai 山崎先生退官記念会, pp. 515-527. Tokyo, 1967.

_____. "Shinmatsu Yōsukō karyūiki ni okeru shien shūdan" 清末揚子江下流域における私塩集団 , *Shakai bunka shigaku* 社会文化史学 #6 (August 1970), pp. 1-23.

Watson, James L. "Chinese Kinship Reconsidered: Anthropological Perspectives on Historical Research," *China Quarterly* #92 (December 1982), pp. 589-622.

Willmott, W.E., ed. *Economic Organization in Chinese Society.* Stanford, 1972.

Wong, R. Bin. "Food Riots in the Qing Dynasty," *Journal of Asian Studies* 41 #4 (August 1982), pp. 767-788.

Wright, Arthur F. and Denis Twitchett, eds. *Confucian Personalities.* Stanford, 1962.

Wright, Mary C., ed. *China in Revolution: The First Phase, 1900-1913.* New Haven, 1968.

Wu Ch'eng-ch'iao 伍承喬 , comp. *Ch'ing-tai li-chih ts'ung-t'an* 清代吏治叢談. Shanghai?, 1936.

Wu Ching-tzu. *The Scholars.* Translated by Yang Hsien-yi and Gladys Yang. Peking, 1964.

Wu Pen-i 吳本一 . "Shan-tung chih shui-yen, shui-cha, shui-che, shui-tui, shui-mo yü yu-che" 刿東之水堰,水柵,水車,水碓,水磨 與油車 , *Che-chiang yüeh-k'an* 浙江月刊 #47 (March 1973), pp. 37-38.

Yabuuchi Kiyoshi 藪內清 . *Chūgoku no sūgaku* 中国の数学 . Tokyo, 1974.

Yamakami Kaneo 山上金男 . *Sekkō zaibatsu ron* 浙江財閥論 . Toyko, 1938.

Yamashita Yoneko 山下米子 . "Hsinhai kakumei no jiki no minshū undō: Kō-Setsu chiku no nōmin undō o chūshin to shite" 辛亥革命 の時期の民衆運動：江浙地區の農民運動を中心 として , *Tōyō bunka kenkyūjo kiyō* 東洋文化研究所紀要 #37 (March 1965), pp. 111-218.

Yamazaki sensei taikan kinenkai 山崎先生退官記念会 , ed. *Yamazaki sensei taikan kinen tōyōshigaku ronshū* 山崎先生退官 記念東洋史学論集. Tokyo, 1967.

Yang, C.K. *Religion in Chinese Society.* Berkeley, 1961.

Yang Lien-sheng. Personal communication. November, 1973.

_____. "Female Rulers in Imperial China," *Harvard Journal of Asiatic Studies* 23 (1960-1961), pp. 47-61.

Yeh Ch'üan 叶权 . *Hsien po pien.* 賢博編 . In *Ming shih tzu-liao ts'ung-k'an ti-i-chi* 明史資料丛刊第一輯 . Shanghai, 1981.

Yeh Lung-yen 葉龍彥 . "Ch'ing-mo Min-ch'u chih fa-cheng hsüeh-t'ang (1905-1911)" 清末民初之法政學堂 (1905-1911), Ph.D. thesis in History, College of Chinese Culture (Yang-ming Shan, Taiwan), 1974.

Yen Chung-p'ing 嚴中平 . *Chung-kuo mien-fang-chih shih kao* 中國棉紡織史稿 . Peking, 1963.

_____ et al., eds. *Chung-kuo chin-tai ching-chi shih t'ung-chi tzu-liao hsüan-chi* 中國近代經濟史統計資料選輯 . Shanghai, 1955.

Yokoyama Himitsu 橫山永三 . "Ro Jin nōto: 'Kokyō' o chūshin ni shite" 魯迅ノート:「故鄉」を中心にして , *Yamaguchi daigaku bungakukai shi* 山口大学文学会誌· 16 #1 (1965), pp. 29-43.

Yü-yao liu ts'ang chih 餘姚六倉志 . 1920.

Yüan Huan-chang 阮煥章 . "Shaohsing K'o-ch'iao tou-fu-kan" 紹興柯橋豆腐乾 , *Che-chiang yüeh-k'an* 浙江月刊 #55 (November 1973), p. 30.

Yung-cheng chu-p'i yü-chih 雍正硃批諭旨· Preface dated 1732. Taiwan photoreprint, 1965.

Glossary

cha-kuan　閘官

chan-hsing hsing-lu　暫行刑律

Ch'ang-chou [county in Soochow prefecture]　長洲

Ch'ang-chou [prefecture in Kiangsu]　常州

Ch'ang-chou jen　常州人

Ch'ang-ho　長河

Ch'ang-hua　昌化

Chang Li　章禮

Ch'ang-shu　常熟

Chao　趙

Chao-lien　昭槤

chao-mo　照磨

chao-wen　昭文

Che-chiang feng-su kai-liang ch'ien-shuo　浙江風俗改良淺說

Che-chiang jen　浙江人

Che-hsi　浙西

Che-Shao hsiang-ts'u 浙紹鄉祠

Che-Shao jen wei shih-yeh 浙紹人為世業

Che-tung 浙東

chen 鎮

Ch'en [name of déclassé family] 陳

Chen-hai 鎮海

Ch'en Lung-cheng 陳龍正

Chen-tse 震澤

Ch'eng-hsien 嵊縣

cheng-shui 爭水

Chi-an 吉安

chi-chi 寄籍

chi-hai 己亥

ch'i-kung 漆工

ch'i-meng-shih 啟蒙師

Chi-shan hui-kuan 稽山會館

ch'ia 卡

Chia-hsing 嘉興

chia-hsün 家訓

Chia-shan 嘉善

Chiang-yin 江陰

chiao-shou 敎授

chiao-yü 敎諭

chiao-yü-hui 敎育會

ch'ien-chuang 錢莊

Chien-hu 鑑湖

ch'ien-ku 錢穀

chien-min 賤民

chien-shang 奸商

chien-sheng 監生

Ch'ien-t'ang 錢塘

Chien-tao-tang 尖刀黨

chien-yeh kung-so	蘭業公所
chih-jan chü	織染局
Chih-li an-ch'a-ssu shu	直隸按察司署
chih-yüan	職員
chin	斤
chin Che-tung chü-chien	盡浙東巨奸
Chin-chien	金鑑
Ch'in Chin-chien	秦金鑑
Chin-hua	金華
Chin-k'uei	金匱
chin-shih	進士
chin-shen	搢紳
Ch'in T'ao	秦濤
Ching-chiang	靖江
Ching-hsi	荊溪
Ching-hu	鏡湖
ching-li	經歷
Ching-ning	景寧
Ch'ing-pai lei-ch'ao	清稗類鈔
ching-shih-shih	經史師
Chiu-chiang	九江
chou	州
Chou [name of landlord]	周
Chou Chien-jen	周建人
chou-p'an	州判
Chou Shu-jen	周樹人
Chou Tso-jen	周作人
chou-t'ung	州同
Chu [name of village]	祝
ch'ü [district]	區
chü [bureau]	局
Chu-chi	諸暨

Chu-chia keng	祝家埂
Ch'u-chou	處州
Ch'ü-chou	衢州
chü-jen	舉人
chu-jen [master]	主人
chu-pu	主簿
Chu Keng	朱賡
Chu ts'un	祝村
chüan	捐
ch'üan-hsüeh-hui	勸學會
ch'üan-hsüeh-so	勸學所
chüan-na	捐納
chüan wei-ju-liu	捐未入流
Ch'üan Tsu-wang	全祖望
chuang ta-chia	椿大家
Chüeh-chih ch'üan-lan	爵秩全覽
Chung	鍾
Chung-hsi hsüeh-t'ang	中西學堂
Chung-wai hsin-pao	中外新報
fa	法
fa-cheng hsüeh-t'ang	法政學堂
fa-kuan	法官
fan-chü chih ch'ü	繁劇之區
Fan Yin	范寅
fang [urban ward]	坊
fang [lineage sub-branch]	房
fei	匪
fei kuo hai	飛過海
fen-kuei	分櫃
Fen-shui	分水
feng-su kai-liang	風俗改良
fu	府

fu-kung	附貢
fu-mu kuan	父母官
fu-pang	副榜
fu-she chiao-yü	復設教諭
fu-she hsün-tao	復設訓導
fu-sheng	附生
Fu-yang	富陽
Hai-ning chou	海寧州
Hai-yen	海鹽
Hang	杭
Hangchow	杭州
Hang-chou jen	杭州人
Hang-chou pai-hua pao	杭州白話報
Hang-hsien lü-shih kung-hui	杭縣律師公會
hao-shih	好事
Ho-i-ho sao-ssu-ch'ang	合義和繰絲廠
hou-hsüan chih-fu	候選知府
hou-hsüan t'ung-chih	候選同知
Hou-sheng fang-chih kung-ssu	厚生紡織公司
hsi fa-chia yen	習法家言
hsi-t'ien	戲田
Hsia-fang-ch'iao	下坊橋
hsia-yü	下愚
hsiang	鄉
hsiang hsien-sheng	鄉先生
hsiang-shih	鄉試
hsiang-yung	鄉勇
hsiao-fei	梟匪
hsiao hsüeh-hsiao	小學校
hsiao hsüeh-t'ang	小學堂
Hsiao-shan	蕭山
Hsieh [name of landlord]	謝

Hsieh Chao-chih	謝肇淛
Hsieh Keng-hsien	謝庚仙
hsien	縣
hsien-ch'eng	縣丞
hsien-sheng	先生
hsien-wei	縣尉
Hsin-ch'ang	新昌
Hsin-ch'eng	新城
Hsin-yang	新陽
hsing-ming	刑名
hsing-mu	刑幕
hsiung-k'un	兇棍
Hsiung Tsai-ch'ing	熊再青
hsü	胥
Hsü [name of landlord]	許
Hsü Chung-fan	徐仲凡
hsü-li	胥吏
hsü-t'u	胥徒
Hsü Shu-lan	徐樹蘭
Hsü Yu-lan	徐友蘭
hsüan-shou	選授
hsüeh-cheng	學正
hsüeh-ch'ü	學區
hsüeh-hsiao	學校
hsün-chien	巡檢 [also written 巡檢]
hsün-tao	訓導
hu [household]	戶
Hu [name of gentryman]	胡
Hu-chou	湖州
Hu Jen-chi	胡仁濟
Hu-t'ang	湖塘
hua-chüan kung-so	花捐公所

huai-hsing   懷刑

Huang Ch'un-sheng   黃春生

Huang tao-shih   黃道士

Hui-chou   徽州

hui-kuan   會館

i-ch'eng   驛丞

i-chuang   義莊

I-hsing   宜興

i-hsü   議敘

I liang-li shan-tsu   宜量力贍族

i-shu   義塾

I-wu   義烏

i-yüan   議員

Jen-Ch'ien   仁錢

jen-chüan   認捐

Jen-ho   仁和

Jih chih lu   日知錄

ju-hsüeh   儒學

Ju-lin wai-shih   儒林外史

k'ai-hsin   開新

kai-hu   丐戶

kai-t'ou   丐頭

k'ang-liang   抗糧

k'o-ch'eng-po i-pen   課程簿一本

K'o-ch'iao   柯橋

Ku   顧

Ku Chien-ch'en   谷劍塵

ku hsiang   故鄉

Ku Yüeh ts'ang-shu-lou   古越藏書樓

Kuan-shan   官山

Kuang-fu hui   光復會

kuan-shen ho-pan   官紳合辦

kuan-shui kuan   關稅官

kuan sung-shih   官訟師

Kuan-ti   關帝

kuan-tsu   官租

Kuei-an   歸安

Kuei-chi   會稽

kuei-hsiang   跪香

Kuei-i min-ch'ing hao-sung   會邑民情好訟

k'uei-lei   傀儡

K'un-shan   崑山

kung-chih ching-shih   供職京師

kung-sheng   貢生

kung-shih   供事

Kuo-fa pu shun jen-ch'ing   國法不順人情

kuo-wen   國文

Lai   來

Lan-ch'i   蘭谿

li [proper decorum]   禮

Li [family name] [landlord's name]   李

li [legal precedent]   例

li [measurement]   里

li-hsü   吏胥

li-kung   吏貢

li-mu   吏目

Li Wei   李衛

li-yüan   吏員

liang-min   良民

lieh-shen   劣紳

likin   釐金

Lin-an   臨安

Lin-ch'ing [in Shantung]   臨清

Lin Ch'ing [rebel leader]   林清

Lin-hai   臨海

Lin-p'u   臨浦

Lin-shan-wei   臨山衛

liu-mang feng-ch'i   流氓風氣

Lou   樓

Lou-chia-t'a   樓家塔

Lou Ching-hui   樓景暉

Lu   陸

lü   律

Lu Hsün   魯迅

lü-shih   律師

Lun to-p'in   論隨貧

Lung   龐

Ma Yung-hsi   馬用錫

mao-chi   冒籍

miao   廟

miao-shen-ch'i   廟神旗

mien-tsu   免租

min-ch'üan   民權

min-kuo   民國

min-tsu   民族

mou   畝

mu-fu   幕府

mu-ou   木偶

mu-t'ing   幕廳

mu-yu   幕友

Nan-ch'ang   南昌

nan-se   男色

Nan-t'ung   南通

Nan yin-chü   南銀局

nei-shen   內神

Ningpo   寧波

Ning-Shao pang	寧紹幫
nü-erh chiu	女兒酒
Nung-kung to-hu hsüeh-t'ang	農工隨户學堂
pai-hsing	百姓
pan-hu	板户
pan-shai-fa	板晒法
P'ang Chao-hsiao	龐兆熊
Pang-hua	邦化
pao-chüan	包捐
pao-chung	保種
pao-kung-t'ou	包工頭
Pao-ting	保定
pei-pang	北榜
pei-pang chü-jen	北榜舉人
pien-i feng-su	變易風俗
po-chiang	箔匠
p'u-chiang	譜匠
pu ho tse ch'ü	不合則去
pu-i	補道
pu-t'ou ch'ien	埠頭錢
p'u-t'ung hsüeh-t'ang	普通學堂
pu-yung tao	補用道
sai-hui	賽會
San-chiang-cha	三江閘
San Tai	三埭
sha-min	沙民
Shan-Kuei i-kuan	山會邑館
Shan-yin	山陰
Shang-yü	上虞
Shao-chün p'ing-t'iao cheng-hsin lu	紹郡平糶徵信錄
Shao-pang	紹幫
Shao tao-kuei	紹刀鬼

Shaohsing	紹興
Shaohsing hsien-kuan	紹興縣館
Shaohsing hsien-kuan chi-lüeh	紹興縣館紀略
Shaohsing jen	紹興人
Shaohsing kun-t'u	紹興棍徒
she	社
she-hsi	社戲
she-min	畬民
shen	紳
shen-hu min-hu chih fen	紳戶民戶之分
Shen I-kuan	沈一貫
shen min	紳民
shen-p'an-t'ing	審判廳
shen-shang	紳商
shen-shih	紳士
Shen Te-fu	沈德符
shen-tung	紳董
sheng-li ti-wu chung-hsüeh	省立第五中學
Sheng-tse	盛澤
Shih [family name]	史
shih	石
shih-chen	市鎮
Shih-men	石門
Shih pao	時報
shih-shen	士紳
Shih-shih-kung	沛施公
shih-yeh	師爺
shu-yüan	書院
shui-k'o-ssu ta-shih	稅課司大使
shui-k'o ta-shih	稅課大使
Shun-te	順德
Shun-t'ien	順天

Soochow	蘇州
Ssu-ming	四明
ssu-yü	司獄
Sun	孫
Sun Ting-lieh	孫鼎烈
Sung-chiang	松江
sung-kun	訟棍
sung-shih	訟師
sung-shih hua	訟師話
Ta Ch'ing chin-shen ch'üan-shu	大清搢紳全書
Ta Ch'ing hsien-hsing hsing-lü	大清現行刑律
Ta Ch'ing hui-tien shih-li	大清會典事例
Ta-hsing	大興
ta p'ao che	大砲者
ta shen	大紳
ta-shih	大使
T'ai-chou	台州
T'ai-hu t'ing	太湖廳
Tai-shan	岱山
tai-shu	代書
T'ai-ts'ang	太倉
tan	石
Tan [family name]	單
T'ang-hsi	湯溪
T'ang-p'u	湯補
tao-pi	刀筆
tao-pi-li	刀筆吏
tao-t'ai	道台
Te-ch'ang-sheng kung-ssu	德昌生公司
Te Ch'ing	德清
ti-fang tzu-chih	地方自治
ti-ma-hsi	的篤戲

t'i-ming lu   題名錄

ti-pao   地保

Ti-ssu-men   第泗門 [also written 第四門]

tien-fei   佃匪

t'ien-hsia wei kung   天下為公

tien-shih   典史

tien-shih i-kuan   典史一官

T'ien-t'ai   天台

t'ien-yen wu-ching   天演物競

t'ing ssu-yü   廳司獄

Ting-hai   定海

Ting Shih-ch'ing   丁仕卿

to   墯

to-min   隋民

to-p'in   墮貧

Tou-men   斗門

tsa-chi jen   雜技人

tsa-i   雜役

Tsai Pei-ching hui-kuan mu-lu   在北京會館目錄

ts'ang ta-shih   倉大使

Ts'ao   曹

tsao   竈

tsao-hu   竈戶

Tso-shih hsü chuan   作事須專

tso-tsa   佐雜

ts'un-ku   存古

tsung-ts'e   宗祠

tsung-tsu kuan-nien   宗族觀念

tu-k'un   賭棍

Tu Te-sheng   杜德勝

t'u-ti-shen   土地神

Tu Ya-ch'üan   杜亞泉

Tuan Kuang-ch'ing	段光清
T'ung-chia	童家
Tung Ch'ing-chang	董慶章
t'ung-chih [comradeship]	同志
t'ung-chih [subprefect]	同知
Tung-fang tsa-chih	東方雜誌
Tung-hsi yang fa-chia chih hsüeh	東西洋法家之學
t'ung-hsiang ching-kuan	同鄉京官
T'ung-hui-kung sha-ch'ang	通惠公紗廠
T'ung-jen hsüeh-t'ang	同仁學堂
t'ung-p'an	通判
Tung-p'u	東浦
t'ung-sheng	童生
Tung-yang	東陽
Tung Yüeh hui-kuan	東越會館
tzu-chuan	自傳
wai-shen	外神
Wan-fu ting-chang ch'üan-an	完賦定章全案
Wan-p'ing	宛平
Wang Chi	王畿
Wang Ch'in	王欽
Wang Ch'un-sheng	王春生
Wang Hui-tsu	汪輝祖
Wang Kuei-lao	王桂老
Wang Ssu-jen	王思任
Wei A-ch'eng	魏阿城
wei ch'ien-tsung	衛千總
wei-yüan	委員
wen	文
Wen-ch'ang-ti	文昌帝
Wen-chou	溫州
wen-i-shih	文藝師

wo-pei	卧 碑
Wu	吳
Wu-chiang	吳 江
Wu-chin	武 進
Wu-hsi	無 錫
Wu-hu	蕪 湖
Wu-i	武 義
Wu T'ai-fu-jen	吳 太 夫 人
Wu Yüeh	吳 越
Yang	楊
Yang-chou	揚 州
Yang-hu	陽 湖
yang-ko-hsi	秧 歌 戲
Yao-chiang	姚 江
Yao Tzu-ch'i	姚 子 祁
Yeh Ch'üan	叶 权
yeh-ju wu-ch'eng	業 儒 無 成
yen-ch'ang-k'o ta-shih	鹽 場 課 大 使
Yen-chou	嚴 州
yen-k'o ta-shih	鹽 課 大 使
Yin-hsien	鄞 縣
yin-shen sai-hui	迎 神 賽 會
Yü-ch'ien	於 潛
Yü-hang	餘 杭
yu-sheng lieh-pai	優 勝 劣 敗
Yü-tu	漁 度
Yü-yao	餘 姚
yüan-chi	原 籍
Yüan-ho	元 和
Yüan she [essay title]	原 社
Yüan-she [place name]	阮 社
yüan-shih	院 試

Yüeh   越

Yüeh-chou   越州

Yüeh she   越社

Yüeh yen   越諺

yung   勇

Yung-hsi t'ang 永錫堂

Index

Except in obvious cases, place names below the county level are followed by the county in parentheses; county names are followed by the prefecture in parentheses; and prefectural names are followed by the province in parentheses.

Ch'ien-chuang (native banks), 10, 25, 27, 28
  run by Ning-Shao natives, in Shanghai, 79-80, 198n34
  See also Banks, Money

Chien-hu (lake in Shaohsing), 216n12
  See also Ching-hu

Ch'ien-ku (tax *mu-yu*), 9, 128, 151, 205n55
  See also Mu-yu

Ch'ien-lung Emperor, quizzes possible Shaohsing native, 199n54

Chien-min (déclassé), 65ff
  See also Déclassé, *To-min*

Ch'ien Mu, 204n45

Chien-shang (unethical merchants)
  See Merchants

Chien-sheng (holders of purchased degree), 30, 108, 111, 117, 124, 153
  as protest leaders, 20
  psychology of, 20
  purchase of degree of, 108, 116ff
  purchase of magistracies by, statistics on, 117-118
  purchase of subofficial posts by, 117, 125
  as subofficials, 101, 102, 116ff
  statistics on, 170, 174, 175
  and tax resistance, 19, 43

Ch'ien-t'ang (Hangchow)
  statistics on, as producer of subofficials, 104, 173, 175
  statistics on purchase of magistracies by natives of, 117

Ch'ien-t'ang River, 22, 60

Chien-tao-tang (Sharp Sword Society), 63

Chih-jan-chü (weaving and dyeing bureau), 198n48

Chihli, 125, 127, 169
  academic success of natives, 87
  and examination system, 108
  natives replace Ning-Shao natives, 84
  Shaohsing natives in, 82ff

  as subofficials, 98ff, 169, 200n4
  as *mu-yu* of judicial commissioner, 128
  See also Hopei, Shun-t'ien

Chin-hua (Chekiang), 48, 76, 131, 199n58

Chin-k'uei (Ch'ang-chou), 173

Ch'in lineage (Kuei-chi), 125ff

Chin-shen (officials), engaged in commerce in Shaohsing, 187n43

Chin-shih (holders of empire-wide degree), 27, 40, 84, 111, 119, 126, 152
  and career patterns, 127
  correlation between production of, and production of subofficials, 175
  and elite status, 17, 19, 127
  lineage "tax" on, 160
  military, 85
  relations with local magistrate, 20
  statistics on, as education-related subofficials, 171
  statistics on, produced by Shaohsing, 126
  from Wan-p'ing and Ta-hsing, as Shaohsing natives, 87

Chin-t'an (Kiangsu), 216n13

Chin Tung-yeh, 107

Ch'in Wen-k'uei, quoted, 102

China Weekly Review, 137

Ching-chiang (Ch'ang-chou), 173

Ch'ing Code (*Ta Ch'ing lü-li*)
  on pettifoggers, 184n19
  reform of, 134
  on salt smuggling, 60
  See also Law

Ching-hsi (Ch'ang-chou), 173

Ching-hsien (Ning-kuo), statistics on, as producer of sub-officials, 104, 201n15

Ching-hu (lake in Shaohsing), 216n12
  See also Chien-hu

Ching-li
  See Prefectural commissary of
    records

Ch'ing-pai lei-ch'ao (Ch'ing Anecdotes
  by Category), 78, 129
  See also Hsü K'o

Ch'ing shih-lu (Veritable Record of the
  Ch'ing [Dynasty]), 116

Ching-shih-shih (classics-and-history
  teachers), 159

Chiu-chiang (Kiangsi), 78

Ch'iu Chin, 63, 182n2
  affair, 146-147, 212n59
  father's background, 193n31
  See also Kuang-fu hui

Chou Chien-jen, 16, 51, 185n2

Chou En-lai, 182n2, 199n56

Chou jail wardens (*li-mu*)
  statistics on Shaohsing natives as,
    in Shun-t'ien, 94
  throughout China, 102, 172

Chou-p'an
  See Second-class assistant *chou*
    magistrates

Chou Shu-jen
  See Lu Hsün

Chou Tso-jen, 10, 14-15, 16, 25, 64, 66,
  107, 108, 162, 182n2, 185n1, 191n92,
  205n61

Chou-t'ung
  See First-class assistant depart-
    mental magistrates

Chü (tenant bureaus), 189n27

Ch'u (districts), 66

Chu-chi (Shaohsing), 12, 17, 49, 51, 55,
  62, 66, 71, 151, 162, 183n5, 185n15,
  189n34, 190n49, 195n66
  characterized, 6, 155
  description of vendetta in, 163-
    164
  gentry-official relations in, 20
  as "lineage society," 155

litigation in, 132
natives of, in Hangchow, 81
population, 7, 77
printing of genealogies in, 161
single-lineage villages in, 157
statistics on
  enrollment in *hsüeh-t'ang* in,
    144-145
natives of, as
  assistant county magis-
    trates in Shun-t'ien, 90
  chou and county jail
    wardens in Shun-t'ien,
    94
  county registrars in Shun-
    t'ien, 92
  jailkeepers in Shun-t'ien,
    95
  local magistrates in Shun-
    t'ien, 89
  postmasters in Shun-t'ien,
    96
  second-class assistant *chou*
    magistrates in Shun-
    t'ien, 91
  subcounty magistrates in
    Shun-t'ien, 93
passers of examination for
  judges from, 136
production of subofficials by,
  100, 101, 105, 173
purchase of magistracies by
  natives of, 117

Chu-chia keng (Chu-chi), 195n66

Ch'u-chou (Chekiang), 76

Ch'ü-chou (Chekiang), 48

Chu Hsi, 48

Chü-jen (holders of provincial-level
  degree), 30, 84, 85, 107, 108, 111,
  116, 118, 124, 126, 136, 138, 193n31
  candidacy for, as minimum
    qualification for residence in
    hui-kuan, 84, 109, 111
  and elite status, 17, 19
  relations with magistrate, 20
  statistics on, as subofficials, 100,
    170, 171, 174
  success of Shan-yin and Kuei-chi

natives in becoming, 109-111
"tax" on, by lineage, 160
See also Pei-pang chü-jen

Chu Keng, 113

Chu Min, 183n4

Chu-pu
See County registrars

Chu-ts'un (Chu-chi), 195n66

Ch'ü T'ung-tsu, 21, 22, 203n42
quoted, 115, 204n55

Chu Tzu-ch'ing, 182n2

Chu Yüan-chang, 66, 75
See also Horizontal tablet, Ming
T'ai-tsu...

Chüan (contributions)
for charity relief, 37
as commercial taxes, 46
See also Likin

Ch'üan Han-sheng, 47

Chüan-na
See Purchase and sale of offices ...

Ch'üan Tsu-wang, essay by, on parish
cults, 37

Chuang ta-chia (pinning down the
rich), 50, 191n90

Chung-hsi hsüeh-t'ang (Sino-Occidental
School)
See Schools

Chung lineage (Chu-chi), proclamation against intermarriage with
déclassé, 71-72

Chung-wai hsin-pao (The Sino-Foreign
News), 33

Clans, 155, 157, 170, 213n3
See also Lineages

Class
conflict, 4, 13, 34, 50
inhibited in periphery, 65
in Shaohsing's core, 15
consciousness in core and
periphery, 13, 38, 167
organization, poor vs. rich, 13

relations after 1911 Revolution, 152
See also Horizontal ties

Clerks, administrative, 9-10, 20, 32, 43,
81
in central government's administration, 111-118, 126, 127, 128,
152, 170, 184n23, 206n76
alliances between, and *mu-
yu*, 207n96
assistants to, in Six Boards,
111-112
cleverer than merchants,
116
déclassé as, 70
as de-facto *mu-yu*, 114
examination for, 206n76
false registration by, 84,
113
hereditary nature of, 113,
203n38
hired as *mu-yu*, 114
knowledge of legal prece-
dents, 114, 203n37
mathematical expertise of,
112
and merchants in Peking,
202n21
Shaohsing natives as, 84,
107, 112, 113, 114-116,
204n45
status of, 114
statutory quotas for, 111
as suboffficials, 101
training of, 111-112
See also Board of Revenue,
Kung-shih
in local administrations, 67, 78,
87, 184n23
allied with pettifoggers,
208n3
collusion with bandits, 63
corruption of, 63, 184n15
exempt from law of avoid-
ance, 201n6
fear of local assemblies,
150
hereditary nature of, 113-
114
as pettifoggers, 132
purchase of posts by,

Mencius, 158
on human nature, 67

Mercenaries (*yung*), in Yü-yao, 33, 35, 37

Merchant-gentry nexus, 25-30
See also Gentlemen-merchants

Merchants, 41, 50, 65, 79, 81, 119
charcoal, 79
condition of, after 1911
Revolution, 152
contradictions within merchant
class, 46
leather, 51
and *likin* tax, 45-46
literacy of tradesmen, 107
natives places of, doing business in
Shaohsing, 51
not as clever as Central Board
clerks, 116
officials engaged in commerce,
187n43
rice, 50
rich
in local and provincial
assemblies, 150, 213n77
mansion of, 213n8
salt, 58-59
Shaohsing,
in Hangchow, 198n45
in Hankow, 197n19
in Peking, 84, 203n21
in Shanghai, 79, 197n32
in Soochow, 198n47
silk, 143
soysauce, 198n47
sugar, 51
tea, 51, 143
unethical, 48-49
varying statuses of, 25
wine, 198n44
See also Gentlemen-merchants,
Guilds, Merchant-gentry
nexus, Peddlers

Meskill, Johanna Menzel, 2, 12

Metropolitan counties
lineage schools in, 158ff
as producers of *chin-shih*,
suboffices, and *mu-yu*, 128-129,

174, 175-176, 201n15
hsüeh-t'ang students from, 148
See also Core areas, Urbanism

Metzger, Thomas, 25, 114

Miao (parish), 36, 37, 38, 189n25
See also She

Miao Ch'üan-chi, 112

Miao-shen-ch'i (banner of the parish
god), 189n25

Military
anti-military bias of Confucianism,
163
chin-shih and functionaries barred
from *hui-kuan*, 85
God of War, 166
martial ethos, 163
in Ch'eng-hsien, 162, 214n33
militarization in the periphery, 62
See also Board of War, Mercenaries,
Militia, Pao-ting Military
Academy, Soldiers, Vendettas

Militia, 35-36
anti-Taiping, 188n25
involvement in vendettas, 163
student, 148

Mills, silk and cotton, 179-180

Ministry of Education
See Education

Ming T'ai-tsu, and *sheng-yüan*
problem, 18, 185n6, 185n12

Missionaries, 33, 40, 77
Catholic, 21
church burned, 81
Jesuit, 10
English, desire to convert
Shaohsing 75, 196n3

Mobility, social
See Social mobility

Modernization, late Ch'ing, 149
educational, 138-149
industrial, 180
judicial reform, 131-138
local self-government, 149-151
of *mu-yu* system, 135ff